ADVANCED THEORY AND PRACTICE IN SPORT MARKETING

**ERIC C. SCHWARZ,
JASON D. HUNTER,
AND
ALAN LAFLEUR**

Routledge
Taylor & Francis Group

LONDON AND NEW YORK

First published 2013
by Routledge
2 Park Square, Milton Park, Abingdon, Oxon OX14 4RN

Simultaneously published in the USA and Canada
by Routledge
711 Third Avenue, New York, NY 10017

Routledge is an imprint of the Taylor & Francis Group, an informa business

British Library Cataloguing in Publication Data
A catalogue record for this book is available from the British Library

Library of Congress Cataloging-in-Publication Data
Schwarz, Eric C.
Advanced theory and practice in sport marketing / by Dr. Eric C. Schwarz, Dr. Jason D.
Hunter and Alan LaFleur. – 2nd ed.
p. cm.
1. Sports–Marketing. I. Hunter, Jason D. II. LaFleur, Alan. III. Title.
GV716.S37 2012
796.06'88–dc23
2012010444

ISBN: 978–0–415–51847–5 (hbk)
ISBN: 978–0–415–51848–2 (pbk)
ISBN: 978–0–203–12338–6 (ebk)

Typeset in Zapf Humanist and Eras
by Keystroke, Station Road, Codsall, Wolverhampton

MIX
Paper from
responsible sources
FSC
www.fsc.org   FSC® C004839

Printed and bound in Great Britain by
TJ International Ltd, Padstow, Cornwall

ADVANCED THEORY AND PRACTICE IN SPORT MARKETING

Effective marketing is essential for any successful sport organization, from elite professional sports teams to local amateur leagues. Now in a fully revised and updated second edition, *Advanced Theory and Practice in Sport Marketing* is still the only text to introduce key theory and best practice at an advanced level.

The book covers every key functional and theoretical area of sport marketing, including marketing research, information systems, consumer behavior, logistics, retail management, sales management, e-commerce, promotions, advertising, sponsorship, and international business. This new edition includes expanded coverage of important contemporary issues, including social responsibility and ethics, social media and networking, relationship and experience marketing, recovery marketing, and social marketing. Every chapter contains extended cases and first-hand accounts from experienced sport marketing professionals from around the world. Following those cases are questions encouraging students and practitioners to apply their theoretical knowledge to real-world situations and to develop their critical thinking skills. A companion website provides an impressive array of additional teaching and learning resources, including a test bank of exam questions, PowerPoint slides, and extra case studies for lecturers and instructors, and useful web links, self-test multiple-choice questions, and glossary flashcards for students.

Advanced Theory and Practice in Sport Marketing goes further than any other sport marketing text in preparing the student for the real world of sport marketing. It is essential reading for any upper-level undergraduate or postgraduate course in sport marketing or sport business, and for anybody working in sport marketing looking to develop and extend their professional skills.

Eric C. Schwarz is Associate Professor of Sport Business and Chair of the Department of Sport Business and International Tourism in the Donald R. Tapia School of Business at Saint Leo University, USA. He is currently President of the Sport Marketing Association.

Jason D. Hunter is Assistant Professor of Parks and Recreational Administration at George Williams College of Aurora University, USA. He is currently developing a Master's Degree program in Sports Management and an online Graduate Recreational Administration Program.

Alan LaFleur is a social media consultant. Having worked for Sports Features Communications he has gone on to found two of his own companies in this sector, Bloom Social and Apprentice Star League.

CONTENTS

FIGURES

TABLES

CASE STUDIES

xi

case studies

CONTRIBUTORS

CASE STUDIES

Ashley A. Bowling, Department of Exercise and Sport Science, East Carolina University, Greenville, North Carolina

David P. Hedlund, St. John's University, Queens, New York

Bob Heere, Assistant Professor, Department of Kinesiology and Health Education, University of Texas at Austin, Texas

James Johnson, Assistant Professor and Graduate Coordinator, Sport Administration, School of Physical Education, Sport and Exercise Science, Ball State University, Muncie, Indiana

Matt Kastel, Manager of Baseball Operations, Maryland Stadium Authority, Baltimore, Maryland

Timothy B. Kellison, Department of Sport Management, Florida State University, Tallahassee, Florida

Chiyoung Kim, Department of Kinesiology and Health Education, University of Texas at Austin, Texas

Jordan I. Kobritz, Professor and Chair of the Sport Management Department, State University of New York, Cortland, New York

Heidi Nordstrom, Teaching Assistant, Health, Exercise and Sport Sciences Department, University of New Mexico, Albuquerque, New Mexico

Charles Parrish, School of Recreation, Health, and Tourism, George Mason University, Fairfax, Virginia

David Pierce, Associate Chair and Assistant Professor of Sport Administration and Undergraduate Program Coordinator, School of Education, Sport and Exercise Science, Ball State University, Muncie, Indiana

Sam Taggart, Creative Strategist, VaynerMedia, LLC, New York

A.J. Vaynerchuk, Co-Founder and President, VaynerMedia, LLC, New York

Matthew Walker, School of Human Performance and Recreation, University of Southern Mississippi, Hattiesburg, Mississippi

Stacy Warner, Associate Professor, Department of Exercise and Sport Science, East Carolina University, Greenville, North Carolina

FROM THEORY TO PRACTICE

Daniel E. Ballou, Director of Sports Sales and Marketing, Albuquerque Convention and Visitors Bureau, Albuquerque, New Mexico

Douglas Blais, Professor of Sport Management, Southern New Hampshire University, Manchester, New Hampshire

Pamela Cheriton, President and CEO, Event Services International, Fort Myers, Florida

Mandy Cormier, Former Merchandise Manager, Norfolk Tides Baseball Club, Virginia Beach, Virginia

Katie Cox, Director of Marketing, Gator Bowl Association, Jacksonville, Florida

Buffy Filipell, Founder and CEO, Teamwork Online, LLC, Cleveland, Ohio

Nigel Jamieson, Principal Lecturer, Centre for Recreation, Sport and Tourism, Adelaide, Australia

Michael Johnstone, Marketing Manager, National Rugby League, Sydney, New South Wales, Australia

Matt Lawrence, Minor League Video Coordinator, Los Angeles Dodgers, Los Angeles, California

Kristopher M. Lull, Marketplace Manager, Baseball America, Durham, North Carolina

Anthony Penna, Director of Florida Operations, Ted Williams Museum and Hitters Hall of Fame, St. Petersburg, Florida

Mark Rodriguez, Director of Ticket Sales, Boston Bruins (NHL) Hockey Club, Boston, Massachusetts

Daniel P. Smith, Senior Vice-President of Marketing, ClickSquared, Inc., Boston, Massachusetts

Frank Supovitz, Senior Vice-President, Events, National Football League, New York, New York

Tracy West, President, Hayson Sports Group, Concord, Massachusetts

PREFACE

The field of sport marketing is infused in virtually all aspects of sport business management. As such, it is inevitable that many students will be involved in some aspect of sport marketing during their careers. As with the first edition, this book is being published with the educator and student in mind, and is specifically aimed at those whose sport management program is housed in the business and/or management department. Most sport marketing books restate concepts learned in an introductory marketing course prior to getting into sport marketing. This is appropriate for sport management programs housed in a department other than business and/or management. However, for sport management programs housed in a business and/or management department, where virtually all students have already taken a "Principles of Marketing" course, the book is simply repetitive. *Advanced Theory and Practice in Sport Marketing* strives to go beyond the introductory marketing course by expanding the knowledge of the student with advanced marketing theory related to ethics and social responsibility; market research and information systems; consumer behavior; product and logistical management; sales, retail, and e-marketing management; communication management, promotions, advertising, and sponsorship; social media and networking; international and global marketing; and emerging sociological concepts.

The other aspect of this book is the application of real-world situations to the text. Professors talk about what goes on in the field of sport marketing based on their limited experience. *Advanced Theory and Practice in Sport Marketing* publishes what goes on in the real world of sport marketing by having professionals in the field provide first-hand accounts of how they entered the field of sport marketing, what their current job entails, and advice to students who wish to enter the field of sport marketing. This allows the instructor to better prepare the student for life in the sport marketing profession. It is the goal of the authors to have this book become a resource that sport marketing educators, students, and professionals will utilize as an everyday reference tool in pursuit of their goals.

The book reflects the authors' extensive research and varied experiences in the field of sport marketing. Eric Schwarz has worked in and with professional, amateur, and non-profit sport organizations, and conducted feasibility studies and developed marketing plans as a consultant in sport facility and event management. He has conducted and presented research in sport marketing and experiential learning in the United States, Canada, Europe, and Australia. In addition, from June 2006 to August 2007 he went on sabbatical in Australia, conducting research in social and leisure marketing and designing an MBA degree. Jason Hunter supplements this knowledge by bringing extensive experience from the physical education,

XV

athletics, and coaching realm, as well as being a former owner of a sport retail firm and a sport facility. Alan LaFleur brings more current knowledge specifically focused on the use of social media and networking to enhance sport industry businesses.

The initial two chapters of the book serve to provide an overview of sport marketing, including a basic review of those topics commonly covered in an introductory marketing course. The remainder of this text will provide the reader with a framework understanding of sport marketing by connecting traditional marketing to sport marketing. Each chapter will cover a specific aspect of traditional marketing and applying it to the field of sport marketing.

SOCIAL RESPONSIBILITY AND ETHICS

The reader will gain an understanding of the various concepts of social responsibility and ethics as related to the multiple aspects of sport marketing. Through an analysis of the various dimensions of social responsibility in sport marketing (economic, legal, philanthropic, and ethical), readers will gain an appreciation of the various concepts inherent to each dimension of social responsibility in terms of application within sport marketing theory and practice. In addition, they will recognize the influence of ethics across multiple applications of sport marketing, as well as evaluate the role of social responsibility and ethics in the implementation of strategic planning in sport marketing.

MARKET RESEARCH AND INFORMATION SYSTEMS

Readers will expand their knowledge of the concepts of market segmentation, positioning, and demand analysis, and use that knowledge to develop basic capabilities in advertising research, competitive analysis, and strategic outcomes assessment in sport marketing. Inclusive of this will be the development and implementation of focus group research, survey research, and experimental studies; the identification, retrieval, and analysis of secondary data; the utilization of qualitative and quantitative research methodologies; and the application of the research method. The reader will also gain an appreciation of the use of information systems for sport marketing goals and objectives through structure, organization, and communication. Inclusive of this will be an examination of sport consumer relationship management for both the internet and non-internet environment using strategic database and software marketing, with the goal of being able to identify market opportunities, develop targets, and manage and evaluate promotional efforts in sport.

CONSUMER BEHAVIOR

Readers will learn how to utilize basic cultural, personal, social, and psychological principles to explain how those factors directly affect individual purchasing and consumption behavior of participants, fans, spectators, volunteers, and community and corporate partners. In addition, there will be an examination of the various types of sport consumer studies, and how individual and environmental factors, socialization, and participation directly influence the decision-making process for sport consumption. Inclusive of this examination will be an analysis of the expected demographic, psychographic, geographic, and behavioristic characteristics of the sport consumer.

PRODUCT AND LOGISTICAL MANAGEMENT

The reader will learn how to distinguish, identify, and classify the various elements of sport products and services, and the stages of the sport product life cycle. In addition, the concepts of branding, licensing, images, marks, and positioning will be identified as related to the sport product. The reader will also be presented with numerous logistical functions that a sport business must manage, including inventory management, team and equipment transportation, warehousing, order processing, and information systems. Both network design and global logistics will be analyzed as a part of this focus. There will also be an explanation of the importance of the integration of these various systems, and the effects integration has on the overall viability of the sport industry.

SALES MANAGEMENT

The reader will be presented with an overview of the strategies and techniques for promoting and selling the sport product, including sales theory models, promotion theory paradigms, and promotion application in sport marketing. In addition, the distribution process of the sport product will be covered, including an analysis of the distribution principles related to time, place, and possession, as well as the process for selecting distribution systems.

RETAIL MANAGEMENT

Readers will gain an understanding of sport retailing and sport retail management through a presentation of various retail strategies and a strategic approach to retailing in the sport field. Inclusive of this chapter will be the concepts of strategic retail management; the factors and skills associated with situation analysis; the ways to target customers and gathering information; the concepts associated with choosing a retail location; the concepts related to managing a retail business; the concepts related to merchandise management and pricing; the various ways of communicating with the customer; and integrating and controlling all aspects of the retail strategy.

E-MARKETING MANAGEMENT

Readers will gain an understanding that in the twenty-first century, e-business and e-commerce have become staples within the field of sport marketing. Information will be offered regarding the factors that drive modern business through digital technologies. Inclusive of this will be concepts of managing digital enterprises via the internet, the World Wide Web, and intranets, including C2B and B2B, as well as potential future technologies. In addition, how sport businesses utilize electronic means to overcome barriers of geographic boundaries to market, produce, and deliver services will be covered.

COMMUNICATION MANAGEMENT AND PROMOTIONS

Readers will gain an understanding of the other elements of the sport promotion mix, including licensing, publicity, personal contact, incentives, and atmospherics. They will learn how to incorporate sport promotion activities into an integrated communications plan, how to plan an event, create pricing, location and distribution strategies, and how to cost-effectively promote them. Areas to be covered will include sports information, media relations, public relations, and community relations. In addition, indirect (word-of-mouth) and direct (sales) promotional strategies will be covered in relation to positioning, building brand equity, increasing credibility, and enhancing image transfer and association.

ADVERTISING

Readers will be provided with an overview of the methods for bringing public attention to the sport product or business through print, broadcast, or electronic media. This will include an examination of copy and design, media planning and buying, portfolio development, video production, broadcast advertising development, billboard/outdoor advertising development, and graphic design. The reader will also discover how to integrate the field of sport and the engagement of interdisciplinary thinking as it relates to all areas of communication. Special emphasis will be placed on journalism, audio-visual communications, development communications, telecommunications, and mass communications.

SPONSORSHIP

Readers will gain an appreciation of the significant role sponsorship plays in the sport promotional mix. Through an explanation of the history of sport sponsorship, the reader will gain an understanding of the various areas of sport sponsorship, including governing body sponsorship, team sponsorship, athlete sponsorship, broadcast sponsorship, facility sponsorship and event sponsorship. Through the articulation of corporate and brand goals, the reader will also learn about the various criteria for sponsorship, and how they are utilized in choosing the companies to partner with, developing sponsorship packages, and engaging in sponsorship negotiations.

SOCIAL MEDIA AND NETWORKING

Readers will gain an appreciation of the evolution of social media and networking as an integral tool for enhancing the implementation of sport marketing practices. Initially, by explaining what social media and social networking are, the reader will be taken through the process of the inner workings of a Facebook page, how to effectively use Twitter for sport marketing, how to utilize the analytics of Twitter and Facebook, and the networking and sales opportunities inherent to using LinkedIn. The reader will also recognize the power of new media through geolocation social media and other mobile applications, and appreciate just how little potential social media have actually reached.

INTERNATIONAL AND GLOBAL MARKETING

Readers will gain an appreciation of the ever-growing internationalization and globalization of marketing in and through sport. This will be accomplished through an examination of the implementation of policies, procedures, and strategies within the parameters set forth by cultural, economic, political, and legal constraints of various worldwide markets. Inclusive of this explanation will be the various elements of alternative dispute resolution inherent to sport marketing management.

EMERGING SOCIOLOGICAL ISSUES

Readers will learn about the emerging sociological issues inherent to sport marketing. The first will involve evaluating the role of relationship and experience sport marketing as applied in the sport industry. Second will be an assessment of the importance of recovery sport marketing during and after a negative situation, and how to recapture a market. Finally, readers will interpret how social sport marketing plays a significant role in expanding sport businesses beyond profit-making operations to include offering intangible social benefits

PEDAGOGICAL FEATURES

Advanced Theory and Practice in Sport Marketing enhances learning with the following pedagogical devices:

- Each chapter opens with a chapter outline and a list of chapter objectives.
- Key terms appear alphabetically at the end of the book in the glossary.
- Each chapter has a case study embedded within the text to enhance critical thinking as related to real-world concepts associated with the text material.
- At the end of each chapter, there is a real-world case written by professionals from the field of sport marketing. These experts are from academia, professional sports leagues and teams, amateur sport organizations, and corporate sport. The information they supply will provide the learner with knowledge of how that individual entered the specific area of sport marketing, about the real world of sport marketing, and advice as to what the learner can do to better prepare for entry into the specified area of sport marketing.
- A summative conclusion at the end of each chapter reviews the chapter objectives and pertinent information gained from the chapter.

CRITICAL THINKING

One of the most important skills for students to develop through their college and university years is critical thinking. This mental process of analyzing and evaluating information is used across all disciplines, and serves as a process for reflecting on the information provided, examining facts to understand reasoning, and forming conclusions and plans for action.

The authors of this book have provided a series of opportunities for students to enhance their critical thinking skills while also verifying their understanding of the materials presented in this text. Each chapter has a case study embedded within it to enhance critical thinking as related to real-world concepts associated with the text material. These scenarios are a collection of "real-world" situations modified with a sport marketing twist to provide the student with the maximum opportunity to analyze, evaluate, and ponder possible solutions to the ethical or global situation. Questions associated with each case study will help students focus their efforts on key theoretical aspects from the chapter, and apply that knowledge to deal with the specific scenario.

This text provides a unique opportunity for critical thinking in association with sport marketing in the corporate or professional setting. "From theory to practice" cases appear at the end of each chapter, written by professionals in the field of sport marketing. Each one provides information about how the individual entered the specific area of sport marketing, the professional world of sport marketing, and advice of what the student can do to become better prepared for entry into the specific area of sport marketing.

COMPANION WEBSITE

The companion website for *Advanced Theory and Practice in Sport Marketing* provides the following additional resources for students:

- an electronic test bank of multiple-choice questions for each chapter
- glossary flashcards
- useful web links.

The companion website also provides the instructor with the following teaching aids:

- PowerPoint presentations for each chapter
- discussion questions for each chapter, which may be used as essay topics or in class discussions
- suggested answers for the discussion questions, and explanations of the answers to the multiple-choice questions
- additional case studies and scenarios for each chapter with suggested discussion topics
- a sample master syllabus.

ACKNOWLEDGMENTS, DEDICATIONS, AND EPIGRAPHS

ERIC C. SCHWARZ

I would like to first dedicate this book to my wife Loan. Your unconditional love in life, as well as your unending support for my work and my writing is the foundation for all of my success. You continue to influence me and give me the strength to be the best person in life. You are the most important person in my world – thank you for making me a better person every day!

In addition, I would like to show my appreciation to my best friend and co-author of this second edition, Jason Hunter. Over the 25 years, regardless of the distance between us, our friendship has continued to be an integral part of my life. I once again thank you for your efforts on this second edition, and more importantly for your friendship.

I would like to also acknowledge our third author, Alan LaFleur. I have been very fortunate to have quality students over the years, including Alan. His involvement in helping integrate current information about social media and networking in the textbook, as well as having a "younger" set of eyes review the manuscript, significantly helps ensure that this book is targeted toward a new generation of students, in addition to relevant academicians and professionals.

And finally . . . To Maxi . . .

JASON D. HUNTER

I owe thanks to Mariann, my wonderful wife, and three amazing children, Zachary, Morgan, and Jake. Without their support and encouragement, there would not have been enough hours in the day to complete this project.

I would also like to thank my friend, colleague, and co-author Eric Schwarz. We have known each other for more than 25 years, since we completed our undergraduate degree from Plymouth State University of the University System of New Hampshire. I am very thankful for the educational opportunities that Plymouth afforded me and for the lasting friendships that developed and continue to grow.

Thank you to my students and colleagues at George Williams College of Aurora University for allowing me to apply my love for lifelong learning both in and out of the classroom.

Finally, I owe special thanks to my parents Jay and Merrylyn Hunter for providing me with the foundation that helped transform me into the person I am today. Without their love, support, and moral judgment, I would never have seen the true benefits of education and strength of family.

ALAN LAFLEUR

To my loving family!

PART I

SPORT MARKETING: THE BASICS

CHAPTER ONE

INTRODUCTION TO SPORT MARKETING

CHAPTER OUTLINE

- What is sport marketing?
- The marketing plan
- Bottom line: what is sport marketing?
- Strategic sport marketing: looking to the future
- Conclusion

CHAPTER OBJECTIVES

The reader will be able to:

- provide an overview of sport marketing
- define what sport marketing is, how it is connected to the business of sport, and the relationship to traditional marketing
- identify the components of the four Cs of marketing analysis (consumer, company, competition, and climate), and STPD (segmentation, targeting, positioning, and delivery)
- examine the role of strategic sport marketing planning in moving sport organizations forward toward implementing strategies, attaining a vision, and future success.

3

WHAT IS SPORT MARKETING?

Prior to describing what sport marketing is, we should take a look at the definitions of the two root words – "sport" and "marketing."

Sport – or is it sports?

First we look at the concepts of sport and sports. Sport is defined as activities, experiences or business enterprises that center on athletics, health and wellness, recreation, and leisure time opportunities. Some of the common misconceptions about sport include the following: (1) there needs to be a competitive situation; (2) the offering must have a standard set of rules; and (3) participants need specialized equipment and facilities. This is true of sports, which simply refers to individual, dual and team sports activities such as soccer, baseball, golf and tennis. Sport is an all-inclusive term covering all aspects that go beyond the playing field, including all the various operations that make the games happen.

Sport and business

Now we look at how the concept of business ties into these previous definitions. Business is defined as individuals or organizations that seek to make a profit by providing products and services that satisfy the needs, wants and desires of the consumer. The business world covers a wide variety of aspects. The internal factors include the primary business activities of management, marketing, and finance, which are centered on business owners, employees, and customers. The external factors include competition, the economy, information technology, legal and regulatory forces, and social responsibility and ethics.

The definition of business and the internal and external factors in the business world are mirrored in the profession of sport management and administration. With regard to whether sport administration or sport management is more appropriate, it seems as though more programs as business utilize the term management over administration; however, there is no significant difference between the meanings of the two terms when it comes to the field of sport. The only difference tends to be curricular-based, and will vary from institution to institution. Therefore, when looking at this field, the major of sport management, and in some cases sport administration, is of greater interest to business educators. This is defended by the following definition of sport management: the collection of skills related to the planning, organizing, directing, controlling, budgeting, leading, and evaluation of an organization or department whose primary product or service is related to sport and its related functions.

However, what is unique about the products and services associated with the sport business industry is that many of the goods are intangible and experiential. While there are the typical sport products such as equipment, merchandise, publications, food, and memorabilia, much of the products and services are ethereal in nature. There are many services that are implemented to enhance the quality and value of the tangible sport product, and hence the satisfaction of the sport consumer. These services may include maintaining sport products (ice skate sharpening), education for using equipment to improve wellness or lifestyle (personal

4

trainers), or enhancing sport products or their extensions (personalized merchandise such as names on jerseys or logos on hats).

In addition to services, there are many intangible aspects of sport products that are experiential in nature. For example, a sport team offers a product of a single game ticket to a home game. While the ticket and the opportunities for purchasing tangible product extensions is available, much of the product is focused on experiential enhancements, including the appearance and atmosphere of the facility, the customer service provided by employees, and either the euphoria of a team's victory or the devastation of a loss. Furthermore, unlike most products, once the game or event takes place, the product disappears and all that remains is the memory of it. This is what makes the marketing of the sport business industry unique.

Marketing

Now that we have a definition of sport, as well as a basis for its relationship to the business world, what is marketing? There is often confusion over what marketing truly is. Marketing is often defined by its components, such as advertising, sales, promotions, product management, pricing, publicity, etc. These components do not define what marketing is – they act to enhance the application of marketing elements.

When many people think of marketing, they are really thinking of marketing tactics. People associate marketing with tactics, including the television commercials we see while watching sporting events, the between-play promotions during live sporting events, and the information published in newspapers or broadcast on a newscast. But tactics in marketing are similar to the tactics of sport. They are very important, but useless without having a sound basis of knowledge.

While this knowledge is a sound basis for the understanding of marketing, the true definition of marketing is simply the functions involved in the transfer of goods and services from the producer to the consumer. The focal point of these functions is in four specific areas known as the 4 Cs of marketing analysis: the consumer, the company itself, the competition, and the climate.

The consumer

Who is the consumer? Is it the traditional shopper who (1) visits stores in person in search of merchandise or bargains; (2) knows what he or she wants and makes the purchase, or (3) repeatedly purchases a commodity or service? Or is it the twenty-first-century consumer who (1) uses his or her followers to acquire information to make a decision on buying a product, (2) the customer who reaches out to the organizer of an event on Twitter to complain about an event, or (3) the person watching the free stream of an event at home on a computer? It is these and much more. By definition, a consumer is an individual or organization that purchases or obtains goods and services for direct use or ownership. As marketing professionals, we strive to please all of these consumers to maximize sales of products and services, and hence maximize profit. But how do we reach these consumers?

5

Segmentation

Segmentation is the concept of dividing a large, diverse group with multiple attributes into smaller groups with distinctive characteristics. These distinctive groups have similar needs and desires, and hence will respond to marketing efforts in similar ways. The concept of segmentation is basic to all marketing efforts, since the goal of segmentation is to identify the market.

One of the biggest challenges for marketing professionals is to determine the appropriate segment to market. Some of the major factors utilized to choose a segment include:

- What is the size of the segmented market?
- What is the purchasing power of the segmented market?
- How can the marketer be sure that the product is what the consumer wants?
- Is it worth marketing the product to the chosen segment?
- What tactics should be used to attract the segment to purchase the sport product?

To answer these questions, marketers use the four bases of segmentation: the consumer's state of being, the consumer's state of mind, product usage by consumers, and product benefits as perceived by consumers.

The consumer's state of being is the concept of belonging to a specified class or group. In marketing, the major states of being include location, age, income level, gender, race and ethnicity, and sexual orientation. Geographic location is used to determine the spread of population as related to the distribution and usage of a product. Age helps to differentiate the needs and interests of consumers, as they differ throughout the lifespan. Income levels help the marketer determine the probable standard of living of the demographic, which in turn influences the manner in which a product is marketed. An example of this would be that a teenage inner-city basketball player who plays at the Rucker from Harlem will be marketed to differently as compared to the suburban soccer mom; the 10-year-old alternative sports fan who is influenced by anything related to skateboarding and BMX bikes; and the millions of people who try to emulate players and game actions through video games and fantasy sports. As marketing becomes more global in nature, understanding the intricacies of various race and ethnic markets is integral to marketing success. In addition, marketing based on sexual orientation is an emerging market; however, there is still some controversy as to whether this should be viewed as a separate and distinct market.

The consumer's state of mind deals with the individual cognitive processes involved in marketing. Among the most prevalent concerns to marketers are individual personality traits, lifestyle changes that are evident throughout the lifespan, and the individual preferences and perceptions of consumers, which are wide and varied.

Product usage by consumers deals with the consumption rates by the various market segments. Central to this concept is the Pareto Principle, otherwise known as the 80/20 rule. The Pareto Principle is generally applied to vendors or customers in a retail setting. This rule assumes that 20 percent of the customers generate 80 percent of the sales, or that 80 percent of merchandise comes from 20 percent of the vendors.

Product benefits as perceived by consumers go beyond the consumer's state of mind to look specifically at the assessment by consumers as to the advantages the products provided. The

6

consumer will always ask the question "What is in it for me?" By understanding the consumer's viewpoint, it allows marketers to (1) describe the products more efficiently and effectively in marketing collateral; (2) better prepare salespeople as to how to sell products, and (3) provide evidence as to how to better differentiate products.

Targeting
In the marketing world, we strive or aim to satisfy our desired market through the concepts of exchange and relationships. The purpose of targeting is to find the best way to get a product's image into the minds of consumers, and hence entice the consumer to purchase the product. The research and development processes described earlier are utilized at this stage to enter the product into the market. This is accomplished through a detailed analysis of the marketing mix, otherwise known as the four Ps of marketing: product, price, place, and promotion (see Figure 1.1). The product may be tangible (goods) or intangible (services), and decisions are made based on concepts such as branding, functionality, and quality. Price is the amount of money or goods asked for in exchange for something else. Place deals with the methods of distributing the product to consumers. Promotion represents how information about the product is communicated to customers, with a goal of receiving positive response from the consumer, and results in product sales.

[Note: Later in the chapter we will elaborate on this concept, and show how, in the realm of sport, the elements of marketing are expanded to the six Ps of sport marketing by moving publicity/public relations out of the category of promotion, since it is such a large factor in the marketing of sport, and expanding on the various ways people influence marketing.]

Product   Price

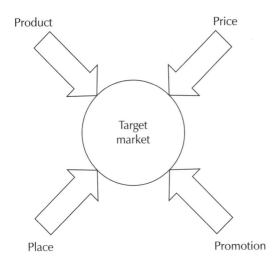

Place   Promotion

Figure 1.1 The marketing mix

Positioning
Positioning is how a company seeks to influence the perceptions of potential and current customers about the image of the company and its products and services. This is accomplished

7

by applying the marketing mix with the goal of strategically placing the product or service firmly in the mind of the consumer. We often talk in society about the concept of "making a good first impression." In positioning, the goal is to get the consumer's mind to react to the implementation of the marketing mix in a positive manner. By creating this knowledge, consumers will develop an impression that is often difficult to change. Hence, if the marketer can send a message that is consistent with what the consumer already believes (the consumer's perceptions), the product will become easier to sell. An example would be a Detroit Red Wings advertising campaign concentrating on Detroit being known as Hockeytown. Hockey consumers are already aware of this fact, and the marketers can play off of this knowledge.

One of the best ways to position a product in the consumer's mind is to be first on the scene. People want who they perceive is first in the market, or the best in the market. This concept of being number one can often overcome other shortcomings of products.

However, not all products can be first on the market, or number one in the market. So how do you position these other products so that the consumer will buy? This is most often accomplished by claiming a unique position in the market. Through applying the marketing mix, the marketer will strive to carve this uniqueness into the mind of consumers, so that they feel they are getting something different and worthwhile for their hard-earned money. In general, when there is a clear market leader, it is often extremely difficult to knock off the king of the mountain. By not challenging the market leader head-on, a company can increase its market share through marketing its uniqueness as compared to that industry leader. To market their uniqueness, marketers look to cater to the specific benefits of the product. In order to do this, the product must often be sold at a low price, since when viewing new products people will value low initial price more than quality.

Delivering

Delivery is the concept of producing or achieving what is desired or expected by the consumer. Through the concepts of segmentation, targeting, and positioning, a framework is created to allow the industry to utilize marketing to deliver an awareness of products to potential consumers. The previous concepts are the development phase and the start of the implementation phase of the marketing concept. Delivery is the completion of the implementation phase, and the start of the management aspect, where the creative and process aspects of the marketing discipline are applied.

The remainder of this book will focus on the delivery of the marketing concept.

Understanding the consumer is central to the ability to engage in marketing. Marketers must know how consumers behave, their motivations, their perceptions, and their preferences. Marketers must have an awareness of their attitudes, their knowledge, and their emotions. In addition, marketers must have the ability to segment the market, analyze the target market, position the product, and deliver it to consumers.

The company

What do we need to know about the company itself? The framework for this is the SWOT analysis (Figure 1.2), which looks at the internal strengths, internal weaknesses, external opportunities and external threats of the organization.

8

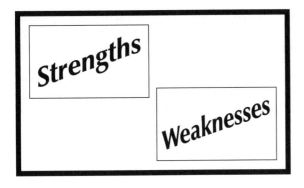

Figure 1.2 The company and SWOT

For starters, the framework of understanding the company is in the first two parts of a SWOT analysis: internal strengths and internal weaknesses. The strengths of a company are its resources and capabilities that may be used to develop a competitive advantage. A competitive advantage is where a company sustains profits above the average for the specific industry. Competitive advantage is usually looked at in two ways: cost advantage (when a company can deliver the same benefits as competitors at a lower cost); and differentiation advantage (when a company can deliver benefits that exceed those of other products in the specific industry). By understanding these concepts, a marketer can gain a better understanding of the company itself. In addition, the marketing professional can implement a more effective and efficient marketing effort by maintaining or improving on strengths, while seeking ways to improve on and eliminate weaknesses. Examples would include having limited time, staff, or funding.

The competition

So, what do we need to know about the competition? The framework of competition is in the last two parts of a SWOT analysis: external opportunities and external threats. By evaluating opportunities and threats, a company can evaluate its current status in the market, and determine which direction the company should be heading. This is most often guided by an organizational mission, through an evaluation of organizational and management options, and outlining the goods and/or services to be marketed. The opportunities are the marketplace openings that exist because others have not entered or capitalized on that part of the marketplace. Threats are those environmental factors that can negatively affect the marketing of a product if the company does not react to them.

The climate

Finally, we should be concerned about the internal and external climate that affects all parts of the sport business organization, but especially the sport marketing functions. The internal climate of an organization focuses on the organizational structure and how that directly affects the culture within the sport business. Organizational culture is a system of shared values, beliefs, assumptions, and understanding that influences worker behavior. A strong organizational culture is characterized by employees sharing the same core values, whereas a weak one is characterized by employees who do not possess common values. Organizational culture has the potential to affect organizational effectiveness, which in turn may have a direct effect on the message being sent by the sport business through its marketing efforts. Sport marketing managers need to create an appropriate organizational culture by setting a vision and getting employees excited about the fundamental purpose of the organization.

If it is deemed that the current culture is not conducive to successful implementation of marketing efforts, then the marketing manager is faced with the challenge of changing the culture. This is especially challenging because, as the global reach of sport marketing increases, there is a need to have a better understanding and acceptance of cultural diversity. As a result of this necessity to expand the understanding of global organizational behavior, sport marketing organizations need to value a wide range of cultural and individual differences and embrace them to achieve the full marketing potential of the sport organization.

The external climate includes the influences from outside the organization that have a direct effect on sport marketing efforts. The major external climatological factors affecting sport businesses today are the economy, information technology, legal and political forces, and social and ethical influences. The economy has a direct effect on the amount of discretionary money and time individuals can afford to partake in purchasing or experiencing the products and services offered through sport marketing efforts. These economic constraints are caused by numerous factors, including inflation, significant competition, high interest rates, and weak economic indicators of future economic conditions.

As new information technologies become standard use in everyday life (iPads, Android tablets, smartphones, Kindles), marketers have to be able to utilize that technology in a way that will reach the end user. We have seen that as smartphones become the norm, applications have been developed to produce a better memory of an event; for example, the MLB application that allows you to order food to be delivered so that you never have to leave your seat or stand in line. However, technology changes so fast that industry needs to constantly learn the new trends. This year the trend could be geolocation social media like Foursquare and next year it could be the next step in geolocation – Augmented Reality – that makes exploring the city around you into a new experience. Imagine passing by Soldier Field on your way to work, holding your phone up, and seeing the upcoming schedule, a button to buy tickets, and a highlight video of their last game. New technology makes it easier to reach a new customer and it is up to the marketer to be able to figure out how to use the technology to grab the attention of consumers who are being bombarded by other companies that are asking for their entertainment dollars.

Legal and political forces have a direct effect on the way in which sport organizations can operate within a given environment. Regulatory forces ranging from federal, state, and local government to administrative law as set by governing bodies and organizations all have a direct effect on the manner in which sport marketing efforts are implemented. Understanding the influence of power and politics is crucial to overcoming conflicts and constraints resulting from external legal and political decisions. Understanding how to work from a position of power by influencing decisions and controlling resources, combined with working within the political structure by using informal strategies and tactics to gain power, develop powerful networks, and establishing alliances, will allow the sport marketing manager to overcome most road-blocks put in place by legal and political forces.

With regard to social and ethic influences (which will be covered in greater detail in Chapter 3), a sport marketing professional must understand the societal values and beliefs that directly affect the implementation of sport marketing efforts. The foundations of these societal values and beliefs are focused on the ethical influences and social responsibility evident in a given society. Ethics are the principles, rules, or standards of right conduct of individuals, groups, or a society. Ethics generally explain a society's way of life, rules of conduct, and moral code. Sport marketers have a duty and obligation to act in a responsible manner in terms of the ethics within a society. As such, sport marketers and organizations must also act in a morally and socially responsible manner, and this generally falls under the realm of corporate social responsibility (CSR). CSR focuses on the responsibility sport organizations have to society beyond that of investors and stakeholders to include philanthropy, volunteerism, and any other efforts that foster relationships that enhance society.

THE MARKETING PLAN

All of the previous information is then compiled into a marketing plan. A marketing plan starts with primary and secondary market research. It is very dangerous to start a marketing plan without appropriate research and by assuming what the intended market wants and needs. Primary market research is gathering your own data through observation, surveys, interviews, and focus groups. Secondary market research uses published information including industry profiles, trade periodicals, and demographic profiles to determine the scope of your market.

The next part of the marketing plan focuses on economics. The key factors when identifying the economy of your market include the following:

- What is the total size of the market?
- What percent share of the market do you intend to capture?
- What is the current demand within the market?
- What are the current and future trends of the market?
- Is there growth potential within the market?
- What are the barriers to entering the market, and how will the company overcome those barriers?
- How could changes in the industry itself, the economy, technology, and governmental regulations affect your company and force changes in your marketing efforts?

The following section should describe the product(s) and/or service(s) to be marketed. Three key concepts that should be articulated in the plan for each product or service should be: (1) a description of the most important features of the product/service, with particular consideration given to what differentiates it from other products/services; (2) a description of the benefits, specifically considering what the product/service will do for the consumer; and (3) a description of the post-sale services (warranties, service contracts, delivery options, consumer support, refund policies, etc.).

Now we need to detail the demographics of our customers. For individuals, we consider such items as age, gender, race/ethnicity, location, income level, social class, occupation, and education. For business consumers, we consider the industry, location, size, and preferences.

Next we detail the competition. It is important to remember in this section to list all competitors (indirect and direct), and differentiate the level of competitiveness – whether they compete across the board, or only in certain product areas. In this section there must also be a comparison of how your product(s) or service(s) will compare with the competition. This competitive analysis will help determine your competitive advantages and disadvantages, and provide data to help determine the best way to market your products within the industry.

After this information has been compiled, a niche can be defined. A niche is a special area of demand for a product or service. On a large scale, companies such as Nike and Reebok design and market athletic shoes for each different sport, and often with specialized models based on specific athletes. On a more direct scale, a niche marketing scheme would be offering specialized golf products such as customized clubs, designer balls and tees, and associated golf gadgets to subscribers of *Golf* magazine. These niches are then used to develop the marketing strategy. Inclusive of this strategy development are the elements of the marketing mix, including:

- the method for setting prices and associated pricing strategies (price)
- the distribution channels to be utilized to sell products and services (place)
- the method for getting information to potential consumers (promotion).

Now that a description of the products, services, customers, markets, and strategy has been completed, the final element of the marketing plan is a sales forecast. Usually this is completed in two ways. First, a "best case scenario" should provide a realistic expectation of sales. Second, a "worst case scenario" should provide the minimum expectation of sales, irrespective of what happens.

BOTTOM LINE: WHAT IS SPORT MARKETING?

In conclusion, marketing is the study of the consumer, the company, the competition, and the climate; specifically relating those areas to market segmentation, target markets, product positioning, and delivery of the product. Then, to engage in marketing, we use the various tactics of marketing, which will be elaborated upon in the remaining chapters of this volume.

OK – so what is sport marketing? Based on the definition of "sport" and "marketing," it shows how complex both concepts are. Therefore, it is safe to assume that combining the two concepts to get sport marketing is probably even more complex. This is very true, because sport marketing is a process of developing and implementing activities related to the production, pricing, distribution, promotion, and publicizing of a sport product. These sport products run the gambit, from sport drinks to sport clothing with team logos, to ticket packages. The goal of this process is to satisfy the needs and wants of consumers, achieve the goals and objectives of the company in relation to their philosophy, mission, and vision, and stay ahead of the competition to maximize your product's and company's potential. This complexity is accompanied by certain characteristics that make the sport product unique.

STRATEGIC SPORT MARKETING: LOOKING TO THE FUTURE

A strategic plan is a comprehensive and integrated plan that is designed to look at the long-term projections of a business. Traditional strategic plan formation focuses on creating a coherent mission for an organization, assessing its internal operational strength and weaknesses, evaluating external opportunities and threats, generating relevant goals and objectives, crafting an appropriate organizational structure to move the business forward, and finally developing an action plan to implement the process. However, the strategic sport marketing plan goes into much more depth to include inputs, constituencies, key success factors, assumptions, key result areas (KRAs), and strategies. As such, the following sections will take a look at the synergistic, all-inclusive strategic sport marketing process in terms of where the sport business is at the starting point, where the sport business wants to go, and how the sport business is going to achieve its vision.

CASE STUDY 1: STRATEGIC PLANNING OF THE JIMMY V CELEBRITY GOLF CLASSIC

Authored and contributed by Ashley A. Bowling and Stacy Warner,
East Carolina University

The V Foundation, named for late coach Jim Valvano who is best known for leading North Carolina State to a national championship in 1983, was created in his memory to raise money for cancer research. The non-profit organization formed in 1993 hosts several events annually. One of the marquee events is the Jimmy V Celebrity Golf Classic held every August. The event includes a raffle, gala, and two full rounds of golf for participating celebrities and sponsors. In 2007 event organizers decided to move the Classic from Raleigh (where it had been held for the previous 13 years) to Pinehurst Resort, a world-renowned course. However, in 2008 construction began on the Lonnie Poole Golf Course at NC State University in Raleigh, and the course was set to open in 2009.

The governing board of the Jimmy V Celebrity Golf Classic used a strategic assessment when faced with the decision to either stay in Pinehurst or return to Raleigh. A SWOT analysis was conducted during this assessment to determine the organizational strengths and weaknesses as well as any opportunities and threats. One of the biggest strengths of the V Foundation is its connection to the basketball community and "Tobacco Road," the small geographical area known for the intense basketball rivalries between UNC, Duke, and NC State. The V Foundation also has a strong relationship with ESPN, which hosts Jimmy V Week every December. A weakness of the organization is its size. There are only three full-time employees and the organization relies heavily on volunteers.

In September 2008, the city of Raleigh unveiled its new convention center. Moving the Classic back to Raleigh would provide a major marketing opportunity and draw more attention to the new Lonnie Poole Golf Course and convention center along with the event itself. The V Foundation, however, would face some challenges, due to hosting the event in Pinehurst for the previous two years. The members of the V Foundation did not want to damage their relationship with the resort, and the opportunity to play at Pinehurst appealed to the golf enthusiasts that attend the event each year. The V Foundation office is located just outside of Raleigh and the Classic did have a 13-year history in Raleigh. Thus, a strong base of sponsors, participants, volunteers, and spectators were readily available.

After a thorough assessment, the V Foundation and the governing board of the Classic decided to move the event back to Raleigh. To continue their relationship with Pinehurst, they maintained hosting the Pre-V event at the famous resort in Pinehurst. In partnering with the Lonnie Poole Golf Course and the Raleigh Convention Center, a marketing plan was developed with the slogan, "You can go home again." One of the top marketing goals for the Classic in 2009 was to raise more money for cancer research than they did the previous year.

Once the marketing plan and the goals were in place, implementation became key to the V Foundation's strategic plan. Implementing the plan involved use of the marketing mix, or the 4 Ps: product, price, place, and promotion. In this particular case, "place" was of particular importance.

The 16th Annual Jimmy V Celebrity Golf Classic in 2009 was relocated back to Raleigh. The event was welcomed by the local community and included appearances by athletes such as Chad LaRose (NHL), ESPN analyst Stuart Scott, and Sidney Lowe, former player of Jim Valvano. At the conclusion of the event, another assessment was conducted to evaluate and assess the event. The event received rave reviews from participants and the results of the evaluation made it clear that the event was considered a success by every measure. The Classic also achieved its goal of raising more funds than the year before. After 18 years, the Jimmy V Celebrity Golf Classic has raised over $15 million for cancer research and continues to donate 100 percent of the funds raised to that cause. The Classic continues to thrive due to its strategic planning and ongoing evaluation and assessment.

This case demonstrates the benefits of strategic planning for an organization. Conducting a SWOT analysis, creating a marketing plan and goals, implementing that plan, and continued evaluation are imperative for an organization to reach its full potential. If strategic planning is designed in accordance with the organizational vision, marketing effectiveness will be greater and the organization will likely thrive for years to come.

Questions for discsussion

1   If you were an event manager of the Classic, what would you measure to gauge the success of the event each year?
2   In light of the case, what are some threats the V Foundation could have faced by changing the location of the Classic?

14

Where is the sport business?

Prior to any quality strategic planning, sport marketers must have a complete understanding of the current situation of the sport business, and how that information has a direct effect on the overall strategic planning process. These include initial inputs to the process, mission, constituencies, key success factors, internal strengths and weaknesses/external opportunities and threats (SWOT), uncontrollable assumptions, and the ideal vision.

The initial inputs to the process are those initiating factors that entice a sport business to enter into a strategic planning process. These start with the core competencies of the sport business, which are the capabilities, skills, and technologies that allow a sport business to provide value to its customers. The challenge in strategic planning is to make sure that they do not become obsolete five to ten years down the road. At the same time, the core competencies need to be a contributor to perceived customer value of consumers, to provide a foundation for entry into new domestic and global markets, and should be viewed as being unique in the marketplace. It is important to not confuse core competencies with assets – core competencies:

- do not appear on balance sheets
- do not depreciate
- cannot be purchased or sold
- strengthen an organization and therefore are not product- or service-specific
- create competitiveness in the marketplace
- require significant investment over time
- involve risk-taking ventures
- need broad support from the entire organization.

Ultimately, core competencies provide consumer benefits, are difficult for competitors to imitate, and can be leveraged across markets and product/service lines. However, there are five additional initial inputs that are integral for successful initiation of a strategic planning process. First are the personal values of the ownership and executive management of the sport business. These will drive the direction of the organization. Next is the history of the sport business, which serves as a framework of the past and will often help in understanding the present and shaping the direction for the future. Third is employee input, since, without engagement and buy-in from those who will eventually implement the strategic plan, there is no chance of success. Fourth are the trends in the sport business industry, the economy, society as a whole, technological advantages, legal changes, and political influences. Finally are the core organizational values of the sport business. Core values are the principles that guide the internal organization and its interactions with external constituencies. Some of the most common core values used in sport business include integrity, responsible stewardship, teamwork, and service.

After evaluating the initial inputs to the strategic planning process, the mission of the sport business is analyzed and integrated into the development of the plan. A mission statement is a short declaration usually of 50 words or less (although some can be as much as a paragraph long) that articulates the purpose of an organization. It is integral that inclusions of the strategic marketing plan work in alignment to the mission of the sport business in terms of the general purpose of the strategic marketing plan, the products and services affected by the plan, the overall values and beliefs of the organization, and the customers of the sport business.

This is directly connected with understanding the constituencies inherent to the strategic planning process. The first involves understanding the needs of consumers through market research, as well as the consumer's role as both a participant and a spectator. Second is the market selection processes embedded in the segmentation, targeting, positioning, and delivery (STPD) process discussed earlier in the chapter. Third is identifying the key success factors (KSF) that will be measured as part of the ongoing evaluation of the plan. The purpose of a KSF is to differentiate successful businesses in the sport industry. Usually sport businesses focus on a maximum of two or three majors KSFs, because these are the area where they need to excel. Fourth is the SWOT analysis of the marketing mix decision about products, pricing, place, and promotions. Internal factors (strengths and weaknesses) are controllable and include organization operations and culture that affect the achievement of goals, objectives, and strategies. External factors include uncontrollable assumptions regarding political, economic, social, and technological (PEST) factors, as well as competition. Finally, an exploration of a clear ideal vision for the plan, including its alignment with the vision for the sport business, is crucial to success. Both visions are short, concise statements of one to two sentences that need to reflect the mission statement, have a forward-looking orientation at least five years into the future, and are measureable and achievable.

Where does the sport business want to go?

With the vision being a forward-looking statement, the obvious next question involves looking into what direction the sport business wants to go by implementing the strategic sport marketing plan. This is accomplished through the development of key result areas (KRAs), the articulation of goals and objectives, and the creation of strategies.

KRAs are the general outcomes for the sport business that are articulated through the strategic sport marketing plan. A KRA serves to bridge the current situation of the sport business to where the sport business wants to be. KRAs also need to be measureable and achievable, as they become the defining concept of responsibility for the sport marketer placed in charge of it. Sport businesses and marketers must develop KRAs that are adaptable to various internal and external influences that will occur over time, and must have the agility to address those changes in a timely manner.

The development of goals, objectives, and strategies takes place under each KRA. Goals are specific accomplishments that are to be achieved within a set time period – either short term (usually within one year), medium term (a period ranging from one to three years), or long term (usually more than three years). Objectives are the steps to be enacted to accomplish the goals. These objectives need to be SMART – specific, measureable, aggressive, realistic, and time-based. Strategies are how the goals and objectives will be achieved, which is then employed through action plans.

How will the sport business get there?

The action plan served to bridge the planning processes documented above to the imple-mentation phase of strategic marketing. An action plan specifically documents who is responsible for implementing the strategic sport marketing plan, what tactics are to be executed to succeed, the timeline for completion of the plan, and the allocation of resources needed to accomplish the inclusions of the strategic sport marketing plan. These include communicating the plan to all relevant parties, coordinating the work that needs to be accomplished, selecting the staff who possess the skills necessary to provide input, implementing a knowledge accumulation process to allow for creativity in the implementation, engaging all aspects of the marketing information system to secure data, and creating a motivation and reward system to reinforce the importance of successful attainment of the vision.

The strategic sport marketing plan is an element of the overall business plan of a sport organization. The action plan is only one element of the implementation process of a strategic sport marketing planning process. Three other elements that are integral to the success of the strategic sport marketing plan are the budget, individual departmental plans, and the operations plan. A budget is an estimate of the expected revenues and expenses to be incurred over a specific time period. It is important to secure the appropriate budgeting to finance the strategic sport marketing plan, as the limitation of funding can severely hamper implementation.

The departmental plans are the micro-strategic plans implemented within each area of responsibility that connect to and aid in the attainment of the vision of the macro-strategic sport marketing plan. The most often used tool to measure performance and success within departments is the Balanced Scorecard, which measures financial, internal business process, learning and growth, and customer factors for a balanced viewpoint to reach a given vision and strategy. The Balanced Scorecard provides a consistent process of specifying objectives, devising measures for these objectives, setting targets, and devising initiatives to achieve these targets.

The operations plan serves as a central document that articulates accurate and current information regarding the operational policies and procedures of the sport organization. The first section of an operations manual usually articulates the philosophy and expectations of the organization. This is often followed by the human resources information, which articulates the policies and benefits of employees including how operations interact with employment and employee relations, and connects operations with the general information and policies/procedures of the sport facility. The final section includes the specific operational procedures of the sport organization. This plan goes beyond being an overview of policies, expectations, and procedures – it serves as a question-and-answer guide pertaining to everyday operations and sport organization policy.

CONCLUSION

The purpose of this chapter is to provide the reader with an overview of the evolution of sport marketing. First, we investigated what sport marketing is by defining the root words. Sport is defined as activities, experiences, or business enterprises that center on athletics, health and wellness, recreation, and leisure time opportunities. The association of sport with business (individuals or organizations that seek to make a profit by providing products and services that satisfy the needs, wants, and desires of the consumer) helps to develop an understanding of the field of sport management as the collection of skills related to the planning, organizing, directing, controlling, budgeting, leading, and evaluation of an organization or department whose primary product or service is linked to sport and its related functions. The marketing aspect of sport focuses on the functions involved in the transfer of goods and services from the producer to the consumer.

The focal point of these functions is in the specific areas known as the four Cs of marketing analysis: the consumer, the company itself, the competition, and the climate. The consumer is an individual or organization that purchases or obtains goods and services for direct use or ownership. To reach sport consumers, sport marketing professional go through a series of processes. Segmentation is the concept of dividing a large, diverse group with multiple attributes into smaller groups with distinctive characteristics. Targeting seeks to find the best way to get a product's image into the minds of consumers, and hence entice the consumer to purchase the product. This is accomplished by focusing on the four Ps of marketing – product, price, place, and promotion, the evolution of publicity as a fifth P, and the ongoing influence of people as the sixth P. Positioning focuses on how a company seeks to influence the perceptions of potential and current customers about the image of the company and its products and services. Delivery is the concept of producing or achieving what is desired or expected by the consumer.

With regard to the company and competition, the framework is centered on the SWOT analysis. The managerial function of the company itself is most concerned with internal strengths and weaknesses. The leaders of the company tend to focus on the external opportunities and external threats posed by competition and the environment. However, they must also address the climate that affects the sport marketing functions of an organization, including internal (organizational structure, culture, and change) and external (the economy, information technology, legal and political forces, and social and ethical influences) factors. All this information is then compiled into a marketing plan, and enhanced with primary and secondary research, economic and financial considerations, and an evaluation of the products and services to be offered.

A strategic plan is a comprehensive and integrated plan that is designed to look at the long-term projections of a business. The strategic sport marketing plan is a synergistic, all-inclusive, forward-looking process in terms of where the sport business is at the starting point, where the sport business wants to go, and how the sport business is going to reach their vision. Initially, strategic planning requires a complete understanding of the current situation of the sport business, and how that information has a direct effect on the overall strategic planning process in terms of the initial inputs to the process, mission, constituencies, key success factors, internal strengths and weaknesses/external opportunities and threats (SWOT), uncontrollable assumptions, and the ideal vision. To determine what direction the sport business wants to go, implementing the strategic sport marketing plan is accomplished through the development of key result areas (KRAs), the articulation of goal and objectives, and the creation of strategies. This is then all compiled into an action plan that documents who is responsible for implementing the strategic sport marketing plan, what tactics are to be executed to succeed, the timeline for completion of the plan, and the allocation of resources needed. The action plan then integrates with the budget, individual departmental plans, and the operations plan to drive the overall sport business plan toward attaining the vision set forth in the strategic sport marketing plan.

18

FROM THEORY TO PRACTICE

FRANK SUPOVITZ, SENIOR VICE-PRESIDENT, EVENTS
National Football League, New York, New York

In my opinion, I have the best job in the world. Sometimes it seems like one of the toughest, but it is certainly the best. In my position as Senior Vice-President of Events for the National Football League, I manage the department responsible for the planning and management of the Super Bowl, Pro Bowl, and the NFL Draft, among many other programs. We work closely with the host cities, stadiums, hotels, sponsors, broadcasters, and support venues that are needed to successfully execute these events, sometimes many years in advance.

Getting to this point in my career was partially a function of being in the right place at the right time, but also about being open to the many exciting possibilities a career can take. That did not mean taking any job that came my way. I evaluated every opportunity to determine whether a new job might provide me with new challenges for my experience and expertise, and whether I could imagine myself happy in a new pursuit not a year later, but ten years later.

I grew up in Queens, and worked evenings after school as an usher at Radio City Music Hall. That part-time job turned into a 16-year run at the Hall, advancing through the ranks through the operations department, then marketing, and finally to director of special events. There, I applied my experience in entertainment marketing with the knowledge of staging corporate, sports, and civic events to projects including the half-time show for Super Bowl XXII. From there, I worked on the U.S. Olympic Festival, the Goodwill Games, and other major programs, eventually ending up at the National Hockey League in 1992. There, I was responsible for NHL All Star Weekend, the Stanley Cup, and the NHL Draft, among many other events. After 13 seasons in hockey, I moved from pucks to pigskin, moving to the National Football League in 2005.

What does it take to plan a Super Bowl? Start with three to five years of working with local business and governmental leaders to prepare a city to host 150,000 inbound visitors, preparing the stadium for the nation's most watched annual event, managing ticketing for more than 70,000 fans, contracting more than 20,000 hotel rooms, hundreds of motor coaches, and tens of thousands of parking spaces. Many elements the public never sees, such as securing two practice facilities with the same playing surface as the stadium, hotels for the competing teams' accommodations and offices, and a media center to house more than 100 radio stations and the NFL Network broadcasting live throughout the week, as well as work space for thousands of accredited reporters and writers. We design and construct tented or indoor hospitality space for up to 8,000 corporate guests, more than 150,000 square feet of space for two major parties, a million-square-foot home for the NFL Experience fan festival, and banner and décor programs for city streets, the stadium, hotels, and other event facilities. We are also concerned with the presentation of the game on the field and scoreboard, create a

300-foot hardened security perimeter around the stadium, and manage a program to credential thousands of game day workers. While this list is by no means complete, it provides a tiny snapshot of why it takes hundreds of people and a number of years to prepare for one game on one day.

None of it is possible without the help of our business partners, and it is also our job to ensure that our sponsors get the best possible value from their association. It is so much more than sponsor signage on site, an ad in the program, or public address announcements. Each sponsor wants their product, service, and message to rise above the clutter, targeting a specific audience, and encouraging sampling or purchase. The trick is to involve sponsors in a meaningful way so they feel a sense of ownership in our events. Visa, for instance, offers special and exclusive experiences in which card holders can win a chance to tour the Super Bowl field before the game, watch the half-time show from the field, or bring Gatorade to the bench (involving yet another sponsor). General Motors is featured as a sponsor of the post-game ceremonies during which the Super Bowl MVP wins a car. Pepsi offers fans and visitors a concert series in the host city. Each of these partners activate their sponsorships with involving and unique experiential marketing programs that their association with the NFL can offer because we understand that our relationship is a true partnership in which both parties can richly benefit.

The pursuit of success in your sports marketing and management career will follow many of the same philosophies as building success on the field. Expand your playbook by staying current with the market and learning all you can about how this amazing business works. Keep your eyes open for changing developments and trends that will help you punch through obstacles and challenges, and be prepared to respond quickly to opportunities.

Settle for no less than excellence in everything you do. The competition for the best positions is fierce!

CHAPTER TWO

MANAGING THE SPORT MARKETING MIX

CHAPTER OBJECTIVES

The reader will be able to:

▪ understand how the sport marketing mix is implemented and managed
▪ recognize the concepts that make sport marketing unique
▪ expand the traditional marketing mix into the six Ps of sport marketing
▪ appreciate the intricacies of the sport marketing plan.

WHAT MAKES SPORT MARKETING UNIQUE?

When we look at sport marketing and what makes it unique, we must complete an in-depth analysis of those market forces that are utilized to meet the needs and wants of the consumers, while ensuring success for the company. What makes this different from traditional marketing? In theory there is no difference. However, in practice there is a world of difference. The primary sport product, and hence the market, is traditionally demand-based, whereas most generic products are marketed based on need.

The characteristics of sport marketing

Sport can be a consumer good, a consumer service, a commercial good, or a commercial service

Sport is an end-product that is produced for mass consumer appeal to spectators and participants. The primary sport product may be both tangible and intangible in nature. At the same time, businesses and corporate entities use sport as a way to reach their consumers and to sell their respective products and services. They also utilize sport (specifically events) as a reward system for their employees. An example of this would be holding an employee night at the local ballpark or arena to reward the employees for their hard work. An additional reward system could be offered if the company owned a corporate suite at the facility. The organization could reward those with the highest level of production with the ability to watch an event from the suite.

The principal sport product is perpetually intangible, subjective, and variable

The consumer experience is constantly subjective because it is subject to various levels of interpretation. This makes it very difficult for the sport marketer because, with so many different consumer perceptions, it becomes challenging to guarantee the satisfaction of consumers.

In addition, since there is no predictability of the results of sport, and there is no guarantee of the quality of play from the participants, it again becomes challenging for the sport marketer to guarantee the satisfaction of the consumer.

Sport has an appeal that is extensive and permeates all aspects of life

This provides the sport marketer with a range of target markets, and thus requires the sport industry to create variations of products. These variations must represent the innumerable demographics of consumers, including age, sex, income level, race/ethnicity, and geographic location.

Sport is normally publicly consumed and consumer satisfaction is directly affected by the external environment

The consumption of sport usually involves social interaction. According to numerous studies conducted, there is a strong correlation between social identification, affiliation with a team, and the decision to attend sport events. In fact, the research shows that less than 2 percent of collegiate and professional sport spectators attend events alone. As a result of this, sport marketers must create products and activities that enhance group attendance, and hence facilitate consumer satisfaction.

The chief sport product elicits a strong emotional connection

Customers have a strong personal identification, both positive and negative, with elements of the sport product. The sport marketing professional must be able to market products to both sides of this affiliation.

22

Sport consumers believe they are the experts when it comes to knowledge of the product

Usually the manufacturers of a product are the experts about that product. In turn, consumers usually trust the opinion of the company producing the product, or the industry where the product is sold. Not so in sport, where consumers believe they are the experts. An example of this is the concept of the "Monday Morning Quarterback" – where fans look back on the game and pass judgment on what the players or coaches should have done. This is intensified by the number of media outlets – websites devoted to sports (especially fantasy sports), Twitter conversations that never cease, sport radio, 24-hour-sport television networks, back-page newspaper coverage, etc.

The sport product (in an event form) is a perishable commodity

In this form, there is no true inventory. The sport event is produced and consumed at the same time. Therefore, the sport marketer must pre-sell the event. To accomplish this, the sport marketing professional must "sell" anticipated performance and projected potential.

As with most demand-based products, consumer demand for the main sport product can vary greatly

With most products, we consider the economic concept of supply and demand. The main sport product is demand-based. This makes it difficult for the sport marketer to develop strategies, as they must read the minds of consumers and identify their needs and desires as related to the sport product.

Sport organizations concurrently compete and cooperate

While sport organizations compete on the court or field, they cooperate away from the competition to assure stability and existence. This challenges sport marketing professionals to market the sport product with both in mind. A great example of this would be the rivalry between the Boston Red Sox and the New York Yankees. While they often compete with each other in the standings, the field of play, and in the minds of fans, they must rely on each other for games to take place on the field. If the Red Sox chose not to show up for a game at Yankee Stadium, there would be no event.

Most of the marketing effort is not placed on the primary sport product; it is placed on product extensions

Since marketing professionals have little or no say about the primary product, they must use product extensions to get the message about the product into the public eye. The main example of a product extension is merchandise. Product extensions serve as a major revenue generation for sport organizations at all levels.

Exposure from the mass media has resulted in a reduced emphasis on traditional sport marketing

The over-saturation of sport in the mass media has resulted in an evolution in the traditional method of controlling and coordinating the marketing mix. This exposure is called publicity. The expanded public relations efforts have forced marketers who traditionally viewed the marketing mix as the four Ps of marketing evolve their theory into the six Ps of sport marketing – product, price, place, promotion, publicity, and people.

CASE STUDY 2: SEATTLE SOUNDERS FC: SUCCESSFUL MARKETING OF A MLS EXPANSION TEAM

Authored and contributed by Heidi Nordstrom, University of New Mexico

Seattle Sounders FC is a soccer club that competes in Major League Soccer (MLS). The Sounders were established in 2007 as a MLS expansion team. The club's majority owner is Hollywood producer Joe Roth and its minority owners are Adrian Hanauer, Paul Allen, and Drew Carey. Soccer has had a great history in Seattle, spanning over four decades, and has included clubs that played in leagues such as the North American Soccer League, the United Soccer League, the Continental Indoor Soccer League, and most currently, Major League Soccer. The first Seattle Sounders soccer team were founded in 1974 and they played in the North American Soccer League. Seattle tried to secure a MLS team in 1994 but could not gain enough season ticket holders and lacked a true soccer-specific stadium (Farrey, 1994).

Knowing that soccer had great popularity and history in Seattle, the owners of the new MLS team wanted to create a connection to the people of Seattle from the very beginning. Fans were able to choose the team name through an online poll, with 14,500 fans registering their vote during the four-day election (Fans Choose, 2008). The Seattle Sounders FC logo was developed to represent the partnership between the ownership, the community, the players, and the fans.

There are several organized groups that rally at CenturyLink Field during each game, including a 53-member marching band called "Sound Wave." Minority owner Drew Carey wanted to emphasize fan association ideas which he found were successfully used in European soccer. The Sounders FC Alliance was formed in 2008 and is the only members' association in professional sports in the United States to offer its members a voice in club matters. Members of the Alliance have the ability to vote on the removal of the General Manager and on other team decisions (Romero, 2008). Season ticket holders become automatic members while non-season ticket holders may buy into the Alliance for a $125 fee. Membership benefits include voting privileges, invitation to an annual meeting, and other team perks. Members can also be elected to the Sounders FC Alliance Council. The first vote on the General Manager is scheduled to be held in November 2012 following Seattle's third season. Carey is Chairman of the Sounders FC Alliance.

24

The Seattle team also gained fan accolades by signing Washington native and star goalie Kasey Keller in their inaugural season. He is a four-time World Cup participant and played in the English Premier League. Keller retired after the 2011 Major League Soccer season in front of a record crowd of 64,140 people (Evans, 2011).

The owners of the Sounders made their team powerful by hiring young, talented, and fearless players from other countries where soccer is the most popular sport. They also created an inventive advertising and PR strategy that sells Seattle as one of the few cities in the United States where soccer's popularity is similar to American football and baseball. The results of their marketing tactics have become very successful, which has helped create a bond between the city of Seattle and the team. The streets become green and blue in the "March to the Match" created by a procession of thousands of fans who march to the stadium before every home game. The diverse Seattle fan base attends games religiously at CenturyLink field in downtown Seattle. The atmosphere is full of energy where nobody sits down during the games and the fans cheer and yell chants similar to European-style football matches (Sharples, 2009). Seattle has sold out every league match, set MLS records for average attendance, and led the league in season ticket sales (Seattle Sounders, 2011). From the very beginning, the Seattle Sounders FC soccer club found the perfect recipe to create a successful expansion team in Major League Soccer.

Questions for discsussion

1   How could you use the Seattle Sounders' marketing methods when promoting a team in a different sport?
2   Could these methods be used in any city? And if not, what made it work in Seattle?
3   Do you see the popularity of the Seattle Sounders continuing for many seasons to come? Or is it short lived?

THE SPORT MARKETING MIX

The heart of the sport market is the sport marketing mix. Central to our understanding of the sport marketing mix are the four areas of marketing analysis – the consumer, the company, the competition, and the climate. These "chambers" of the heart must be understood so that the marketing mix can be controlled, coordinated, and implemented within the overall marketing effort. As covered in Chapter 1, our analysis of consumers includes segmentation, targeting, positioning, and delivery. For the company, we analyze internal strengths and weaknesses, as well as competitive advantages including cost and differentiation. As far as competition is concerned, we consider external opportunities such as marketplace openings, and external threats such as environmental factors. With regard to climate, we are concerned about the internal climate in terms of organizational structure, culture, and change; and the external climatological factors including the economy, social networking, legal and political forces, and social and ethical influences.

Once we understand the components of the sport market, we can now manipulate our efforts through the elements of the marketing mix. There is a significant difference in the traditional view of the marketing mix when it comes to sport. As a rule in marketing, the marketing mix was always viewed as the four Ps of marketing. However, in sport marketing, there is an expanded role that publicity and/or public relations play. These are the methods and activities utilized to establish and promote awareness with the public by disseminating information through various media outlets. With this expanded role of publicity, that aspect has been broken away from being a part of promotion into its own elements. Hence, the sport marketing mix has evolved into the five Ps of sport marketing – product, price, place, promotion, and publicity.

The emergence of social media has put an even bigger weight on publicity. The person following on Twitter now has just as much control over distributing information as do the traditional media. If the person is very influential, he or she could have more control than the traditional media. In fact, influential people could possibly add a sixth P to the marketing mix – people.

The successful interaction of the marketing mix with the target, as well as between the elements themselves, is crucial to a successful marketing effort (see Figure 2.1). This interaction has a direct affect on the sport marketing professional's decision-making process. Included in this process is the realization that interactions are not always positive in nature. How does the sport marketer deal with this?

This is where strategy comes into play. The marketing mix can only be utilized if it is in conjunction with understanding the four Cs of competitive analysis (the chambers of the heart of sport marketing) – the consumer, the company, the competition, and the climate. We talk about segmentation, targeting, positioning, delivery, differentiation, marketplace openings and environmental factors – but how do we develop a strategy which takes into account all the facts that are important, while at the same time having a full understanding of the cross-impact of all of these factors? Unfortunately, many in the field of sport marketing do not know how, or do not wish to spend the time. They often make decisions based on unfounded, preconceived notions, or knee-jerk reactions. However, there are a series of questions, falling into three categories, which if answered can provide the information necessary to make more effective and efficient decisions related to the sport marketing mix as a whole:

1   Product impact

■   What is the level of impact the marketing effort will have?
■   Will the product increase the return on investment?
■   Would the introduction of a broader product range increase the possible return on investment?

2   Potential risks

■   What is the probability that the marketing effort will be successful?
■   Is it based on a theory that success has a low or high probability of occurring?
■   Are competitors likely to respond with a better option?
■   What are the risks of not pursuing the marketing strategy and being left behind?

3   Feasibility

■   Is the marketing effort feasible from a technical point of view (enough resources – space, staff, and customers)?

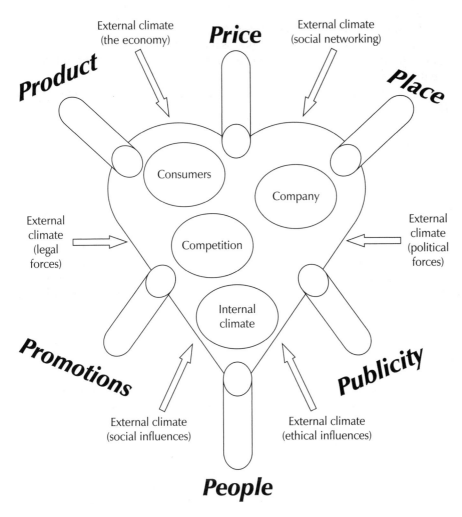

Figure 2.1 The heart of the sport market: the sport marketing mix

- Is the marketing effort feasible from a financial point of view (affordability, cash flow, and net income implications)?
- Is the marketing effort feasible from a political point of view (support from stakeholders)?

Once these questions have been answered, the sport marketing professional can then effectively create a value chain for the effort. Adding value is a crucial factor in marketing a product. The goal is to identify, evaluate, and understand the consumer's value chain and investigate the potential impact of the organization's value chain on the consumer. The value chain shows the amount of value that is added during the marketing process, which in turn facilitates differentiation. Differentiation is the concept of being creative and demonstrating distinct and specialized characteristics of sport products and services as compared to those of its competitors. In the sport market, efforts toward differentiation are centered on the following:

27

- *Purchasing*: quantity discounts, package deals
- *Products*: improve features of extensions such as merchandise
- *Distribution*: faster delivery, ease of purchasing products, increase opportunities to purchase the product
- *Marketing communication activities*: public relations, media relations, community relations
- *Sales activities*: appropriate pricing of products, selling products with the features consumers need and want
- *Customer service activities*: convey product information to customers, availability to deal effectively and efficiently with customer problems and questions.

Sport marketing differentiation strategies are doomed to fail if the product feature is not perceived as an influencing or determining factor by the consumer. This includes charging a price that consumers perceive as being too high relative to the additional features, or that the features have not been well conveyed to the consumer. Basically, if there is no understanding of or attempt to identify how consumers define value, the marketing professional cannot implement an appropriate marketing plan, and hence the goal of differentiation will fail. This, in turn, will affect the profitability of the organization, which eventually could lead to its downfall.

Escalator concept

To stay on the cutting edge of providing value for the sport consumer, the sport marketing professional strives to establish ways to attract new consumers into the sport market while enticing current sport consumers to become more involved with the sport product. Earlier with regard to product usage we talked about the Pareto Principle, otherwise known as the 80/20 rule. The utilization of the 80/20 rule by marketers is fundamental to the development of segments, but how do marketers then develop the segment over time? The concept that is essential to this development process is the escalator concept. This concept is utilized to represent the movement of consumers to higher levels of involvement with a specified product. This concept is shown in Figure 2.2.

Non-consumers

A non-consumer is an individual who does not use a good or service. There are three levels of non-consumers with whom the sport marketing professional must attempt to identify. The non-aware non-consumer is an individual who does not know about the sport product, and therefore is not a user of the sport product. The sport marketer strives to make this demographic aware of the product so that he or she might choose to become a consumer in the future. The misinformed non-consumer is an individual who is aware of the sport product, but does not purchase because, based on the information, he or she does not associate him- or herself with the sport product. The aim of the sport marketing professional is to change this image of the product in the mind of the misinformed non-consumer by providing information that creates an association with the sport product. The aware non-consumers are probably the most difficult to address, because they have knowledge of the sport product and its benefits, and

28

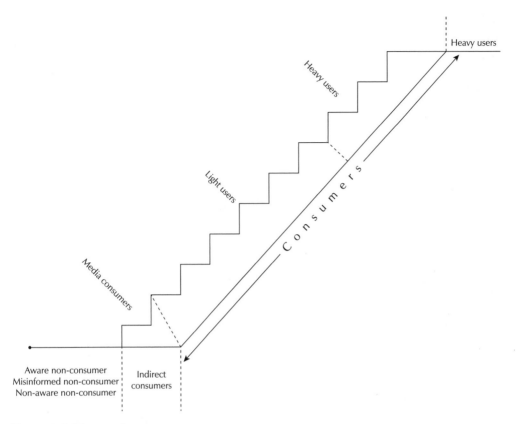

Figure 2.2 The escalator concept

Source: Adapted from Mullin, B. J., Hardy, S., and Sutton, W.A. (1999). *Sport Marketing* (2nd edn). Champaign, IL: Human Kinetics, p. 36.

have chosen not to consume the sport product. Often, these aware non-consumers are so knowledgeable that they can sense when the sport marketer is trying to influence them. The sport marketer must attempt to change perceptions about a sport product, which involves a detailed understanding of this aware non-consumer's value chain. Getting this type of non-consumer on to the bandwagon often involves a lot of effort.

Indirect consumers

Indirect consumers in the sport market are those who utilize the sport product from a distance through the use of intermediate or intervening opportunities. For the sport product, this may include only watching sport on television, only being a part of a fantasy league, or only purchasing peripheral products such as hats and shirts. The goal of the sport marketer is to entice these sport consumers to increase their level of involvement by purchasing more peripheral products, or, more realistically, attending events in person.

Light users

The light users are those who are actively involved as indirect consumers, but who also attend an event once or twice a year. The goal of the sport marketing professional is to get them more involved by having them attend more events. This is most often accomplished through ticket packages and group plans.

Medium users

Medium users are even more involved. They probably attend as many as half of the events related to the sport product. The sport marketer attempts to entice these sport consumers to move to the top of the "escalator" by showing them the benefits of having season tickets, leasing a sky box, or attending a hallmark event (Super Bowl, All-Star Game) associated with the sport product.

Heavy users

Heavy users are sport organizations' bread and butter. These are individuals who are fully engaged in the culture of the organization at a maximum consumer level. The sport marketing professionals must work to maintain this level of expectation through their efforts, continually apprising the heavy users that they are important and receiving the maximum benefits possible.

The key is to strive to increase the level of involvement in the sport product over time, while limiting having anyone fall off or go down the escalator. However, it is important not to forget those who do reduce their involvement. By understanding their reasons for decreasing the connection with the sport product, sport marketers learn valuable lessons to improve their tactics as as to work toward preventing a recurrence of this dip in image and involvement.

Another challenge which sport marketers face is that, depending on the sport product, individuals can fall on different parts of the escalator. For example, one individual may be a heavy user of football but a light user of basketball, and an aware non-consumer for baseball. Marketing efforts must not only differ based on the level of consumer or non-consumer, but also for each sport product. With so many sport products on the market, the task for the sport marketing professional is challenging and never-ending.

Developing a sport marketing plan

Now that we have an understanding of the different levels of sport consumers and non-consumers, a sport marketing plan must be developed to address their needs and wants. Sport marketing plans are comprehensive frameworks for identifying and achieving a sport organization's marketing goals and objectives. The process used in developing a sport marketing plan is a ten-step process.

Step 1: Identifying the purpose of the sport marketing plan

All individuals involved with a sport organization must be involved in the process of writing mission and vision statements, as well as developing goals and objectives. This is to ensure that all members of the sport organization will be committed to carrying out the plan acting in accordance with the organizational philosophy.

Step 2: Analyzing the sport product

The sport product is three-dimensional: tangible goods, intangible support services, and the game or event itself.

1   *Goods* include tangible items such as clothing (e.g., shoes, licensed apparel) and equipment (e.g., bats, balls, racquets).
2   *Intangible support services* include activities or programs that are supplementary to sport but necessary for its operation (e.g., game officials, operations staff, office support).
3   *The game or event itself* is composed of two parts: the main product and the product enhancements. The main product of the event is the actual competition taking place. The product enhancements are the extras during the event, such as the mascot, music, half-time entertainment, concessions, and cheer-leaders. These serve to enhance the overall experience for the customer.

Step 3: Forecasting the market climate

Assessing the sport climate requires examining internal and external factors as they affect marketing efforts. Assessing the past market climate enables managers to identify factors associated with successful or failed marketing efforts. Forecasting the future market climate requires re-examining the organization's mission. This involves the aforementioned SWOT analysis – assessing the strengths and weaknesses of an organization or event and the opportunities and threats faced by an organization or event.

Step 4: Positioning the sport product

When positioning the product, the sport marketing professional must take into account six distinct markets for sport. Three are considered primary markets, and three are considered secondary markets:

- Primary markets
    - *participants* – athletes, coaches, and game officials
    - *spectators* – stadium attendees, television viewers, radio listeners, and newspaper or magazine readers
    - *volunteers* – social hosts at sport events, statisticians, team managers.
- Secondary markets
    - *advertisers* – use sports to target and communicate their products to large groups of spectators
    - *corporate sponsors* – use sports to target and communicate positive and distinctive images about their products to large groups of spectators
    - *athletes' endorsements of products and licensed products* – personalities and celebrities or distinctive symbols, logos, or trademarks encourage consumers to perceive products as popular or prestigious.

Step 5: Segmentation and targeting consumers

This step involves grouping consumers according to common characteristics. Segmentation is most commonly analyzed using demographics, psychographics, or based on media preferences. Demographic segmentation refers to grouping sport consumers based on their age, gender, income, race or ethnicity, education, and place of residence. Psychographic segmentation refers to influencing consumers' attitudes, interests, and lifestyles. Market segmentation based on media preference categorizes consumers based on their sport media preferences (such as television, radio, internet, magazines, or publications). This helps identify smaller groups to be targeted, and allows the sport marketer to develop an effective and efficient strategy to reach the target market.

Step 6: Packaging the sport product

This is the way the consumer will view the sport product. Since consumers view products in different ways, it is necessary to present the sport product in different ways. Packaging tangible or industrial sport products involves explaining the benefits of the products such as the strength and longevity of metal bats, the comfort and safety of helmets, or the expanded sweet spot of oversized tennis rackets. Packaging the core product of sport (the game or event itself) involves communicating about the expectations of the product and providing information before the point of purchase. Another aspect of product packaging is the manner in which product enhancements (discussed in step 2) are included in the overall sport experience.

Another aspect of packaging the sport product is the associated licensed merchandise. For example, many sport teams and events offer goods such as hats, T-shirts, jackets, and other apparel. They also offer non-apparel such as novelty items and sport memorabilia that are perceived as extensions and representations of the respective teams.

Also utilized to package the sport product is sponsorship. Sponsorship involves an agreement between a sport organization and a corporation where the corporation pays a fee to the sport organization to acquire rights to affiliate with the organization or an associated event for the purpose of deriving benefits from the partnership. Sponsorships can help corporations increase sales, change attitudes, heighten awareness, and build and maintain positive relationships with consumers.

Step 7: Pricing the sport product

Price is the factor that is most visible and flexible, especially as a result of sales, discounts, rebates, and coupons. Creating a strategy for pricing is integral to the success of the sport organization because it has a significant impact on the success of the overall sport marketing plan. Sport marketers must consider the four Cs described early in the chapter within the "heart of sport marketing" – the company itself, the sport consumer, the competition, and the climate – especially the external factors of the economic climate, government regulations, and politics.

sport marketing: the basics

Step 8: Promoting the sport product

Promoting sport products involves implementing a mix of activities that will communicate the preferred image of the sport product to selected targets, educate the target audience about the sport product and its benefits, and ultimately persuade the sport consumer to purchase the product. The following elements compose a promotion strategy:

- *Advertising*: Presenting a one-way paid message about the sport product (newspapers, magazines, television, radio, direct mail, scoreboards, in-arena signage, pocket schedules, game programs, posters, outdoor advertising)
- *Community relations*: Activities and programs arranged by a sport organization to meet the interests and needs of the public and, by so doing, establish good faith relationships with the public (youth sport clinics, athlete autograph signing opportunities, collecting food items at arenas to help people in the community, a meet-up where the fans that follow the team on Twitter get a chance to mingle with various faces of the team, also called a Tweet-Up)
- *Media relations*: Maintaining positive relations with networks and individuals in the media to obtain positive media exposure for a sport product (scheduled informal and formal information sessions with media representatives)
- *Personal selling*: Direct face-to-face communication with individuals, groups, or organizations to sell tickets, luxury suites or boxes, or sponsorships
- *Promotions*: Activities and inducements to encourage consumers to purchase the sport product (giveaways, coupons, free samples, cash refunds, contests, raffles)
- *Public relations*: A sport organization's overall plan for communicating a positive image about its product to the public, including implementing community and media relations activities and programs
- *Social media*: Engaging the social networks to create a bond between the fan and the team (creating content about the product on Facebook for fans to like and share, giveaways to Twitter followers so that the followers can share their experience, and contests to see who can create the best video about the product)
- *Sponsorship*: Forming a partnership between sport organizations and corporate entities as a form of promotion.

Step 9: Distribution (place) of the sport product

Place refers to the location of the sport product (stadium, arena), the point of origin for distributing the product (ticket sales at the stadium, sales by a toll-free telephone number), the geographic location of the target markets (global, national, regional, state, communities, cities), and other channels that are important to consider regarding whether target audiences may access the product (such as time, day, season, or month in which a product is offered, as well as the media distribution outlets consumers may use to receive the product experience). Factors related to the physical location of the sport can have a favorable or unfavorable impact on the marketing plan as well.

33

Step 10: Evaluation and feedback about the sport marketing plan

This evaluation requires obtaining feedback (from inside and outside the organization) about the marketing plan. The feedback must then be analyzed and evaluated. The evaluation should focus on determining the extent to which the plan helped the organization achieve its mission by acting in accordance with the core values of the organization.

Why the theory and plans do not always work

All the sport marketing plans in the world are great in theory, but they do not always work. The major reason for this is having a lack of vision. There is a tendency to look for instant gratification – what is going to be successful right now. This lack of foresight in sport marketing ventures is known as a marketing myopia. A summary of research shows that the major reasons why there is a marketing myopia in sport are:

- There is a tendency to produce and sell goods, rather than identify needs and satisfy customers. This is a result of sport organizations failing to spend time and money on quality market research, which in turn has led to a major shortfall in data collection and analysis.
- There is a belief that winning equals sales, which in most cases is not true.
- There is confusion between what marketing is and what promotions are.
- Sport organizations tend to be shortsighted – the "I want it now" principle.
- Since there is such an overabundance of people wishing to enter the sport field, starting salaries are often very low. There is an effort to offset these low salaries by including commissions, but the lack of guaranteed income can scare many quality potential marketers away.
- With sales being driven by quotas and commissions, organizations tend to put little emphasis on training, tactics, and sales as a strategy. If a sport marketer can sell, only then will time be put in. This has created a slow growth of professional sport marketing staff.
- The speed of new technology and how what works with a marketing plan now might be obsolete in the near future. There is a constant need for sport marketers to evaluate new technology and adapt their tools to more efficiently reach the customer. New technology consists of smartphones, computer tablets, social networks, web applications, ticketing systems, payment methods, etc.

CONCLUSION

Sport marketing is unique for numerous reasons, but most importantly because the primary sport product, and hence the market, is traditionally demand-based, whereas most generic products are marketed based on need. These concepts are elaborated upon in this chapter, as well as the impact of the sport marketing mix, the escalator concept, and the elements of the sport marketing plan.

Sport marketing is unique to traditional marketing in numerous ways:

- The sport product takes many forms including a consumer good, a consumer service, a commercial good, or a commercial service.
- The main sport product is perpetually intangible, subjective, and variable.

34

- Sport and hence the sport product has an appeal that is wide and varied.
- The sport product is normally publicly consumed and consumer satisfaction is directly affected by the external environment.
- Sport product elicits strong emotional connections.
- Sport consumers believe they are the experts when it comes to knowledge of the product.
- The sport product is a perishable commodity.
- Since the sport product is demand-based, the consumer demand for the main sport product varies greatly.
- Sport organizations concurrently compete and cooperate.
- Sport marketing efforts focus more on product extensions than the primary sport product.
- Influences from mass media have resulted in a reduced emphasis on traditional sport marketing.

The over-saturation of sport in the mass media has resulted in an evolution in the traditional method of controlling and coordinating the marketing mix. This exposure is called publicity. The expanded public relations efforts have forced marketers who traditionally viewed the marketing mix as the four Ps of marketing evolve their theory into the six Ps of sport marketing – product, price, place, promotion, publicity, and people. Strategic implementation of the sport marketing mix can only be utilized if it is in conjunction with understanding the four Cs of competitive analysis – the consumer, the company, the competition, and the climate in terms of product impact, potential risks, and feasibility. Ultimately this analysis seeks to determine how to provide value to sport consumers, and enticing them to become more involved with the sport product. The concept that is essential to this development process is the escalator concept. This concept is utilized to represent the movement of consumers to higher levels of involvement with a specified product – whether they are non-consumers, indirect consumers, light users, medium users, or heavy users.

A sport marketing plan must be developed and utilized to address the needs and wants of the sport consumer. Sport marketing plans are comprehensive frameworks for identifying and achieving a sport organization's marketing goals and objectives. The process used in developing a sport marketing plan is a ten-step process:

1 Identifying the purpose of the sport marketing plan.
2 Analyzing the sport product.
3 Forecasting the market climate.
4 Positioning the sport product.
5 Segmentation and targeting consumers.
6 Packaging the sport product.
7 Pricing the sport product.
8 Promoting the sport product.
9 Distribution (place) of the sport product.
10 Evaluation and feedback about the sport marketing plan.

Sport marketing plans are great in theory, but they do not always work. The major reason for this is having a lack of vision. There is a tendency to look for instant gratification – what is going to be successful right now. This lack of foresight in sport marketing ventures is known as a marketing myopia. It is the goal of the sport marketing professional to avoid these pitfalls by engaging in a sport marketing effort that is efficient, effective, and which addresses the wants and needs of the sport consumer.

35

FROM THEORY TO PRACTICE

ANTHONY PENNA, DIRECTOR OF FLORIDA OPERATIONS
Ted Williams Museum and Hitters Hall of Fame,
Tropicana Field, St. Petersburg, Florida

The opportunities I took advantage of during college led me to where I am today. Proudly, I can say that I am the Director of Florida Operations for the Ted Williams Museum. From a young age, I knew what I had a passion for. I am a hardworking, dedicated, risk-taking individual who lives for sports. As a student, I was presented with an opportunity to work at the World Baseball Classic in Orlando, FL during my spring break of my freshman year. While others were looking forward to lounging on the beach, I was ecstatic that I was going to be a part of a major yearly gathering of professionals. Taking advantage of this opportunity was just the beginning of what was to come. I have always tried to stay ahead of the game and this quality helped me attain internship positions with notable baseball organizations.

During my college career, there was not a time where I was not working full time at an internship in addition to being a full-time student. I worked with the Brevard County Manatees, Dunedin Blue Jays, and the Clearwater Threshers. It was during spring training at the Philadelphia Phillies training complex that I met my current boss. My enthusiasm and clever approach to business got me noticed. He was the Executive Director of the Ted Williams Museum. My personal career goal was not to work for a nonprofit organization but rather, I had my sights on an Assistant General Manager or General Management position. However, my willingness to try new things led me to my current position. My experiences coordinating events, managing other interns, and generating new marketing campaigns made me an ideal candidate for a position with the museum.

Leading up to this offer, I spent the majority of my free time applying and interviewing for positions in Major and Minor League Baseball. My advice to college students is to sell yourself – keep track of *everything* you have accomplished and learned how to do relative to the position, be confident, and sell yourself! I had experience pulling tarp, being a mascot, managing concessions stands, and generating intern schedules, just to name a few. All of these experiences mattered. Having the opportunity to learn such a wide variety of skills made me a well-rounded individual ready to take on any task. Employers will ask about field experience and want to know what you have done. This is your chance to make everything count.

The marketing mix is an important aspect of my daily responsibilities on the job. If we do not pick the right product, set an appropriate price, pick venues with interested fans, create exciting promotions, and attract the right people we will not be able to meet our goals or give back to our community. Our main source of income comes from silent auctions held during baseball games. Since I have been employed with the Ted Williams Museum, we have branched out and been able to obtain contracts with the Miami Dolphins, Minnesota Twins, and Tampa Bay Lightning.

It is of the utmost importance that we carefully select venues to bring our product to. We look at numbers that relate to their average attendance, their record at their home venue, and if we would face competition. The selection of product keeps me on my toes. I carefully select memorabilia that is suitable for the specific game. Predicting the crowd (our customers) is one of the challenges we face every time we prepare for a silent auction at a game. The process of selecting pictures and product along with scheduling signings with players is never ending. Being on top of trades, trends, and fan attitude is critical to our success. Carefully selecting inventory and maintaining an appropriate stock can be difficult. We have to always be aware of player injuries, potential decline in fan approval, and the projections of a wide range of players. Sometimes it makes sense to stock up on an injured player's memorabilia at a cheaper price in hopes of selling it when they make a comeback. This idea does not always hold true though. We take risks daily when it comes to purchasing.

We have been fortunate to branch off and not only do silent auctions, but also to coordinate charity dinners. My experience with event coordination made this possible. Once we partnered with a player, it was up to us to make it happen. Getting the word out to people who would be interested was crucial. We thought this first annual dinner would be a great opportunity for us to reach out to our established base of clients who contribute to the museum via silent auction regularly. We attract people to our events, auctions, and to our museum by offering them a unique product and experience. They return to us because we are willing to go the extra step to meet their needs. Sponsors also play a big role in the success of this foundation. The Ted Williams Museum is a unique means of marketing because it reaches a vast variety of people in an unconventional way. We ensure that our sponsors see the benefits of their donation and we work hard to establish a lasting relationship.

The success of your sport marketing and management career starts with a willingness to work hard and think outside the box. As a student, you cannot get caught up in obtaining an ideal, glamorous position. Once you get into the field, you will be amazed at what goes into making these sport operations function. It is important to take advantage of every opportunity presented to you. The experiences you have will ultimately make the information you learn through your textbook come to life. It is much easier to relate to the ideas presented in class when you can apply them to an actual experience. Do not discount an opportunity because you do not think it is what you want to do in your future. You never know who you will meet or what door will open along the way. Give everything 110 percent effort because people do pay attention to you and will notice your work ethic.

CHAPTER THREE

SOCIAL RESPONSIBILITY AND ETHICS IN SPORT MARKETING

CHAPTER OUTLINE

- Social responsibility
- Ethics
- Relationship of social responsibility and ethics in strategic sport marketing planning
- Conclusion

CHAPTER OBJECTIVES

The reader will be able to:

- compare and contrast the concepts of social responsibility and ethics as related to the various aspects of sport marketing
- distinguish between the various dimensions of social responsibility in sport marketing
- analyze the various concepts inherent to each dimension of social responsibility in terms of application within sport marketing theory and practice
- recognize the influence of ethics across multiple applications of sport marketing
- evaluate the role of social responsibility and ethics in the implementation of strategic planning in sport marketing.

SOCIAL RESPONSIBILITY

A sport marketing professional must understand the societal values and beliefs that directly affect the implementation of sport marketing efforts. He or she is also expected to act in a morally and socially responsible manner. One of the foundations of these societal values and beliefs is focused on the social responsibility evident in a given society. By definition, social responsibility is a sport organization's obligation to increase its positive impact on society as a whole while decreasing any negative impact. This is often accomplished by being a quality marketing citizen, which entails adopting a strategic focus to maximize social obligations to stakeholders in terms of economic, legal, philanthropic, and ethical considerations.

Corporate social responsibility (CSR) and sport marketing

Corporate social responsibility (CSR) focuses on the responsibility sport organizations have to society beyond that of investors and stakeholders to include philanthropy, volunteerism, and any other efforts that foster relationships that enhance society. When considering CSR and its relationship to sport marketing, one must understand the marketing environment in terms of the ability to collect information about marketing forces through environmental scanning via observation, primary market research, and secondary information. The assessment and inter-pretation of the information must define the environment accurately, consistently, and include information that is significant to the marketing effort. Sport marketers should also work towards having a proactive approach in environmental analyses, as sport organizations want to shape and influence the environment with its strategies rather than be reactive and have to adjust to change created by competition and other controllable external forces. At the same time, sport marketers must be able to effectively address the uncontrollable external factors including changes in the economy, fluctuations in the sport business industry, changes in laws and rules from regulatory powers, advances and changes in technology, and the continued evolution of sociological forces centered on demographic diversity and cultural influences (Figure 3.1).

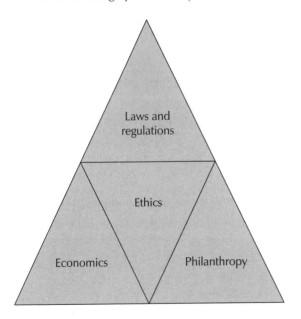

Figure 3.1 Dimensions of social responsibility

Corporate social responsibility focuses on two main concepts that the sport marketer must fully understand. First is having an understanding of the stakeholders who have a vested interest in the products, services, industries, operations, and outcomes of a given sport organization. Second is the concept of marketing citizenship, where the sport marketing strategy focuses on the needs of the stakeholder in terms of economics, legal issues, philanthropic activities, and ethics.

From an economic standpoint, regardless of social mission or vision, the ultimate goal for any business is to be profitable, and hence the sport marketer must keep in mind the fact that all marketing efforts must consider the end result of profit. In doing so, the sport marketer must accomplish this within the framework of the laws, rules, and regulations in society, and understanding the concepts of what is right and wrong. At the same time, organization have a social obligation to be a good corporate citizen by contributing to the community and improving the quality of life through philanthropy. Sport marketers are often responsible for implementing such activities in line with the laws, rules, and regulations set forth by governing bodies. In accepting these responsibilities, sport marketers must also recognize their responsibility to do what is fair, just, right, and without harm to people; hence acting in an ethical manner in all that they do. With this basis of understanding, let us take a look at each of these dimensions of social responsibility in more detail.

Economic dimensions of social responsibility

Regardless of the other numerous goals and objectives of a sport organization, the number one goal of any business is to make a profit. The economic dimension of social responsibility is no different; hence the sport marketer must understand how to integrate social responsibility into the concepts of consumerism, and the profit responsibility which an organization has to its owners and stockholders.

Concept of consumerism

The concept of consumerism involves the systematic efforts of sport organizations, including individual sport marketers and sport marketing groups/departments, to protect the rights of consumers. This concept was enacted into law under the administration of President John F. Kennedy in 1962 under the Consumer Bill of Rights, which put into law the ethics of exchanges between buyers and sellers. Originally applied to lobbying government officials and agencies, boycotts, letter-writing campaigns, public service announcements, and any coverage by broadcast media, consumerism has expanded into all realms of ethical business including sport marketing. Ultimately, the goal is to ensure consumers the rights of safety, to be informed, to have a choice, and to be heard.

The growth of consumerism has led to a significant overuse of sport marketing efforts across the sport industries, and has created a need to ensure that social responsibility be extended across the spectrum of stakeholders ranging from government to businesses to consumers. This is as a result of the need to overcome three of the major challenges presented by consumerism – manipulation, organization, and culture.

40

Manipulative techniques in sport marketing create a connection between consumerism and the need to persuade customers to expand their needs and wants, which can often be interpreted as forcing the customer to purchase product extensions and expansions that they do not need. This is most often as a result of overmarketing through advertising and sales management techniques. As a result of this overmarketing, there is a perception that this increases materialism and also creates the need for advertisers to push the envelope with more risqué types of advertising to attract the interest of consumers. So how do sport marketers meet the needs and wants of consumers while being socially responsible and at the same time maximizing profit without exploiting consumers? This is a significant challenge, and actually forces sport organizations to change their focus from being totally profit-driven to become a more responsible business by making enough profit to cover future costs. Being socially responsible through consumerism focuses on the ability to exercise social power to a maximum number of customers while maintaining a high level of economic profitability and creating an organizational culture that supports it.

Speaking of the organization and culture, social responsibility efforts force a modification of behaviors and actions as related to marketing sport organizations. A great majority of current sport marketing efforts focus on the short-term needs of consumers rather than their long-term welfare. In addition to customers, this focus on short-term needs has equally been applied to the environment – especially the physical environment; not considering the long-term, reciprocal impact of environmental resources and the consumer marketplace. The need to employ a societal marketing concept has in many cases superseded the traditional marketing concept, in that it is important to satisfy the needs and wants of consumers better than competitors not only with the products and services they offer, but also in terms of the overall social well-being of employees, competitors, supply chains, and society as a whole, and in consideration of economics, legislative, ethics, and in discretionary areas such as volunteerism and service.

Profit responsibility to owners and stockholders

As with any sport business, the ultimate goal is to make a profit, and as such to ensure a return on investment (ROI) to owners and stockholders. As noted earlier, one of the greatest challenges for sport marketers is to implement strategies that will hopefully aid in maximizing profits for the organization (and hence investors make a greater ROI) while balancing social responsibility which limits profit maximization to profit optimization – or making enough profit to deal with forecasted costs. This shift in profit philosophy needs to be instilled in all aspects of the organization starting with the sport organization's business philosophy, and needs to flow down through all aspects of the organization through the mission, vision, goal and objectives, and policies and procedures. From the sport marketing effort, this means engaging in normative marketing that is focused on meeting the needs and wants of consumers within the parameters of the organization's moral standards. Thus, any organization that can engage with investors who understand the concept of profit optimization, and employ sport marketing efforts that can strive to improve profitability and revenue generation within those parameters, can remain financially successful and become more socially responsible. This is a significant challenge for many organizations, especially since the initial shift of their philosophy often results in increased economic costs (and hence decreased profits). However,

41

the end result has the potential to create both tangible financial and intangible societal profits for owners and stockholders.

Legal dimensions of social responsibility

While the number one goal may be to make a profit, there are parameters set forth through the legal environment to ensure that there is a clear framework of what is right and wrong. Sport marketers must understand both the laws set forth by governmental regulatory agencies as well as the rules created by self-regulatory agencies.

Sport marketers must understand the laws set by local, state, federal, and in some cases international governmental regulatory agencies in terms of what they are allowed to do from a legal standpoint. The three major areas of law to be considered include statutory law, constitutional law, and common law. Statutory law includes those laws created and passed by legislative bodies, and which are only binding in the jurisdiction of the entity that passed the law. Constitutional law is dictated by the constitution of a country or region, and is the supreme ruling document over all others. Common law embodies laws that have been built on the past decisions of courts. The precedence from previous cases forms the parameters for future legal actions, and cannot be overturned or eliminated without overruling by a higher legislative body.

Sport marketers must also understand the rules and regulations set by self-regulatory agencies. These organizations may include an individual sport organization, professional sports leagues such as the National Basketball Association (NBA) or English Premier League (EPL), associations such as the National Collegiate Athletics Association (NCAA), committees such as the International Olympic Committee (IOC), federations such as the Fédération Internationale de Football Association (FIFA), and agencies such as the World Anti-Doping Agency (WADA). These rules fall under the area of law known as administrative law, where the laws, rules, and regulations that are developed, adopted, and enforced have been created by a specific governing body, and the members who voluntarily choose to align themselves with the governing body must abide by those laws, rules, and regulations.

Philanthropic dimensions of social responsibility

Philanthropy is defined as the social obligation an organization has to be a good corporate citizen by contributing to the improvement of the quality of life of people ranging from an individual or community to society as a whole. In sport marketing, philanthropy is most often managed through the community relations department. This department works with public interest groups and the general public using initiatives to better the population they are focused on while increasing brand awareness. Community relations departments most often implement the concepts of cause-related marketing, strategic philanthropy, and environmental marketing as their philanthropic efforts.

42

Community relations

Community relations is the process of the sport organization interacting and connecting with the target population within a specific area. Community relations is an integral part of any sport organization whether the relationship is player, team, or league initiated. Community relations efforts can be initiated in many ways (individual organizations, individual players, events, leagues, etc.), but are usually focused on associations with public interest groups or the general public. The main goal of community relations by a sport organization is to foster goodwill in the community and develop a long-term relationship with individuals and the community as a whole. This type of effort is a monumental and fragile undertaking, as it only takes one negative comment or action to erode years of goodwill.

Cause-related marketing

Cause-related sport marketing is the process of creating a relationship between a sport organization and a specific social cause. This relationship, which can range from a one-time partnership to a long-term association, needs to be mutually beneficial. While the sport organization associates itself with a cause as part of its marketing strategy for both charitable reasons and corporate self-interest, the organization overseeing the social cause needs to receive monetary or donated product benefits from the sport organization. Cause-related marketing's strategic potential as an effective management tool for connecting sport organizations with consumers is significant. The perception that an organization is involved with a cause-related marketing program increases the customer's interest in the sport organization, and plays a role in both attendance/use and repeat attendance/use. In addition, it is hoped that the relationship between the sport organization and a charity will encourage attendees/users of those sport products and services to benefit the social cause through their own involvement or charity. Ultimately, the sport organization hopes to see an increase in attendance and/or product usage, media attention as related to their involvement, and a more positive public image.

Strategic philanthropy

Strategic philanthropy is a concept where a sport organization seeks to use all of its core competencies to address the interests of its stakeholders to achieve both organizational and social benefits. A key point with strategic philanthropy is that is goes well beyond cause-related marketing, because it involves both financial and non-financial contributions. As such, concepts such as enhancing public awareness and volunteerism are an integral part of the strategic philanthropic endeavor. More importantly, cause-related marketing focuses on the direct link of a sport organization's products and services to a charity, whereas strategic philanthropy involves corporate giving and associated philanthropic activities to be a synergistic fit with the sport organization's philosophy, mission, goals, objectives, and vision. Hence, in order for the sport organization to operate and grow, strategic philanthropic activities are engrained in the culture of the organization. This level of involvement creates an even greater organizational image with customers and the public, but takes it a step further by including all levels of the organization, which in turn improves employee loyalty, morale, and commitment to the organization.

Environmental marketing (natural/ecological environment and green marketing)

An area of significant growth in philanthropic social responsibility involves environmental marketing, which includes the natural environment, the ecological environment, and the concept of greening. These concepts collectively fall under the umbrella of green marketing, which focuses on developing products, pricing strategies, promotion activities, and delivery methods that do not damage the natural environment. The reality is that there is a great push from consumers to not only provide an experience with sport products and services that improves quality of life, but to also do so while promoting a healthy environment that enhances everyone's standard of living. Hence sport organizations, as part of their social responsibility, need to consider concepts such as conservation, pollution reduction, green product development and manufacturing, waste management, and overall environmental sustainability as integral parts of the overall operational and marketing strategy for sport organizations. As we become more environmentally conscious as a society, sport organizations need to realize a number of facts, including that green products and services are mainstream, often work just as well as non-green products and services, and consumers are savvier in their understanding of products and services that are organic in nature. Therefore, sport organizations need to be more aware of how products are manufactured, packaged, consumed, and disposed of; and whether the resources being used to produce the product and service for the sport organization have a reputation for environmental responsibility (i.e., guilt by association). This has a direct effect on marketing efforts for the following reasons:

- People no longer buy a product only because of what it does, but also what it stands for.
- Sustainability is as important a product quality concept as its usefulness.
- Green products often represent the newest technologies and business concepts being used in the marketplace.
- Consumers engage in green marketing as a result of being influenced strongly by opinion leadership such as friends, family, and trusted organizations via word of mouth and social networks.
- The perception is that current consumers prefer to be associated with organizations that recognize society as being as important a customer as the stakeholders themselves.

CASE STUDY 3: MARKETING PRO-ENVIRONMENTALISM IN NORTH AMERICA'S GREENEST CITY: AT&T PARK AND THE SAN FRANCISCO GIANTS

Authored and contributed by Timothy B. Kellison, Florida State University

In response to the emergence of environmental sustainability as an area of global concern, many businesses have developed eco-friendly products or adopted "green" practices to attract environmentally conscientious consumers. In North America, professional sport organizations are becoming increasingly engaged in green initiatives. One of the most visible demonstrations of a team's pro-environmental commitment is a green arena, ballpark, or stadium, which requires significant investment and planning. In the past five years, a number of professional sport facilities have received Leadership in Energy and Environmental Design (LEED) certification by the U.S. Green Building Council, which is the most predominant green building accreditation in the United States (Nalewaik & Venters, 2008). Complemented by eco-friendly business practices and fan initiatives, green-certified facilities have become focal points for several professional teams marketing themselves as forward-thinking organizations.

Major League Baseball's San Francisco Giants is among the teams most actively engaged in pro-environmental behavior. At the heart of the Giants' pro-environmental endeavors is its stadium, AT&T Park, which obtained LEED status in 2010. In addition, the Giants have a number of ongoing initiatives in place to demonstrate their commitment "to making AT&T Park the 'greenest' ballpark in the country" (San Francisco Giants, 2012). For example, Gilroy Garlic Fries, one of the ballpark's most popular concession stands, was completely retrofitted with new energy-efficient appliances, lighting, paint, signage, and food containers. All in-park designated smoking areas were eliminated, making AT&T Park a completely non-smoking facility. Over 5,200 surrounding homes are now being powered by 590 solar panels installed at the ballpark. A GREEN TEAM was established to assist spectators with disposing of recyclable and compostable waste. Lighting systems throughout the stadium were overhauled to reduce energy usage, highlighted by the installation of a new state-of-the-art scoreboard that increased efficiency by 78 percent (compared with its predecessor, which was installed in 2000). The recycling and composting program has reduced physical waste, while an advanced irrigation system aids in water conservation. Even in the front office, updated equipment and policies have reduced paper and printing waste (San Francisco Giants, 2012).

Such initiatives are highlighted throughout AT&T Park on signage, in the media guide, and in public address announcements. In addition to the potential benefits the organization itself may receive from reputation enhancement, the Giants' pro-environmentalism may also inspire fans to adopt sustainable practices at home. In-stadium messages highlight eco-friendly practices – including novel ways to recycle and recommendations for installing energy-efficient light bulbs – that can be applied in fans' personal lives. Through this kind of social marketing, broadly defined as any cause-based promotion intended to induce behavioral change among individuals, Giants fans are encouraged to act in ways that improve their community and the environment.

In addition to benefitting by marketing to existing fans, teams may also reach out to the community to foster relationships with new consumers. While teams in cities such as Atlanta, Pittsburgh, and Washington also compete in LEED-certified venues, have similar pro-environmental initiatives, and engage in forms of social marketing, the Giants stand to benefit by promoting their pro-environmental practices to San Franciscans, an environmentally aware demographic. *TIME Magazine* recently ranked San Francisco the greenest city in North America (Walsh, 2011). Suspecting that community members may be motivated to patronize eco-friendly businesses, the Giants also engage in marketing efforts intended to generate new consumer interest in the organization by promoting their pro-environmental initiatives to the community. For instance, the Giants have formed partnerships with other local organizations to highlight their programs, including Pacific Gas and Electric Company (PG&E), which is leading a community outreach initiative called "Let's Green This City." Together, the Giants and PG&E began rewarding local students with tours of AT&T Park highlighting the team's and stadium's green initiatives. This partnership has been well publicized in the local press and provides the Giants with additional community exposure of their pro-environmental programs.

The Giants' social marketing initiatives reflect a growing trend across professional sport. Both teams and leagues have instituted campaigns to educate fans about pro-environmental behaviors. These social marketing endeavors may inspire both positive social change and goodwill toward organizations. In the case of the Giants, however, marketing efforts directed at environmentally conscientious San Franciscans might provide additional commercial benefit.

Questions for discsussion

1   How can teams competing in cities where environmental issues are less recognized by its citizen's benefit from having pro-environmental initiatives?
2   What motives might the Giants have for engaging in social marketing?

Ethical dimensions of social responsibility

Regardless of the economic, legal, and philanthropic issues inherent to sport organizations, they have an obligation at all times to act in an ethical manner. As such, sport marketers accept the responsibility to ensure that all of their efforts are fair, equitable, and right. In addition, the efforts cannot cause undue physical or emotional harm to people.

Sport marketing ethics is defined as the principles and standards that sport organizations must follow to ensure appropriate marketing conduct in the view of their stakeholders. The implementation of the sport marketing ethics process focuses on analyzing problems, situations, and opportunities that require action, but also involve determining whether that action is right/ethical or wrong/unethical. To truly comprehend how ethical influences relate to social responsibility, we need to have a better overall understanding of how ethics relates to sport marketing.

ETHICS

Sport marketing professionals, in understanding the societal values and beliefs that directly affect the implementation of sport marketing efforts, must also understand the foundation of the ethical influences evident in a given society. Ethics are the principles, rules, or standards of right conduct of individuals, groups, or a society. Ethics generally explain a society's way of life, rules of conduct, and moral code. Sport marketers have a duty and obligation to act in a responsible manner in terms of the ethics within a society.

Ethical issues in sport marketing

Ethics should be infused in all aspects of sport marketing efforts. Without having a strong ethical foundation in sport marketing, deception and dishonesty will create a negative perception in the minds of the sport consumer about the product or service being marketed, and in turn will have a negative impact on the successful completion of strategic goals and objectives of a sport organization. As such, sport marketing professionals need to understand how ethics and ethical behavior affect multiple elements of sport marketing, including understanding the sport consumer, product management, sales management, retail management and e-business, promotions (including advertising and sponsorship), social media and networking, and international/global connections. Examples of ethical issues for each element are provided in the following sections.

Understanding the sport consumer

Analysis of data compiled from examining the marketing mix, assessing data collected through marketing research and the marketing information systems, and evaluating the behavior of consumers in a reliable and valid manner is crucial to successful and ethical sport marketing.

When we look at the elements of the sport marketing mix (product, price, place, promotion, publicity, people), issues of ethical influence permeate the six Ps. Examples include:

1   *Product*: marketing a new piece of exercise equipment, making the choice to be deceptive and not disclose potential defects that could cause injury to a consumer, or perhaps not being truthful in performance information to entice consumers to purchase a product that does not meet their needs.
2   *Price*: pricing a product to sell at a sale price, but in fact the sales price noted is not a reduction of the regular price.
3   *Place*: the biggest issue in this area is the distribution of counterfeit products – that is, making the claim that a product is an original, but in fact it is a knock-off.
4   *Promotion*: there are many realms of this, but the most common is the use of deceptive advertising by promoting false statements or misleading safety claims about a product or service.
5   *Publicity*: publishing misleading or untrue information about an individual through broadcast, print, or internet media sources.
6   *People*: taking advantage of the relationship with consumers by not acting with integrity in marketing – being untruthful, deceptive, dishonest, deceiving, etc.

In marketing research and information systems, the need to collect reliable and valid data for sport marketing efforts is mandatory for ethical decision making. The role of sport marketing researchers is to collect data while viewing the sources in an unbiased manner, hence not allowing external influences such as politics, or internal influences such as emotions, to affect their research. From a problem-solving standpoint, if bias enters the equation, there may be invalid, unreliable data that will prevent appropriately defining the problem or determining the most suitable method for solving the problem. From a data-entry standpoint for the internal reports system, if there is not a way to validate the information where the research comes from (such as with a lot of the information found on the internet), the actions of an organization may be incorrect. From an operational standpoint, using unethical, unreliable, or invalid

47

information, as well as not being truthful or honest in one's actions when engaging the intelligence system, will have a direct effect on the ethical decision-making process for the organization, and hence the way in which products and services are marketed to consumers.

With regard to consumer behavior, sport marketers focus on the internal (attitudes, learning processes, motivations, perceptions) and external (culture, setting, class) factors of consumers. Sport marketers can be unethical in their efforts simply by enticing consumers to purchase a product through connections with their compulsive behavior. Practices of tempting consumers to purchase products by associating their use with alcohol and sex are prevalent in sport marketing, and in many cases are borderline unethical. More concerning is the directing of this marketing to children, whose savvy in ethical understanding the true implications of these marketing efforts is immature at best.

Product management

Ethics as a field of management has been slowly deteriorating for decades. Business ethics usually address the most outrageous abuse, generally dealing with human rights violations or extensive financial losses. The reality is that the so-called minor infractions happen on a daily basis. These infractions routinely go unpunished internally. The leading causes of many infractions are consumer dissatisfaction, employee turnover, and ineffective quality improvement and training efforts. This damages a corporation's branding which in turn may cost the company its market share.

If this loss of market share for world-class organizations runs between 10 and 15 percent of total sales revenue, management ethics in the best world-class companies is costing companies billions annually. If the average were to continue or increase, it could pose an extraordinary opportunity for improvement or cause the collapse of the corporation.

Most quality improvement projects deal with visible processes such as customer service operations. It is entirely possible to address the processes but still have unresolved issues involving people. If people do not want to cooperate and work together, or if tensions are high, process improvement becomes increasingly difficult.

It is a human tendency for management to seek single causes for failure when multiple, systematic causes are at work. In most cases blaming is placed on the failure of leadership. The common cause of below-par performance can usually be traced to ethics patterns. The ability of corporations to manage ethics at this personal level will yield significant economic returns.

Ethical management, when done correctly, is a comprehensive program that continuously improves thinking and behavior patterns rather than just some high-visibility issues and ethics policies. Many corporations spend millions on training and quality improvement initiatives without ever addressing the leading constraints to quality or performance improvement, which are ethics failures within the corporation.

Employees are more than just a collection of skills and capabilities. They are a system with a culture of their own. This culture is so powerful that it ultimately has more of an impact on what, where, and when decisions become reality than on the decision makers themselves. The importance of hiring employees who share a similar core ethical belief to that of the

48

corporation is monumental. This core of ethical beliefs is directly tied to the success or failure of the corporation.

Quality ethical management identifies the ethics needs before training or policy implementation even begins. An ethics policy without regard to the specific needs of the organization is ineffective. An ethics policy addresses the underlying root causes of unethical behavior. Unethical behavior hinders organizational performance. The speed at which we resolve ethical issues directly benefits performance. By focusing on the corporation's ethics, and not just policy, ethics management removes constraints to performance and reduces risks of large-scale ethics failures in the process.

Sales management

Shady practices may close more deals in the short run; however, relationships with customers and the bottom line of the corporation will suffer in the long run. Because sales representatives typically have personal interactions with clients and potential clients, their actions are more readily visible, and unethical behavior can have a profound effect on the branding of the company. Some would argue that the commission structure of compensation would encourage unethical behavior from sales representatives. Research has not been able to validate this belief. In other words, the sales representatives were no more likely to recommend a particular product when a high commission was associated with that product compared to the same product when a flat fee for sale was offered.

Salespeople tend to be excited over the products they are selling and may use mild exaggeration in describing the product. The ethical question is how much is too much. Apparently there is a gray line between ethical business practices and unethical business practices. This topic is important because each day salespeople must make ethical decisions that can affect their family, corporate status, and their relationships with the clients, and the bottom line.

There are many variables that can influence one's ethical perspective; for example, personal or family life, job performance pressures, and competitive drive. These internal and external factors are forever changing and the judgment or lack of judgment today does not guarantee repetition. Many people will allow minor ethical infractions to slide by without giving them a second thought. It is only in the major unethical acts that the salesperson begins to reflect on his or her own ethical decision making. Given these situational and personal lapses in judgment, it is not surprising that research has been inconclusive in its predictions of salesperson action in ethical and unethical situations.

Retail management and e-business

The potential for a corporation to run into financial and legal difficulties due to unethical decisions, especially those operating in a retail setting (either "bricks and mortar" or electronic) is staggering. In many cases, because of greed, executives have tried to make the company look more successful that it really is. The need to raise capital, increase stock prices, borrow capital from banks, or earn personal performance bonuses are all potential reasons for unethical management.

49

In retail management, sport marketing managers must deal with the ethical climate of the retail operation. One area of significant concern is addressing inappropriate business ethics shown by salespeople, retail managers, and ownership; and its effect on marketing a retail operation. The problems caused by the pressures of having to fulfill sales quotas, dealing with customers making returns and exchanges, and in some cases the lack of sales training regarding how to act in an ethically sound manner, may ultimately negatively affect the operation and perceptions of the business. Sport marketing managers need to be involved in ensuring that ethical behavior permeates the entire operation.

However, a sport marketing manager cannot control all things, and hence may need to change the perceptions of customers in order to entice them to purchase products offered by a retail outlet. For example, one of the biggest issues in retail management is choosing whether or not to sell products manufactured in third world nations by child labor. From a business standpoint, this may save money for the corporation. However, the decision to manufacture and sell products produced in this manner can cause a marketing nightmare for a sport marketer. There are many who believe that companies are exploiting children in third world countries to save money in production. Sport marketers often need to address these attitudes, beliefs, and perceptions by educating the general public or seeking to put a positive spin on the situation.

Beyond traditional retail operations, technology has allowed a number of things that were never possible before to become reality. E-business technology allows both employees and consumers to be watched and profiled in ways never before imaginable. Employees have at their fingertips the means of using the internet for personal transactions and/or ethically and morally provocative sites. There are allegations made by companies against employees, such as invasion of privacy. There are also allegations of companies against consumers through invasion of privacy, unauthorized data collection, price fixing, or sale of personal information. Unethical uses of the internet to steal identity, vandalize, and commit corporate espionage are all possible from an employee's desk.

Although these legal and ethical lapses have a monumental impact, many companies have used the government's lapse in positive ways. This has allowed large corporations to expand their market share by offering individualization of their products. An example of this is Nike's customization program for licensed apparel. This customization has allowed large corporations to gain market share with the mom and pop shops who were providing after-sales services. This has also allowed the mom and pop shops to compete globally with their products, mostly through a touch of the keyboard. With little overhead cost, small businesses that can integrate retail and electronic business strategies can often gain market share and compete in markets that were never open to them before.

Promotions

Promotions are the most visible form of sport marketing, as they involve communicating information about the sport product or service to consumers. While ethics permeates all aspects of sport promotions, the most significant areas of ethical concern focus on advertising and sponsorship.

Advertising

To identify and explain the ethical issues in sport advertising, advertisers must consider that the basic economic principles that guide the evolution of advertising also have social and legal effects. When they are violated, social issues arise and the government may take corrective measures. Society determines what is offensive, excessive, and irresponsible; government bodies determine what is deceptive and unfair. To be law-abiding, ethical, and socially responsible, as well as economically effective, advertisers must understand these issues.

From a business standpoint, advertising helps to establish the corporate image or what the corporation wants as its image. The consumer interprets the advertising and promotional imprint and develops the corporate brand. Advertising can announce a number of possibilities to consumers. Some of the ethical issues in sport advertising include the following:

- *Truth*: advertising shall tell the truth, and shall reveal significant facts, the omission of which would mislead the public.
- *Substantiation*: advertising claims shall be substantiated by evidence in possession of the advertiser and advertising agency, prior to making such claims.
- *Comparisons*: advertising shall refrain from making false, misleading, or unsubstantiated statements or claims about a competitor or his or her products or services.
- *Bait advertising*: advertising shall not offer products or services for sale unless such offers constitute a bona fide effort to sell the advertising products or services and is not a device to switch consumers to other goods or services, usually more highly priced.
- *Guarantees and warranties*: advertising of guarantees and warranties shall be explicit, with sufficient information to apprise consumers of their principal terms and limitations or, when space or time restrictions preclude such disclosures, the advertisement should clearly reveal where the full text of the guarantee or warranty can be examined before purchase.
- *Price claims*: advertising shall avoid price claims which are false or misleading, or saving claims which do not offer provable savings.
- *Testimonials*: advertising containing testimonials shall be limited to those of competent witnesses who are reflecting a real and honest opinion or experience.
- *Taste and decency*: advertising shall be free of statements, illustrations, or implications which are offensive to good taste or public decency.

Sponsorship

Two of the biggest ethical challenges in sport marketing today are popular athletes being touted as role models and ambush marketing.

The use of sport personalities as role models

Rightly or wrongly, children see the success of professional athletes and equate specific sports talent as someone to emulate. The use of popular athletes in advertising has existed in North America for many years. Baseball players such as Babe Ruth or Ty Cobb were some of the first to allow their names and likeness to be mass produced for the sale of candy and tobacco products. Many athletes have appeared to represent a higher physical ideal and their superb individual performances, whether as Olympians or as professionals. These accomplishments make athletes commercially attractive to corporations for the purpose of endorsing a product or a brand.

In 1969, Joe Namath shattered the idea of the clean-cut, speak-only-when-spoken-to image. Namath was cocky, opinionated, anti-establishment, but good-looking and a winner. Namath ushered in the notion of a young hero who was ready to replace traditional sport icons.

In the past 30 years, a new dimension has been added to the use of sports celebrity role models. Many companies have taken deliberate action to recruit the not-so-nice athlete. Nike was the first to promote a non-conventional athlete (Steve Prefontaine). Nike also changed its marketing approach to have athletes who stood out promote their products. Non-traditional, controversial athletes such as tennis players John McEnroe, Andre Agassi, and basketball player Charles Barkley became Nike advertising icons.

Celebrity endorsers are influential as role models because of their ability to attract attention to a commercial, product/service, or organization. However, the use of sport endorsers benefits the product or brand in many more complex ways.

Role models change with the passing of time. Active sport athletes become retired sport athletes and younger athletes are there to take their place. An active athlete may be viewed in a number of different and unpredictable performance contexts. These contexts include winning, losing, honor, good sportsmanship, dirty play, and/or emotional outbursts. Any of these be used in a commercial format. These athletes are placed on a pedestal made of gold. Children only see the end-product and equate this type of promotion with success. If I want to be like Mike, I have to wear Nike shoes and Hanes underwear, eat at McDonald's, and drink Gatorade.

Marketing firms and corporations are not focusing on making future leaders of the world or even future Michael Jordans and LeBron James. Their focus is on getting children to purchase these products for the rest of their lives. Hopefully there is a true role model in their lives to explain the difference.

The ethics of ambush marketing at sporting events
Ambush marketing is a method used to attach a corporation's products or services to an entity without the permission of that entity. The rapid growth of sponsorships has resulted in a number of opportunities designed to maximize profits. However, while this outburst of sponsorship opportunities has ensured that companies can purchase rights to any aspects of an event, it has also created some difficulties. As the number of sponsorship possibilities increases, so too do the loopholes in contracts and potential litigation over rights of sponsorship. Because there is so much money at stake and so many facets of a game or event, the potential for many sponsors creates conflicts of interest.

Ambush marketing first appeared at the 1984 Los Angeles Olympic Games because of the exclusivity within product sponsorship categories. Competitors were explicitly excluded from obtaining sponsorship rights; some sought alternative means implying an association with the Olympic Games. This illegal practice reduces the effectiveness of the sponsor's message while devaluing the sponsorship opportunity.

This tactic is used to attribute goodwill to a company which may not deserve it and which has definitely paid for it. Some ambush tactics included activities such as sponsoring the broadcast of an event sponsored by a competitor, or sponsoring sub-categories of the same event. Other tactics include purchasing advertising spots during a broadcast, then placing the alleged ambusher's brand with the event. More recently, some companies have developed images that are similar to those used by official sponsors and have allegedly ambushed an event, many of which have been dealt with by the courts.

Ambush marketing usually falls into two categories: flagrant and ambiguous. Flagrant infringements would include breach of copyright or unlicensed use of trademarks. Ambiguous infringements exploit the so-called gray area of contract law.

The law provides limited support; sponsors need to create a climate in which companies engaging in this unethical behavior are exposed and held accountable. The IOC has attempted to shame alleged ambushers into discontinuing their tactics by producing and running advertising that describes the companies as cheats. This serves to educate the public about the existence of ambush marketing. Increasing emphasis is thus now placed on the legal aspect of contract and trademark law, and the coordination between event owners and broadcasters has reduced the likelihood that naming rights and broadcast rights to the same event would be divided. Given the global nature of sponsorships, and differences in trademark registration, event owners need to register the images they use in every market they currently trade in, or in which they may wish to trade.

Social media and networking

Social media and networking allow for a brand to reach more customers on a personal level than ever before. However, it is important that the brand does so in a respectful and trustworthy manner. On the social web, a brand that is not trustworthy will be ignored quickly, so it is only in an organization's best interests that it maintains the trust of its followers. This means that when sharing content, the content should not go to websites with malicious software or untrustworthy sales practices. An organization should not spam the timelines of its followers. Constant messages entering the timeline of an organization is a quick way to lose a fan-base.

Brands should be careful with the data they accumulate through their social media endeavors and not tread on the right of their customers' privacy. The selling of data gathered through social networking sites should not be done whatsoever unless the user has given permission.

International and global connections

Over the years, a number of scandals have come to light concerning the production or marketing of potentially harmful products in less developed countries (LDCs). Well-known examples from the 1970s and 1980s include high-dosage contraceptives sold over the counter; baby food promoted using high-pressure sales methods; continued sales of pesticides and high-tar cigarettes after forced withdrawal from Western markets; inadequate health and safety precautions during production of asbestos; and the explosion of a chemical plant due to lax safety standards. One might reasonably wonder why well-educated, professionally trained managers, who work for companies with international reputations, might take decisions that risk provoking censure by the world business community. Is it just the result of the "profit motive" run rampant? Is it merely the "ugly face of capitalism?" Or are there other reasons that might explain the apparent willingness of Western managers to run the risk of jeopardizing the health and well-being of consumers in the developing world?

53

Marketing in LDCs is often characterized by an imbalance of power because the foreign corporation controls access to information about the product, its use, likely effects of misuse, and the availability of safer alternatives. Consumers in LDCs may be vulnerable to exploitation insofar as they lack, to a greater or lesser degree, the basic skills and knowledge that typify consumers in Western markets. In addition, the consumer environment in many LDCs lacks agencies and organizations to monitor company action, such as the Better Business Bureaus and Consumers Union in the United States.

The term "vulnerable" is used here to describe consumers who, for various reasons, find themselves at a disadvantage relative to a global corporation in not being fully able to express, claim, or defend their rights as consumers. Since the Consumer Bill of Rights was issued in the United States in the early 1960s, at least four basic rights have been identified: the right to safety; the right to be informed; the right to choose; and the right to be heard (i.e., to have one's interests fully and fairly considered in the formulation and administration of government policy).

While this list appears to offer considerable protection, it assumes that consumers are willing to be involved in the purchase and consumption of a product, and that they are able to defend their rights. This assumption may not hold true in the case of children, the elderly, or the uneducated poor because they may not have the necessary cognitive ability with which to defend their rights to information, choice, and due consideration. With regard to safety rights, the burden of responsibility would appear to fall on the sellers of goods and the local government or its agencies. Consumer vulnerability is particularly prevalent in LDCs, being associated with the poverty and illiteracy typical of lower levels of economic development. Even when willing to stand up for themselves, consumers in LDCs may not have the necessary education and confidence with which to express and claim their rights.

Generally, sport marketing professionals are obligated to avoid and prevent causing harm with marketing efforts, and to act in a moral, ethical, socially responsible manner where the result is a positive impact. Unfortunately, there is variability in legal and ethical values, attitudes, and standards even among the developed nations of the world, leaving aside the developing world. However, the ethical climate should have little effect on one's acceptance of various norms. As a result, this is an area where individual factors dominate and whether or not one's firm embraces the importance of ethical behavior is irrelevant. On the other hand, a sense of idealism and income level were both closely linked to acceptance of all the norms tested. Since income may be a surrogate measure of success, the results may indicate that those who were more successful tended to have stronger marketing-related norms.

Another major ethical concern is consumer vulnerability, especially as associated with low levels of economic development and lack of supervision of the marketplace. Consumers' emancipation is inhibited by the cumulative effects of the lack of education, lack of opportunities to acquire consumer skills through store and price comparison, lack of information about products and potential hazards, lack of availability of alternative choices, and so on. As a result many consumers in LDCs may be completely unprepared or insufficiently armed to evaluate marketing offers made by any company, whether global or local.

RELATIONSHIP OF SOCIAL RESPONSIBILITY AND ETHICS IN STRATEGIC SPORT MARKETING PLANNING

In order to strategically move a sport organization forward through marketing planning, there needs to be an understanding of the relationship between social responsibility and ethics. Social responsibility is the overall effect that sport marketing plans and decisions will have on society in its entirety. Ethics involves the individual and group decisions made by the sport organization in terms of being right or wrong. In both the organizational operations plan, the human resources manual, and the strategic sport marketing plan, sport organizations need to articulate the expected code of conduct for all employees in terms of social responsibility. This includes communicating the rules and standards expected by the company in terms of its philosophy, mission, goals, objectives, and vision. As a result of these ethically and socially responsible expectations, sport organizations should be able to better respond to the needs and wants of customers and increase the reputation and image of the sport organization.

CONCLUSION

A sport marketing professional must understand the societal values and beliefs that directly affect the implementation of sport marketing efforts. Social responsibility is a sport organization's obligation to increase its positive impact on society as a whole while decreasing any negative impact. From a corporate standpoint, sport organizations focus on the responsibility which sport organizations have to society beyond that of investors and stakeholders to include philanthropy, volunteerism, and any other efforts that foster relationships that enhance society. Corporate social responsibility focuses on two main concepts that the sport marketer must fully understand. First is having an understanding of the stakeholders who have a vested interest in the products, services, industries, operations, and outcomes of a given sport organization. Second is the concept of marketing citizenship, where the sport marketing strategy focuses on the needs of the stakeholder in terms of economics, legal issues, philanthropic activities, and ethics.

From an economic standpoint, the social mission or vision of the organization must be able to work collaboratively with the capitalistic concept of consumerism and the profit responsibility organizations have to owners and stockholders. From a legal point of view, organizations must act within the framework of the laws, rules, and regulations set forth by local, state, federal, and international governmental regulatory agencies; as well as self-regulatory agencies including the sport organization itself, leagues, associations, committees, and federations. From the philosophical dimension, sport organizations have the social obligation an organization has to be a good corporate citizen by contributing to the improvement of the quality of life of people ranging from an individual or community to society as a whole. This is accomplished through community relations, cause-related marketing, strategic philanthropy, and environmental marketing.

And then there is ethics – the principles and standards that sport organizations must follow to ensure appropriate marketing conduct in the view of their stakeholders. These rules of right conduct of individuals, groups, or society generally explain a population's way of life, rules of conduct, and moral code. Sport marketers have a duty and obligation to act in a responsible manner in terms of the ethics within a society. As such, sport marketing professionals need to understand how ethics and ethical behavior affect multiple elements of sport marketing, including understanding the sport consumer, product management, sales management, retail management and e-business, promotions, social media and networking, and international/global connections.

Sport organizations need to articulate the expected code of conduct for all employees in terms of social responsibility. As a result of these expectations, sport organizations should be able to better respond to the needs and wants of customers and increase the reputation and image of the sport organization.

FROM THEORY TO PRACTICE

NIGEL I. JAMIESON, PRINCIPAL LECTURER
Centre for Recreation, Sport and Tourism – TAFE SA North,
Adelaide, South Australia

In addition to my current position, I have been a Visiting Professor at Daniel Webster College, New Hampshire, USA, and have held management positions in Rugby Union, Lacrosse, Australian Rules Football, and the YMCA in Australia and have been involved in organizing and marketing National Championships (both open and age) and a range of events and activities associated with recreation, sport, and tourism. In addition, I have been a Professional Event Organizer for a major regional center in my home state of South Australia, and owned, operated, and marketed a fitness training program, fitness organizations, and served on numerous advisory boards.

Previously, I have had consultancies in recreation sport and fitness – Pheidippides Fitness (reflecting my early Bachelor of Arts in Classical Studies and History), In the Zone Sport Management (conducting sport for primary schools in my home state as a District Convener for the South Australian Primary School Sports Association), an event management company (Movers and Shakers which organized the SA National Aerobic Championships for ten years) and extensive employee fitness programs, including the Adelaide Corporate Challenge which is a lunchtime sport for office workers that is approaching its 25th year of operation.

You may pay lip-service or false homage to the "ethical Gods" but in reality the need for ethics in sport marketing is real and powerful. In a sports world bombarded with messages, both sublime and "in your face," the need for believable, honest, and ethical marketing has never been so acute. We are an increasingly cynical and disbelieving public, and rightly so with some of the less than scrupulous "operators" continuing to make outrageous claims and raising the levels of bad taste in our industry. As an industry we also have some of the most media-savvy and discerning public to market our products and services to who can very easily see through false and dishonest marketing messages. All of these factors combine to make the need for ethics in sport marketing acute and critical in our current times.

Ethics I believe refers to the principles and concepts of right and wrong in terms of personal and professional conduct and decisions. I have adopted my own "creed" or code of ethics and try to act in a manner that is without reproach and continues to be a "beacon" to other administrators and players that I am associated with. I believe that this is essential to my continued success in the industry over a long period of time. I also do not believe that this should be isolated only to my professional career as I continue to teach right and wrong in all aspects of my life. I applaud those professional associations which have adopted their codes of conduct or standards of behavior in an attempt to raise the "bar" in our industry – all power to them!

I would like to suggest that everyone involved in the administration and marketing of sport should adopt a code of ethics for competition (players, spectators, and officials) and for business practices to enable the sport, organization, or competition to be beyond reproach. My lunchtime sporting competition – the longest running multi-sport corporate program in Australia – has a simple code of ethics that every player gets a copy of and is readily available on the competition website (www.adelaidecorporatechallenge. com.au).

Do not exhibit any bias or prejudice toward player selection and treat everyone as truly equal, officials included! Do not allow false or unethical marketing claims to emanate from your organization or sport and be true to yourself and your sport at all times.

One of the most powerful forces in sport, and indeed society as a whole, is the peer group pressure of following the "pack" and facing continual temptation to use business practices and marketing that may be less than ethical. My one piece of advice for people in the management and marketing of sport is to hold onto your good values even in the face of criticism and peer group pressure to follow the next person or organization – stand up and show your moral fiber! Act responsibly and without fear of retribution – do not blame others or shirk from your responsibilities as an administrator and "bastion" of your game – if you do not, who will? And remember: in order to be considered ethical an action must be voluntary, without fear of compromising those values you hold dear – stand up and be counted! Live your life and your sport in the most ethical manner.

The most popular new word for our industry in Australia at the moment is sustainability. Not the focus that we sometimes treat warily because of the association with that disparaging term "tree huggers" but the triple bottom line which needs to be followed in order for a sport or business to be truly sustainable. One of the major pushes I have witnessed in association with this aspect of sustainability has been the term corporate social responsibility. Whether sporting groups or organizations truly believe or not, at least the term has goaded many into action and, perhaps more importantly, introspection about what sort of corporate citizens they really are. All aspects of their operations have been examined with a view to being more responsible and in turn more sustainable in the long term. Two of the biggest sports in Australia, cricket and Australian rules football, have spent considerable time, effort, and resources to consider their corporate social responsibility and I am happy to report that they have put their "money where their mouth is" and have demonstrated a commitment to this aspect of ethical behavior that is commendable. In particular cricket's outreach programs with Indigenous youth in this country have been outstanding and football's work with the disadvantaged in places such as South Australia and even western Sydney has been exemplary. Smaller, less well-resourced sports have at the very least adopted causes and have become aware of being better corporate citizens with simple measures such as equipment lending banks, concession membership fees, and waiving fees for instruction in poorer schools and lower socio-economic areas. This shift in focus has been welcomed, and many sports are reaping the benefits of being more socially responsible.

Everyone is responsible for ethical behavior – it is not optional and fair play is the respect all constituents of your sport or organization must display; no one is exempt from this responsibility and make sure you impress that on your organization all the time. My strong belief is that if prospective employees do not hold ethical behavior in such high esteem as I do then perhaps they are the wrong people to employ. I cannot instill ethical behavior in them; it must be innate and is one of the first things I look for in prospective employees. They must "walk the talk" and I value this quality highly in my current employees, and I simply do not tolerate any unethical marketing practices.

What can we do in sport to help raise ethical marketing standards?

I believe we must be united in our condemnation of the behavior that we currently see in sport marketing and general business practices that does not do our cause any good. Bring pressure to bear on those who have a role in terms of funding and "control" of the sports that have transgressed, and exercise some disdain and condemnation of those who have transgressed and do not make excuses for them. My other piece of advice is to be beyond reproach in your sport and act as a model for others in sport and society.

We are facing many challenges in sport marketing at the moment. Those challenges include restrictive privacy laws, marketing "clutter," and the get-rich-quick "characters" who still surface from time to time. This attracts unwanted criticisms from those who have rightly stepped up to the plate and given us a "hammering" (to borrow from the sporting vernacular). Please weather the current storm and show respect, fairness, justice, and responsibility and be caring, trustworthy, and ethical! It is the least we can do for our sport, our organization, and our employees!

Keep the faith! It will be more than worth it in the long run!

PART II

UNDERSTANDING THE SPORT CONSUMER

CHAPTER FOUR

SPORT MARKETING RESEARCH AND INFORMATION SYSTEMS

CHAPTER OUTLINE

- What is a sport marketing information system?
- Components of a sport marketing information system
- Value of an integrated sport marketing information system
- Conclusion

CHAPTER OBJECTIVES

The reader will be able to:

- recognize the purpose and uses of a sport marketing information system
- recognize the differences between the components of the sportmarketing information system
- recognize the purpose and uses of sport marketing research
- distinguish between the steps of the sport marketing research process, including realizing the importance of each step and the development process associated with those steps
- know the variety of research services in sport marketing research and how to access them
- understand the difference between sport marketing research and online sport marketing research
- understand how the research system interacts with the internal reports system, the intelligence system, and the decision support system, as well as with each other, to implement a most efficient and effective sport marketing information system.

WHAT IS A SPORT MARKETING INFORMATION SYSTEM?

Sport organizations are increasingly investing time and resources into the creation of a sport marketing information system (SMIS). This structure consists of all aspects of the sport organization (people, equipment, goal and objectives, policies and procedures, etc.) being responsible for gathering, organizing, analyzing, evaluating, and distributing marketing information across the sport organization for the purpose of efficient and effective decision making.

The first part of the system is sport marketing research, which is the collection and analysis of information about sport consumers, market niches, and the effectiveness of sport marketing initiatives. Sport marketing research serves as the foundation of the studies that are undertaken for specific problems. However, to have an efficient and effective sport marketing information system, there needs to be interaction from three other components – the internal reports system, the sport marketing intelligence system, and the sport marketing decision support system.

The internal reports system involves information that is generated by the internal operations of the sport organization. Internal reports include all aspects of the accounting information system, including asset and liability management, revenue and expense operations, and administration of owner's equity. The sport marketing intelligence system involves the procedures and sources that the organization utilized to obtain everyday information about developments regarding external opportunities and threats. The sport marketing decision support system, or sport marketing DSS, encompasses the primary and secondary data previously collected by the sport organization, the tools and techniques utilized to interpret those data, and the process by which that information is used in the decision-making process.

COMPONENTS OF A SPORT MARKETING INFORMATION SYSTEM

Sport marketing research

Sport marketing research is the collection and analysis of information about sport consumers, market niches, and the effectiveness of sport marketing initiatives. This is accomplished by first identifying and defining market opportunities and threats, and then designing, implementing, managing, and evaluating marketing actions via the marketing plan. Sport marketing research is a comprehensive ten-step process as follows:

1 Determining the need for sport marketing research.
2 Defining the problem.
3 Establishing sport marketing research goals and objectives.
4 Choosing the appropriate research methodology.
5 Identifying sources of information and determining methods for collecting data.
6 Designing data-collection forms.
7 Determining sample size.
8 Collecting data.
9 Examining data and drawing conclusions.
10 Preparing and presenting the final research report.

62

Sport marketing research process

Determining the need for sport marketing research

Research is needed for many purposes within sport marketing. In some cases, research is conducted when there is a lack of information about what is going on within the targeted market, and the organizations cannot make informed decisions about their marketing efforts. In other cases, research is utilized to examine the perceptions of sport consumers in relation to myriads of areas ranging from attendance at events to sponsorship and brand awareness. Sport marketing research is needed even when there is existing information, but the application of the information is unknown.

The purpose of sport marketing research is twofold. First, it is used to determine if there are opportunities in the market for the sport organization to take advantage of. This may include a lack of competition overall, a market niche void of competition, or an opportunity to offer better products or services than that of the current members of the segment. Second, it is utilized to determine the threats to the sport organization. This involves an evaluation of marketing performance and determining whether the marketing efforts are working. If they are not, the sport marketing professional must modify current marketing strategies, or create new marketing actions.

Sport marketing research ultimately will significantly decrease the uncertainty in making marketing decisions. Unfortunately, many sport organizations are not willing to spend the time necessary to conduct appropriate sport marketing research. Some of the reasons include a lack of time, funding, or resources. However, a major reason that most sport organizations do not conduct research is because they do not know how to do so in an efficient and effective manner. Those who enter the sport marketing profession with a clear understanding of how to manage the sport marketing research process become a significant asset to the sport organization.

Another major problem is not being able to separate being a marketing manager and a marketing researcher. In larger organizations these may be two separate positions – the marketing manager controls the marketing resources and efforts of the sport organization, whereas the marketing researcher investigates the needs of the sport organization and plans for meeting those needs. However, in most sport organizations, the sport marketing manager must also conduct the research for the organization. Therefore it is imperative that the sport marketing professional knows how to separate those roles.

The role as a sport marketing researcher is to generate and ask questions, and to develop the techniques necessary to accomplish the task at hand. Sport marketing researchers must view the organization in an unbiased manner – they cannot allow politics or emotional involvement with the organization to affect their research. If bias enters the equation, there may be invalid, unreliable data that will prevent appropriately defining the problem or determining the most suitable method for solving the problem.

In general, the sport marketing researcher is conducting a cost–benefit analysis to determine the loss to the organization if the problem is not addressed. Therefore, sport marketing research is conducted when problems or changes in the market take place, new marketing objectives are implemented that result in changes in marketing action, there is an opportunity to secure a competitive advantage in the market, or there is a need to re-evaluate the status of the competition.

Defining the problem

Once it has been determined that there is a need to conduct sport marketing research, the problem must be defined. This is the most important step in the sport marketing research process. Without a clear understanding of the purpose of the research, appropriate goals cannot be developed, actions cannot be planned, and a solution cannot be achieved.

One of the major problems within sport marketing today is confusing symptoms of problems with the actual problem itself. An example of this would be a baseball team seeing a 10 percent decline in ticket sales. Typical conclusions that have been drawn include increasing the amount of advertising, offering ticket promotions, or giving rewards or incentives to customer who attend (example: US$1 off French fries at McDonald's after the game). However, has the organization actually determined the problem? These snap decisions are typical with sport organizations due to lack of time, money, or resources. However, if the organization simply took stock of the situation, sat back and completed some basic research, it could determine the true problem and direct its marketing efforts accordingly.

So how do we define the problem? First, there must be a full evaluation of the sport organization, including history and culture, products and services, strengths and weaknesses, perceived opportunities and threats, resources available, and any recent marketing strategy changes. The researcher must also understand what the overall mission, goals, objectives, and vision for the sport organization are. By evaluating all this information, the sport marketing researcher can get a full understanding of the sport organization, and potentially discern patterns or deviations from norms.

After assessing the organizational situation, the sport marketing researcher then clarifies the situation in terms of indicators of change. Some of these indicators include changes in sales volume, market share, profit, and complaints. The sport market researcher cannot look at each indicator at face value only – often he or she must delve into each indicator in significant detail to determine any potential underlying causes of the problem.

As the researcher collects this information, he or she is evaluating all the data in an effort to pinpoint the actual problem. For every problem there is an underlying cause of that problem. Therefore, as the data are evaluated, indicators that are determined not to be a cause of the problem are eliminated from consideration. This allows the sport marketing researcher to narrow the focus and target the most likely causes of the problem by creating a list of probable causes. These probable causes will eventually lead to the development of the true problem statement.

After these probable causes are determined, the sport marketing researcher must come up with potential solutions to address these causes and hence resolve the problem. These solutions can range from changing the price of a product or service, improving service, modifying products, implementing new promotions, and making changes to the channels of distribution. A word of caution when making these changes – the sport marketer must ensure that the solution does not have a negative impact on other parts of the sport organization.

Establishing sport marketing research goals and objectives

The aforementioned potential solutions are then articulated in terms of research goals and objectives. Sport marketing research goals are the list of items that need to be accomplished

64

to rectify a problem. The objectives are the steps that will be undertaken to accomplish each goal. These goals and objectives formulate the backbone of the sport marketing research plan.

Research goals and objectives must be accurate, detailed, clear, operational, and measurable. To facilitate the development of these goals and objectives, the sport marketer must develop constructs and operational definitions, define or create relationships between those constructs, and identify the model(s) to be used to conduct the research. A marketing construct is the item which is to be examined or measured. The operational definition is how the construct will be measured. This is usually in a question format that will be used in a specific measuring tool. The sport marketer will then look for relationships between the constructs, which will identify significant links between two or more constructs and help in the development of concise outcomes. The development of these concise outcomes will then be logically ordered and research questions developed. At this point, the sport researcher will choose an appropriate research method to answer the research questions.

Choosing the appropriate research methodology
The research method is a plan for a study that steers the collection and analysis of information that was gathered. There are two major sources of information in sport marketing research. Primary data are information collected by the sport marketer specifically for the research project. This is normally achieved through personal contact, either by mail, telephone, email, or face-to-face. The methodologies utilized in collecting this type of data will be discussed later in the chapter.

Secondary data is information that has been collected by another source or for another purpose prior to the current research project, and is being evaluated for use to solve the problem at hand. The availability of secondary data is endless, so the sport marketer must understand the various classifications and sources of these data. One of the common misconceptions is that secondary data can only come from external sources outside the sport organization, such as from the internet and research studies. While these sources are very important, some of the most vital secondary data may be found within the sport organization. Data such as sales records, surveys, and questionnaires administered by other departments, end-of-year reports, and program and operational evaluations can be utilized as a solid starting point for any research effort. In addition, internal databases that collect generic information for the sport organization can also be extremely valuable. All of these internal secondary data start to tell a story about the sport organization, how it works, and possible directions in which to take the research.

As noted above, external sources including the internet and research studies are also valuable sources of secondary data. With regard to the internet, it continues to be the fastest growing source of information not only for sport marketing research, but for all types of research. However, one of the cautions of using internet-based information is guaranteeing the reliability of the source, and validity of the data. Almost anyone in the world can post something on the internet. Determining the data that are most important to your organization, while ensuring that they are from an appropriate source, is quite a challenge.

Hence this is why most researchers tend to use research studies. The sources are usually valid and reliable, accepted on a global scale across the industry, and are generally issued through a publisher, syndicated service, or database. Some of the major sources of secondary data in the sport marketing field include marketing journals such as *Sport Marketing Quarterly* (www.smqonline.com), online databases such as the Sport Business Research Network (www.sbrnet.com), sports marketing research companies such as American Sports Data (www.americansportsdata.com), and independent market research studies conducted by numerous corporations and organizations around the world. Some of the key demographic and general sources of secondary data often used in sport marketing include the United States Census Bureau (www.census.gov), the United States Government Printing Office (www.po.gov), the Survey of Buying Power (www.salesandmarketing.com), and *Demographics USA* published by Bill Communications. With the increasing popularity of lifetime sports and alternative sports, the *Lifestyle Market Analyst* (http://www.srds.com/frontMatter/ips/lifestyle) published by SRDS has become an increasingly important tool in understanding lifestyle marketing, customer relationship marketing management, and consumer experience marketing management.

The type of primary or secondary data to be utilized depends on which one of the three major methods for conducting research is used – exploratory, descriptive, or causal:

- *Exploratory research* is conducted when there is little or no information about an opportunity or threat. This is the most difficult method of research because it is impossible to create a plan of action in advance, instead working with impressions and assumptions based on personal experience or expertise. The gathering of information is usually informal and unstructured. This means that the sport marketing researcher will collect as much data as possible in order to gain as much information about the situation as possible. As the problem become clearer, the collected data are evaluated and a determination of which information should be kept and which may be discarded is made. Eventually the problem will become evident, and a plan of action can be created. Sport marketing professionals often do not wish to engage in this type of research because of the time needed to complete the process. They would often rather use a "best-guess" scenario and hope to stumble upon the right conclusion. However, quality exploratory research can reveal significant background information, clarify problems, define concepts, generate hypotheses, and create a list of research priorities.
- *Descriptive research* utilizes data that describes the "who, what, when, where, and how" of a potential problem. This information is very factual and accurate, but does not take into account the cause of the situation. Although this method is most often used in sport marketing circles via observations and surveys, there is still a major fear in conducting this type of research because of mathematics. Many people have a fear of numbers and commonly misinterpret the difference between math and statistics. Math involves the actual solving of equations, whereas statistics is the collection, organization, and interpretation of solved mathematical equations. If more people understood that descriptive research involves looking at what the numbers mean rather than solving equations, more sport marketing researchers would be willing to take more time conducting this type of research.
- *Causal research* is utilizing experimentation and simulations to determine the cause-and-effect relationship between the sport organization and the problem at hand. This type of research is extremely complex because there is no certainty that the results are not being influences by other variables. As a result of this, and the need for time, money, and resources, this type of research is rarely conducted by sport marketing professionals.

66

Identifying sources of information

The source of information will be directly affected by the type of research design. Qualitative research involves collecting, analyzing, and interpreting data by observing what people do, or how they answer open-ended questions. This research tends to involve a small number of respondents who represent a segment of the population. The respondents focus on the qualities of a sport product or service by articulating the values and beliefs which they perceive the specific brand to have. In contrast, quantitative research involves collecting, analyzing, and interpreting data collected from a larger sample via a structured questionnaire or survey. The data are analyzed in statistical terms, and the results produced in a numeric form. At times, both qualitative and quantitative data will be used concurrently. This is known as pluralistic research.

The source of information to be utilized for a research study will depend not only on the research design, but also on the type of primary or secondary data available, and the preferred method of collecting data.

Exploratory sources of information

1 Secondary data analysis

As implied earlier in this chapter, secondary data analysis involves using existing data that have been collected by another source or for another purpose prior to the current research project. The secondary data that come from sport research studies are usually classified in one of four categories. Narrow-Random studies are usually conducted by leagues, individual teams, and sponsors on an as-needed basis to gather specific information on consumer demographics, behaviors, attitudes, product use, and media consumption. Extensive-Random studies are usually only performed by large corporations because of the significant resources (money, time, and people) needed to broaden the study using a large or national sample. As a result of this cost, these types of studies are done on an irregular basis. Narrow-Standard studies deal with specific samples and populations, and are conducted on a regular basis to provide a clearer view of trends. Extensive-Standard studies are more generalized to a large or national sample and tend to look at categories in a generic sense without consideration for individual differences caused by culture, location, or demographic make-up.

2 Case study analyses

Case study analyses are a special type of secondary data analysis. Case studies are published accounts of situations that have occurred to a business or industry, and may be viewed as serving as a guide to answer current research questions. This allows the sport marketer to get a firsthand view of a similar situation and to see how another organization dealt with the circumstances. It is important, however, to use case studies with care. Even though situations may be similar, the solutions may not be viable or appropriate for the organization. Therefore, it is important to look at case studies and determine the relevancy to the current research questions. The more relevant the case is to the research being conducted, the more valid and reliable the solutions will be.

3 Focus groups

Focus groups are interviews that involve eight to 12 people at the same time in the same group, and are used to evaluate products and services, or to test new concepts. To plan for a focus group, the major objective of the meeting must be decided upon. Once the main objective is chosen, the facilitator must design a series of questions (usually numbering six to eight) that will serve to gain a better understanding of the stated objective.

When planning for the session, an average of four questions may be asked per hour, as the focus group is basically a series of individual interviews. Therefore, most focus groups last between one-and-a-half to two hours. The best place to hold focus group sessions is in a room free from distraction with good air flow and lighting, such as a conference room. Offering refreshments during the session would be appropriate.

It would be proper to provide an agenda prior to the meeting (one week), and review that agenda at the start of the session. Setting ground rules for the focus group will keep the session flowing freely. Those ground rules should help keep the group focused, the meeting moving, and bring resolution to each question.

The make-up of the focus group should include individuals with similar characteristics, but who do not know each other. The focus group members should have a willingness to be thoughtful in analyzing the questions, and to share their responses to the questions. The focus group members should also be willing to have the meeting recorded so that the facilitator can review the meeting afterwards.

The job of the facilitator of the focus group is to welcome the members of the group, ask the questions, ask follow-up questions that are geared to clarifying the original answer, and ensure even participation from all members of the focus group. It is best that the facilitator should have a knowledge of the concepts related to the objective, but should be independent from the organization to limit bias. At the end of the focus group meeting, the facilitator should thank everyone for their participation, and guarantee that they will receive a copy of the report from the meeting.

4 Sentiment analysis

Sentiment analysis is the science of analyzing comments made across various internet platforms (i.e. consumer blogs, Twitter, Facebook, etc.). This method relies on being able to take text and break it down into categories like positive, negative, and sometimes neutral.

For most sport marketer researchers there will be simply too much text to sift through, so they will need to opt for an automated process that involves analysis through natural language processing (NLP). The problem with an automated process is that a machine cannot decipher language accurately some of the time.

At the time of writing, sentiment analysis as an automated technology is still in its infancy. However, when the technology becomes more accurate it will be the most cost-effective means of exploratory research to which the sport market researcher has access.

5 Experience surveys

Experience surveys refer to collecting information from those who are considered to be experts in the field of interest. These experts may be part of a direct network, through recommendations of members of the direct network, or from research conducted about the area relating to the research questions or objectives. These differ from traditional surveys in that they are specifically fact finding in nature; therefore the results are not being compared to other individuals or groups.

6 Projective techniques

Projective techniques are used to allow respondents to verbalize their true opinions or beliefs about products and services. When asked directly, respondents often will not address their true attitudes or motivations due to assuming what the interviewer wants the answer to be, feeling pressure that their attitude or belief is not correct, or simply not wanting to have their name tied to their response. Projective techniques, such as tests using word association, sentence completion, or thematic perceptions can allow the respondent to answer in a non-threatening environment. Third-person techniques, such as role playing, also allow the respondent to reply in terms of another.

Descriptive sources of information

1 Cross-sectional studies

Cross-sectional studies measure components from a sample within a population at a specific point in time. Since these are one-time measurements, they are often referred to as a snapshot of the population. The main type of cross-sectional study utilized in sport marketing research is a survey. Surveys can be administered in paper form or online, and are used to gather information from a sample. It is expected that the sample is representative of the entire population.

2 Longitudinal studies

In contrast, longitudinal studies measure components from a sample within a population repeatedly over a period of time. These multiple measurements seek to show trends related to the research being conducted. Two major methods of longitudinal study are panels and market tracking studies.

Panels represent a group of individuals who have agreed to being involved with market research studies at periodic intervals to measure changes over time with a consistent sample. Panels may be continuous or discontinuous. Continuous panels are asked the same questions repeatedly over the period, hence tracking trends related to the specific objective. Discontinuous panels vary the questions asked, therefore allowing the researcher to track various related topics within a specific research area.

Market tracking studies do very much the same as panels, but without the human interaction. These studies measure one or more variables over a period of time using data available from other research studies.

1   Test marketing

Most experiments in sport marketing take place in the real world. A common phrase utilized in sport marketing to describe these field experiments is "test marketing." Test marketing usually involves determining the sales potential of a new product or service, or the acceptance of a product previously entered into the marketplace. Test marketing for sport organizations often centers on the variability of the sport marketing mix and how changes may influence future sales.

Test marketing can take place via normal distribution channels, but owing to the lack of time and resources these experiments are usually outsourced to research firms who will conduct testing in one of three ways. Controlled testing is where distribution of information or products will be through the research firm's predetermined number and type of distribution network. Electronic testing is a limited methodology involving a panel of sport consumers carrying a card that they present when making a purchase (or obviously their lack of product purchase). The information is then fed into a computer and the results compiled. Simulated testing is even more limited in the fact that a small sample of data is collected from consumers, assumptions about the specific population made, and information about generic marketing programs collected. All the information is then put into a theoretical model, and likely results of sales volume and product interest are generated.

2   Secret shopping

Secret shopping (also known as mystery shopping) is a tool utilized in market research to investigate products and services of competitors by sending individuals to act as buyers. Usually what happens is that a sport organization wants to measure the level of service offered by a competitor, or needs to collect data about specific products. The sport marketing professional will hire individuals to either act as shoppers or legitimately shop on behalf of the organization in return for either payment or the opportunity to keep what they purchase. Secret shoppers are provided with the expected behaviors to be exhibited, questions and/or complaints to discuss, specific purchases to be made, and data to be recorded. Sport organizations then use this information to adjust pricing, modify services, or justify the methods already being used.

Determining methods for collecting primary data

As defined earlier in the chapter, primary data is information collected by the sport market researcher specifically for the research project through personal contact. The most basic method for collecting primary data is by observation. While it seems very simple and basic to watch someone or something and then record what was seen or heard, it is easier said than done. In fact, most observations rely on recording devices ranging from tape-recorders or video to the most basic of observational recording methods – written notes. The main importance of recording information in a tangible form is because while the mind is one of the most comprehensive computers known to man, the complexity of retrieving every detail of information on an "as-needed basis" is difficult and often lacking necessary intricate details.

For obvious reasons, the time and resources needed to conduct observations for all research is impossible. Therefore, other methodologies need to be utilized to conduct the extensive

70

marketing research needed by sport organizations. The most common method used is the survey. Surveys are used to collect information from respondents about their attitudes, values, opinions, and beliefs via telephone, mail, face-to-face, and online. A survey may consist of anywhere between five and 500 questions; however, those surveys that are concise and short, with directed, easy-to-answer questions usually reward the researcher with a larger amount of information that tends to be more reliable and valid.

There are a number of advantages to utilizing surveys for sport market research. First is the ability to standardize the survey. This allows for consistency in the measurement, since all respondents will answer the same questions in the same order and following the same scale. Second, it is easy to administer a survey. In most cases the respondents fill out the survey without assistance from the researcher.

Surveys also allow the sport marketing researcher to gain information about concepts that are unobservable. From a demographic interest, we can solicit more accurate information about many topics including a person's income level, occupation, and distance traveled to the event. From a business standpoint, an example would be asking a question about how many times a person has attended a sporting event during the season. Unless we saw the person every time they entered the facility, or we have a computer tracking program that could accurately tell us who used a ticket, we would not know the answer. The responses to the survey questions may be used to tell us where this customer falls on the "escalator", and how we can more effectively market toward that individual to entice him or her to make additional purchases.

The ease with which we evaluate the data received via surveys is also a great advantage. All the data from a survey can be statistically analyzed using computer-processing programs such as Minitab and SPSS, or be evaluated by creating your own statistical analysis format using a spreadsheet program such as Excel. These programs offer the ability to process small and large amounts of information for tabulations, correlations, probabilities, and numerous other statistical analyses. This also allows for coding of data to take into account individual, segment, and subgroup differences.

Types of surveys
There are three major ways to collect data – self-administered surveys, interviews, and computer-administered surveys. Prior to initiating the process, the sport marketing researcher completes an analysis of: (1) time available to collect and analyze data; and (2) the budget available to administer the survey. The sport marketing researcher will use this information to determine which data-collection method will provide the highest quality amount of data within the stated constraints.

1 Self-administered surveys
A self-administered survey is where individual respondents complete the survey on their own. This is the most commonly utilized survey method because the cost is low, the respondent is under no pressure to complete the survey, and there is usually no undue influence placed on the respondent by the surveyor. However, the responses to the survey may not be totally accurate due to misunderstanding questions, not following directions in answering the survey, or just not fully completing the survey because of lack of time or interest. The two main types of self-administered surveys are mail surveys and drop-off surveys.

Mail surveys involve mailing the survey to potential respondents and encouraging them to fill out the questionnaire and returning it via mail. To entice respondents to take the survey seriously and increase the likelihood of a response, sport marketing researchers will often include a self-addressed, stamped envelope with the survey. In addition, some will put a coupon or even a one-dollar bill into the envelope as an incentive.

Drop-off surveys are given to the respondent to fill out. Then the following option may be offered: (1) the researcher will come back at a later time to pick up the completed surveys; (2) a drop box will be set up for the respondent to return the completed survey; or (3) the ability for the respondent to return the completed survey by mail, fax, or email is provided.

2 Interviews

Interviews are basically person-administered surveys. The interviewer reads the questions and then records the answers from the respondent. This can be accomplished either in person or on the telephone. The advantages of this type of surveying include being able to build a rapport with the respondents so that they are in a comfort zone, being able to ask follow-up or clarifying questions instantaneously, and the ability to control quality and adapt questions and methods throughout the process. On the other hand, since this type of surveying takes a longer period of time, the use of this method has significantly decreased. The reasons for this include the advent of computer technologies and their use in surveying, the limited amount of discretionary time people have to meet or talk, and the desire not to be bothered at home during family time to participate in a survey. Regardless of this, it is important to understand the various methods because, while not as widely used, they are still important tools in the acquisition of data.

Telemarketing is the old-fashioned telephone call to a person's home. These may be administered in two ways. The most common method is the central location telephone interview. This is where a group of individuals work for a research firm or data-collection company and make standardized interview calls to a list of individuals, businesses, or even just a series of phone numbers. Usually a supervisor keeps track of the callers by listening in to the conversation and providing instant quality control to the telemarketer following a call. When a company does not have the ability to set up a call center, another method is where individual callers work from their home and have a list of people, businesses, or phone numbers assigned to them.

Another method of interviewing takes place as a result of our need to shop. Shopping intercept surveying occurs when a researcher stops shoppers in malls, supermarkets, outlets, and other retail establishments to get individual opinions. Often shoppers will be enticed with a discount or free item if they participate in the survey. The major limitation of this type of survey again involves time. Since the person you are interviewing is shopping, and often only has a set amount of time, the survey needs to be concise, and the enticement must be of interest to the consumer.

3 Computer-administered surveys

As mentioned earlier, with the advent of advanced computer technologies, surveying has entered a new era. In the latest data published by the Economics and Statistics Administration (www.esa.doc.gov):

72

- More than half of the United States population (71%) is now online using the internet. People using broadband internet is at 68 percent.
- Approximately three-quarters of the population in the United States use computers on a regular basis.
- Nearly one in two people use email on a regular basis.
- Over one-third of the American population (36%) use the internet to search for products and services.

With these types of numbers it was inevitable that surveying via this method would come. There are numerous advantages to computer-administered surveys. The main advantage is fast, error-free data collection. In addition, the sport marketing researcher can include pictures, videos, graphics, and other informational data to supplement the information provided to the respondent. The only down side to computerized surveys is specifically for detailed surveys, where there may be some high set-up costs.

The most commonly used computer-administered surveys are online/internet-based questionnaires. In some cases, individual respondents would be emailed the survey via attachment, and they would then download the survey, reattach it, and reply. However, in most cases, respondents would go to a specific website to fill out the questionnaire. Sport marketing researchers would design and post the survey via the website, and the responses would be tabulated and forwarded by the internet site company. Some of the most popular sites in use for surveys today are www.surveymonkey.com; www. zoomerang.com; www. surveyshare. com, and www.websurveyor.com; even Google Docs has a form feature that may be used to administer surveys.

Two other methods of computer-administered survey are computer-assisted telephone interviews (CATI), and fully computerized interviews. CATI is where the survey questions pop up on a computer screen, the interviewer reads the question to the respondent, the respondent gives the answer, and the interviewer enters the answer into the computer. Fully computerized interviews take the interviewer out of the equation. The respondent sits at the computer, questions show up on the screen, and the respondent enters his or her answer directly into the computer for tabulation.

Designing data-collection forms
Regardless of the type of survey or interview to be administered, there are some constant functions that must be considered in designing a tool to collect data. What form should questions take? How are the results to be measured? Am I using the best scale of measurement? Can I guarantee reliability and validity?

There are three fundamental response formats for questions. Closed-ended questions are when the sport marketing researcher provides specific options of answers for the respondent. Open-ended questions have no answer options provided by the sport marketing researcher to the respondent. Scaled-response questions use a scale developed by the sport marketing researcher, and the respondent's answers are based on both his or her perception and the scale defined.

Closed-ended survey questions may be developed using two formats – dichotomous and multiple category. Dichotomous closed-ended questions require a choice of two responses,

73

such as yes or no, or (a) or (b). Multiple-category closed-ended questions are where there are more than two response options. These types of surveys are used most often by researchers because of the ease of administration, the limited amount of time needed to complete the survey, and the ease of tabulating results.

Open-ended survey questions tend to take longer to answer, as they require respondents to elaborate on their answers. This type of survey is also complex to tabulate as there are often no standard answers, and extended time is often needed to analyze the results. An unprobed format tends to be easier to tabulate and evaluate as the sport marketing researcher simply wants an exact answer from the respondent. If the survey is developed in a probing format, the sport marketing researcher is giving the respondent a chance to elaborate on answers. While this may provide additional information, there is no guarantee that the data will be helpful to the study.

Scaled-response survey questions generally fall into two formats. If utilizing an unlabeled format, it is a numbered format where a descriptor is given to the end-points. An example would be "Rate the service level of the following utilizing a scale of 1–5, where one is poor and five is excellent." A labeled format gives a descriptor for each level of the scale, such as:

1=outstanding 2=very good 3=average 4=need improvement 5=unacceptable

So how do sport marketing researchers choose the proper type of question and response format for their survey? The type of answer being looked for is the most important feature. Following that, other considerations include what has been utilized in similar studies in the past; the method by which the data will be collected (i.e. telephone, mail, email, face-to-face); past history of how respondents prefer to answer questions; and the statistical analyses needed for reporting the findings.

The way in which responses are measured provides one with pertinent information about the subject being sought by the sport marketer. It also helps to provide parameters as far as what the information shows and what it does not show. These limitations help with the accuracy of disseminated information and serve to focus on the most important information needed by the sport organization. These parameters will also dictate the statistical analyses to be used by the sport marketing researcher.

There are two major considerations to reflect upon when planning to measure responses. The first is the characteristics of the scale to be utilized. There are four main characteristics – description, distance, order, and origin. Description refers to how the scale is to be labeled. Distance represents the numeric range between responses. Order signifies the size of the scale descriptors (more than, less than, equal to). Origin deals with the starting point of the data. While the data starting point is often "0", it is important to remember that in sport marketing research the zero point may be an arbitrary point based on previous data. This is especially true in sales where commissions are not paid until reaching a certain sales level. Assuming a salesperson must make US$50,000 in sales prior to receiving commission, the zero point in this case is US$50,000 in the mind of the salesperson.

The other consideration is the levels of measurement for the scales. In sport marketing research there is a hierarchy of scales based on the number of characteristics evident. The most basic of scales is the nominal measurements of scale, where the responses use labels, and hence only have the characteristic of description. Ordinal measurements of scale describe the data

74

and rank order those data. Interval measurements of scale use distance as descriptors to designate the range of responses, as well as ordering and describing the data. Ratio measurements of scale show all four characteristics, including a true zero point.

In sport marketing research there are two major scales of measurement utilized for survey data. The first is the Modified Likert Scale in which respondents are asked to indicate their degree of agreement or disagreement on a symmetric agree–disagree scale for each of a series of statements. In sport marketing research the most common form is the 5-point scale as follows:

1=strongly disagree 2=disagree 3=neutral 4=agree 5=strongly agree

The second is the Lifestyle Inventory, which centers on the measurement of psychographic data. This modified version of the Modified Likert Scale takes into account the values and personality traits of people as reflected in their unique activities, interests, and opinions toward their work, leisure time, and purchases.

The questionnaire development process

Now that a framework for data-collection methods has been described, the development of the questionnaire can begin. The starting point is to determine the goals and objectives of the survey. The goals articulate the plan of what the sport marketing professional wishes to find out, and the objectives are the steps within the questionnaire that will seek to answer those questions. Once this has been determined, a review of the data-collection methods is undertaken to determine the most appropriate form the questionnaire should take.

1   Designing the questionnaire

The first step in designing a questionnaire is the development of the individual questions. When writing a question, one of the basics is to keep questions very specific, focusing on a single topic (see Figure 4.1). Therefore, the questions should be brief but directed. In addition, the questions should have universal interpretation. This will increase the level of reliability and validity of the responses. The best way to ensure this is to use basic vocabulary and simple grammar that is utilized across the majority of demographics within the population or sample.

There are also some things that should be avoided when designing questions for a survey. The biggest "no-no" is making assumptions with questions. It is the job of the question designer to specify the criteria upon which judgments are to be based, and not allowing the respondent to assume the criteria. In addition, the questions need to be as general as possible. Questions that are too specific or which use an example will direct the respondent to focus on the example instead of the broad application of the concept being questioned.

Questions should not be beyond the scope and understanding of the respondents. This includes the memory of the respondents, since most individuals remember things in generalities rather than in specifics. If questions are not general in nature this may force respondents to answer at two extremes, guess at the response they think the surveyor wants, or exaggerate the answer so that it appears that the respondent is knowledgeable.

Three final "do not's" when designing questions. Do not ask questions that the respondent cannot relate to – such as asking them which cable television station they watch sports on, but there is no choice for those who do not have cable. Second, avoid what is called "double-barreled" questions, where there are two questions within one. An example would be "Were

Do's	Do not's
➤ Focus on a single topic	➤ Make assumptions with questions
➤ Be very specific	➤ Be specific with questions
➤ Be brief and directed	➤ Use specific example
➤ Design questions with universal interpretation	➤ Go beyond the understanding of the respondents
➤ Use basic vocabulary and simple grammar	➤ Force the respondent to guess at a response
	➤ Compel the respondent to exaggerate his or her answer
	➤ Ask questions that the respondent cannot relate to
	➤ Use "double-barreled" questions
	➤ Use leading questions

Figure 4.1 Question design

you satisfied with the concessions and merchandise offered at the stadium?" If the answer is yes, were they satisfied with the food offered? Food taste? Beverage variety? Offerings in the pro shop? Service? You cannot tell from the answer to the question, and therefore the response is useless. Finally, questions should not lead the respondent to a specific answer. To avoid this, refrain from loading the question with statements or words that will direct the respondent into a biased response. An example would be "How did you like your experience at the game?", and the responses are (a) extremely well; (b) very good; (c) OK; and (d) not too well. Since only positive answers are provided (not too well still focuses on the positive – "well"), this is a biased and leading question.

Once all the questions are created, an initial evaluation process is started to reword and rework questions. During this process, each question is evaluated based on the do's and do not's listed above, and modified if necessary. The goal is to ensure that the questions meet the standards set forth to decrease the potential of generating unreliable, inaccurate, or invalid responses.

2 Organizing the questionnaire
There are four steps to organizing a questionnaire – the introduction, question sequencing, pre-coding, and approval process. The introduction is usually a cover letter or paragraph at the top of the questionnaire giving general information about the study. The first item of consideration when writing the introduction is whether the sponsor of the study, or the individual/company administering the questionnaire, is to be identified. If they are identified, it is known as an undisguised survey. If they wish to remain anonymous, it is a disguised survey.

76

The next part of the introduction explains the purpose of the research. This should be a brief and simple one- to two-sentence explanation of the study. This is followed by a one-sentence explanation of how and why the respondent was chosen for this study.

The last part of the introduction is the part that makes or breaks the research – the request for participation in the survey. People have less discretionary time in today's society – what is going to make them take time out of their busy schedule and complete your survey? The answer is incentives! Incentives can range from money to product samples to discounts and coupons. For some, a copy of the study when completed is desirable. The goal is to match the incentive to the respondents.

One other note with regard to the introduction: there will be some who will only complete a questionnaire if they are guaranteed either anonymity or confidentiality. Anonymity assures the respondent that he or she will not be identified in conjunction with the data collected or the study. Confidentiality means that the researcher knows the individual respondents, but the name of the respondent will not be divulged, or information relating to the study will not be attached to the individual without the expressed consent of the respondent.

Once the introduction is completed, the questions will be sequenced. However, one step that is added to some questionnaires at this point is screening questions. Screening is the process by which a research can conduct a preliminary appraisal of potential respondents to determine their suitability for the study. These questions are asked at the beginning of the questionnaire to eliminate those who do not meet the necessary qualifications for the study. For example, if this is a general questionnaire to determine perceptions of service and quality at a particular baseball stadium, a question might be "Have you attended a baseball game at this stadium?" If the response is no, you would thank the respondent for his or her time and move on to another potential respondent.

Next is the sequencing of questions. Usually a questionnaire starts with warm-up questions. These questions are usually simple, easy to answer, and create further interest in the study. An example of a warm-up question would be "How often have you attended a baseball game at this stadium?" After the warm-ups, transitions are used to let the respondent know that the format of the questions will be changing. For example: "For the next series of questions you will be asked about your views of service and quality for various areas of the stadium." Sometimes, skip questions will be used as a part of this section. A skip question is where the answer to that question will affect which question to ask next. An example would be "Have you made a purchase from any merchandise booth with the stadium during this season?" If the answer is yes, move on with the questionnaire; if the answer is no, the respondent will be directed to skip a series of questions about merchandising and move on to the next section.

As a rule, easier questions are placed early on in the questionnaire, with complicated questions appearing toward the end. The reason for this is that once you have a respondent who has invested some time in the survey, the likelihood of their just not completing the questionnaire because of a difficult question is very low. Therefore, the sport marketing research uses the easy questions as a hook, and once hooked the respondent is committed. Another way to ensure that respondents do not quit is to inform them that they are almost finished, as there are usually a limited number of difficult questions. An example of a complex question would be "Rate each of the following services on a scale from 1 to 7."

The final section of the questionnaire is classification and demographic questions. In years past, these questions were found at the beginning of a questionnaire, but studies have shown that asking for that information up front discourages people from completing surveys because they did not want to give personal information. Even if it was noted on the questionnaire that the section was optional, the perception of this information being at the front was that it was most important to the study. Therefore these questions now appear at the end. The respondents have already provided the sport marketing researcher with information and now, whether they wish to provide this information or not, the research has the data. The demographic and classification information is important to the research in order to do additional statistical analysis on the data, so it is important to ask questions that allow for anonymity and confidentiality should the respondent wish for that.

The next step in the questionnaire development process is pre-coding questions. This information is utilized to help in data entry and dissemination. The goal of pre-coding is to associate each possible response with a unique number and/or letter. Numbers are preferred because there are more statistical analysis programs that identify with numbers than with letters. The key is that pre-coding cannot interfere with the respondent answering questions by confusing them. In fact, with the use of computer tabulation, most pre-coding is put into the statistical software instead of on the actual survey, and as data are entered the pre-coding will automatically be implemented.

The final step is to gain approval of the survey from the client. It is important to remember that although the sport marketing researcher may be the expert in the field, it is ultimately the client (i.e. the management of the sport organization) who must approve the research tool. Often this process requires explanation to the management, who may not understand the process.

3 Pre-testing and revisions

After the questionnaire has been approved, the sport marketing researcher must ensure that the questionnaire works through the process of pre-testing. In this process, the sport marketing researcher is actually conducting a "dry run" of the process by testing the survey on a small, representative sample of respondents. Generally, five to ten respondents are used to not only answer the questions but also to ask the sport marketing researcher questions regarding confusions or misunderstandings. The sport marketing researcher will analyze these concerns and make revisions as necessary. Once revisions are finalized, the questionnaire is ready for mass use.

Determining sample size

A sample is the most basic element of sport marketing research, since the factors taken from a small group are representative of the characteristics of an entire population. The population is the entire group that is defined as being under study as per the research questions. Information about populations, and hence samples, most often comes from the census (www.census.gov).

A sport marketing researcher will start with a sample frame, which is a master list of the entire population (example: All Los Angeles Lakers fans who have attended at least one game at Staples Center). There may be errors in the listing, such as those season ticket holders which

78

may be a corporation and which give the tickets to various people who use them, individuals who buy tickets for someone else, and those who have paid cash for the ticket but may not even be in the database. This is known as the sample frame error – the degree to which the sample frame does not encompass the entire population.

Next, a sample is selected; for example, Los Angeles Lakers season ticket holders. Again, there may be a sampling error, which is caused either by the method by which the sample is chosen, or by the size of the sample. In the scenario listed above, an error could be that a season ticket holder may not be representative of a person who can only afford to go to one game per year, or that the season ticket holder sample may not statistically be a large enough sample to reliably and validly represent the entire Los Angeles Lakers ticket population.

However, the reality is that it is less expensive and time consuming to take a sample instead of attempting to survey the entire population. In addition, it would be almost impossible, even with computer assistance, to analyze the massive amount of data that would be generated from such a large population. Therefore, we use one of two methods of sampling – probability and non-probability.

1   Probability sampling
Probability sampling is most often used in sport marketing research when looking at current customers. It utilizes random selection from the known population. There are four methods of probability sampling – simple random sampling, systematic sampling, cluster sampling, and stratified sampling.

Simple random sampling is where the sport marketing researcher uses some chance method which guarantees that each member of the population has an equal chance to be selected into the sample. The most common of these are the blind draw method (pulling names out of a hat) and the random numbers method (every member of the population is given a number and a computer generates a random list of numbers for the sample).

Systematic sampling is less time consuming than the simple random method. Starting with a list of the entire population, each is given a number. Then a skip interval is calculated. This skip interval represents how many names would be skipped when selecting the sample. This is calculated by taking the entire population list and dividing it by the desired sample size. For example, let us say there are 10,000 ticket holders, and we want a sample size of 1,000. The skip interval would be 10. Therefore, every tenth name on the list would be entered into the sample.

Cluster sampling is where the population is divided into groups, any of which could be considered as a representative sample. Most of the time clusters are based on demographics (geographic location, age range, sex, race). While this is a faster method of dividing groups, there cannot be a guarantee that the cluster is truly representative of the entire population.

Stratified sampling is utilized when there might be a large divergence in the population that would cause a skewed distribution. This skewed distribution is a result of extremes in the population – for example, if the majority of the population has an average income of US$50,000 +/– 25% ($37,500–67,500), but a significant percentage is making over US$100,000. In this case the population would be separated into different strata, and a sample would be taken from each.

79

2 Non-probability sampling

Non-probability sampling is most often used in sport marketing research when there is no way to guarantee the representation in the sample. Therefore, the desired population does not have a guarantee of being a part of the sample. There are four methods of non-probability sampling – convenience sampling, referral sampling, judgment sampling, and quota sampling.

Convenience sampling is where the sport marketing researcher goes to a high-traffic area such as a mall or shopping center to survey potential respondents. Errors occur as a result of there being no guarantee that users will be within the population at the chosen location.

Referral sampling is where the respondents to a survey are also asked to identify other individuals who would likely qualify to take part in the survey. Again this is a biased sampling method as those who are not well known, not liked, or who have caused conflict in the eyes of the respondent will not be included.

Judgment sampling occurs when the sport marketing researcher uses either his or her own opinion, or that of someone considered to be an expert, to determine who will be a part of the sample. This is a subjective method of sampling; therefore beliefs, feelings, attitudes, and perceptions could play a significant role, and hence may bias the sample.

Quota sampling goes a step further than judgment sampling, but also seeks to enhance convenience sampling. This method seeks to balance the proportion of selected respondent characteristics by setting quotas on how many individuals from a specific group may respond. Groups may be capped based on demographic features, product use, or service features utilized.

Examining data and drawing conclusions

The goal of this section is to introduce the student to basic methods of describing the data and being able to draw basic conclusions utilizing one of five statistical analysis methods – descriptive, inferential, difference, associative, and predictive. All of these statistical methods are used to reduce the large quantity of data available in drawing conclusions for the study. The data are summarized and explained in logical order, while communicating patterns of behavior or action and generalizing the sample to an entire population. It is recommended that individuals who wish to gain more extensive experience in data analysis take a market research class or a probability and statistics class.

1 Descriptive analysis

Descriptive statistics are used early on in the analysis of data and serve as a foundation for future, more detailed analysis of data. As the title states, descriptive statistics use basic data reduction and summarization to describe the respondents, the sample, and the population. The methods utilized for descriptive analysis are mean, median, mode, frequency distribution, range, and standard deviation – each is defined in Table 4.1.

2 Inferential analysis

Inferential statistics are used to generalize the results and draw conclusions simply based on the population characteristics and the data collected. This method is used to estimate values, test hypotheses, and determine significant differences. The two main methods for completing an inferential analysis are standard error and the null hypothesis. Standard error is used to

80

Table 4.1 Definitions of descriptive statistics

Mean	The average value of a set of numbers (sum of all responses/number of respondents)
Median	The middle value of a distribution (50th percentile)
Mode	The value occurring most frequently in the data
Frequency distribution	The number of times a value occurs during the study. These distributions can be documented as individual cases (frequency), percentages, and running totals (cumulative)
Range	The distance between the lowest value and the highest value
Standard deviation (SD)	Measures the spread of values throughout the data. For a normal curve, which is used most often, the midpoint is the mean and the standard deviation is measured from that point

measure the variability in the sample distribution. This is accomplished by taking the standard deviation from the mean and dividing by the total number of respondents (SD / N). This allows us to apply that error to determine the similarity or dissimilarity of the sample based on the spread of the distribution and the associated percentages. Also associated with the standard error are confidence intervals. These are utilized to calculate the degree of accuracy that the researcher prefers. Most researchers seek a 95 percent level of confidence in their studies.

Hypothesis testing is the articulated expectation of the sport organization, the sport marketer, or the sport marketing researcher. There is a five-step process to hypothesis testing as documented below:

1   Make a statement about something that exists within the population.

■   *The owner of an Af2 Arena football team states that attendance is only at 60 percent capacity because the community at large is not aware of the team's presence.*

2   Draw a probability sample and determine a sample statistic (mean is most often used).

■   *The sport marketing department outsources to a market research firm and asks for a systematic sampling method to be used on residents within a 40-mile radius. At the end of the study, results show that 83 percent of the geographic target is knowledgeable about the team. Additional information shows that 61 percent of the respondents did not attend a game for two associated reasons – high ticket prices of arena football, and choosing to spend their discretionary money on the minor league baseball team in town.*

3   Compare the statistic to the original statement (hypothesis).

■   *The 60 percent stated by the owner does not equate to the 83 percent stated by the research.*

4   Decide if the statistic supports the hypothesis.

■   *The researched 83 percent does not support the owner's original statement.*

5   If the sample does not support the hypothesis, reject it and revise.

■   *We reject the owner's statement and start a plan to address the reason why 40 percent of the arena is empty – including a review of ticket prices, and a modification of marketing and promotional efforts to address the competition.*

3 Difference analysis

Difference analysis is utilized when there are variations that exist between targeted groups. This is very apparent in sport marketing research, especially with the aforementioned escalator concept. Heavy users (season ticket holders, luxury suite owners) will view satisfaction with sport products and services very differently from light users (who attend a game once or twice a year).

Two main statistical concepts are utilized to measure differences between groups. The first is the *t* test, which assesses whether the means of the two groups are statistically different from each other. Marketing efforts can be directed to the two groups in a similar fashion only if the difference between the means is statistically insignificant. The other test is the analysis of variance (ANOVA). ANOVA testing is utilized when there are more than two groups being compared.

4 Associative analysis

Associative statistics evaluate whether two specific variables within a study are related. An example would be: Are ticket promotions in the local newspaper resulting in more tickets purchased? There are three main methods for evaluating association – cross-tabulations, chi-square analysis, and Pearson product moment correlation. These are defined in Table 4.2.

Table 4.2 Methods for measuring association

Cross-tabulations	Basic tabular comparison method using raw data, frequencies, or percentages
Chi-square	Known as a "goodness of fit" test; it seeks to take the obtained frequencies from the sample and compare them to the statistical hypothesis
Pearson product moment correlation	Also known as the correlation coefficient; creates a linear association between two variables

5 Predictive analysis

Predictive statistics are used mainly by sport marketing researchers in prediction and forecasting the future by evaluating previously collected data. A variety of regression analyses are utilized to engage in predictive analysis including bivariate regression analysis (two variables), and multiple regression analysis (more than two variables). Regression measures a dependent variable and its relationship to one (bivariate) or more (multiple) independent variables.

Research reports and services within sport marketing research

Once all the information has been compiled, the results need to be communicated to the sport organization through a sport marketing research report. Sport marketing research reports cover a wide range of areas, including but not limited to customer satisfaction, economic impact, needs assessment, organizational behavior, and risk assessment. This report presents factual information based on research results, recommendations from the sport marketing researcher, and conclusions about what could happen if necessary change is not implemented. This report is then used by the management of the sport organization as a foundation for their decision-making process. For this reason, the information presented in the sport marketing research report must be organized, concise, accurate, and clear. Visuals, including tables, pie charts, bar graphs, line graphs, maps, photos, and flow diagrams, can all be used to enhance the report and simplify the message for those who may not read it in its entirety. It would also be appropriate for the sport marketing researcher or professional to include an oral presentation with the report to highlight the most important sections.

Online and web-based sport marketing research
With the expansion of electronic technologies and the internet, online and web-based sport marketing research has become more prevalent. The main reason the online and web-based technologies are becoming the preferred method for conducting research is because of their effectiveness (ease of use) and efficiency (minimal time and resources needed). There are numerous other advantages to online and web-based research, including:

- It can be effectively utilized at all stages of the sport marketing research process.
- It can be used for both qualitative and quantitative research.
- It can be used to administer surveys, as well as conduct observational research both in real time and asynchronously.
- It allows respondents to participate in a place of their choice (home, work, internet café, etc.).
- Researchers and organizations can view data in real time.
- Researchers can provide supplemental information (videos, pictures, advertisements, simulations) for respondents to view and re-view as a part of the research.

There are also a number of challenges with online and web-based research. First, it is difficult to determine with full reliability and validity whether the data collected are truly representative of the entire population. It is challenging to verify the authenticity of the person responding to the research. This is also true for the secondary information published on the web. It is important that researchers verify that the source of the information is reputable.

Another challenge is getting people to complete surveys via the web. Spam (unsolicited email) and pop-up advertisements have inundated online and web-based systems to the point of people downloading pop-up blockers, and having unknown email go to a junk email folder for deletion.

CASE STUDY 4: SPORT MARKETING POTENTIAL IN CHINA
This is a two-part case study. The first section will cover the marketing research effort that targets consumers' influences and financial implications as being a worthwhile sport marketing effort. To implement effective marketing strategies in a specific country, it is pertinent to understand consumer behavior in that country, which will be covered in the second part of the case study and will appear in the next chapter.

From the marketing research effort, a questionnaire was administered to 2,155 mainland Chinese consumers in ten selected cities, and different economic, social, and personal factors in the China's environment are determined.

INTRODUCTION

With a quarter of the world's population and a fast-growing economy, China is rapidly turning into one of the busiest market centers in the world. Sport marketing has the potential to emerge not only as an effective vehicle in imitating the development of the Chinese economy; it also affects the Chinese culture and lifestyle.

Since sport marketing in China has not been analyzed or researched, it is appropriate to study the consumer as well as general financial implications. A look at American success in sport marketing will be helpful. However, implementing such strategies in China creates special considerations owing to the existence of cultural and economic differences between the two countries. This study attempts to identify the proper marketing strategies in China through an analysis of Chinese consumers' behavior, attitudes, and buying patterns.

METHODOLOGY

The methodology used in this study consisted of exploratory research of interviewing managers of retail outlets, secondary research of literature review, and primary research of a total of 4,000 questionnaires distributed in ten selected cities (Beijing, Chendu, Guangzhou, Nanjing, Qindao, Shanghai, Shenzhen, Tianjin, Xian, and Xiamen) in China. Questionnaires were administered to a judgmental quota sample and assigned to one of four age groups with equal males and females.

The rate of response was 53.9 percent; 2,155 questionnaires were returned.

The analysis of the data includes editing, coding, analyzing coded observations, and interpreting results for solutions to the research problems. Tabulations and measures of central tendency were used to describe the distribution of characteristics in the subject population. Cross-tabulation and chi-square statistics were also used to show relationships between consumer segments.

SURVEY FINDINGS

Eleven major factors affecting consumer purchasing emerged from the questionnaire data analysis:

1 *Purchasing reasons*: the major reason why people purchased sport products was "for exercise."
2 *Purchasing experience evaluation*: approximately half of the respondents indicated that their purchasing experience was "positive."
3 *Income level relative to the expenses level:* the Chinese consumers' income levels range from less than US$173 per year to over US$863 per year. The middle-income level accounted for 72 percent of the respondents. However, most respondents indicated that they spent "less than US$40 per year" on the purchase of sporting goods.
4 *Types of sporting goods purchased*: "shoes" were the No. 1 favorite type of sporting goods for Chinese consumers. Females tended to purchase apparel; males were more likely to purchase all types of sporting goods.
5 *Product factors affecting purchasing*: "quality," "style," and "price" were the three most important factors influencing purchasing decisions.

6 *Purchasing:* "boy- and girlfriend" had the most important influence in the decision process. "Parents" had the least important influence.

7 *Sources of information about where and how to purchase:* the major information channel for Chinese consumers was their "going to a shopping mall" experience.

8 *Influence of advertisements:* Of those responding to the survey, more than half said they either "occasionally" or "rarely" believe advertisements.

9 *Brands consumers prefer:* Adidas, Asics, Nike, and Reebok were identified by the Chinese consumers.

10 *Where goods are purchased:* most of those surveyed purchased their sporting goods from either "a sporting goods store" or "a department store."

11 *Time spent in sport activities:* almost 90 percent of the Chinese consumers spent "less than five hours a week" participating in sport activities. However, three meaningful findings emerged: (a) those who participated "less than five hours a week" in sport activities spent more money purchasing sport products than those who participated "over five hours a week" in sport activities; (b) those in the income level of "US$402 to US$863" spent more time participating in sport activities; (c) young adults and "unmarried" persons spent more time per week participating in activities than those who were "married" or elderly.

Source: Adapted from: Geng, L., Lockhart, B., Blackmore, C. and Andrus, R. (1996). Sport marketing strategy: A consumer behavior case analysis in China. *Multinational Business Review.* Retrieved March 17, 2006 from http://www.findarticles.com/p/articles/mi_qa3674/ is_199604/ai_n8756626.

Questions for discsussion

1 Utilizing a questionnaire for this type of research can be quite a challenge due to the spread of the 2,155 mainland Chinese consumers in ten selected cities, and the different economic, social, and personal factors in China's environment. In a country of over 1 billion people with a land mass of over 9.5 million square kilometers (3.67 million square miles or the size of the United States) it is very difficult to determine an appropriate sample. Considering the sampling methods discussed in the chapter, what methods of probability and non-probability sampling could have been used for this study? Explain in detail as to your reasoning why you believe this method could be used. Choose the one method you would use and explain why in terms of ensuring reliability and validity of the data collected.

2 You are the marketing director of a sport apparel company who wishes to enter this market now. Assume the market research information provided in this study has remained static. By analyzing each of the 11 factors affecting consumer purchasing that emerged from this questionnaire data analysis, would you move forward and enter this market? If yes, how would you proceed? If no, why not?

3 Again as marketing director, you determine that the data collected for this study is outdated. How would you go about replicating the study? Would you use all the same questions? If not, which ones would you change and how? Would you implement the questionnaire differently? How?

Many of these challenges have forced sport organizations to review the way in which they conduct research. This has resulted in more sport organizations investing time and resources into the creation of a sport management information system (SMIS). This structure consists of all aspects of the sport organization (people, equipment, goals and objectives, policies and procedures, etc.) being responsible for gathering, organizing, analyzing, evaluating, and distributing marketing information across the sport organization for the purpose of efficient and effective decision making. The following sections of the chapter will explain the remaining components of the sport marketing information system.

Internal report systems

The internal report system is the basic information system used by sport marketing professionals to examine the internal operations of the sport organization. The internal reports consist of all facets of the accounting information system, including asset and liability management, revenue and expense operations, and administration of owner's equity. This allows the sport marketing professional to review reports of orders, sales, costs, inventories, cash flows, receivables, payables, and debts on an ongoing basis. This information is available quickly, because most sport organizations produce these reports of financial management on a monthly, and even weekly, basis.

Any sport organization that has been in business for any period of time has more information available than it realizes. Therefore, much of this information often remains underutilized because the information does not leave the department which created or collected it. The individuals in those various departments do not always realize how the data could help sport marketing professionals in their decision-making process. In addition, many sport marketing professionals fail to appreciate how information from other areas might help them and therefore do not request it.

The internal records that are of immediate value to marketing decisions are orders received, inventory, and sales invoices. By comparing orders received with invoices, a sport marketing professional can establish the extent to which the sport organization is providing an acceptable level of customer service. Evaluating inventory records with orders received helps a sport marketer determine whether the marketing efforts are addressing the current demand patterns, and if changes need to be made. This often occurs with ticket sales for less desirable match-ups. For example, when the New York Yankees host the Boston Red Sox, there is usually not a ticket to be had. However, for other teams such as Pittsburgh Pirates or Kansas City Royals, there is less of a demand to pay a premium price for those games. The sport marketing professional can look at ticket inventory levels, see which games are not selling, and design programs to entice customers to purchase tickets and attend the games.

However, there is a lot of information that the various departmental, managerial, and administrative areas within the sport organization can provide that would enhance the sport marketing information system. Table 4.3 provides a sample list of internal operations that can provide internal report information to the sport marketing information system.

Table 4.3 Internal operations that provide internal reports

Organizational area	Information to be provided	Use of the information
Accounting and finance	Product pricing and costing Marketing and sales expenses	Profitability potential by sport product or service
Customer service	Customer feedback on product reliability and performance	Ability to review files for new product or service ideas Ability to review problems that need to be addressed
Corporate planning	Goals and objectives for the sport organization	Measuring tool to determine progress toward attaining goals
Data processing	The system for organizing data	Understanding of the capabilities of the system Articulation of what the system needs to provide
Human resources	Background on sales and marketing employees Performance review data	Learning curve for salespeople Review criteria for future hires

Marketing department	Types of new sport products and services with market possibilities
	Customer response to current sport products and services
	Strategic marketing plans
	Promotional campaigns
		Data for market analysis of current sport products and services for:
		   Prospects
		   Current customers

Merchandising/ticketing	Inventory status	Forecast promotional needs to be attached to selected inventory
Sales department	Sales figures Feedback from customers	Streamline and improve methods of securing sales

Order-to-payment cycle

The focal point of the internal records system is the order-to-payment cycle, which includes all of the activities associated with the completion of a business transaction. The process starts with a request for purchase. This request can range from a merchandiser or concessionaire placing an order with a supplier, to an individual clicking on buttons to find tickets online, to a fan placing an order for food at the concession stand. The request for purchase is any situation where a buyer wishes to make a purchase from a seller.

The cycle continues with the seller providing information on the price to be paid. For the merchandiser or concessionaire, it is the receipt of an invoice. For the sport consumer purchasing tickets online, it is the screen that tells how much the cost will be. At the concession stand, it is the vendor telling the customer how much it will cost for the food ordered. The order-to-payment cycle concludes with the payment and delivery of the products.

The more efficiently and effectively the cycle works, the more orders can be processed, the more sales are transacted, and the potential for higher profit by the sport organization is realistic. From the standpoint of the sport marketing professional, access to the order-to-payment cycle is crucial. The order-to-payment cycle spans most business processes. The sport marketing professional may need access to information from any of those processes at a given time based on a problem at hand. Therefore the sport marketing professional can address market changes, opportunities, and threats more quickly. In addition, sport marketers can send messages to prospects and customers that the sport organization addresses consumer needs, wants, and desires quickly. This, in turn, has the potential of increasing sales and enhancing the image of the sport organization.

Point-of-sale system

As with many sport marketing functions, time is of the essence. If a demand need is not addressed quickly, another organization will swoop in and take advantage of the opportunity. Therefore, many sport organizations have increased the speed with which sport marketing professionals and management can access information by moving their internal report systems to a computer-based intranet. Advances in technology have provided sport marketing professionals with more comprehensive information at their fingertips by providing instant access to information about their prospects and customers through sales information systems. These sales information computer systems for internal reports are also known as point-of-sale (POS) systems. Table 4.4 lists a variety of POS hardware that can collect information that may be ultimately used by the sport marketing professional.

Table 4.4 Types of point-of-sale (POS) hardware

Name of hardware	Variations of hardware
Barcode scanner	Handheld, Hands-free, and Countertop
Barcode printer	High-speed direct thermal and thermal transfer label printers
Receipt printer	High-speed thermal and impact receipt printers
Credit card reader	Standard
Check reader	Standard
Portable age/ID verifier	Identity verification via driver's license or state-issued/military ID
Palm pilots	With integrated barcode scanner or wireless communication
Cordless scanners	Long range and short range; cordless and wireless
POS keyboards	With integrated credit card or check reader
POS monitors	Touch screen

In addition, there are a number of software programs that take the information collected and disseminate those data into an easy-access format. Some examples of the software programs available include the following:

- eClub Logic by KI Software
- Intuit Quickbooks POS
- Microsoft CRM
- Microsoft Retail Management System

- Seta Systems Golf Club Management Software
- TangentPOS by Venue1
- Windward's SportsStorePOS for Retail Sport Stores.

Data mining of transactional data

One of the major growth areas in sport marketing is transactional data collected as a result of data mining. Data mining is the process of collecting and analyzing data from non-traditional perspectives, categorizing the data, and summarizing relationships. An example of this would be a baseball team using a fan loyalty reward card to analyze buying patterns at the stadium and associated merchandise outlets. They may discover that men who buy a ticket to the game on average also purchase two beers, approximately US$15 of food, and spend about US$10 on merchandise. It can also show what the most popular food and merchandise items are. It could also be used to offer promotions on low-selling items, and hence be able to move that merchandise out of inventory and replace it with other types that may increase revenue.

This concept of data mining of transactional data has served as the foundation of current sport consumer relationship management programs, which will be discussed in Chapter 15. The two main companies that are engaged in data mining of transactional data for sport organizations are AIM Technologies and EDCS. AIM Technologies focuses on collecting information about the demographics and psychographics of fans, whereas EDCS's Top Prospect system collects information and translates purchases into a points system similar to a frequent flyer program for airlines. The more fans use their card, the more points they get and the more benefits they receive. Under both programs, sport marketing professionals are able to use the data to design promotions and other specials through the programs.

These data-mining efforts allow sport marketers to analyze and correlate hundreds if not thousands of different segments that were targeted differently. However, with this mass of information, sport marketing professionals can get lost in the quantity. The key is that each transaction is not of interest; the patterns and associations of transactions to evaluate areas where coordinated sport marketing efforts can be utilized to save time and resources for the sport organization.

The data collected may also be utilized to grade the sport customer, which is another emerging method of sport marketing productivity. Most of the data collected may be given a grade or score, and hence sport marketing professionals can evaluate the success or failure of a sport marketing campaign – just as a teacher would evaluate a research paper handed in by a student. As long as the sport marketer has developed outcomes that can be broken down into measurable terms, these grades may be used to more effectively and efficiently target potential and current sport consumers.

In addition to the grading of transactional data, sport marketing professionals must also categorize information using RFM analysis. RFM (recency, frequency, monetary) analysis is used to determine the most profitable customers for the sport organization based on: (1) if the customer has purchased recently; (2) how often the customer has made a purchase; and (3) how much the customer spends with the sport organization. This RFM analysis serves as the foundation for the Pareto Principle (or 80/20 rule) discussed in Chapter 1, where 80 percent of a sport organization's business comes from 20 percent of its customers. The RFM analysis also provides the sport marketer with the ability to conduct a long-term value analysis.

Long-term value with regard to the sport consumer is an evaluation of what that sport consumer is worth to the sport organization in terms of sales and profit over a period of time. A long-term period usually refers to a minimum of three years, but can be as long as a lifetime.

The internal reports system serves as a framework for the sport marketing information system by affording the sport marketing professional the ability to examine the internal operations of the sport organization and improve upon marketing efforts. Utilizing the information collected from various departments through inputs from the order-to-payment cycle, the point-of-sale system, and data mining, the sport marketing professional is better able to understand the sport organization itself, and its relationship to prospective and current customers. However, as discussed in the introduction, this is only the second of four components that make up the sport marketing information system.

Sport marketing intelligence system

The sport marketing intelligence system is a set of procedures utilized by sport marketing professionals to secure everyday information about developments in the marketing environment regarding external opportunities and threats. Earlier in this chapter we discussed the difference between primary data and secondary data. The same concept applies in the sport marketing intelligence system – primary intelligence and secondary intelligence.

Primary intelligence is information collected by the sport organization through direct contact with customers, the distribution network, competitive analysis, and the internal sport organization itself. To enhance the collection and dissemination of primary intelligence, sport marketing professionals will work with the sport organization in two ways. First, they can create an internal marketing information department that is responsible for being the central location for all data gathered from marketing research and collected via marketing intelligence. The department would be accountable for providing information throughout the sport organization to help enhance the marketing efforts in all areas. Second, the sport marketing department can work with the sales department to train salespeople not only to sell, but to also observe and report on the perceptions, values, and beliefs of customers.

Sport marketing professionals can also obtain primary intelligence by communicating with all channel members (suppliers, manufacturers, distributors), and work to share intelligence so that all have a detailed awareness of each other's activities. Having an integrated system of intelligence will help all parties to understand roles and create a more effective and efficient network.

Another method is to collect intelligence from competitors, especially those who have products in direct competition with the sport organization. Being aware of the opportunities and threats created by competition and addressing those issues promptly is crucial to success in sport marketing. Some of the methods used to collect competitive intelligence are drive-by and on-site observations such as secret shopping, cold calling the organization to obtain information by asking generic questions a normal customer would, and contacting community sources such as a chamber of commerce to secure additional information.

Secondary intelligence is information collected by the sport organization from previous published sources such as books, trade journals, newspapers, and reliable sources on the internet. In addition, many sport organizations will purchase data from syndicated sources. Table 4.5 provides a sample list of external areas that can provide intelligence information to the sport marketing information system.

Table 4.5 External sources of information for intelligence

External area	Information to be provided	Use of the information
Competition	Products and services offered Product and service literature	Offering comparisons Technology comparisons Opportunity analysis Threat analysis
Customers	Demographic, psychographic, geographic profiles Sales data	Customer segmentation Customer profile analysis Product and service sales history
Database and internet information retrieval system	News abstracts about current events, industry news, products and services, the economy, and market analysis	Potential changes in product and/or service positioning Understanding of economic impact and the influence of current events on markets
Governmental (federal, state and local) data	Industry comparisons Competitor comparisons Demographic and geographic comparisons Economic and financial data	Competitive analysis Market segment analysis Organizational profiling
Industry reports	Data analysis by industry Industry news	Industry growth statistics Trend analysis
Suppliers, wholesalers, and distributors	Market conditions General consumer analysis	Sales analysis Pricing changes Promotion ideas Segmenting and targeting Introduction of new products and/or services

Scanning of the environment

Although the goal is to approach sport marketing intelligence in a deliberate fashion as described above, much of the actual collection of intelligence is mainly acquired through informal observations and conversations. The process is known as scanning. In sport marketing intelligence gathering, scanning may be undertaken in a number of ways. Formal scanning is a systematic search for information where there is a specific goal for the intelligence gathering. The scope of the search is narrow, but less rigorous than a full marketing research effort. Informal scanning involves a limited, unstructured effort in collecting data for a specific goal. This usually involves making inquiries to individuals on an impromptu basis. An example

91

would be a sport marketer walking around a partially full stadium, sitting down next to a fan and asking generic, yet structured questions about his or her satisfaction with the experience.

Semi-focused scanning is where there is no specific intelligence being sought or goal to attain, but a general inquiry is conducted to discover any piece of intelligence that may become evident. With this type of scanning, sport marketing researchers will usually limit where they attempt to gather intelligence. For example, they may pose generic questions to full season ticket holders, but not to partial plans holders or fans who purchase single game tickets. A final type of intelligence search is unfocused scanning, where sport marketing professionals expose themselves to information they deem to be useful based on what they have read, heard, or seen. Although this activity is unfocused, it is an intentional attempt to gather intelligence. An example would be a sport marketer with a minor league baseball team reading in the local newspaper an editorial about a fan's displeasure with the concessions offered at the stadium. At the following home game, that sport marketer will work his or her way around the facility, standing on various concession lines and talking informally with fans. The hope is to gather enough information to address the issues of concern with the concession stands.

Dissecting intelligence from scanning

Regardless of the method of scanning chosen by the sport marketing professional, there is a process for scrutinizing the information that has been collected. While the sport marketing researcher may be the leader of the scanning process, it is important to utilize as many resources as possible to collect data. In addition, it is important that all individuals involved in scanning the external environment be open-minded and unbiased in the gathering of marketing intelligence.

The first stage begins with an evaluation of the intelligence, and associating that information to relevant trends. These associations are analyzed using trend-impact analysis, which is a forecasting method that allows a sport marketing researchers and the organization to track trends, apply the intelligence that has been collected to those trends, and examine the impact on potential future events that are a part of the overall organizational strategic plan. When determining whether or not to move forward, the sport marketer and the management of the sport organization must determine how advantageous moving forward would be – in other words, what is the probability of success? This is determined by looking at the feasibility of the organization to make any changes that are needed based on the time and resources available. This is especially true in the marketing area as changes could directly affect advertising, promotions, consumer behavior, and methods for completing future market research.

The second stage starts when the organization agrees to move forward with change based on the intelligence. At this point, the sport marketing professional will work with the management of the sport organization to complete a cross-impact analysis, which examines the relationships between outcomes. The newly created outcomes from the previous stage (the future organizational impact) are correlated with current organizational impacts (philosophy, mission, goals, and vision).

Upon completion of the cross-impact analysis, the results are evaluated in terms of the organization's strengths and weaknesses. This third stage of entering the data into the internal part of the organization's SWOT analysis, with the objective of determining whether the changes coincide with the philosophy of the organization, requires the creation of additional or new goals and objectives, and/or necessitates a change to the vision for the sport organization. Changes to goals and vision may be appropriate within any sport organization. However, changes that impact upon organizational philosophy should be looked at very closely, since those changes may significantly shift the entire value and belief system of the organization.

If change is deemed to be appropriate, the fourth stage would be twofold. The sport marketing professional would draw up plans to evaluate the marketing impact of these changes. At the same time, the management of the sport organization will look at how to best integrate the changes within all aspects of the organizational strategic plan. The groups would then come together to reach a final decision and make one of three choices:

1   *Opposition*: decide that the change is not appropriate for the sport organization.
2   *Modification*: take the necessary steps to integrate the changes across the sport organization. This often requires the sport marketing department to act quickly to inform relevant constituents (distribution network, customers, media) of the changes. In addition, the sport marketing professional will need to examine how the changes affect the current marketing mix and segments, and to what new segments the sport organization could be opened.
3   *Relocation*: the decision that takes place only in dire situations where the sport organization must change to a different market. This type of change is done only in extreme circumstances.

Sport marketing decision support system (DSS)

The sport marketing decision support system (DSS) is the fourth component of the sport marketing information system. The sport marketing decision support system assists sport marketing professionals and other decision makers within the sport organization by taking advantage of information that is available from the various sources. The sport marketing DSS comprises three major parts: (1) the primary and secondary data previously collected by the sport organization; (2) the approaches and methods utilized to decipher and explain the data; and (3) the process of utilizing the information in the decision-making process of the sport organization. This coordination of data, systems, tools, methods, people, and infrastructure serves as a central clearing-house for information used to make strategic decisions, control decisions, operational decisions, and marketing decisions.

The sport marketing decision support system has an effect on both the decision process and decision outcomes. These two components are interrelated, since the outcome depends on the result of the decision process. The outcome for any decision in sport marketing must lead to a better performance in the marketplace by the sport organization. To accomplish that, the decision process must involve decision makers who can identify the core decision variables that have the strongest relationship to positive performance. This in turn will enhance the quality of decisions that are made.

High-quality decisions are made when the change in the selected marketing variable leads to higher profits, a stronger and more positive image, or increase in sport consumer satisfaction.

To test and determine whether these changes will work, those involved with the sport marketing decision support system will run simulations by performing "what-if" analyses. Each outcome is usually integrated with each relevant element of the sport marketing mix to determine whether the desired effect would take place. However, sport marketing decision makers must make sure that they understand their information-processing limitations. The human mind is limited in its ability to process and recall information. When there is an over-abundance of information, the decision maker must spend an extensive amount of time organizing the information instead of solving the problems. This is especially true when there is irrelevant information included in the data. This slows down the process, and may divert the decision maker from finding relevant data quickly.

Key factors of the sport marketing decision support system

There are two factors that play an important role in the framework of the sport marketing decision support system. The first factor is the cognitive abilities of the decision maker. Cognitive abilities refer to the perceptual and intellectual capabilities of individuals. These abilities include comprehension, judgment, learning, memory, and reasoning. Cognition has a direct effect on the decision-making style of an individual and may be viewed from two extremes. High-analytical decision makers break down problems into smaller parts, resulting in a set of causal relationships. Then the decision variables are manipulated to address those relationships with the goal of reaching decisions that will provide optimal success for the sport organization. Low-analytical decision makers look at a problem as an absolute, and seek feasible solutions to the entire problem based only on past experiences and previously solved problems.

The second factor is the time pressures associated with decision making. Sport marketers realize that due to the ever-changing marketplace, acting fast is as important as acting correctly. Hence this time pressure has a direct effect on the ability to appropriately utilize the sport marketing decision support system, since using it takes additional time and the benefits from the system focus on effectiveness rather than efficiency. Time pressure often reduces the amount of information searching and processing conducted by the sport marketing professional, which often results in simplifying strategies and being more conservative with decision making.

Engaging the sport marketing decision support system

This is the most difficult component of the sport marketing information system to employ. Sport marketing professionals tend to be highly analytical, and, as a result of the profession of marketing in general, usually have a significant level of time pressure placed upon them. As a result, many sport marketing schemes, promotions, and activities are not successful over the long term. The key is to expand the likelihood of long-term success. This is done by first addressing the changing environment quickly, and then engaging the sport marketing decision support system to evaluate the change, make recommendations on further modifications, and implement those recommendations within the sport marketing environment. However, it is important to remember that whatever decision is made, it must be able to interact with the other related sport marketing mix efforts including product strategies, sales efforts and pricing tactics, place distribution, and advertising and promotional plans.

94

VALUE OF AN INTEGRATED SPORT MARKETING INFORMATION SYSTEM

A carefully designed sport marketing information system will produce information that is significant and useful to the sport marketing professional in making sport marketing decisions. It is important to understand that while the ultimate goal of the sport marketing information system is to help the sport marketing professional make better decisions in the shortest period of time possible, management wants a system that will provide a positive return on investment. One of the common misconceptions by management is that the cost, time, and appearance of needing extensive resources, owing to the involvement of all departments and the need for a significant computer infrastructure, is not worth it. In fact, many organizations believe that the sport marketing information system is a facade that makes the sport organization appear to be current by implementing the latest marketing ideas. However, as with any product or service offered by the sport organization, we look at the information collected in terms of marginal cost versus marginal value. Marginal cost is the total cost that is incurred based on the quantity produced. Marginal value is the worth to the sport organization of producing one more unit of the product in comparison to other products. Therefore, a sport marketing information system that is valuable to a sport organization must show that the value of the information being collected, analyzed, and used is equal to the cost of that information.

CONCLUSION

The purpose of a sport marketing information system is to collect the various data available in one place for use in making efficient and effective sport marketing decisions. A sport marketing information system is a structure of interacting people, infrastructure, and techniques to gather, sort, analyze, evaluate, and distribute relevant, well-timed, accurate information for use by sport marketing professionals in sport marketing plan development, implementation, and management. The sport marketing information system is made up of four components: the marketing research system, the internal reports system, the sport marketing intelligence system, and the sport marketing decision support system (DSS).

The marketing research system is the process of designing, gathering, analyzing, and reporting information that is utilized to solve a specified sport marketing issue or problem. The sport marketing research process starts with determining its need as a result of a lack of information available about a target market. As a result of a problem being defined, the sport marketing professional comes up with a list of potential solutions, which are then articulated in terms of goals and objectives, and then utilized to develop modified policies and procedures. At this point, the sport marketing researcher must choose the appropriate research methodology based on the type of primary and secondary data available. Research will be conducted using one of three methods – exploratory research, descriptive research, or causal research. Often, the sport marketing researcher needs to collect additional primary data, which is secured through personal contacts via observations, self-administered survey questionnaires, person-administered surveys (interviews), and computer-administered surveys. Once the response format for the questions is chosen, the sport marketing researcher must determine how the results will be measured. There are two major issues to consider when planning to measure responses: the characteristics of the scale to be utilized and the levels of measurement for the scales. Now that the response format and measurement scale has been determined, the survey questionnaire can be developed and the sample size determined. The tool is then implemented, data analyzed using any number of statistical methodologies, and the results are then articulated through a sport marketing research report. It is important to note that with the complexity and variety of methods of research utilized in sport marketing, the conclusions drawn are consequently used in a wide variety of ways. Since the specific aspects of sport marketing vary widely, the use of collected research data will be discussed accordingly within each future chapter.

The internal reports system serves as a framework for the sport marketing information system by affording the sport marketing professional the ability to examine the internal operations of the sport organization and improve upon marketing efforts. Utilizing the information collected from various departments through inputs from the order-to-payment cycle, the point-of-sale system, and data mining, the sport marketing professional is better able to understand the sport organization itself, and its relationship to prospective and current customers.

The sport marketing intelligence system is a crucial element of the sport marketing information system because it opens the door to understanding the external environment that affects the sport organization. By using the primary and secondary intelligence collected through the various methods of scanning, and evaluating those data through the scanning dissemination process, the sport marketing professional gains a better understanding of the opportunities, threats, and trends that can affect the sport organization. In addition, this intelligence is utilized to enhance the internal reports of the sport organization, and can serve as a framework for future sport marketing research.

The sport marketing decision support system (DSS) assists sport marketing professionals and other decision makers within the sport organization by taking advantage of information that is available from the various sources and using that information to make strategic decisions, control decisions, operational decisions, and marketing decisions. This system looks at both the decision process and decision outcomes, with the goal of making changes in selected sport marketing that lead to higher profits, a stronger and more positive image, or increased sport consumer satisfaction. The key factors of the sport marketing DSS are the perceptual and intellectual capabilities of the decision makers (cognitive abilities), and the time pressures associated with decision making. The most difficult component of the sport marketing information system to implement, the overall goal of this component is to make decisions that interact with all parts of the sport organization, as well as with the other, related sport marketing mix efforts including product strategies, sales efforts and pricing tactics, place distribution, and advertising and promotional plans.

The sport marketing information system collects data from the marketing environment, including information from channels, competitors, customers, the economy, the law, markets, politics, and secondary research. The information is disseminated into one of three areas – the sport marketing research system, the internal reports system, and the sport marketing intelligence system. All of that information is then fed into the sport marketing decision support system to make strategic decisions, control decisions, operational decisions, and marketing decisions. The decisions must produce results that are valuable to a sport organization by showing that the information being collected, analyzed, and used is equal to the cost of that information.

96

FROM THEORY TO PRACTICE

DOUGLAS BLAIS, PROFESSOR OF SPORT MANAGEMENT
Southern New Hampshire University,
Manchester, New Hampshire

I am currently a Full Professor of Sport Management in the School of Business at Southern New Hampshire University, and have a Ph.D. in Sport Management with a concentration in marketing from the University of Connecticut. I have had extensive experience conducting market research for a variety of sport organizations including the Boston Celtics, Manchester Monarchs (AHL affiliate of the Los Angeles Kings), a PGA Champions Tour event, Eastern Mountain Sports, and the Verizon Wireless Arena.

Sport marketing research is a crucial element to the success of a sport organization. Strong marketing research provides timely information to identify new opportunities, evaluate the current market, determine market segments, and aid in marketing mix decisions.

The Manchester Monarchs of the American Hockey League are consistently in the top half of attendance in the league. The Monarchs attribute their success to understanding the needs and wants of their fans. The Monarchs have made a commitment to market research. The organization conducts extensive market research every year. This research takes on various forms including a brief fan survey conducted every game, focus groups, in-depth fan surveys, secret shoppers, arena observations, Facebook, and Twitter.

The in-depth survey has been one of the most critical elements in the organization's research. Examples of the survey questions are as follows:

- What is your zipcode?
- What are your favorite radio stations?
- Do you listen to the Monarchs on the radio?
- How many games do you expect to attend this year?
- What is the number of times you visit the Monarchs' website?
- Where do you obtain schedule information?
- What starting time for the games do you prefer?
- Who was the decision maker for attending the game?
- Do you follow us on Facebook?
- Do you follow us on Twitter?
- Please list your three favorite promotions.

The Monarchs use this information in a variety of ways. The Monarchs are able to give sponsors demographic information, determine which promotions to continue or eliminate, and check the effectiveness of their website to disseminate information, and the best ways to reach their target audience.

The in-depth survey allows the Monarchs to sample a large number of fans and obtain research on a number of areas. The focus groups, while limited to a much smaller sample,

97

allow the Monarchs to obtain more qualitative research. The Monarchs conduct focus groups annually with season ticket holders, individual game attendees, and a sampling of fans with partial ticket plans. Fans are given the opportunity to express what they like best and least about the organization and game presentation. An example of information obtained during a focus group was the displeasure of fans when other fans left their seats during play. The research indicated that this was occurring more often in the 200 level compared with the 100 (lower) level of the arena. The Monarchs developed additional announcements incorporating clips from a television sitcom educating fans to wait for a stoppage in play before leaving or returning to their seats. Additional ushers were placed in the 200 level to apply this policy.

The Champions Tour golf tournament used fan surveys to answer many of the same questions used in the Monarchs surveys. Additional research questions include:

- how the tickets were obtained (from a sponsor, own company, gift, promotion, etc.)
- the number of days attending the tournament
- number of golf rounds played per year
- golf handicap
- reason(s) for attending (fan of golf, meet players, business, family outing, etc.)
- how they learned about the event.

The tournament also conducted focus groups of fans who had attended in previous years and did not attend in the past year. The focus group allowed for participants to voice their opinions as to why they had stopped attending the event. The above research aided tournament officials in deciding how to best develop their marketing mix.

Students interested in conducting marketing research should:

- Be familiar with spreadsheet software (Microsoft Excel) and statistical software (SPSS).
- Volunteer with local organizations. Professional market research is expensive and many minor league and non-profit organizations cannot afford to hire a firm. Organizations such as the Special Olympics, YMCA, Boys and Girls Club, or your local organization (i.e. Kiwanis) that sponsors a running road race would all be interested in your services.
- Conduct research that will give you experience in designing, collecting, analyzing, interpreting, and reporting data.
- Understand the importance of the market research process in the success of any organization.

CHAPTER FIVE

SPORT CONSUMER BEHAVIOR

CHAPTER OBJECTIVES

The reader will be able to:

▪ utilize basic cultural, personal, social, and psychological principles to explain how those factors directly affect individual purchasing and consumption behavior of participants, fans, spectators, volunteers, and community and corporate partners
▪ examine the various types of sport consumer studies and how individual and environmental factors, socialization, and participation directly influence the decision-making process for sport consumption
▪ analyze the expected demographic, psychographic, geographic, and behavioristic characteristics of the sport consumer.

WHAT IS SPORT CONSUMER BEHAVIOR?

Sport consumer behavior is the conduct that sport consumers display in seeking out, ordering, buying, using, and assessing products and services that the consumers expect will satisfy their needs and wants. In general, there are two major types of consumers that sport marketers want to understand. First is the personal consumer, who is an individual who buys goods and services for his or her own use. This personal use is not always limited to individual use – it often extends to household use, use by a family member, or use by a friend or colleague. An example of this extension would be a family buying a set of tickets to a game. Second is the organizational consumer, which is a for-profit or nonprofit business or industry entity that buys goods, services, and/or equipment for the operations of the organization. An example of this would be a baseball team purchasing equipment, balls, and bats for use in practices.

INDIVIDUAL FACTORS AFFECTING SPORT CONSUMERS: WHAT MAKES THEM TICK?

The personality of the sport consumer

From an individual standpoint, the sport marketer must be able to understand numerous concepts. The first is the consumer's self-concept. This self-concept goes beyond self-image; it includes recognizing who the sport consumer wants to be (ideal self), how the sport consumer believes he or she is viewed by others (perceived self), and how the sport consumer interacts with his or her reference group (reference group self). Sport marketers must also be aware of the stage in the life cycle of which the target is a part. Sport consumers change as they transition through life, which in turn modifies an individual's attitudes, values, and identities.

These concepts serve as the foundation for the individual personality. Personality is defined as the unique and personal psychological characteristics of an individual which reflects how he or she responds to the social environment. An individual's personality reflects his or her individual differences. While personality can change, it is generally permanent and consistent.

Personality has been examined by many theorists; however, a majority of sport consumers and consumer researchers in general tend to apply the personality theories of Sigmund Freud to consumer behavior. It is generally held in Freudian theory that consumer purchases are a reflection of the personality of the consumer. Freud believed that the unconscious needs or desires of people motivate them to do something. In sport consumer behavior, that "something" is the purchase of a sport product. To understand Freudian theory, the sport marketing professional must comprehend the three elements of the theory: the id, the superego, and the ego. The id is the primary process of the unconscious mind that focuses on gratification (such as instant gratification and release) and primitive instinctual urges (such as sexuality and aggression). The superego is the morality of an individual, which in turn formulates the ethical framework of individual values, beliefs, and codes of conduct. The ego is the balancing part of the mind between primitiveness and morality, which includes internal and external consciousness, individual character differences, and the relationship between emotions and actions.

100

The goal of the sport marketer is to arrive at an optimum stimulation level. According to the theory of optimal stimulation level, individuals attempt to adjust stimulation until their specific optimal level is reached. The sport marketing professional must be able to determine these changes in stimulation level as these variations will have a direct effect on the behavior of sport consumers.

There are two levels of sport consumer consumption that are directly affected by stimulation levels. The first is materialistic sport consumers. These individuals place a value on acquiring and showing off their accumulated sport products. These are the "I have to have it" sport consumers who believe that possessions equal status. These materialistic sport consumers see their possessions as a representation of self. Having the sport product often improves their self-image, or provides them with a higher status as viewed by their external influences.

The second is the fixated sport consumer, otherwise known as the fanatic. These individuals have a strong interest in a particular sport product category and are willing to go to extreme lengths to secure items in that category segment. They are willing to spend as much discretionary time and money as is necessary to search for and purchase the specified sport product. While not all sport consumers fall into these two categories, the sport marketer will often target these demographics as they often result in the greatest return on marketing efforts.

The learning processes of sport consumers

Sport marketers must understand how the sport consumer learns. Some will want to learn about a specific offering prior to creating an opinion, and hence becoming involved with the sport product (learn→feel→do). An example would be someone who is interested in rugby – researches and learns how to play – then becomes a fan. Others will develop an attitude toward a sport product, then consume the product, and as a result of satisfaction, learn more about it (feel→do→learn). For example, a boy whose father is a football fan may be influenced to become a fan at an early age, and as he grows older he looks into the team and its history. A third manner in which the sport consumer learns is by trying out a sport product, and if satisfied will learn more and develop a more detailed view of the sport product (do→feel and learn). This is evident in the example where someone with no prior interest in basketball participates in a pick-up game with some friends, then enjoys the game and becomes a fan.

Sport marketers also have to educate the sport consumer where to buy, how to use, and how to continue using the sport product. This is most often accomplished through a process of teaching theory and providing experience to the sport consumer about the purchase and consumption behavior of a sport product. This learning process may be a result of a careful search of information (intentional) or by accident (incidental). Regardless, sport marketing professionals must use a number of techniques to educate the sport consumer. Through motivation (which will be examined later in this chapter), the sport marketer strives to influence the sport consumer toward a specific goal such as a purchase. Sport marketers often use signals, sounds logos, and associations to motivate the sport consumer. They also use reinforcement to entice the sport consumer to repurchase the sport product.

To effectively teach the sport consumer, the sport marketing professional must be aware of various learning theories – both behavioral (learning that takes place as a result of observable responses to external stimuli) and cognitive (based on problem solving and information processing).

Behavioral learning theories

Classical conditioning refers to the process of using an existing relationship between a stimulus and response to bring about the learning of the same response to a different stimulus. There are three strategic applications utilized by sport marketers regarding classical conditioning. First is repetition, which increases the connection with the sport product while at the same time preventing the sport consumer from overlooking the sport product. This has a direct relationship to exposure, which is a significant concern of sport marketers with regard to sport product awareness. It is generally accepted that three exposures to an advertisement is the minimum necessary for it to be effective.

The second application of classical conditioning is stimulus generation. This is the inability of the sport consumer to differentiate between similar stimuli. In this respect, the sport marketer utilizes numerous techniques to differentiate the sport product through product extensions, branding, and licensing. The final application of classical conditioning is stimulus discrimination, where the sport consumer is able to perceive differences between sport products. This tells the sport marketer that he or she has accomplished effective positioning of the sport product.

Another behavioral learning process is operant conditioning. Sometimes also called instrumental conditioning, this is where no automatic stimulus–response relationship is involved, so the sport consumer must first be induced to engage in the desired behavior and this behavior must then be reinforced. This theory is more of a trial-and-error process when reinforcement plays a significant role in determining customer satisfaction. The goal is to provide the sport consumer with a favorable experience as related to the sport product in order to shape the learning of the sport consumer, and result in repeating the behavior (i.e. repeat purchase of the sport product).

Operant conditioning is widely utilized by sport organizations. The goal is to equate the activity, product, or service with pleasure, entertainment, and enjoyment. Think about your typical football game – why are there cheerleaders? How come music is played during intermissions? Why do they put trivia questions or other contests on the big screen? Why do organizations use Twitter and other applications to get fans to interact with each other? How about participatory activities such as "Fling-A-Football", where you get to throw a Nerf ball from your seat onto the field and hopefully land it on a target for prizes? Why do they have short pee-wee football games on the field during half-time? All of these activities are an effort to engage the spectators over and above the game, entice them into a positive behavior, have them leave the facility with a feeling that they were entertained (even if their team lost), and encourage them to repeat their purchase behavior.

Cognitive learning theories

Cognitive learning focuses on the information processes that are important to the sport marketing professional. Primary in this focus is the concept of retention, which involves the ability to recall or recognize something that has been learned or experienced. Information is stored in the human memory either in the order in which it was acquired, or based on major categories. The sport marketer must be able to figure out how to retrieve those memories through marketing efforts, which in turn should aid in the retention of the sport consumer.

Another concept important to cognitive learning is involvement. Involvement was defined earlier as creating a close connection with something. The sport marketer seeks to stimulate the process of acquiring knowledge about a sport product through media strategies. The strategies are often directed toward creating a relationship between the sport consumer and the sport product through persuasion. Marketing strategies that focus on the specific attributes of the product are used to persuade those sport consumers who are already highly involved with the sport product. For those who need to be persuaded to become associated with the sport product, alternative methods involving cues such as setting (playing in a new facility) and endorsements (equating a favorite player with a sport product) are used.

The sport marketing professional, regardless of theory, must be able to measure the effectiveness of consumer learning. This is accomplished through a number of measures. The most basic is through recognition and recall of the sport product through advertisements and other marketing collateral. This can be completed through aided or unaided recall. Another method is through an evaluation of cognitive responses, when an evaluation of the sport consumer's comprehension of the intended message is conducted. Similar to this are attitudinal measures and behavioral measures, where the feelings of sport consumers, and responses by sport consumers to promotions, are evaluated to determine the effectiveness of message delivery. The overall goal, regardless of method, is to determine whether the sport consumer has learned enough about the product to become brand loyal.

The process of motivating sport consumers

Motivation is the influence that initiates the drive to satisfy wants and needs. For the sport consumer, this is achieved through motives such as accomplishment, fun, improvement of skill, health and fitness, or the desire for affiliation with or love for a player or team. For sport consumers, it goes beyond their needs and wants; it also involves tension and drive. Tension is mental or emotional stress, while drive is the desire to accomplish a task. When sport consumers have wants or needs, they stress about how they will fulfill it. They then come up with a plan to fulfill the need with influences from their own personality and learning process. The result is the creation of a behavior that will hopefully lead to the fulfillment of the want or need. This fulfillment then reduces tension and the sport consumer is satisfied.

Prior to understanding how motivation works, the sport marketing professional must recognize what motives are. A motive is an emotion or psychological need that acts to stimulate an action. Emotional motives involve the selection of goals according to individual or subjective criteria. Rational motives entail selecting goals based on objective criteria. In general, motives will never fully satisfy needs, because new needs develop as a result of the satisfaction of old needs. In other words, as individuals achieve their goals, they set new (and often higher) goals for themselves.

In general, in order to motivate the sport consumer, the sport marketing professional is required to focus on three specific needs: power, affiliation, and achievement. Power is where sport consumers want to have control over their environment. Sport marketers strive to provide this feeling to the sport consumer, but still keep control of the situation. Affiliation is the most basic concept of social interaction. Human beings need interaction with other human beings. Sport marketers make every effort to provide an atmosphere of this connectedness and belonging, not only with the sport product, but also with other users. Achievement involves the need for personal accomplishment. Sport consumers want to have feelings of self-fulfillment, high self-esteem, and prestige. Sport marketers work to control the attitude of sport consumers and to provide them the perception of a positive experience as related to the sport product.

How the attitudes of the sport consumer are formed and changed

An attitude is a state of mind or behavioral predisposition that is consistently favorable or unfavorable with respect to a product or situation. Attitudes are formed in many different ways, but most often they are formed either from personality factors or learned from environmental influences. As mentioned at the end of the previous section, sport marketers strive to control the attitudes of the sport consumer. But how is that accomplished?

There are a number of models for attitude formation and identification. The most prevalent of these is the tri-component attitude model, where cognitive, affective, and conative factors are considered. The cognitive component focuses on the knowledge and perceptions of the sport consumer that are acquired from a direct experience with an attitude object – in this case a person, behavior, or event related to the sport product. The affective component involves the emotions or feelings of the sport consumer as related to the specific sport product. The conative component centers on the likelihood that the sport consumer will carry out a specific action or behavior as a result of the interaction with the attitude object.

Another model is the multi-attribute attitudes model. These series of models examine the make-up of sport consumer attitudes in terms of the attributes of the sport product. The first is the attitude-toward-object model, where the sport consumer will have a positive attitude toward the sport products they feel have an acceptable level of attributes that they want, and a negative attitude toward sport products they feel do not have what they are looking for. Next is the attitude-toward-behavior model, which states that the attitude of the sport consumer toward a specific behavior related to the sport product is a function of how strongly he or she believes that the action will lead to a specific outcome. The final model is the theory-of-reasoned-action model. This is a theory that interprets the interrelationship between attitudes, intentions, and behavior, which in turn should lead to better explanations and predictions of sport consumer behavior.

There are two other models of attitude formation that are utilized by sport marketing professionals. The trying-to-consumer model tries to account for an attempted purchase of the sport product by investigating personal and environmental barriers. The attitude-toward-

104

the-ad model simply investigates the feelings and judgments of sport consumers based on their exposure to sport-related advertisements. The measurement involves the attitudes toward both the advertisement and the sport product.

Since different sport consumers may like or dislike the same sport product for different reasons, a practical framework for examining attitude functions of sport consumers can be very useful for the sport marketing professional. In general, there are four basic attitude functions sought in the sport consumer. The Ego-Defensive Function suggests that since most sport consumers want to protect their self-images from inner feelings of doubt, they seek to replace their uncertainty with a sense of security and personal confidence. The Knowledge Function stresses that sport consumers usually have a strong need to know and understand the people and things with whom they come in contact. The Utilitarian Function states that when a sport product has been useful or helped the sport consumer in the past, the attitude toward that sport product tends to be favorable. The Value Expressive Function maintains that attitudes are an expression or reflection of the sport consumer's general values, lifestyles, and outlook.

In understanding these functions, the sport marketing professional must understand the various strategies employed to implement attitude change. This can be accomplished in a number of ways, including:

- changing the basic motivational function of the sport consumer
- associating the sport product with a respected group or sport event
- working out a conflict between two attitudes, preferably moving from negative to positive
- changing components of the multi-attribute attitudes model to meet the needs of the sport consumer
- altering the beliefs of sport consumers as related to the brands of the competitors of the specific sport product.

Sport consumer attitude formation and change has a direct relationship to the other behavioral concepts through attribution theory – which attempts to explain how people assign the concept of cause and effect to the sport product on the basis of either their own behavior or the behavior of other sport consumers. There are a number of issues related to attribution theory that have a direct effect on its implementation. They include:

- *Self-perception theory* suggests that attitudes develop as sport consumers look at and make judgments about their own behavior.
- *Internal attribution* is the sport consumer giving credit to him- or herself for an outcome as a result of the sport consumer's own ability, skill, or effort.
- *External attribution* is the sport consumer giving credit to factors beyond his or her own control.
- *The foot-in-the-door technique* is based on the premise that sport consumers develop attitudes by looking at their own behavior.
- *Attribution toward others* is when the sport consumer feels that another person is responsible for either positive or negative sport product performance.
- *Attribution toward things* is when the sport marketers and researchers are trying to find out why a sport product meets or does not meet the expectations of the sport consumer.

These elements of attribution theory are qualitatively tested and measured by sport marketing professionals in a number of ways. First, through distinctiveness, the sport marketer can determine the distinguishing traits between sport consumers. Sport marketers can also track consistency over time, or repetition of purchasing patterns. Finally, the sport marketer can draw a consensus as to the attitude of the general sport consumer population.

The perceptions developed by sport consumers about sport products

Perceptions involve gaining an understanding of the individual values, attitudes, needs, and expectations of the sport consumer by scanning, gathering, assessing, and interpreting those insights. For the sport consumer, perception involves the process of interpreting and selecting a sport product based on awareness obtained through any of the five senses, but especially via sight or hearing. Basically, it is the way sport consumers see the world around them. The three elements that formulate perception are sensations, images, and affections. Sensations are the most basic element of perception, as they are the immediate and direct responses from the sensory organs. Images are the pictures that are formed in the mind to differentiate what is perceived. Affections are the actual emotions emitted as a result of the perception.

Perception may be viewed in three distinct ways. The first is perceptual selection, which is based on the previous experiences and the present state of mind of the sport consumers. Selective perception is made up of a number of sub-concepts including selective exposure, selective attention, perceptual defense, and perceptual blocking. Selective exposure deals with knowing that sport consumers choose whom they listen to, what they watch, and they only obtain specific types of information. Selective attention is that, at any given point, sport consumers can only digest so much information and that they only pay attention to those they believe are most important at the given time. Perceptual defense is when sport consumers protect themselves from an awareness of something unpleasant or threatening. Perceptual blocking is the process of the sport consumer putting up obstacles to prevent perceptions from influencing them.

The second manner is via perceptual organization. This is the concept of grouping perception in a manner where the individual sport consumer can interpret the perception and chart a plan of action. Unfortunately there are perceptual distortions which may prevent appropriate interpretation of perceptions. These may include similarities in physical appearance, stereotypes, misinterpreted first impressions, and jumping to conclusions. There is also a concept called the halo effect where a sport consumer may form an overall positive impression of a sport product because of one good characteristic; however, the sport consumer may not have the expertise to pass judgment in an effective manner to truly determine the quality of the sport product.

The third aspect of perception is interpretation. This is the area most sport marketing professionals concentrate on as this interpretation focuses on the imagery and emotions of the sport consumer, and gives the sport marketers information as to whether their marketing efforts are successful. This determination of sport consumer imagery focuses on positioning, price, quality, and risk.

Positioning involves establishing a specific image for a sport product in relation to competing products. A sport marketer will utilize perceptual mapping to determine the best position to enter the marketplace. This research method gives sport marketers the opportunity to

106

graphically analyze perceptions concerning the attributes of specific sport products. Depending on the evaluation, a number of methods of positioning could be implemented to enter a sport product into the marketplace. For direct positioning, the sport marketer may position the sport product directly against the competition, or position the sport product based on a specific benefit. More broad positioning efforts include positioning the product for several markets, and umbrella positioning – covering all aspects of the marketplace. There are even times where a sport marketer may position a product in an unknown position, taking a risk and hoping for the reward.

Pricing strategies are focused on perceived value of the sport product. Pricing based on perception is based on three factors – satisfaction, relationships, and efficiency. Central to this strategy is acquisition-transition utility. Acquisition utility represents the consumer's perceived economic gain or loss associated with the purchase of the sport product. This is determined by the utility of the sport product and the purchase price. Transaction utility deals with the perceived pleasure or displeasure associated with the financial aspect of the purchase by the sport consumer. This is based on the internal reference price of the sport consumers (the price at which they perceive the sport product to be valued) and the actual purchase price.

Perceived quality of sport products depends on the form the sport product takes. If a sport product is tangible in nature, the perceived quality comes from internal beliefs and environmental influences. If the sport product is intangible or variable (as most sport services are), the product is viewed as perishable. In addition, because of the nature of the sport product, the quality is variably perceived due to the fact that the sport product is often produced and consumed at the same time. There is a direct correlation between price and quality, as the perception of price is an indicator of product quality. It is believed that if a sport product has a high price, then that product is of a higher quality.

Probably the least controllable factor of perception is risk. This is the extent of uncertainty perceived by the sport consumer as to the outcome of a specific purchase decision related to the sport product. These risks may include functional risk, physical risk, or financial risk. While sport consumers cannot totally control risk, they can reduce the likelihood by staying up to date on the latest information about the sport product, staying loyal to known sport products, selecting sport products based on image, and searching for reassurance from external influences.

EXTERNAL FACTORS AFFECTING SPORT CONSUMERS: THE ENVIRONMENT IS EVERYTHING

For the business of sport, consumer behavior is a complex process because the sport organization has limited control over the end results. However, it is crucial to have a better understanding of the core environmental and individual elements that contribute to success in marketing sport. From an environmental standpoint, there are a number of external factors over which the sport marketer has limited control, but has the opportunity to manipulate to his or her advantage. These include targeting the consumer behavior of those associated with the sport consumer (family, friends, colleagues), and the opportunity structure of sport. The opportunity structure of sport is critical to the development of marketing opportunities as it is the foundation of involvement in sport activities. The opportunity structure and the associated involvement are influenced by a number of geographic concepts such as climate and geography, and psychographic concepts such as norms, values, and beliefs.

However, the area of greatest interest is demographics. Demographics are the categories of traits that characterize a group of people. The generic categories that most sport marketing professionals look at are age, gender, race and ethnicity, household size, annual income, and geographic location. Age is an important factor because it is important to understand who in the family is responsible for decision making. While the parent may have the purchasing power, the children have the influencing power. In addition, younger people purchase items for different reasons than older people. This is also true for gender. Males tend to make more impulsive decisions, while females tend to be more analytical in their purchasing. Race and ethnicity is significant because of the variety of beliefs and values based on cultural differences. Household size will have a direct effect on purchasing power and the types of product purchased.

Geographic location, especially in sport, has a gigantic effect. For example, a baseball fan who lives in Nassau County on Long Island, New York has two choices: travel 15 to 30 miles to Yankee Stadium in traffic that could take between one and two hours, or go five to ten miles to Citi Field to see the Mets and not have to fight as much traffic. If a person does not have an allegiance to one team or the other, the decision will be clear in most cases – take the shorter trip. However, if you are a fan of the New England Patriots or Boston Red Sox, where the team is marketed as a regional team for Maine, New Hampshire, Vermont, Massachusetts, Rhode Island and Connecticut, individuals will travel up to six hours to go to a game.

In sport marketing, especially with the expansion of global influences, these concepts are expanded beyond the traditional concepts to include culture, subculture, cross-culture, and social setting.

Culture

Culture is the principal attitudes, behaviors, values, beliefs, and customs that typify the functioning of a society. In sport consumer behavior, culture often regulates the level to which marketing efforts are accepted. The sport marketing professional must understand how sport consumers learn within their culture, and what factors affect their problem-solving and decision-making processes. Culture is "learned" in four distinct ways. Formal learning is typically classroom-based and highly structured. Informal learning is an independent learning style where learning rests primarily in the hands of the learner. Incidental learning comes as a result of the activity in which the individual is participating, such as task accomplishment, interpersonal interaction, sensing the organizational culture, trial-and-error experimentation, or even formal learning. Technical learning is the combination of education and training. The eventual goal is for the sport marketing professional to understand these cultural differences so that marketing efforts such as advertising can be directed in such a way that the sport consumers view the sport product as being socially acceptable.

Two qualitative measurements are used to assess culture and cultural learning: content analysis and consumer fieldwork. Content analysis is a method for systematically analyzing the content of print, and verbal and/or visual communication to determine the current social values of a society. Consumer fieldwork involves site observation within a normal environment, often without the knowledge of the consumer, to observe behavior.

For the sport marketing professional, these two qualitative techniques seek to draw conclusions based on the attitudes and motivations of sport consumers. In sport marketing, these conclusions are used every day. When Ichiro came to the Seattle Mariners from Japan and Hideki Matsui came to the New York Yankees, new marketing opportunities arose immediately. Seattle's influence in the significant Japanese market in their city instantly increased. The New York Yankees started putting advertisements in Japanese in the stadium. Both resulted in more people from the Japanese culture going to games and buying merchandise.

This is also true of Yao Ming when he was drafted to play for the NBA's Houston Rockets. He single-handedly brought a new Asian-American fan base to basketball. The presence of Dominican Republic flags in the stands at Major League Baseball games whenever prominent Dominican players play is evident across the league, to the point where many teams now have Latin American Heritage nights. In fact, teams have even expanded those cultural nights to a series of Theme, Community, and Heritage dates, including Greek Night, Korean Night, Meringue Night, Italian Night, Pakistani Night, Irish Night, Hispanic Heritage Night, Jewish Heritage Day, Oktoberfest, and Polish Heritage Day.

Subculture

A subculture is a distinct cultural group differentiated by an identifiable segment within a larger population. Subcultures are usually identified based on their demographic segment – gender, age, geographic region, race, nationality, ethnicity, social class, occupation, and religion. Some would even argue that sport is a subculture. Market segmentation recognizes that different consumer groups have assorted wants and needs that justify the development and offering of different products and services. Sport marketers have utilized a variety of approaches to segment the sport, entertainment, and leisure service and retail markets; however, each of the traditional segmentation approaches has limitations. Marketing methodologies, including segmentation strategies, need to mirror and harmonize with the target subculture.

Cross-culture: international and global interaction

As transportation and technology innovation bring the far reaches of the world closer, there is obviously more interaction both internationally and globally. This is especially true in the sport market. The United States has been known for hundreds of years as "the melting-pot" but may be more aptly described today as a "mosaic" – many different cultures and subcultures overlapping to create twenty-first-century American society. As this interaction grows, the sport marketing professional learns to not only understand the similarities and differences among sport consumers, but often the process of acculturation. Acculturation is the modification of a culture or subculture as a result of contact with a different culture. As more and more athletes come from overseas to the United States to play professional sport, the sport marketing professional must not only market to the behavioral aspects of the sport consumer, but also to the ever-expanding cultural aspects of the sport consumer. This forces the sport marketing professional to not only have a solid understanding of the business of sport, but also of the humanities and social science aspects that can be directly related to this new global society.

Social setting and social class

While culture, subculture, and cross-culture issues are important to the sport marketing professional, ultimately the social setting is the most direct concern of the sport marketer. The understanding of these reference groups within the target market is ultimately going to determine those who will purchase the majority of the specific sport product. A reference group is a group – two or more people making up a unit – with which a sport consumer identifies, and hence probably shares similar attitudes, values and beliefs. In sport marketing we acknowledge four categories of reference groups: (1) normative reference groups are what individuals look to in order to determine how they should behave; (2) in comparative reference groups, individuals look at other individuals and groups to compare and gauge their behavior; (3) multiple reference groups reinforce the idea that an individual can access more than one reference group; and (4) indirect reference groups are individuals or groups with whom a person identifies but does not have direct contact.

When sport consumers identify themselves as part of a reference group, they usually conform to the norms (attitudes, values, and beliefs) of that reference group. The sport marketing professional often targets elements of the reference group to spread the word about a sport product. This provides a vehicle to inform all members of the reference group about the sport product, and to legitimize the decision to use the same sport product as the rest of the group. Sport marketers attempt to influence the members of the reference group as a whole by associating the sport product with factors such as attractiveness, credibility, and expertise. Sport marketers at the same time try to influence individual group members by marketing the sport product in terms of the need for affiliation, the need to be liked, and the fear of negative evaluation as related to the reference group.

The most powerful reference group in today's society is family. The function of the family includes emotional support, a suitable lifestyle, and a stable economic foundation. Families influence each other throughout the lifespan to make decisions about purchases. The sport marketer must understand the roles of the family in the decision-making process to determine the best way to influence those sport consumers to purchase the sport product. There are five roles in the family decision-making process:

1   *Initiators* are any members of the family who can express the need for a product or service, such as a boy asking his father to buy tickets to a baseball game.
2   *Influencers* are people whose views carry some weight in the final decision. An example would be a mother suggesting to a father that it would be good to go on a family outing to a baseball game.
3   *Deciders* are family members who assume responsibility for choosing the characteristics of the product and executing the decision with regard to the brand, the vendor, the timing, and the payment method. This decision is based on the information collected in

110

the previous stages. For example, the father deciding that the family will attend a minor league baseball game next week, and he will buy the tickets online.

4   *Buyers* refer to the family member(s) who are physically involved in the process of purchasing a product. This would be the father actually going online and making the purchase. It is important to remember that the retailer still has an influence on the sport consumer. If the purchase is difficult because the website is too complex, the buyer may choose to go elsewhere.

5   *Users* are the members of a family who are beneficiaries of the product. It is imperative to identify who actually qualifies as the end-user of the product, and how satisfied the user is with different aspects of the product. An example would be that the father purchases the tickets, but, because he has to work, only the mother, son, and his son's friend use the tickets.

Since so many family members have influenced the purchase decision, it is possible that user satisfaction may vary on different counts, which is reflected in their post-purchase behavior. The users may or may not recommend the product to others on the basis of their satisfaction levels. This has serious implications for the marketer since word of mouth plays a very important role in the purchase of consumer durable products.

The sport marketing professional must have a keen understanding of the different social settings and social classes when attempting to influence the sport consumer. Depending on the social class, sport consumers from similar geographic areas may view the sport product very differently. Some may view the sport product in terms of being fashionable and a status symbol, while others may view the sport product as a treat or appropriate use of discretionary time and/or money. So once the sport marketer understands all of these factors, how does he or she actually go about influencing the sport consumer to purchase the sport product?

THE MARKETING CONCEPT FOR SPORT

To deal with the inner workings of sport consumer behavior, the sport marketer must have a clear understanding of the marketing concept, a consumer-oriented philosophy which suggests that satisfaction of consumer needs provides the focus for product development and marketing strategy to enable the firm to meet its own organizational goals. The development of the marketing concept for sport is centered on three sub-concepts: sport production, the sport product, and the selling of sport. Sport production is centered on the premise that sport consumers are primarily interested in the availability of the sport product at reasonable prices.

The sport product makes an assumption that sport consumers will purchase the product offering the highest quality, the best performance, and the most features. The selling of sport relates to a belief that sport consumers are not likely to buy a sport product unless they are enticed to do so. The combination of these ideas is central to the marketing concept for sport in that in order for a sport organization to be successful, the needs and wants of the target markets must be met at a higher level as compared to the competitors.

Who are the sport consumers?

There are two major groups of sport consumers that sport marketers are concerned with: spectators and participants. Spectators are defined as individuals who observe a performance, such as a sporting event. When sport marketers consider this fairly narrow definition of spectators, their main concern is attendance at events. There are numerous factors that the sport marketing professional must consider to attract as many spectators as possible to a sport event.

A central factor to consider with spectators is motivation. Motivation (which will be discussed in more detail later in this chapter) is a psychological concept that stimulates an individual to work toward accomplishing a desired goal, which in turn gives purpose and direction to an individual's behavior. In sport, there are numerous motivational factors that influence spectators to attend an event. Intrinsic motivation is the desire to satisfy natural needs and interests, including knowledge, accomplishment, and experiences. Extrinsic motivation involves rewards or incentives used by an individual to bring about desired behavior in another person. Amotivation is where there is no influence intrinsically or extrinsically. Sport marketers must have a clear understanding of these motivational factors to entice sport consumer to consume the sport product. Some of these factors include self-esteem enhancement, diversion from everyday life, entertainment value, eustress, economic value, aesthetic value, the need for affiliation, and family ties.

On the other hand, the definition of participants tends to be broad in nature. By definition, participants are individuals who take part in an activity. However, the manner in which the participant takes part in the activity varies greatly. Participant consumer behavior is defined as actions performed when searching for, participating in, or evaluating the sport activities the consumers believe will satisfy their needs. As with spectators, the participants have internal and external influences that affect their level of involvement in sport. Internally, the decision of the participant is affected by his or her personality, motivation, ability to learn, intrinsic perceptions, and personal attitudes. Externally, decisions are affected by culture, social class, reference groups, family, friends, peers, and colleagues.

Why do people consume sport?

There are numerous individual and environmental factors that have an effect on consumer behavior. For the sport consumer, there are three sub-factors that seem to have the most influence on the sport consumer: socialization, involvement, and commitment.

Socialization is defined as the process by which individuals acquire attitudes, values, and actions which are appropriate to members of a particular culture. In sport culture, sport marketers look at the process by which individuals develop and incorporate skills, knowledge, attitudes, and items/equipment necessary to perform sport roles.

Socialization in sport demands some type of involvement, which is defined as creating a close connection with something. Involvement in sport is as easy as ABC. Affective is the attitudes, feelings and emotions directed toward a sport activity, such as sadness when your team loses a play-off series. Behavioral are the actions or reactions directly related to the internal and

112

external stimuli sport provides; for example, cheering and giving "high-fives" with other people in a sports bar when your team makes a great play.

Cognitive is the process of acquiring knowledge about a sport activity, including researching information on the internet, listening to experts on sports radio, and asking questions about an activity of someone who understands that activity.

Commitment is the process by which an individual is emotionally or intellectually bound to a course of action. In sport, commitment refers to frequency, duration, and intensity of involvement in a sport. A sport marketer must understand the thought processes of the sport consumer as it relates to concepts such as willingness to spend their valuable discretionary money, time, and energy. This understanding of commitment directly relates to the concepts presented in Chapter 1 regarding the escalator concept. As sport consumers become more committed to the sport product, they move up the escalator. An example of this would be the 2003 Florida Marlins. During the regular season, the Marlins average only 22,792 fans per game, and that average increased significantly during the last month of the season when the team appeared to be headed to the play-offs. However, once they had made the play-offs and made it to the World Series, they were averaging 65,900 fans. The same happened with the Tampa Bay Rays in 2008 and 2010. During the regular season they only averaged about 22,370 in 2008 and 23,148 in 2010; but when the play-offs came around, they averaged 36,048 in 2008 and 36,973 in 2010.

PROBLEM SOLVING AND DECISION MAKING

The previous sections provided a basic description of who the sport consumers are as well as their philosophy as to why they consume the sport product. But the understanding of the values and beliefs of sport consumers is useless if the sport marketing professional fails to understand how the sport consumer ultimately makes a decision. Hence, an analysis must be conducted of how the sport consumer determines what he or she wants, and how the sport consumer sets goals and objectives that result in making a choice. This is the framework for the problem-solving and decision-making processes.

Problem solving

Problem solving is a cognitive process by which an individual uses critical thinking to work out and answer a problem. To understand problem solving, the sport marketing professional must first understand the problem-solving cycle. This is an organized, step-by-step approach that involves brainstorming, formulating various solutions, analyzing all solutions to determine a course of action, implementing the course of action, evaluating the success of the course of action, and repeating the cycle until an optimal solution is reached. The problem-solving cycle involves the steps as shown in Figure 5.1.

The first step involves understanding the stated problem(s). These statements can be in many forms, from simple open-ended questions, to existing conditions in need of change.

▪ *Example – The GM asks you to come up with a plan to increase attendance for the last month of the season. The team is in last place and attendance is down 15 percent.*

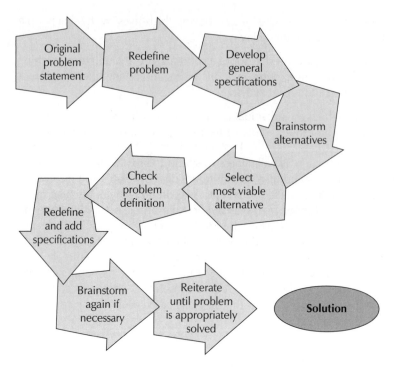

Figure 5.1 The problem-solving process

Source: Adapted from http://thayer.dartmouth.edu/teps/

Second, the problem(s) needs to be redefined by the sport marketer in terms that are clear and void of bias. Often when individual customers encounter a problem, they put an internal spin on the necessity for a solution because of vested interest or perceived need. Sport marketing professionals seek to remove those biases so that the root problems can be identified and solved with an optimal level of success.

■ *Attendance is down 15 percent.*

The third step is to set general specifications. As the sport marketing professional gains an understanding of the problems at hand, a plan is created to focus on the core problems. This plan involves setting parameters for solving the problem, while considering constraints to the problem-solving process such as legality and ethical issues. To ensure optimal effectiveness, the parameters must always be defined and justified, and, if economics are involved, also quantified.

■ *A 15 percent decrease in attendance not only affects the team's bottom line in ticket sales. It also affects concessions, merchandising, parking, and potentially the morale of the players and coaches. The plan must address all of these areas. It also means that there is probably no additional money to enact a plan.*

The fourth step is to identify alternative solutions. This is where the brainstorming process begins, ideas are contemplated, and a list of various possible solutions is created. This process often takes place in a group setting, without criticism, and with maximum creativity. The longer the list of possible solutions, the better the chance for success.

■ *Some possible solutions include: buy one ticket get the second half-price; meet-and-greet autograph sessions before and after the game; discounts at merchandise and concession stands; buy two tickets to a game and receive a voucher for one free ticket to a game the following season (with the purchase of another ticket); give away tickets on Twitter and Facebook to those followers that share content and talk about the team (in hopes that their own supporters will start following the team and attending games).*

Next, the most viable alternative must be selected. The solution list is analyzed in depth, determining the advantages and disadvantages of each alternative. The process for examining the alternatives involves categorizing the alternatives, determining a scale for critiquing each alternative, pooling the best alternatives, and then ranking those solutions from most desirable to least. This part of the problem-solving process often involves experimentation and market research to justify the best option, and a clarification of unclear alternatives.

■ *With concessions and merchandising already losing money, there may be a reluctance to decrease prices. Meet-and-greet sessions before the game may interfere with game preparation – after the game may be easier. Buy two, get one for next year eats into potential profits in the long term, and may not be looked upon too fovorably by the ownership. Therefore the most viable options are buy one get one half-price, where at least there is the potential to get some revenue from tickets, and may help merchandising and concessions. Then supplement that with some free autograph times after the game. This keeps people watching to the end even when the team may be losing, and allows an opportunity to improve image.*

Once the best option has been determined, the sixth step involves the sport marketer revisiting the problem to ensure that the brainstorming process did not go off track, and that the option chosen has the best opportunity to solve the base problem. Upon completion of this redefinition, the next two steps take place. The first (step 7) involves refining and adding specifications that are directly related to the chosen alternative. Then (step 8), a second brainstorming takes place to become more focused on the alternative chosen, and to determine any sub-alternatives that may arise from the redefinition.

■ *Seems like the plan can address the problem of attendance being down 15 percent. However, we note that there is one series of games against the World Champions, and we have already sold 80 percent of our seats for the series. Therefore, this offer needs to be limited to the series where attendance is significantly less than average.*

The final step involves the implementation of the selected alternative. If the selected alternative works to solve the problem, you have succeeded! If the option does not work, the sport marketer must utilize the feedback and measurements provided, revise the problem-solving methodology, and repeat the process until the problem is solved.

■ *Create flyers, radio, and TV spots promoting the discount. Put the information on the website. Make sure all members of the organization, especially the sales staff, are aware of the promotion. Time the promotion so that there is a chance for purchase, but not too soon around the practically sold-out series so that those customers do not feel they got a raw deal.*

115

Now that the generic problem-solving cycle has been discussed, the sport marketing professional must understand how the sport consumer uses this process to solve problems. There are three levels of problem solving: routine response behavior, extensive problem solving, and limited problem solving. Routine response behavior has the lowest level of problem-solving involvement by the sport consumer. In the mind of the sport consumer, there is no problem to solve because the sport product is frequently purchased and the perception is that there is little risk involved with the purchase of the product. An example of this would be purchasing tickets to a game. As a result of this habitual problem solving, there is limited information search, and the process of evaluating alternatives is eliminated. For the sport marketing professionals, there is very little they need to do with these sport consumers, and hence need to spend little money to develop marketing plans directed to this type of problem solver.

Extensive problem solving is the other end of the spectrum – where the involvement in the problem-solving process by the sport consumer is at the highest level. The sport consumer extensively evaluates the sport product, conducts a significant information search about the sport product, and refuses to enter the decision-making process before having an abundance of alternatives to choose from. This may be when an active mogul skier is seeking to purchase a new pair of skis. The sport marketer must spend extensive money and resources geared toward this level of problem solving and must provide a broad spectrum of data in order to persuade this type of sport consumer to consider the sport product.

In between these two extremes are the sport consumers who engage in limited problem solving. When a problem is recognized, they first complete an internal information search, relying on data they already know. They may then supplement their data with an external search, such as via the internet, but this is not always necessary. This type of problem solver considers a limited number of alternatives, but those alternatives are more generic – involving alternative forms of entertainment. An example would be a person buying a new pair of shoes, but their purchasing is going to be limited to Nike, Reebok, and Adidas. The sport marketer must focus on selling the sport product by demonstrating that spending discretionary dollars on the specific sport product will provide value to the sport consumer.

Decision making

Decision making is a cognitive process by which an individual consciously makes a tactical or strategic choice that results in executing an action. In sport consumer decision making, there are four views that are utilized by sport marketing professionals enabling them to understand this process. The economic view is a systematic process where sport consumers make the most rational personal choices and identify the resulting opportunity costs of involvement with the sport product. The passive view is where sport consumers are submissive to marketing efforts, and hence will not object to or resist the promotional efforts of sport marketers. The cognitive view is a knowledge-based form of decision making, where the sport consumer is a thinking problem solver who is not driven by internal desires, but who is also not automatically shaped and controlled by environmental influences. The emotional view is simply based on the mood of the sport consumers. If they feel like purchasing the sport product, they will – it does not matter what efforts the sport marketer has employed.

116

Setting and attaining goals

In understanding these views, and prior to entering into the decision-making process, sport marketing professionals must understand how sport consumers set and pursue their goals. Figure 5.2 illustrates the sport consumer goal development process.

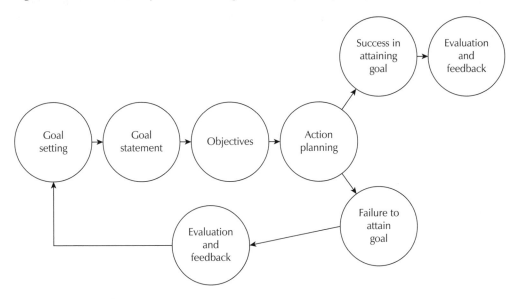

Figure 5.2 The sport consumer goal development process

The first step is to set a goal, which is a specific task that will serve to meet the overall mission of an organization or individual. These goals are often generic in nature. After you have a base goal, the second step is to clarify the goal by creating a goal statement. There are four major sections to a goal statement. The action is what one is going to accomplish. The object is the actual thing that will be acted upon. The amount is the quantification of the goal. The deadline is the time limitation on the attainment of the goal. An example of a goal statement for a sport consumer would be "To obtain a donation from the New England Patriots of signed memorabilia for the silent auction fundraiser by two weeks before the event." The action is "obtain", the object is "New England Patriots signed memorabilia", the amount is "donation" (implied no cost); and the deadline is "by two weeks before the event."

The third step would be to set objectives, which is the development of the specific steps an individual will take to attain the goal. Some objectives that might be set in conjunction with the goal statement from above would be: (1) mail a letter to the community relations department at the New England Patriots to request a donation; (2) contact a local sport memorabilia store to request a donation to the silent auction; (3) attend an autograph signing by a New England Patriots player and obtain his signature on a piece of memorabilia.

The fourth step is the action process. This involves creating a plan of action to accomplish the goal. This includes determining what deliverables must be produced, how they will be produced, who will produce them, when the deliverables are to be ready, and initiating the use of the deliverable to attain the goal.

The fifth step is goal attainment or failure. Eventually, you will either accomplish the goal based on the objectives set forth, or the objectives failed to bring results. Either scenario leads directly into the sixth step – evaluation and feedback. At this point, if the goal is attained, an appraisal of the process is made and a determination of final success is completed. If the goal was not attained, the appraisal process looks at why the objectives could not be accomplished, and a return to the first step is made for re-evaluating the goal and setting a new course of action.

The decision-making process

As the sport consumer sets and attains goals, the decision-making process begins. This process involves three stages: (1) pre-purchase decision making (including problem or need recognition, pre-purchase information search, and evaluation of alternatives); (2) the actual purchase; and (3) post-purchase evaluation.

Pre-purchase decision making: problem and need recognition
The first part of this first stage involves problem or need recognition. The making of a decision by the sport consumer is a result of wanting to move from an actual state to a desired state. The sport consumer will determine whether it is important to engage in the decision-making process based on two considerations: (1) the size of the problem or need; and (2) the importance placed on needing to make a decision.

Pre-purchase decision making: information search
Once the sport consumer determines that a decision needs to me made, he or she will engage in the pre-purchase information search. At this time, the sport consumer seeks to obtain relevant information that will help resolve the problem. The sport consumer will utilize both internal sources and external sources to start making a decision. The information that is based on previous exposure and personal experience serves as a framework for the internal information search.

External sources are environmentally based, and come from a number of sources. Personal contacts such as friends, peers, relatives, co-workers, colleagues, neighbors, followers on social networks, and salespeople; and impersonal sources such as newspaper and magazine articles, consumer reports, direct mail brochures, product advertisements, influential bloggers, question-and-answer websites like Yahoo! Answers, and customer reviews from sites like Amazon are primary sources of information the sport consumer will utilize.

This is often in direct correlation to concerns about perceived value. There are a number of reasons why the sport consumer places value on a product, including: whether the product is discretionary instead of necessary; the alternatives have both desirable and undesirable consequences; family members disagree on product requirements or evaluation of alternatives; product usage deviates from important reference groups; the purchase involves ecological considerations; and there are many sources of conflicting information.

Information from the actual sport product also has a direct effect on the pre-purchase information search. Some of these factors include time between purchases, changes in the make-up and style of the sport product, diversity of purchasing options, the actual price of

118

the specific sport product, and the alternative brands and features available in the various sport product segments. The sport marketer has a direct effect on how the product is viewed by the sport consumer by understanding the individual differences of those consumers. This is often accomplished through an effective use of market research – especially demographic, psychographic, and behavioristic characteristics.

There are also a number of other external sources that can serve to provide information to aid in making a decision. Experiential learning about a product will vary from consumer to consumer. Those who have had a positive experience with a product will require less effort to make a decision. However, when the sport product is being purchased for the first time, the product is new to the market (hence no past experience), or the sport consumer has had an unsatisfactory experience with the product in the past, the sport marketer's efforts toward re-education of the sport consumer is often wide, varied, and detailed.

Another external source directly relates to the concept of social acceptability. When a sport product is socially visible, and other sport consumers purchase the sport product on a regular basis, there is a psychological reaction that entices other sport consumers to decide to purchase. On the other hand, a sport consumer may, in fact, avoid a desired product because of reference group or peer pressure. An example of this would be a Yankees fan living in Boston whose friends would not be too happy with him wearing Yankees merchandise.

Another concept within social acceptability involves gifting. Whether the purchase is for a gift for oneself or another person, it elicits gifting behavior. Gifting behavior falls into five subdivisions as noted in Table 5.1.

Table 5.1 Gifting behavior

Interpersonal gifting	Individual to individual	A father giving a skateboard to his child for his birthday
Inter-category gifting	Individual to another group	A Boys' and Girls' Club giving a skateboard to an underprivileged child
Intrapersonal gifting	Individual to self	A child buys a skateboard for his or her own use
Intergroup gifting	Group to another group	A school fundraiser collects skateboards to give to a local Boys' and Girls' Club
Intragroup gifting	Group to the group	An after-school program raises money and buys itself some skateboards

Gifting is a significant concept that sport marketing professionals must understand, as they can use these relationships to focus their marketing efforts. Some of the circumstances for gifting include celebration of accomplishment, a reward for completing a goal, having some extra discretionary income, or as a reward system to motivate individuals.

So how does the sport marketing professional effectively reach the sport consumer and influence the information being received? It is a difficult process in today's society because it seems that consumers are less loyal to sport products for a number of reasons including:

(1) an over-abundance of choices; (2) an over-saturation of available information; (3) a feeling that the sport consumer is entitled to the product at a reasonable price; (4) an aggravation with the commoditization of sport, and (5) insecurity about the stability of the sport product – especially in light of work stoppages in the NHL (2004–2005) and NBA (2011), and multiple bankruptcies after the start of the Global Economic Recession in 2007 (examples include in the MLB – Los Angeles Dodgers, Texas Rangers; and the NHL – Dallas Stars, New Jersey Devils, Phoenix Coyotes).

Pre-purchase decision making: evaluation of alternatives
The purpose of this section is to use the information acquired during the information search in order to evaluate each alternative proposed. The criteria used to evaluate each alternative are based on the important features and characteristics of the specified sport product. There are three ways that sport consumers look at sport products. The evoked set is the sport product to which sport consumers give their greatest consideration. The inept set is the sport product that the sport consumer excludes from purchase consideration. The inert set is the sport product that sport consumers are indifferent toward because the product is perceived to have no significant advantage. The sport marketers strive to promote their sport product so that it falls within the evoked set of potential sport consumers.

This is accomplished by understanding the criteria used by the sport consumer to evaluate sport products, and then developing marketing strategies to meet the needs and desires of the sport consumer. These strategies are developed based on an understanding of the various sport consumer decision rules.

The compensatory decision rule is how a consumer evaluates each sport product in terms of each important attribute, and then chooses the sport product or brand with the highest overall rating. The non-compensatory decision rule is that the positive evaluation of an attribute of a sport product does not counteract a negative evaluation of another attribute belonging to the same product. The conjunctive decision rule is the sport consumer establishing a minimally acceptable grade for each attribute evaluated. For each sport product that falls below the established grade on any attribute, that sport product is eliminated from purchase consideration. The affect referral decision rule is a simplified decision rule by which sport consumers make a sport product choice based on previously established overall ratings of the sport product. These ratings are directly affected by brand awareness, advertisements, salesperson influence, emotions, feelings, and moods.

The actual purchase
Participation is the most important outcome of the decision-making process, as this is when the sport consumer makes a purchase of the sport product. In sport, we are concerned with three types of purchases. A *trial purchase* is the concept of sampling the sport product before repurchase. The goal of the sport marketing professional is to provide as positive an experience as possible to entice this sport consumer to repurchase. A *repeat purchase* is the ensuing sales of the sport product after the initial purchase. The sport marketer is concerned with consumer satisfaction as related to this purchase because the higher the level of satisfaction, the higher the level of retention and repeat sales. *Long-term commitment purchases* are where the sport consumer is in a state of being bound emotionally or intellectually to a sport product. As with

120

the repeat purchase, the sport marketer is concerned with satisfaction; however, they will offer additional incentives and programs to maintain the sport consumer as a high-volume user of the sport product.

Post-purchase evaluation

The work of the sport marketing professional does not end with the purchase – there is often significant work that goes into post-purchase evaluation. A primary concern that sport marketing professionals have is consumer satisfaction and dissatisfaction. As stated in the previous section, to maintain long-term commitment of sport consumers and repeat purchasers, an evaluation of their satisfaction must often be completed. Of equal importance is consumer dissatisfaction, which can result from the sport consumer having a negative perception of the sport product, or the sport product not meeting pre-purchase expectations of the sport consumer.

To evaluate the outcome of the sport product, sport marketers look at six levels of assessment: (1) actual performance of the sport product matches the expectations of the sport consumer; (2) actual performance of the sport product significantly exceeds the expectations of the sport consumer; (3) actual performance of the sport product is significantly below the expectations of the sport consumer; (4) the sport consumer has a neutral feeling about the performance of the sport product; (5) actual performance of the sport product is better than expected (positive disconfirmation); and (6) actual performance of the sport product is worse than expected (negative disconfirmation).

Another significant concern during the post-purchase evaluation is cognitive dissonance. In general, the human mind tends to embrace thoughts that minimize the amount of conflict between cognitions, which may include attitudes, emotions, beliefs, or values. When two cognitions have a conflict between each other, the sport consumer falls into a state of cognitive dissonance. Sport marketers are very concerned with cognitive dissonance because people tend to subjectively reinforce decisions they have already made. Therefore, if sport consumers feel they may have made the incorrect choice, they will change their perceptions to make their decision seem better. The sport marketer strives to prevent this conflict. If this is not possible, the gear shifts toward reversing this modified decision so that the sport consumer repeats purchase of the sport product.

Factors that affect the decision-making process: decision variables and external influences

During the decision-making process, there are decision variables and external influences that have a direct effect on the end results of the process. Decision variables are those individual behavioral factors that make sport consumers unique. These qualities include: (1) the personality of the sport consumer; (2) the learning process of the sport consumer; (3) the process of motivating sport consumers; (4) how the attitude of the sport consumer is formed and changed, and (5) the perceptions developed by sport consumers about a sport product. External influences are also known as the "circle of social influence." These external influences include: (1) culture; (2) subcultures; (3) international and global interaction (cross-culture); (4) social setting; and (5) social class.

CASE STUDY 5: CONSUMER INFLUENCES IN CHINA

This is the second part of a case study that started with the marketing research effort discussed in the previous chapter. As you may recall, a questionnaire was administered to 2,155 mainland Chinese consumers in ten selected cities, and different economic, social, and personal factors in China's environment were determined. Eleven major findings related to the unique behavior, attitudes, and buying patterns of Chinese sport consumers were determined. The marketing implications of the Chinese culture and lifestyle as related to findings were considered in terms of economic, social, and personal influences. These three categories have unique Chinese environmental and cultural meanings and thus need to be considered when engaging in marketing in China.

ECONOMIC FACTORS

Unlike in the past, when most income was spent on basic necessities such as food and clothing, today's Chinese consumer spends more money on entertainment and durable goods. However, the general tendency of Chinese consumers to have stronger purchasing power and the fact that their buying decisions reflect creative purchasing beyond bare necessities are not reflected in sport marketing. It could be concluded that not all Chinese consumers are willing to spend a certain percentage of their income on sport products. This phenomenon may be explained either by consumers' lack of sufficient income or too high a price for sport products. On the other hand, however, a great potential exists for marketers who appeal to the Chinese consumers with creative strategies. Those who know desires and needs in specific areas, while being sensitive to economic restraints, may capture a slumbering Chinese market.

SOCIAL AND CULTURAL FACTORS

With the implementation of an "open-door policy" in China, the lifestyle of the Chinese people changes constantly. Several social and cultural trends may stimulate marketers to be optimistic about Chinese consumers:

- The most important trend is growing fitness consciousness. No matter the gender, age, occupation, and education of those surveyed, all tend to tie their purchase of sport products with exercise and entertainment.
- A second trend the survey revealed is a movement toward use of sport products for casual reasons. Chinese consumers are embracing a more casual and health-conscious lifestyle.
- There is a growing consumer preference for international products. The Chinese people, especially the younger generation, are very fond of wearing and using brand name sporting goods from around the world. Owning high-grade sporting goods seems to be a symbol of wealth and a new fashion for these young consumers.

The social and cultural trends discussed above will lead to different pricing, promotional, and distributional strategies. Since marketing principles are applicable throughout the international arena, what has proved successful in the American market could basically be transferred and applied to the Chinese market.

However, to implement a successful marketing strategy in China, several environmental differences must be taken into account:

- "Shopping on Sundays" is a hobby for Chinese consumers. Marketers should create an attractive shopping environment in a prestigious shopping center.
- Chinese consumers believe what they see rather than what they hear. They know that some imitation products exist in the market, and dishonesty in advertising is publicized. Marketers should increase their image by eliminating imitation products and dishonesty advertising.
- Although consumers' attitudes toward international sport products are positive, devotion or loyalty to brands is subject to rapid change. Marketers should have a strategy to keep consumers' loyalty.
- Non-athletes have greater purchasing power than most athletes or sportspersons. Non-athletes buy sporting goods either to impress others or simply because their friends have those items. Marketers should consider how to design sport products with attractive sport features.
- The types of sporting goods desired by the older and younger generations are widely dissimilar. In addition, a large gap exists between the desire to purchase and the ability to purchase sporting goods. It causes problems of bringing the right products to the right person and establishing an appropriate price policy.
- The purchasing decision of Chinese consumers is heavily influenced by social values and the social environment. Marketers should establish an educational program to either match or lead a social value.

PERSONAL FACTORS

Because of recent social changes, Chinese consumers have learned much from other cultures. They are more independent and more knowledgeable about commerce and business. There are at least three particular changes which may create opportunities for marketers:

1 The nuclear family has become the basic economic unit, and it has more power to make purchasing decisions. With the implementation of the "one child per family" policy in China, the nuclear family, consisting of parents with one child, has replaced the traditional clan family which consisted of two or more generations living as one family.
2 Chinese wives are viewed as decision makers for goods purchased in families. Since wives control the family finances, it is important to target wives.
3 Individuals who live in urban locations have stronger purchasing power. The Chinese government predicts that by the end of 1995, people in large urban areas will increase to 30 percent of the population. This modernization movement will undoubtedly create business opportunities.

Source: Adapted from: Geng, L., Lockhart, B., Blackmore, C. and Andrus, R. (1996). Sport marketing strategy: A consumer behavior case analysis in China. *Multinational*

Business Review. Retrieved March 17, 2006 from http://www.findarticles.com/p/articles/ mi_qa3674/ is_199604/ai_n8756626.

Questions for discsussion

1 It has been generally accepted that a great potential exists in the Chinese sport market. However, questions concerning political stability, the uncertainty of economic development, and cultural differences have not only slowed Chinese sport marketing efforts, but have caused confusion and indecisiveness among sport marketers who strive to implement effective marketing strategies in China. How has the influence of the following changed these views and improved sport marketing efforts in China?

   a Yao Ming, Yi Jianlin, and other Chinese basketball players being drafted and playing in the National Basketball Association (NBA)?

   b Beijing hosting the 2008 Summer Olympic Games?

   c The NBA looking to form NBA China?

2 Changes to the traditional management of the sport marketing mix had to be modified to accommodate the Chinese situation. They include:

   a choosing target market segments;

   b determining the services and products to be offered;

   c selecting appropriate pricing strategies;

   d designing promotional programs;

   e providing a proper distribution system.

   You are the international marketing manager for a sport organization of your choice. How would you address each of these areas?

INFLUENCING THE SPORT CONSUMER

What is opinion leadership?

Sport marketing professionals strive to understand how the sport consumer solves problems and makes decisions. Sport marketers, once they gain this understanding, strive to find ways to influence the sport consumer. Influence is a central concept in the definition of leadership. Sport marketers seek to utilize opinion leadership, which is the process by which the sport marketer, or the opinion leader, informally influences the consumption actions or attitudes of sport consumers, who may be classified as opinion seekers or opinion recipients. The main reason why opinion leadership is an effective tool for sport marketers is that the sport consumer views the source of the information (the sport marketing professional) as being credible. Typically, the opinion leader is held in high esteem by those who accept his or her opinions.

There are a number of communication processes that may be used. This is representative of the interpersonal flow of sport communication. There are two models that we utilize in sport marketing. First is a modification of the two-step flow communication model, which is a direct method of communication from a source (owner of the sport product) to the sport marketer

124

(opinion leader), then on to the sport consumer (opinion seekers and opinion receivers) through to the mass media and networks. This is illustrated in Figure 5.3.

Figure 5.3 Two-step flow communication model

A hybrid of the previous model is a modification of the multi-step flow model of communication. In this model, there is information flowing from the source (owner of the sport product) to the sport marketer (opinion leader), but also directly to the sport consumer (opinion seekers and opinion receivers). At the same time that sport consumers receive information about sport products, sport marketers and the owners of the sport product receive feedback from the sport consumers that may be used to market the sport product more effectively and efficiently. This is illustrated in Figure 5.4.

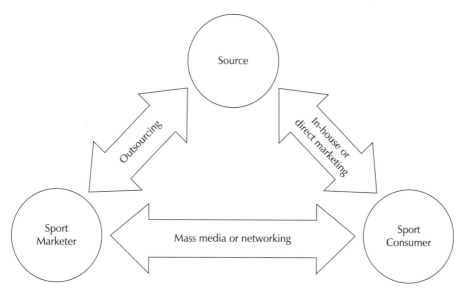

Figure 5.4 Multi-step flow communication model

Viral marketing

However, specifically from the viewpoint of the sport marketer, opinion leadership seeks to pass marketing messages about the sport marketer to as many people as possible, creating the potential for exponential growth in the influence the sport marketer has, as well as exposure of the sport product. This type of marketing is commonly called viral marketing; however, it has also been referred to as buzz marketing or avalanche marketing. There are six elements involved in viral marketing. While an effective strategy does not have to involve all six elements, the more elements it embraces, the more powerful the results are likely to be.

The first is to give away valuable products or services. People in general are naturally attracted to the word "FREE." This powerful word in all aspects of marketing will attract the attention of consumers. The goal of this first element is that, once you have the sport consumer hooked, you can then try to sell additional sport products to him or her. This is very similar to the concept of "to make money you need to spend money." In this aspect of viral sport marketing, the sport product is given away with the goal of selling additional products in the future, hopefully on a permanent basis. For example, the growth that the American Drag Racing League experienced was due to their decision to give away free tickets, but this saw a rise in profits from parking, concessions, and souvenirs. However, each person who takes free tickets has to give out their contact information for ADRL's sponsors. This is great for sponsors and leads to bigger sponsorship deals.

The second element is to provide an effortless transfer of the marketing message to others. This is accomplished by sport marketers by keeping the message short, hence making it easy to communicate to the potential sport consumers. In this day of the digital revolution, it has become increasingly easy to send and replicate these sport marketing messages through mediums such as websites, sms text messages, Tweets, Facebook page updates, online video, emails, digital television, digitized scoreboards, and on-site advertisements.

The third element is the ease with which one can scale the marketing efforts from small to very large. As the marketing messages spread exponentially, more and more opinion seekers and opinion receivers will hear and potentially answer the message. The sport marketing strategy must be able to have the ability to answer potential questions about the sport product in response to the message, or, in a best-case scenario, produce the sport product at an optimal level to deal with the response.

Fourth is to exploit common motivations and behaviors. As discussed earlier in this chapter, understanding the cognitive processes that are utilized to problem solve and make decisions is crucial to success in sport marketing. The fifth element is to utilize existing communication networks. Many people may limit this element to media-based networking such as print, radio, television, or the internet. However, human networking is still the most powerful tool the sport marketer has to communicate sport products to potential consumers. Human networking is a viral sport marketing opportunity for significant and valid exponential growth. Individuals have a broad network that consists of innumerable contacts including family, friends, peers, and colleagues.

The fifth and final element is to take advantage of the resources of others. Sport marketers use many affiliated opportunities to get across the marketing message. In sport marketing, this can range from sponsorship of an event, to news and press releases that appear in newspapers or on the scroll across the bottom of a television screen, to having a link from another's website to your own. Sport marketers, while they wish to have as much control of the message as possible, need the assistance of outside sources to spread the message to a wider audience.

How to measure the effectiveness of opinion leadership

One of the key tasks of a sport marketer is to measure the outcomes of their efforts to determine the level of success of the marketing strategy. In the area of opinion leadership, sport marketers look at four key determinants of success: (1) did the marketing program influence sport consumers; (2) did the advertisements and other collateral materials stimulate sport consumer purchases; (3) was the spread of information about the sport product via word of mouth done in an effective and controlled manner; and (4) was there a creation of a secondary level of opinion leader to further promote the sport product?

Another method of outcome assessment is related to determining whether the marketing efforts reached the opinion leaders in the target market. There are a number of ways to measure these outcomes. The self-designating method is the measurement used most often in marketing. It involves asking a series of AIO (activity, interest, and opinion) questions using surveys to have the respondents determine whether they view themselves as opinion leaders. The sociometric method is where a segmented population is asked to identify those individuals whom they give advice to, and to whom they go for advice. This aids in identifying when people see themselves as opinion leaders, and when they see themselves as opinion seekers and opinion receivers. The key informant method is a form of data collection that involves individuals selected to participate in interviews or focus groups for the purpose of identifying those who are viewed as opinion leaders in society. A final method is the objective method, where individuals are put in a position of being an opinion leader, and an independent analysis of their efforts is conducted to determine success rate.

DIFFUSION AND ADOPTION PROCESSES

Now that we have a strategy for sending the message, how does the message spread to sport consumers? There are two major ways: the diffusion process and the adoption process.

The diffusion process

The diffusion process is where the acceptance of a sport product is spread through communication channels to sport consumers over a period of time. The four key elements within this process are the innovation of the sport product, the sport communication channels, the sport consumer social system, and the time period.

The innovation of the sport product begins with the first two stages of the product life cycle – introduction and growth. During this period, different constituencies define the sport product and give it its own personality, including the producer itself, the product itself, the market, and the sport consumer. Many of these concepts will be discussed in more detail in Chapter 6.

The sport communication channels are wide and varied, including print, radio, television, digital, and internet. These concepts will be addressed further in Chapter 10. The sport consumer social system includes culture, subculture, cross-culture, group, reference group, and social class. This was discussed earlier in this chapter in the section on the external factors affecting sport consumers.

Of the four elements, the innovation of the product is the most significant in the diffusion process. The product characteristic is the only element over which the sport producer and the sport marketer have considerable control. One reason has to do with relative advantage, which is the extent that potential sport consumers perceive a sport product as being superior to existing substitutes. Another reason has to do with compatibility. This is the level at which sport consumers feel that a sport product is able to be integrated with their needs, values, and practices. A third reason is complexity – the degree to which the sport product is very intricate by nature, and hence difficult to understand or use. Fourth is trialability (or divisibility), which is the degree to which the sport product is able to be offered and tried by a number of people on a limited basis. A fifth and final way to control the sport product is through observability (or communicability). This is where the sport product is readily visible to and consumable by the sport consumer.

As a result of controlling the characteristics of the sport product, three distinct levels of innovation result. Continuous innovation is where a sport product is an improved or modified version of an existing product rather than being a totally new product. Traditionally, this alteration has had very little effect on the consumption pattern of the sport product. A second level of innovation is called dynamic continuous innovation. This level takes continuous innovation a step further by actually having a changing effect on the consumption patterns of the sport product. Finally, there is discontinuous innovation, where the sport product is entirely new, and there needs to be the establishment of consumption practices.

The adoption process

The adoption process (Figure 5.5) is made up of the stages that the sport consumer passes through when making a decision to try/continue or not to try/not to continue using a sport product, and Figure 5.6 shows where sport consumers fall in terms of the five categories of adopters.

Innovators, who represent 2.5 percent of the overall population, are adventurous individuals who are willing to try new products. These consumers are usually highly educated, will use

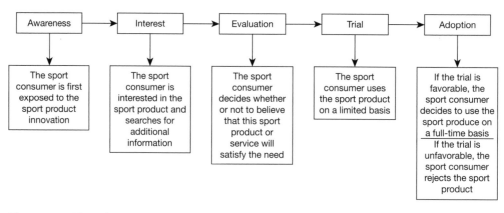

Figure 5.5 The adoption process

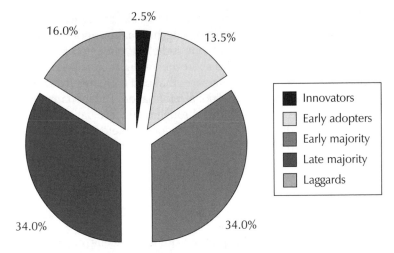

2.5%

16.0%   13.5%

- Innovators
- Early adopters
- Early majority
- Late majority
- Laggards

34.0%   34.0%

Figure 5.6 Sport product adopter categories

multiple information sources to make decisions, and are more willing to take risks. These consumers tend to stay within their own adoption category, and hence rarely communicate about products outside their adopter category.

Early adopters represent 13.5 percent of the overall population, and are usually the leaders in social settings. These individuals tend to be more integrated within local social systems, and hence tend to earn more respect than any other adopter category. Hence, the early adopter tends to be the most influential over people, which results in their being the ideal opinion leader and role model.

The early majority represents 34 percent of the overall population. These consumers tend to be extremely deliberate in their decision making and adopt new ideas/products in an average amount of time. They usually do not hold leadership positions – they would rather be more of an opinion seeker.

Of an equal percentage are the late majority, who tend to be very skeptical of change. As a result, these adopters tend to be followers rather than leaders, and therefore the adoption process is usually as a result of either economic necessity or peer pressure. This group makes up a majority of opinion receivers – and hence tends to be a follower of trends.

The final group, representing 16 percent of the overall population, are called laggards. These individuals are traditionalists in the truest sense of the word. They are happy with the status quo and are the last people to adopt an innovation. They are extremely happy in their comfort zone – living in the past and very suspicious of new products.

Getting the message out

Sport marketing professionals utilize the information from these analyses combined with opinion leadership strategies to influence the sport consumer into purchasing the sport product. By means of the diffusion process, the sport marketer seeks to influence sport consumers to accept and purchase a sport product by spreading information about the sport product through numerous communication channels (print, radio, TV, the internet) over a period of time. By way of the adoption process, the sport marketing professional brings awareness of the sport product to the consumer, and influences the sport consumer to become interested in the sport product and hence search for additional information. The sport marketer continues to work toward influencing the sport consumer throughout the evaluation process and entices the consumer to try the product. Ultimately, the sport marketer strives to have the sport consumer believe that the sport product meets and satisfies his or her needs, resulting in the sport consumer purchasing and using the sport product.

CONCLUSION

Sport consumer behavior is the conduct displayed by sport consumers in seeking out, ordering, buying, using, and assessing products and services that the consumers expect will satisfy their needs and wants. In general, there are two major types of consumers that sport marketers want to understand – the personal consumer and the organizational consumer. The sport marketing professional must understand the internal and external factors that affect sport consumers. The internal factors that make the sport consumer tick include the personality of the sport consumer, the learning process of sport consumers, the process of motivating sport consumers, how the attitudes of the sport consumer are formed and changed, and the perceptions developed by sport consumers about a sport product. External factors resulting from environmental influences include culture, subculture, international and global interaction, social setting, and social class.

In order to effectively understand sport consumer behavior, sport marketing professionals must understand the marketing concept, which is a consumer-oriented philosophy which suggests that satisfaction of consumer needs provides the focus for product development and marketing strategy to enable the firm to meet its own organizational goals. The development of the marketing concept for sport is centered on three sub-concepts: sport production, the sport product, and the selling of sport. The marketing concept focuses on two major groups of sport consumers: spectators and participants. It also focuses on three individual and environmental factors that have an effect on why people consume sport: socialization, involvement, and commitment.

Problem-solving and decision-making techniques must be effectively utilized in order to efficiently analyze sport consumer behavior. This will allow the sport marketing professional to analyze how sport consumers determine what they want, and how they set goals and objectives that result in making a choice. The problem-solving process is an organized, step-by-step approach that involves brainstorming, formulating various solutions, analyzing all solutions to determine a course of action, implementing the course of action, evaluating the success of the course of action, and repeating the process until an optimal solution is reached. The decision-making process involves four views – economic, passive, cognitive, and emotional – that form the foundation for setting and attaining goals. The decision-making process then focuses on pre-purchase decisions (problem and needs recognition, information search, and evaluation of alternatives), decisions during the actual purchase, and post-purchase evaluation.

Sport marketers utilize opinion leadership in order to influence the sport consumer. This concept focuses on the process by which sport marketers informally influence the consumption actions or attitudes of sport consumers. Opinion leadership seeks to pass marketing messages about the sport marketer to as many people as possible, creating the potential for exponential growth in the influence the sport marketer has, as well as exposure of the sport product. This type of marketing is commonly called viral marketing. The five major elements of viral marketing include giving away valuable products or services, providing for an effortless transfer of the marketing message to others, making it easy to scale the marketing efforts from small to very large, exploiting common motivations and behaviors, and taking advantage of the resources of others. Ultimately, sport marketers look at four key determinants of success: (1) did the marketing program influence sport consumers; (2) did the advertisements and other collateral materials stimulate sport consumer purchases; (3) was the spread of information about the sport product via word of mouth done in an effective and controlled manner; and (4) was there the creation of a secondary level of opinion leader to further promote the sport product?

The message is spread to sport consumers through either the diffusion process or the adoption process. The diffusion process is where the acceptance of a sport product is spread through communication channels to sport consumers over a period of time. The four key elements within this process are the innovation of the sport product, the sport communication channels, the sport consumer social system, and the time period. The adoption process is made up of the stages (including awareness, interest, evaluation, trial, and adoption) through which sport consumers pass when making a decision to try/continue or not to try/not to continue using a sport product.

Ultimately, the sport marketing professional utilizes the various processes in sport consumer behavior to influence the sport consumer into purchasing the sport product. The overriding goal is to have the sport consumer believe that the sport product meets and satisfies his or her needs, which in turn results in the sport consumer purchasing and using the sport product.

FROM THEORY TO PRACTICE

PAMELA CHERITON, PRESIDENT AND CEO
Event Services International, Inc.,
Fort Myers, Florida

When I graduated from theater school I never thought that I would make my living in the sporting world. And yet, thanks to the growing consumer desire that entertainment be both engaging and interactive, here I am with close to 20 years as a major league fan event manager. This experience includes 11 years as the Operational Staffing consultant for Major League Baseball's Events and Entertainment Department (MLB All-Star FanFest); 12 years with the National Hockey League (NHL All-Star FANtasy); and ten with the National Basketball Association (NBA All-Star Jam Session). In addition, I was involved with running the Super Bowl XXX Street Spectacular in Tempe, AZ, and the 2006 NCAA Hoop City at the Men's (Indianapolis) and Women's (Boston) Final Four.

Having both witnessed and participated in the FANomenon, I am a firm believer that fan fests are one of the most successful innovations of sport marketing and promotion: the perfect vehicle for fan appreciation, community relations, sport branding, and sponsor recognition. Celebrating and showcasing the best of the sport, these events have captured the market and set the standard for fan entertainment. As an ancillary event that accompanies an All-Star Game or the opening day activity in a team's parking lot, these types of events have become an excellent means of bringing the community in and getting the message out.

Most obviously the target audience for these events is the sports fans, and by extension, their family and friends. All of these events have been geared to appeal to fans of all ages and skill levels from the fanatic to armchair participant – they are truly a family affair. Exit surveys show that the majority of attendees are families with young children and adults in the 36-plus range. In the early years, a participant would stay at the show for approximately three hours but over the past five years that time has expanded to an average of five to seven hours! That is an excellent amount of "face" time for participating sponsors and partners and also a goodly amount of time for snacking, drinking, and shopping for souvenirs and memorabilia.

Because the ticket price is comparable to the host city's other entertainment options, often less, exit surveys consistently show that event attendees consider them a FANtastic bargain. They most often respond that the appeal of these fan fests lies in the fact that they offer a "total" sport experience under one roof: interactive activities for the player participants, legacy and memorabilia displays for the history buffs, player/coach appearances with autographs and skill clinics for the die-hard fans; add the theatrical enhancement of the sounds, sights, and "feel" of the sport and it is heaven on earth for the fan – a consumer's dream come true.

The other noteworthy (albeit quiet) consumers at these events are the volunteers who comprise 80 percent of the staffing of these shows. A fan fest can be as physically large as three football fields and can run for up to 12 hours a day, six-plus days in a row – requiring a team of over 2,500 people. Since it would be fiscally impossible to use the ticket or sponsor revenues to offset the salaries for such a large staff, these events are perforce required to rely on the willing participation of their most active and committed sports fans.

Traditionally these volunteers are people who have either a real love of the game or are motivated by their sense of civic pride – usually it is a healthy combination of the two. A common characteristic is the active desire to share their enthusiasm with the event attendees. As the representative face of the hosting city, they come from a variety of backgrounds; usually range in age from 18 to 80, with the majority in the 18–25 and 35–55 range and are an equal mix of males and females. Almost all have high school education and many have post-secondary degrees, and while most are still working there are usually a good number of retirees and college students. In fact, at least one-third of the total numbers are students who are pursuing their degrees in some kind of sport marketing or management or communications program.

For these students, volunteering at an event of the magnitude and caliber of a major league fan fest offers them the unique opportunity to get some valuable "mega-event" experience under their belts and the distinct possibility of being "discovered" by the professional event staff. I know of several cases where students have been able to parley their aptitude and attitude as "star" volunteers (ever willing, ever able) into on-the-job interviews resulting in future employment.

Another strong motivation for volunteering at fan events is the social aspect of meeting like-minded individuals in a fun and productive environment. Having some longevity in this particular arena, I have been privileged to work with approximately 500 "return" volunteers who plan their vacations around the event in a new city. According to them, it is the perfect way to play: a few "structured" hours of enjoyable activity, an opportunity to meet the "locals" close up, and then it is off to explore the new place – armed with the insider details they picked up during their shift.

Regardless of their reasons, these most excellent people are the life-blood of any event, and it is of the utmost importance that their valuable contribution be loudly recognized and appreciated. They are the ultimate grass-roots marketers who, through enthusiastic word of mouth, can spread the "great event" reviews much further afield than even the media partners – and quite likely to a better, more receptive target audience: their fellow fans.

PART III

SPORT MARKETING LOGISTICS

CHAPTER SIX

SPORT PRODUCT AND LOGISTICAL MANAGEMENT

CHAPTER OUTLINE

- Elements of sport products and services
- Purchasing
- How supply chain management affects sport product management
- Sport product and service management
- The sport product and service life cycle
- Positioning, differentiation, and branding
- Conclusion

CHAPTER OBJECTIVES

The reader will be able to:

- distinguish, identify, and classify the various elements of sport products and services
- understand the steps in the purchasing process and how those are applied to sport marketing, sourcing, and cost management
- identify and appreciate the importance of supply chain management as an integral function of logistics in sport marketing, including inventory management, team and equipment transportation, warehousing, order processing, and information systems
- identify and understand the stages of the sport product life cycle.

137

ELEMENTS OF SPORT PRODUCTS AND SERVICES

A sport product is something that is produced which is bought or sold in the sporting goods industry. Usually, tangible products are referred to as "goods," while intangible products are called "services" or the "experience." A sport service is the process of providing quality, value, and satisfaction to the sport consumer. Intangible products also include "indirect goods," in which customers have the opportunity to stylize tangible products as they wish. Intangible services involve providing a quality standard work, an offering, and/or duties generally expected by the sport consumer. These traditional services are provided to enhance the experience.

Tangible sport products and services

In today's society, consumers want to touch the baseball and feel the jersey. Consumers want to customize their shoes and put their marks on hats. Examples of tangible products include the program that consumers purchase at the gate and the big "number one" foam finger they buy at the merchandise stand. Tangible services might include access to and use of a personal trainer, or ice skate sharpening. Not only do tangible services help the consumer recognize or differentiate a specific product or service from others, they allow consumers to show others their choice and in turn advertise by word of mouth.

Intangible sport products and services

Intangible sport products are the merchandise and extensions that we cannot touch or hold. For example, intangible sport products would be the appearance of the ballpark, the usher who helped you find your seat with a friendly smile, and the sights, sounds, smells, and euphoric feeling of your team's victory. Intangible sport services could be the customer service fans receive when they purchase goods at the ballpark, such as tickets, food, or memorabilia. In some ways, the intangible sport products and services, when negative, have a longer lasting effect as compared to the tangible products. Customers remember how a game was ruined for them because of foul language, weather, or getting to the park late because it was difficult to find parking within a reasonable distance more than they remember the great hot dog, exciting home run, or friendly ticket taker.

PURCHASING

The two general forms of purchasing arrangements are partnership sourcing and competitive sourcing. Partnership sourcing involves the commitment between customers and suppliers to create a long-term relationship based on understood and agreeable objectives that work toward maximizing capability and competitiveness. Competitive sourcing is where suppliers study the nature of the activity, and then determine the best performance for the given activity without input from customers. This performance may include eliminating an activity, modifying a product or service for greater efficiency, or outsourcing to another department, division, or

138

company. Improvement of performance drives this type of sourcing, with competition driving the process.

Partnership sourcing is more preferable because it leads to long-term partnership based on trust between buyer and supplier. Once a level of mutual trust has been established, business partners usually give preferential treatment to repeat customers in the form of price breaks. Partnership sourcing implies that both the buyer and the supplier have mutual reasons to be successful. Competitive sourcing is every company for itself. Competitive sourcing in the short term is a more cost-effective way to do business. However, this competition does not lend itself to building lasting supply chains.

Purchasing today is not about squeezing suppliers but rather strategic supplier management, which involves measuring supplier performance and risks as well as determining the optimum degree of profit. As logistics costs become an increasingly larger part of total costs, proactive supply chain management is the most important factor in keeping purchasing costs low. This supply chain is the link between the purchasing process, production, and logistics management.

Purchasing process

In an era of global sourcing, the multinational company's success often hinges on the most appropriate selection of its foreign suppliers. International suppliers are very complicated and risky owing to a variety of uncontrollable and unpredictable factors affecting the decision. These factors may include political situations, tariff barriers, cultural and communication barriers, trade regulations and agreements, currency exchange rates, cultural differences, ethical standards, and quality standards.

Sporting goods companies have been focused on providing the best possible quality for the lowest available price. Price is what the consumer equates to the value of a good or service. Value is what the consumer is willing to pay for a product. Both price and value are influenced by market trends, corporate climate, and competition for suppliers. These purchasing objectives have forced companies to seek third world labor forces and partner themselves with long-term suppliers that have similar company values. Because of the high labor cost in the United States, it has been more economical to ship raw materials to the third world, have them produce the good, and then reship the finished product to its destination. This purchasing process stretches the supply chain and increases the number of logistical variables.

Purchasing in sport marketing

The single biggest cost-saving measure to the sporting goods industry has been technology advances in the internet. Electronic Data Interchange (EDI) has affected 100 percent of the supply chains. In only a matter of months, the change in the way supply chain partners move product from concept to point of sale resembles the difference between walking the basketball up the court and running the fast break.

The internet continues to tear down communications barriers from geography to cost. This technology will be leveraged through new, web-based communities referred to in today's business world as e-business or exchanges. The impact in purchasing will be on product cost, inventory, time-to-market, market responsiveness, and market share.

With the standardization of sporting goods purchasing, exchanges on the web are popping up at an incredible pace, with leading industry companies, software vendors, venture capitalists, and dot.com start-ups moving aggressively to capture early market share. With a 24-hour, seven-days-a-week venue that is not constrained by geographical location or time zones, the opportunity for cost-cutting measures is endless. Computer companies have developed a web-based marketplace where industry-related businesses will conduct commerce. In return for providing this forum, owners may seek a subscription fee or a percentage of the business transactions made through the exchange. While this sounds like an ingenious way to create revenue for exchange owners, its potential value to consumers is even greater.

With the matching of inventory and/or qualified production capacity to demand, opportunities to lower overheads in the supply chain through bidding processes can be exploited. This model may be applied to raw materials and other supply chain services like transportation. Retailers and branded manufacturers will be able to go direct to source, significantly altering or eliminating the role of agents, brokers, and other middlemen in the process. This translates into retailers with a better bottom line and consumers with high-quality sporting goods at a lower price.

Sourcing

Should retailers concentrate most of its stock purchases in one wholesale supplier (single sourcing) or balance its purchases between two or more suppliers (balanced sourcing)? A concentrated purchasing strategy makes the retailer an important customer to its wholesaler, meriting preferential treatment, by ordering a larger volume. However, concentrated sourcing can also increase the retailer's dependence on the wholesaler. Reducing dependence, in turn, entails diversifying purchases, splitting them between at least two wholesalers, which, unfortunately, increases transaction costs and reduces the retailer's importance to either of its suppliers. The tradeoff is further complicated when retailers operate in a small or closed market with few suppliers and high barriers because genuine options are limited. In most cases, retailers tend to use balanced sourcing, or to split their purchases more evenly between the two wholesalers as opposed to concentrating most of their purchases in a single wholesaler. Current trends suggest that over the long term retailers would prefer to move away from concentrated sourcing. One of the reasons for this preference for balanced sourcing is a desire to avoid over-dependence and opportunistic or unethical behavior on the part of wholesalers.

In 2005, quotas on imports of apparel products were eliminated from World Trade Organization (WTO) countries, including the United States. The new accord originates with what is known as the "Uruguay Round" of trade discussions, which were concluded in 1994 in Marrakesh, Morocco. In that agreement, a ten-year tenure was established to progressively excise apparel and textile quotas.

Unlike the textile industry, which has systematically lost American-based jobs to overseas competitors, the elimination of quotas on apparel imports is generally viewed positively by sporting goods companies sourcing abroad. The lifting of quota restrictions affords U.S. sporting

140

goods vendors and retailers the ability to source apparel products indiscriminately and significantly cheaper, which in turn offers a potential windfall. With the majority of apparel already being sourced offshore, American-based retailers and distributors will now be able to source an entire line, for example, from the country offering the least expensive manufacturing process.

China has emerged as the potential leader in sporting goods suppliers. The unanswered questions are whether China can produce high-quality product at a low price with consistency and on time. With those critical factors in mind, many vendors and retailers sourcing their own branded or private label products are implementing a diversified balanced sourcing strategy. This strategy allows for the most competitive prices with the most reliable delivery.

Cost management

Cost management considers competitive manufacturing and logistics costs, by optimizing the amount of stored materials, keeping capacities filled, achieving economical purchasing prices, and ensuring efficient transport and storage processes. Short processing times accomplish a high level of service and flexibility even in the case of short-term customer demands.

With web-based exchange technology providing a less constrained and more timely flow of information and fewer middlemen in the supply chain, it is possible to dramatically reduce overall lead times. Time-to-market and market responsiveness will have new lead-time benchmarks recorded in days and weeks, eclipsing the current benchmarks measured in months and years. These combined factors will allow for a faster flow of goods at a lower cost with lower supply chain inventories. As this trend continues, companies will have an opportunity to liquidate the slower moving competition.

Two areas with specific applications to the sporting goods supply chain are emerging. The first is the area of inventory liquidation. For example, Tradepac.com provides a place to post merchandise for liquidation, including a category specifically designated for sporting goods and apparel.

Another early exchange player with implications for the sporting goods industry is the transportation services category. An example is Celerix.com. Celerix's exchange goes beyond creating a community for transportation services buyers and sellers to meet. Celerix has also started to provide supply chain visibility through tracking components and alliances with other supply chain exchanges and software providers. Other sporting goods exchanges that provide more comprehensive services, including building and operating e-commerce networks between retailers and manufacturers, are EB2B.com and iCongo.com.

Sporting goods supply chain partners should be actively monitoring this market and swiftly determining how and when to get into the game. As this change to exchanges occurs, old organizational, process, and information technology models will require major overhauls.

HOW SUPPLY CHAIN MANAGEMENT AFFECTS SPORT PRODUCT MANAGEMENT

Supply chain management (SCM) is the combination of art and science that goes into improving the way sport organizations find the raw components they need to make a product or service and deliver it to customers. The following are five basic components of SCM.

1   *Plan*: this is the strategic portion of SCM. You need a strategy for managing all the resources that go toward meeting customer demand for your product or service. A big piece of planning is developing a set of metrics to monitor the supply chain so that it is efficient, costs less, and delivers high quality and value to customers.
2   *Sourcing* : choose the suppliers that will deliver the goods and services you need to create your product. Develop a set of pricing, delivery, and payment processes with suppliers and create metrics for monitoring and improving the relationships. Put together processes for managing the inventory of goods and services you receive from suppliers, including receiving shipments, verifying them, transferring them to your manufacturing facilities, and authorizing supplier payments.
3   *Production*: this is the manufacturing step. Schedule the activities necessary for production, testing, packaging, and preparation for delivery. As the most metric-intensive portion of the supply chain, measure quality levels, production output, and worker productivity.
4   *Logistics*: coordinate the receipt of orders from customers, develop a network of warehouses, pick carriers to get products to customers, and set up an invoicing system to receive payments.
5   *Returns*: the problem part of the supply chain. Create a network for receiving defective and excess products back from customers and supporting customers who have problems with delivered products.

Before the internet, the aspirations of supply chain software devotees were limited to improving their ability to predict demand from customers and make their own supply chains run more smoothly. Now, companies can connect their supply chain with the supply chains of their suppliers and customers together in a single vast network that optimizes costs and opportunities for everyone involved. This was the reason for the B2B explosion; the idea that everyone in the same business could be connected together.

Most companies share at least some data with their supply chain partners. The supply chain in most industries is like a big card game. The players do not want to show their cards because they do not trust anyone else with the information; but if they did show their hands they could all benefit. Suppliers would not have to guess how many raw materials to order, and manufacturers would not have to order more than they need from suppliers to make sure they have enough on hand if demand for their products unexpectedly goes up. In addition, retailers would have fewer empty shelves if they shared the information they had about sales of a manufacturer's product in all their stores with the manufacturer. The internet makes showing your hand to others possible, but centuries of distrust and lack of coordination within the industry makes it difficult.

The pay-off of timely and accurate supply chain information is the ability to make or ship only as much of a product as there is a market for. This is the practice known as just-in-time manufacturing, and it allows companies to reduce the amount of inventory that they keep.

142

This can cut costs substantially, since you no longer need to pay to produce and store excess goods.

Some of the road-blocks when installing supply chain automation are uniquely difficult because the company extends beyond the company's walls. Employees will need to change the way they work, as will the employees from each supplier that is added to the network. Only the largest and most powerful manufacturers can force such radical changes down suppliers' throats. Most companies have to sell the suppliers on the system. Moreover, the goals associated with installing the system may be threatening to those suppliers. To get supply chain partners to agree to collaborate, all stakeholders have to be willing to compromise and help them achieve their own goals.

An extended supply chain is a clever way of describing everyone who contributes to a product. So if you are publishing a sport textbook, your extended supply chain would include the factories where the books are printed and bound, but also the company that sells you the paper, the mill where that supplier buys their stock, and so on. It is important to keep track of what is happening in your extended supply chain because it could end up having an impact on you (as the old saying goes, a chain is only as strong as its weakest link). For example, a fire in a paper mill may cause the textbook manufacturer's paper supplier to run out of inventory. If the textbook company knows what is happening in its extended supply chain it can find another paper vendor.

Inventory management

Retailers grow in different ways; some plan their growth well in advance, conduct copious amounts of research on regional demographics, identify the best real estate, and stay away from new markets until they are fully prepared. Others, like many sporting goods retailers, have grown rapidly through expansion or gradually through the addition of new store locations or competitors' attrition.

As chains have grown, the logistics of managing multiple retail locations has created many new challenges. The knee-jerk reaction is to standardize everything we can. Of course, this is desirable when it comes to point-of-sale (POS) procedures or supply purchasing. But when applied to assortment planning we have taken standardization too far. The quest for consistency, specifically in floor layouts and fixture types, is at odds with the need to tailor assortments to the demands and demographics of local consumers. Each market, with its distinct customer profile, geography, and local competition, can put a different spin on every store, even stores within the same trading area.

Inventory is usually a retailer's single largest asset unless we dissect the way we sort and allocate merchandise to stores. A portion of eroding sales and profits can be attributed to what can only be described as misuse of inventory. Our automated information system provides huge amounts of data, most of which is after the fact. The automated system might show, for instance, that backpacks sell better in one location than in another. In some cases we find the obvious answer that the store is near the university. Companies should not need detective work to find out why something sold better in one location than in another. Companies should have planned, with all the information at their disposal, where their products would sell better, and stocked the store to maximize the opportunity.

Every day, companies compile and store information that customers divulge. But when companies plan for the next season's products, where do we look? Why, to last year, of course, so that they can perpetuate what they already know. The nuances of most of our customers' shopping habits and expectations are never built into the mix during the planning process.

Tailoring store assortments is not only desirable from an inventory management standpoint but also critical if we are to retain our credibility. What can employees possibly be telling customers if they run out of youth soccer shin guards in August but always have them in stock in January? That we are a full-fine sporting goods store? No, it just confirms that the company has the right goods at the wrong time, or in the wrong place.

For large chains, standardization is just the easiest way to make a predictable presentation on a floor plan design and can be easily executed. Senior management thinks it is great that the store in Montgomery, IL looks exactly like the store in Montgomery, AL. This gives management a warm, fuzzy feeling that stores are following the corporate directives. But the benefit stops there. The local customer could not care less. In today's competitive environment, where consumers can buy what they want through the internet, companies need to manage inventory the smartest way they know how, not the easiest.

Certainly, it requires more skill to manage variable assortments and timing across multiple doors. But in Illinois, you had better have ice hockey equipment, and plenty of it; year-round in fact. In Florida, the only hockey they are playing is on the streets, on wheels, and they need to look cool, not stay warm.

There is a new opportunity for the supply chain called "Dropshipping." This service provides online retailers with an easy method to get their products to the consumer. Dropshipping allows the online retailer to hold no supply whatsoever because when an order is received, the dropshipper takes the order and creates the product, ships the product, and handles customer service for the product. It is outsourcing to the extreme and the costs are hard to keep down, but if a sport organization does not have the means to run its own shop, it can use a dropshipper to alleviate most of the headaches.

Transportation methods

Transportation is one of America's largest industries. Its sectors range from automobiles and trucks to airplanes, trains, ships, barges, pipelines, and warehouses. Traditionally, the transportation industry accounts for about 10 percent of the GDP and employs nearly 22 million people, or about 15 percent of all workers in the United States.

At a little more than 10 percent of America's economic activity, transportation is remarkably efficient, considering the fact that it is a vital service to every other sector of the economy. In fact, thanks to the increasing use of advanced information systems and such strategies as intermodal use of containers (sending freight via containers that are easily transferred from ship to railcar to truck as needed, without repacking), the transportation industry's productivity level is excellent. The ratio of tons–miles of freight shipped in the U.S. per dollar of GDP declined by a remarkable 35.3 percent from 1970 through 2011. Meanwhile, transportation is growing rapidly.

The introduction of intergraded databases that can track inventory levels and shipments on a global basis has streamlined the supply chain. As a result, supply chain technology has been one of the fastest growing segments in the information field.

The rapid adoption of outsourcing has led many companies that find shipping to be vital to their business to turn to logistics services providers for all manner of shipping support, including warehousing and distribution services. The sectors of transport, supply chain management, and logistics services are permanently intertwined, creating efficiencies once undreamed of in the transportation arena.

The transportation, supply chain, and logistics industry is going global along with just about every other major industry. These companies, however, hold a unique position because they are the very entities that make globalization possible. This industry is made up of companies that supply the systems and software, run the warehouses, provide the consulting and operate the airplanes, boats, trucks, and trains that move raw materials, finished goods, packages, documents, and people throughout the world.

Offshoring (that is, the transference of manufacturing, customer service centers, and other labor-intensive work from nations like the U.S. and U.K. to developing countries such as China and the Philippines) has been one of the biggest contributors to international commerce in recent years. To facilitate the offshoring of manufacturing work, it has become essential to ship cargo between distant locations, bringing the right goods to the right locations and doing it cheaply, efficiently, and above all, on time.

The needs of modern business have spurred many transportation and logistics sectors to become technologically advanced and to build a truly global presence. This trend has forced many smaller companies to consolidate and merge into larger entities in order to compete effectively. The parcel delivery business is a prime example. Business demands have created courier giants such as UPS, FedEx, and DHL. Major enterprises have the ability to create global networks of offices and warehouses, purchase vast quantities of equipment such as trucks and aircraft, and invest in the expensive and complex information systems necessary to track shipments as they are moved around the world.

With the need to ship massive amounts of goods across long distances came the need to have vast supply chains monitored, organized, and controlled. This led to the advent of logistics companies, which specialize in handling goods on the way to market. Most products in today's marketplace are the result of a global effort. Raw materials for a product may be produced in one country, assembled in another, and finally marketed to consumers in dozens of different nations at once. The key to making such manufacturing systems work is modern supply chain technology – the use of specialized software and networks in a coordinated effort to design, manufacture, ship, assemble, and distribute components and completed products.

The challenges faced by supply chains are multifaceted: coordinating the arrival of supplies in factories; bringing together all the necessary parts and assembling them into consumer-ready products; and distributing them across oceans, highways, and airways to arrive in the correct locations in the right quantities, colors, and styles to satisfy consumer demand, all at the lowest possible cost. Compounded by delays and mistakes that can be made along the way due to bad weather, communication breakdowns, accidents, inspections, or simple human error, these challenges can quickly become catastrophes. In order to prevent mishaps and manage

145

day-to-day supply issues, companies hire supply chain managers and utilize advanced data systems. In some cases, supply chain services are outsourced altogether.

Third-party logistics companies (known as 3PLs) are quickly assuming a vital role in the supply chain. Logistics services are generally defined as services added onto regular transportation activities, including freight forwarding, which is the handling of freight from one form of transport to another (for example, the movement of containers from ship to truck or railcar to truck). Transportation managers determine the most viable mode of transport (by train, truck, boat, plane, or a combination). Warehouses store the stock of other companies and ship the stock out as needed. Supply chain management (SCM) software makers specialize in software that can track or allow communication between the different parts of a supply chain.

Many freight and parcel shipping companies have jumped on the 3PL bandwagon to provide their customers with turnkey shipping services. Deutsche Post, UPS, and FedEx have all made logistics acquisitions as they battle for market share. British-based Exel plc, the largest provider of logistics services in the world, has made several strategic acquisitions in order to offer domestic and international supply chain management from beginning to end, with services including freight forwarding, warehouse management, multi-modal planning. and powerful information technology. However, the industry has not consolidated to the point where there is no longer room for small or start-up companies. Many regional or specific service specialists have achieved a great deal of success in their own niche markets.

Use of electronic means for delivery

With the increase of use of the internet and other electronic means of communication (SmartPhones, iPads, etc.), the need to be connected becomes important. For example, Adidas-Reebok is already working with certain retailers on pilot programs to reduce the supply chain line and auto-replenishment system. Adidas-Reebok outlined the supply chain matrix used by all the major shoe companies. The creative portion of the process typically takes 12 months. The procurement function takes another six. Adidas-Reebok's goal is to reduce that time period by 50 percent in three years. For a start, Adidas-Reebok is closely linking its supply chain efforts to sales and marketing strategies.

This may seem logical, but it is not standard operating procedure in the shoe industry. Adidas-Reebok is also working with its factories to improve their operating performance and place its new products closer to the market. The company is investing in three-dimensional digital software that can reduce the timeline by at least ten weeks. The company also hopes to lop a month off the delivery phase by shipping directly to retailers, bypassing the warehouses. The company is currently testing a labeling and special handling program with some of its factories. Other retailers should demand to know what the other brands are doing to shorten the supply chain time cycle.

The use of the electronic industry is extremely competitive and highly volatile. A company's competitors can often turn on a dime. Outsourcing logistics is not always just a matter of saving money; often it is driven by the need to remain competitive. UPS, FedEx, and other similar companies help manufacturers and marketers of sporting good products to get their product to market quickly and successfully. Getting your product through the supply chain in a quick and efficient manner is not enough. Great business plans are often like produce; they can be highly perishable.

Performance metrics

Supply chain measurements or metrics such as inventory turns and backorders are used to track supply chain performance. Supply chain metrics can help the company to understand how it is operating over a given period of time. Inventory turns are the number of times that a company's inventory cycles or turns over per year. It is the most commonly used supply chain metric. Also used are backorders, which is defined as an unfilled customer order in demand (immediate or past due) against an item whose current stock level is insufficient to satisfy demand.

Supply chain measurements can cover many areas including procurement, production, distribution, warehousing, inventory, transportation, and customer service. However, a good performance in one part of the supply chain is not sufficient. Supply chains are only as strong as their weakest link. The solution is for the company to measure all key areas of its supply chain. Tracking the company's metrics allows the company to view performance over time and guides it to optimize a supply chain. It allows management to identify problem areas, and to compare the company to other like companies through like industry benchmarking.

Measurements alone are not the solution to the company's weak areas. The solution lies in the corrective action that the company takes to improve the measure. The solution comes from process improvements. Using the correct set of metrics can lead the company to the solution to the question: Do we have the right balance between service and cost?

Tracking and measuring the performance of various supply chain functions is necessary but not sufficient for today's extended enterprise. Tying that performance to corporate strategic goals and closing the loop on execution to ensure continuous improvement are keys to effective performance management.

Establishing metrics to track supply chain performance seems, on its face, like a fairly simple and straightforward undertaking. If one is interested only in measuring individual functional performance, this perception is true. But most companies today need to understand per-formance in terms of the overall inter-enterprise supply chain and be able to tie that overall performance to strategic corporate objectives – a far more complex task.

Breaking out of traditional metrics begins with top-level strategic planning. Companies need to ask: what is our strategy? Given that strategy, what does our supply chain need to excel at doing? Maybe it needs to be really fast, or really flexible, or really inexpensive. Whatever it is, the company need to pick metrics designed to measure that capability.

A strategic approach to supply chain performance is also being driven by the growing use of balanced score-cards at many large companies. At the beginning of the year these companies establish their most important financial goals as well as goals in other areas. Many of these top goals have supply chain components. For example, if a company wants to improve its cash flow, supply chain managers and line employees may seek to drive certain key performance indicators (KPIs) – those factors that influence the effectiveness of products and processes. In this situation, the KPIs to be driven may include speeding up order processing and improving order accuracy and fill rates.

Establishing the proper KPIs, and targets for each, is an important next step and one that can be especially difficult when cross-functional or cross-enterprise agreements are required. Targets for each KPI capture the level of improvement desired. There is no point in setting very aggressive targets and having nothing to back them up, so the company must have initiatives that are going to move toward the goal.

The final step is actual implementation, where a company identifies data sources, starts collecting the data and creates an appropriate format for communicating it, and commits to reviewing the information.

SPORT PRODUCT AND SERVICE MANAGEMENT

Sport product and service management focuses on the approach taken by sport marketers and organizations to define and market their products and services. There are a number of issues a sport marketing professional must consider when managing products and services, including the following:

■ choosing the appropriate sport products and services to produce and sell
■ deciding what new sport products and services to add or discontinue
■ deciding how to introduce sport products or services to a market
■ calculating the amount of time it will take for a sport product or service to penetrate the market
■ ascertaining the sport product and service life cycle considerations that need to be addressed
■ deciding how to develop positioning and differentiation strategies for sport products and services
■ establishing the branding and licensing structures to be utilized for sport products and services
■ determining the levels of protection (patents, marks, copyrights) that need to be implemented for sport products or services.

Sport product and service management usually starts as a function of the sport marketing planning process. This process involves the development of the sport organization's products and services marketing strategies, including the tactics and programs to be implemented during the life span of the plan. There are a series of functions that are undertaken during this planning process to determine the appropriate method for managing the specific sport product or service. First is defining the competitive set, which is the process of determining the direct competitors to a sport organization in the specific product or service area. Those organizations most closely defined as competitors are those which offer similar sport products and services, or are generic competitors in the marketplace.

Once the competitive set is defined, the company or organization engages in category attractiveness analysis. This involves developing a general understanding of the market segment category in which the organization operates, and whether continued investment in that segment will yield an appropriate return. There are three main areas of concern in completing a category attractiveness analysis. First is the category of aggregate marketing factors, which are the indicators of the appeal of the sport product or service in the specific segment or category. These factors include category size, market growth potential, the sport product and service life cycle, the sales cycles and seasonality present in the segment, and profitability potential. The second category is the segment factors, which are the underlying opportunities and threats that affect the segment or category. This includes the threat of current competitors and new entrants to the segment, the bargaining power of buyers and suppliers, and the saturation of sport products and services within the category or segment. The final category is environmental factors that are beyond the control of the sport organization. These include technological innovations, politics, economic changes, legislative mandates, and changes in societal views.

In addition, there may be some businesses inside the trade radius offering similar products and services, but which are not competitors owing to differences in target market, class of product or services being offered, or target clientele. An example of this would be a pro shop at a hockey arena selling team merchandise and a "mom and pop" sporting goods store. The pro shop is targeting season ticket holders and fans on game day, while the sporting goods store is targeting the general public. Thus, the two stores are not of major concern to one another.

This analysis elicits some questions related to competitor analyses and consumer analyses. These questions include:

- How well is the sport organization doing as compared to the competition?
- Have our customers been pleased with our current sport products and/or services?
- Can we forecast the needs, wants, and desires of our customers going forward?
- What factors might cause customer behavior to change?

By collecting consumer-based research that is truthful, reliable, and valid, answers to these questions will serve to help the sport organization move forward with confidence. The answers to these questions will also serve as a primer to develop the further management processes necessary in sport product and service management. This is especially important when determining market potential. By estimating the maximum possible sales of a sport product or service, a sport organization will gain valuable knowledge about the amount of sport product or service to make available. If an estimate is too low, it may result in a marketer determining that the segment or category has reached maturity too fast, and cloud his view on any untapped potential that may be present. If an estimate is too high, the sport organization may offer new sport products and services or extensions to current sport products or services which are not truly wanted, needed, or desired by the segment or category. The information about the market potential also serves to help the sport organization to make appropriate pricing, advertising, delivery, promotion, and publicity decisions (the sport marketing mix). It also helps the marketer focus on the continued development, introduction, and growth of particular products and services, as well as evaluating the products' eventual maturation and decline, through the sport product and service life cycle.

THE SPORT PRODUCT AND SERVICE LIFE CYCLE

The sport product and service life cycle encompasses six stages: internal development, introduction to market, growth, maturity, saturation, and decline. All stages are bound by the realities of competition, saturation, and change. A typical life cycle is similar to a bell curve as illustrated in Figure 6.1.

149

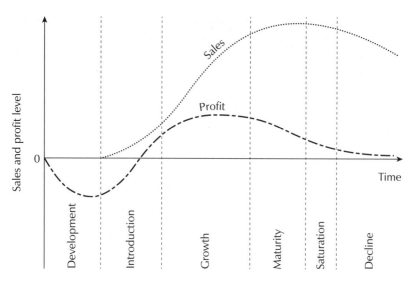

Figure 6.1 The sport product and service life cycle

No market is infinite. Competitors will always want to gain more market share, and someone will always think of a new twist to an old idea. Researching the product life cycle can provide the answer to the following questions. How do I determine if my business is considered to be small, medium, or large? If I am small, how do I compete against larger companies? How do I figure it out and does it matter? How do I know when a product or service has reached saturation point? What are the implications of this? When do I need to find something new to offer, when do I stay the course and do more advertising? These questions and more appear often these days. In the sport industry, the buying marketplace heats up for some and cools down for others more quickly than other industries. Entrepreneurs and business owners need to realize and understand that success or failure is directly linked to the speed and accuracy with which we answer these questions. These questions can be addressed by market research. Market research can be desk or field based, can use face-to-face or telemarketing techniques, and can use focus groups and/or qualitative or quantitative research methods depending on the sport product or service.

Each stage of the sport product and service life cycle has attributes that will influence your decisions on whether this is the appropriate time for your business to grow. Continuous market research will help you avoid pitfalls such as not correctly anticipating demand, overhead expenses, and other variable factors.

Internal development

The internal development stage begins with the idea of a new product or service or a new twist on an existing product or service. How does the company make the idea or invention a reality? This stage offers some of the largest road-blocks. What material should the company use for the invention? Can the company's services be offered to anyone? What are the technological needs? Should this product or service be patented, branded, licensed, trademarked, or copy written? Who will lend the capital in order to mass produce the product? This stage is where the company develops a marketing plan. Has any company produced the same type of product and what were some of the problems they incurred?

A marketing plan for the sport product or service is a formal written statement of marketing intent that summarizes the key points of the operational sport marketing process. These steps include: market research, mission, marketing objectives, financial objectives, target markets, positioning, and market mix:

- *Market research*: is defined as the organized methodical discovery of information about a marketplace.
- *Mission*: defined as an attempt by a corporation to encapsulate its purpose in a simple paragraph or phrase.
- *Marketing objectives*: defined as what the organization is trying to achieve through its marketing activities during a specified period. This is closely linked with corporate objectives.
- *Financial objectives*: defined as goals related to returns that a firm will strive to accomplish during the period covered by its financial plan.
- *Target market*: defined as actively pursuing specific population segments for the purpose of research or sales.
- *Positioning*: defined as the work that a company may undertake to try to position its offering, brand, or service in a specific place relative to competing offerings in the minds of their target market.
- *Marketing mix*: defined as gathered information serves to help the sport organization make appropriate pricing, advertising, delivery, promotion, and publicity decisions.

The marketing plan enables the company to understand which stage a product is entering, leaving, or passing through at any given time. Market data are available through print and media, and with the emergence of the internet more information is at our fingertips than ever before. It is important to consider the source of the information. Just because it is the latest and greatest news does not mean that the consumer cannot change his or her mind.

Some of the questions your research should answer or address are:

- How many competitors are there?
- Who has the best idea and is it the leader?
- How strong is the business that is leading?
- How can I place my sport product or service competitively?
- How many suppliers are entering the market?
- What are potential buyers thinking about buying?
- How much research and development is being done by your competitors, relative to the current product or service, vs. new ones?
- What is the size of the market?
- How long is the life cycle of similar sport products or services?

Using desk or field-based, face-to-face, telemarketing, focus groups, and/or qualitative or quantitative research methods will provide answers to the questions above in a quick, concise, and accurate manner. This research provides an organization with a sales forecast that is

151

believable. This approach to internal development of a sport product or service, and the accompanying marketing plan should point out some of the problems encountered by sport organizations. These problems include not knowing what stage of the market the product is entering, a changing or poorly determined price point, and a higher than estimated number of competitors, all of which can lead to loss of capital investment.

Introduction to market

Now that we have an answer for all of the questions from the marketing plan, it is time to put the plan into action. Through market research, the company has determined a price point that will be competitive. How does the company know the segment of the market it should enter? Having many competitors could indicate maturity or at least a large enough demand that could yield market share; having only a few competitors indicates either an early or late stage cycle. Ideally, a company should enter the market before the growth stage.

The influx of competitors is a general indicator of the transition from stage one to stage two. When this second stage – introduction to market – begins, it is time for the organization to put its product or service into action and start capturing market share. When competitors begin dropping out of the market, the product is either in the maturity stage or is passing maturity and heading to the consolidation and decline stages. This is the time for the company to launch additional products or services in order to reposition the product or service, or it is time to decrease inventory through a price cut and move on.

Growth

The growth stage of this cycle separates the competition. The company with the best product, price, and/or service rises to the top. The establishment of the sport product or service in the market results in an increase in sales and the need to spend money on building the brand. In general, sport services tend to have a longer period of growth as compared to sport products. This is because it is easier for competitors to react to sport products. As a result, the increase in sales and profits will eventually peak as a result of the increased competition. Roller blades were like this. When they were first released, consumer demand spiked. Everyone had to have a pair – and the accessories that went with them – and sales and profits sky-rocketed. Once more competitors entered the market, though, sales of roller blades began to slow, profits dropped, and consequently, prices leveled out.

Maturity

Maturity refers to the time at which the sport product or service has maximized profits and is seeking to maintain a stable place in the market. Competitors have a direct influence on the sport organization's pricing practices, due to both new sport products and services entering the market, and alternative sport products and services being more popular. At this stage, the organization must decide whether to withdraw its product or service from the market, or to make modifications that will continue to maintain the product or service within the market.

If the company desires to maintain a presence in the chosen market, the sport marketing professional, in conjunction with the sport organization, must determine whether it is appropriate to take the risk of over-extending the company's reach. In the maturity stage of the life cycle, the marketer continuously re-evaluates his or her marketing strategy and seeks to determine how much of the market the company can reasonably expect to control. This determination of appropriately choosing whether the sport organization should stay in the market for the long haul will ultimately define the destiny of the sport product or service.

Saturation

Eventually, the sport organization may come to the realization that it needs to re-evaluate the sport product or service life cycle. When the gaining of market share begins to slow, it is usually a sign of market saturation. In turn, market saturation is the first sign that the sport product or service is going to be entering the decline stage. At this point the product or service has little hope of future profits, either because there are too many competitors or because the popularity and interest in the product or service has significantly decreased. ESPN is a good example of this. For a number of years, ESPN was the only national service provider of its kind. Today, though, there are a number of competitors for ESPN's market share, such as Fox Sports Net, NBC Sports Network and many regional sport networks. ESPN has had to try to retake the market by creating other channels including ESPN 2, ESPN News, and ESPN U, and revolutionizing the way programming can be delivered through ESPN 3, in order to maintain its place in sports news and coverage.

Decline

The decline stage is the last stage before obsolescence. At this stage of the cycle, the business should have introduced new services or a next generation of the product. The business that finishes with the most market share gives the company name and brand recognition. With this recognition, it is easier to implement the next generation product or service. The company that gains the largest market share should have the stocks for replacement parts for your product if parts are required. This latter reason can dramatically increase the length of this stage.

The longer the life cycle, the longer a period the company has to acquire market share, make money, and continue research and development. A short life cycle requires more advertising to quickly position the product or service in the market. Sport products and services vary in the speed with which their life cycles are completed. In every case, however, there is no room for mistakes. Slower life cycles allow for traditional advertising and promotion such as print media. Quicker life cycles need an approach such as e-commerce or e-business, which involves the advertising, buying, and selling of goods and services through the internet.

POSITIONING, DIFFERENTIATION, AND BRANDING

Positioning and differentiation are integral processes in the ultimate success or failure of marketing the sport product or service. Positioning is the process of influencing the perceptions of potential and current customers about the image of the company and its products and services. This is accomplished by applying the six Ps of marketing – product, price, place (distribution), promotion, publicity, and understanding people – with the goal of strategically placing the product or service firmly in the mind of the consumer.

Differentiation is creating or offering a similar product or service with the intent to influence demand. This means that a company has developed a strategy of providing a similar product by a competing company to its customers with the claim that its product is better, stronger, faster, or lasts longer than its competitors' products or services. The company hopes that this different offering will better satisfy the needs of its particular customers. Using such a strategy may help reduce the need to compete solely on price.

This strategy could allow the company to differentiate its offerings from larger players and to gain market share and become more effective for its market share. An example of this would be the choice that Chicago baseball fans have. Sport consumers can choose to spend their money on the White Sox who in most years play competitive baseball in a modern stadium, or they can choose to spend their money on the north side where they have not won a World Series since 1908. The Cubs or "lovable losers" have fewer seats, no parking structure, and higher ticket prices. Yet they have differentiated themselves in a city of nearly three million people by selling the folklore and atmosphere of Wrigley Field, the second oldest remaining baseball stadium, and surrounding neighborhoods.

To position and differentiate a sport product or service from others in the marketplace, sport organizations create branding strategies. A brand is a name, term, design, symbol, or feature that identifies one sport product or service as being different from another. A brand can identify a single sport product or service (Celtics) or a group of sport products or services (Nike). Branding is what consumers think of, whether positively or negatively, when they see or hear the name of a sport organization or business. By defining the brand, a foundation is created for all other components of the sport organization to build on. The internet has allowed brand definition to serve as the measuring stick in evaluating the demands of customers by communicating directly with the consumer and bypassing the middleman.

Sport organizations can begin to develop their brand or identity by answering some very simple questions:

- What products and/or services do you offer?
- What are the core values of your company, products, and services?
- What is the mission of your company?
- Who is your target market?
- What is the essence of your company and what message do you think it sends to consumers?

Authored and contributed by Charles Parrish, George Mason University

INTRODUCTION

In Argentina association football dominates the sport marketplace. In spite of the migration of its most talented players to higher paying foreign leagues the appeal of the top level domestic professional league (*Primera A*) transcends social class divisions and generates substantial revenue. In contrast, Rugby Union football in Argentina is a niche middle- and upper-middle-class sport. Although the number of people playing rugby in Argentina is estimated to be over 102,000 (Chadwick, Semens, Schwarz, & Zhang, 2010) the domestic league is a comparatively underdeveloped sport market that has maintained its amateur status for over 110 years. Surprisingly, the country's national rugby team (*Los Pumas*) has performed exceptionally well at recent Rugby World Cups. Further, in 2011 Argentina was admitted into the southern hemisphere's most prestigious international tournament, The Rugby Championship (formerly Tri-Nations). However, the addition of *Los Pumas* was in part contingent on the *Unión Argentina de Rugby* (UAR) further developing the rugby consumer market in Argentina to maintain the tournament's exceptional brand image and maximize revenue for international stakeholders.

RUGBY IN ARGENTINA

Rugby, like association football, was first introduced into Argentina in the late nineteenth century by the British (Mangan, 2002; Ryan, 2008). These particular immigrants established enclave communities with exclusive educational institutions and athletics clubs (Wilson, 2007). It was within these clubs and private schools that rugby (and modern sport in general) took root in Argentina. By the early 1900s association football had gained in popularity as the *criollo* population across the country began participating in and consuming the sport at increasingly high levels (Archetti, 1998, 1999). In contrast, rugby remained a diversion primarily for middle-class Anglo-Argentines and hence did not realize substantial growth within the emerging national popular sport culture (Parrish and Zorilla, 2012). As association football transcended social classes it morphed into *fútbol* and by 1931 the sport was professionalized (Archetti, 1998; Goldblatt, 2006). In the wake of *fútbol's* transformation in style and purpose, the British communities in and around Buenos Aires continued to embrace the sport of rugby (Rodríguez, 2005), which reaffirmed the "games ethic" and maintained their collective identity (Mangan, 1998).

THE DILEMMA

Rugby Union football "officially" remained amateur across the world until the International Rugby Board (IRB) lifted payment restrictions to players in 1995. Media coverage would aid an already surging consumer pattern, spawning a highly commercialized sporting venture for stakeholders (Harris, 2010). However, professionalization has yet to occur in Argentina and it was only recently that the national team was included in a major sanctioned transnational competition beyond the Rugby World Cup.

Currently, the Argentine Rugby Union comprises 25 individual regional unions which promote the sport and organize regionally based competitions and championships. Each regional union is made up of a network of member clubs that field amateur players. The largest and traditionally most successful union in terms of national championships is the Buenos Aires Rugby Union (URBA) (Parrish and Zorilla, 2012).

Given the amateur nature of rugby union in Argentina the country's best players opt for professional contracts abroad. This talent migration impacts upon the quality of rugby being contested in the domestic league and restricts the appeal of the sport for domestic and international audiences. Further, the sport is practiced and consumed primarily by the middle and upper-middle classes in a country where the working class is a significant demographic in the sport consumer market.

In an attempt to increase the number of skilled players beyond the national team talent pool the UAR created the Pampas XV in 2010 (Unión Argentina de Rugby). Team members are awarded modest professional contracts by the UAR and spend part of their "off-season" competing in South Africa's Vodacom Cup tournament. Following the tournament, most of these players return to Argentina to compete for their respective amateur clubs. Many fear this will exacerbate the existing competitive imbalance for the domestic league as nearly half of the 2011 Pampas XV squad competed for teams within the Buenos Aires union.

To mitigate the social class fragmentation rugby faces in the sport consumer market in Argentina, some have suggested aligning rugby with established athletic clubs that sponsor association football teams (among other sports). The goal of the strategy is to tap into the brand of the existing athletic clubs, which enjoy high levels of support across the strata of society. Fan and club reactions to this strategy have been mixed.

Questions for discsussion

1   What types of branding and marketing strategies might the UAR implement to further develop the rugby market in Argentina?
2   Beyond sponsoring the Pampas XV team, how might the UAR and its member regional unions and clubs enhance the actual and perceived quality of the domestic rugby league as a product?
3   Why is the competitive imbalance issue relevant and how might the UAR mitigate the issue? Consider this in terms of positioning and differentiation in the domestic and global marketplace.

By using the information gathered in sports marketing plans, a sport marketing professional can create a personality or essence for a sport organization that can exude anything, including innovation, creativity, energy, and sophistication. This may then be used to build a relationship with the chosen target market that the research has defined. The way in which the targeted sport consumers react to the personality or essence of the sport organization or its products and services will determine if the brand will be successful. Examples of this include footwear makers Nike and Timberland. Nike revamped its website so that the consumer could personalize his or her shoe in real time on screen, allowing customers to alter and/or approve the shoe design before confirming and purchasing the item. Timberland's website encourages each consumer to "build a boot as original as you are." Starting with a work boot silhouette, the consumer can select from a variety of colors and styles to create personalized footwear. This customization builds brand loyalty in today's marketplace.

CONCLUSION

A sport product is something that is produced which is bought or sold in the sporting goods industry. Tangible products are referred to as goods, while intangible products are called services. Intangible products include indirect goods, in which customers have the opportunity to stylize tangible products as they wish. Intangible services involve providing a quality standard work, and are often provided to enhance the experience.

Sport marketing logistics involves identifying your customers, identifying their needs, and combining the company's resources to meet those needs through purchasing and supply chain management. The purchasing process involves offering products and services at a price customers are willing to pay (value), with the goal of creating a long-term relationship between the supplier and the customer. Effective supply chain management involves finding the best suppliers who can respond to needs through an efficient network. The major components of the supply chain management are the strategic plan, sourcing, production, logistics, and returns. One of the major advances in supply chain management for sport marketing is just-in-time manufacturing, where the pay-off of timely and accurate supply chain information equals the ability to make or ship only as much of a product as there is a market for. This has allowed sport organizations to reduce the amount of inventory that they keep and cut costs substantially, since they no longer needed to pay to produce and store excess goods.

Sport product and service management focuses on the approach taken by sport marketers and organizations to define and market their products and services. Sport product and service management usually starts as a function of the sport marketing planning process. This process involves the development of the sport organization's products and services marketing strategies, including the tactics and programs to be implemented during the life span of the plan. It starts by defining the competitive set, which is the process of determining the direct competitors to a sport organization in the specific product or service area. Then the sport organization engages in category attractiveness analysis, in which aggregate marketing factors, segment factors, and environmental factors are considered. This is followed up with competitor and consumer analyses.

The sport product and service life cycle encompasses six stages: internal development, introduction to market, growth, maturity, saturation, and decline. All stages are bound by the realities of competition, saturation, and change. The internal development stage begins with the idea of a new product or service or a new twist on an existing product or service. Introduction to market is the time when the sport organization puts its plan into action and starts capturing market share by introducing products and services to the market. The growth stage is when the organization with the best product, price, and/or service rises to the top and separates itself from the competition. Maturity refers to the time at which the sport product or service has maximized profits and is seeking to maintain a stable place in the market. At saturation point, the sport organization comes to the realization that it needs to re-evaluate the sport product or service life cycle because it is no longer increasing the company's market share. The decline stage is the final stage before obsolescence, and the sport organization should either have introduced new services or a next generation of the product, or it will need to exit the market.

Ultimately, positioning and differentiation are integral processes in the ultimate success or failure of marketing the sport product or service. Positioning is the process of influencing the perceptions of potential and current customers about the image of the company and its products and services. Differentiation is creating or offering a similar product or service with the intent to influence demand. To position and differentiate a sport product or service from others in the marketplace, sport organizations create branding strategies through the use of a name, term, design, symbol, or feature to identify one sport product or service as being different from another.

FROM THEORY TO PRACTICE

TRACY WEST, PRESIDENT
Hayson Sports Group, Inc.,
Concord, Massachusetts

My undergraduate degree is in Finance and Economics and I have a M.B.A. in Marketing from Michigan State. Upon graduation in 1988, I held several positions in Marketing Research, Product Management and Forecasting & Research at a major insurance company and a major office furniture manufacturer.

My family instilled in me a strong sense of community and "giving back." While working at my "corporate" jobs, I became involved in the Grand Rapids Jaycees in Michigan volunteering for several community projects. One of those projects was the SENIOR PGA TOUR professional golf tournament which the Jaycees owned and operated. I had the privilege of volunteering for that tournament for three years in various corporate hospitality and media functions. The group of Jaycees that managed the event was a small, tight-knit group of friends. Each of those individuals had a successful career and was busy "climbing the corporate ladder," but also made the commitment to volunteer many hours a week in management of the tournament. The experience we each gained from doing so was invaluable. We were all fairly young but here we were running a multi-million-dollar professional sporting event in our "off-time." The challenges we faced directly correlated into wonderful learning experiences which then had a direct impact on our careers moving forward. Many of us enjoyed managing the tournament more than our current jobs because by operating the tournament as a group, we were exposed to all facets of business management much quicker than in the limitations of a one-dimensional position in a large corporation.

Being talented does not always lead you to your perfect career in life . . . many times it is all about timing. While working at the 1991 tournament in Grand Rapids, I had the great fortune of meeting the current Tournament Director for a new SENIOR PGA TOUR event in Minneapolis. He was at our tournament reviewing the good things we did at that event and searching for an Assistant Tournament Director to help him begin the tournament in Minneapolis. Knowing he was coming to our tournament, I sent him my résumé prior to his trip. We literally spent about 15 minutes together interviewing during event week in between all the normal event chaos. The following Monday morning he made me an offer to come to Minneapolis, which I promptly accepted. I knew that I was leaving a more financially rewarding and comfortable position at my Fortune 500 Company, but many times in life you need to take a step back financially to make a hopeful leap forward. In addition, to me it is more important to spend your life doing something that you enjoy . . . you will hopefully never then think of yourself at a "job" but at a career. In addition, by accepting the position in Minneapolis, I knew that I would be raising money for charity. What a better way to go through life!

The first tournament in Minneapolis was an operational and financial success. The SENIOR PGA TOUR staff were thrilled with our team's performance. Over a drink in the Rules Office on Sunday night after the tournament was over, one of the Rules officials remarked that he wished our team managed more of the events on the Tour. A light bulb went off and the Tournament Director and I, along with a few other partners, formed our first company, Pro Links Sports, within the next two months. A month after that, we landed the management contract for the 1996 U.S. Senior Open. We went on to become the most successful management company on the SENIOR PGA TOUR (now PGA TOUR's Champions Tour) operating, at various times, eight Champions Tour events and three U.S. Senior Opens. One of those tournaments was the Champions Tour event in Boston, of which I specifically became Tournament Director in 1999.

In 2004, I formed my own professional golf and events management company, Hayson Sports Group, and continue to operate the Boston event while pursuing other professional golf management opportunities.

There are obviously a multitude of important skills necessary for success in the sport marketing and management field and in operating a professional sporting competition. However, the first and foremost thing to remember is that a professional sport is truly just a standard business. Just because it is a professional sport does not mean that you do not need to remember all your basic business skills and apply them appropriately to your unique setting. The other important item of note is not to have the fantasy that professional sport is always glamorous. The majority of people who work in this industry work long, hard hours in behind-the-scenes operations and rarely have any direct contact with professional athletes.

A professional golf tournament is more unique than most other professional sports in the lack of control you really have over your final product. You have to recruit your product (the players) as they are independent contractors, not part of a team. You have to recruit and retrain your "staff" each year (the volunteers). Your customers range from US$20 (standard ticketholder) to multi-million dollars (title sponsors). You do not have a stadium in which to host your sport . . . you must rebuild your "arena" each year (bleachers, hospitality tents, restrooms, concessions, etc.) and your business is dramatically impacted by Mother Nature. All combined, it can be quite daunting to host a professional golf tournament.

The first message I would send to future sport marketing professionals is to make them realize that ethical issues arise in professional sports management just as they do in all other industries. Buyers have the opportunity to take kick-backs. Accountants have the opportunity to cook the books. The key to remember is that, in the end, all you have is your good name and your word. These should be protected no matter what industry you work in.

The second message is related to the importance of positioning and differentiation in the marketplace. One of the most important things you can do to have your business succeed is to be sure you have a tangible way to differentiate your product from that of your competitors. The Champions Tour is the most fan-friendly, interactive professional sport. Each Champions Tour event strives to provide opportunities for fans to interact with the pro golfers via clinics, autograph sessions, player panel discussions, and walking inside the ropes with pro groups. However, it is not only important to have these distinctions with your product; you must communicate them to your potential customers. At the Champions Tour event which we manage, this communication is a constant focus of our staff with our work through multiple media channels, our volunteers, and our corporate partners. We view our existing volunteers, fan, and corporate partners as our best spokespersons in the marketplace and work diligently with those groups to spread the good word about our tournament.

CHAPTER SEVEN

SALES MANAGEMENT IN SPORT

CHAPTER OUTLINE

- What is sport sales management?
- The sport sales organization
- The sport buying process
- The sport sales process
- Non-store-based inventories for sales in sport
- Conclusion

CHAPTER OBJECTIVES

The reader will be able to:

- understand the characteristics of sport sales, and the relationship between sport sales and sport marketing in sport
- appreciate the complexity of the sport organization, including design, management, and human capital
- recognize the stages of the buying and selling processes
- understand the steps involved with managing a sport sales force, and the complexity involved with training, determining sales territories, forecasting sales, budgeting and setting quotas, and motivating, leading, evaluating, and compensating the sales force within ethical and legal boundaries
- comprehend the distinctiveness of sport sales as related to advertising, naming rights, sponsorships, and ticket sales.

WHAT IS SPORT SALES MANAGEMENT?

Sport sales management is the process of directing and controlling those responsible for selling sport products and services (sales force), and achieving the desired level of exchanges between the sport organization and sport consumers. Integral to sport sales management is the ability to understand multiple levels of the sales environment including the role of salespeople, the tasks of sales managers, and the complexity of the design, management, and human capital within the sport organization.

Sales involves the multiple stages of the buying and selling processes. Sales management involves directing and controlling the sales force, including sales training, determining sales territories, forecasting sales, budgeting and setting quotas, and motivating, leading, evaluating, and compensating the sales force within ethical and legal boundaries. In sport sales management, there are distinctive inventories that are sold including advertising, naming rights, sponsorships, and ticket sales.

The relationship between sales management and sport marketing is significant in a number of ways. Within the sport marketing decision-making process, the development of goals and objectives often centers on sales processes. When targeting sport consumers, one of the components of the marketing mix to be considered is price – the price at which a sport product or service is to be sold. By offering the desired sport product or service at the appropriate price through proper channels of distribution, and implementing promotional efforts that create positive image and increase awareness, the exchange process of sales will be enhanced and the likelihood of a customer going to a competitor to make a purchase diminished.

THE SPORT SALES ORGANIZATION

The sport sales organization is made up of three components. Organizational design in sport sales focuses on how the buying and selling process is implemented. The key in organizational design is to create a buying and selling process that takes into consideration sport products and services available for sales, the most effective exchange process to entice the sport consumer to make a purchase, the most efficient methods for delivering the sport product or service to the sport consumer based on geographic location (local, regional, national, international, and global), and to integrate functional processes within the sport organization that allow for maximizing sales. These functional processes focus on the other two components of the sport sales organization – sales managers and salespersons.

Sales managers

A sales manager is responsible for many functions within the sales organization. From a financial and economic standpoint, the sales manager develops sales plans and budgets, creates objectives and quotas, estimates demands, and develops sales forecasts. Managerially, the sales manager determines the number of salespersons needed, and then recruits, hires, trains, leads, and evaluates the sales force. The sales manager is also responsible for developing and administering compensation models, incentive programs, and bonus packages.

162

This interrelationship of planning, organizing, guiding, monitoring, administering, and staffing is integral to the sales manager's ability to effectively direct the day-to-day operations of the exchange function within a sport organization. The sales manager must have a broad view of the entire organization, and understand how each function directly affects sales. This is especially true with the sport marketing function, since it directly relates to the communication process between the sport organization and sport consumers.

To accomplish this, the sport sales manager must develop a sales force that meets the goals and objectives of the sport organization. Since many goals are driven by profit, and sales are the primary revenue function of a sport organization, the effectiveness of the sales manager is of further importance. In addition, the increased revenue and success of the sales function is integral to moving the sport organization forward toward reaching the vision most sport organizations have – growth and maturity.

There are a number of skills and attributes that a sport sales manager must have to be successful. As with most positions within a sport organization, the ability to effectively communicate with all functional areas is crucial to success. If the sales force does not understand the goals and objectives of the sport organization, or does not know the sport product or service being sold, then the downward communication process from manager to employee is not working. In addition, if the sales manager does not communicate with the other functions within the sport organization, or does not work with upper management to recognize what is important to the sport organization, the upward communication process is failing.

The best sales managers are also leaders of the organization. They influence the sales force to complete objectives, accomplish goals, and exceed expectations. Some of the attributes of a quality sales manager include being flexible as a result of the ever-changing sales environment, and remaining persistent and resilient to road-blocks in the sales process. The sales manager also needs to show empathy toward the sales force and sport consumers in understanding problems, needs, desires, and wants. This will result in happier staff and customers. Finally, the sales manager must show integrity and honesty, both important in developing trust among all within the sales process.

Sport marketing is involved with the internal and external environments of a sport organization. Invariably, the sales function must also deal with both environments. The role of the sport sales manager is to be the intermediary between the two environments. Internally, the sport sales manager has to have a grasp on the organizational behavior present within the cultural, political and social structures of the sport organization. The sport sales manager must also be able to scan and understand the multifaceted and complex external environment, including the competitive climate, political and legal influences, economic and socio-demographic situations, technological advances, and sport consumer behavior.

Sales managers serve as an integral part of the sales system. They decipher the marketing strategies set by sport marketing professionals and organizational management based on the available marketing mix. The sales manager then translates those strategies in terms the sales force can utilize in making sales. The sales manager also directs and controls the sales force to maintain necessary levels of sales volume and mix. Ultimately, the sales manager is responsible for the financial performance of the sport organization, including maintaining positive levels of growth, market share, and net profits.

Salespeople

The goal of any sport sales manager is to recruit, train, and hire the most competent sales staff possible. But what makes a good salesperson? Someone who is intelligent and knowledgeable? Flexible yet persistent? Self-motivated, disciplined, and dependable? Creative? Personable? It is all of these qualities and much more that make up a quality salesperson.

Many studies have been conducted to determine the most predominant skills that successful salespersons have. In general, they are centered on five skills sets – communication, logic/critical thinking, organization, time management, and knowledge. Communication skills are the set of abilities that allow an individual to convey information that can be received and understood by another individual. This is crucial for sport salespeople because the way they communicate can make the difference between making a sale (success) or not (failure). The first minute of an encounter between a salesperson and a potential customer is critical. The tone of voice, body signals, eye contact, and positive attitude are all vital to beginning the sales process. After that, being able to provide information in a concise yet complete manner educates the potential buyer about the attributes of the sport product or service. Finally, knowing when to stop talking, listen to the potential customer, answer questions, and eventually make the pitch to close the sale comes with experience and learning how to read the customer.

Analytical skills involve logical and critical thinking to understand the needs, wants, and desires of the sport consumer. Knowing the problem or issue at hand is only half of the process; knowing how to resolve the problem and answer the questions provides the sport consumers with the information they need to make an informed decision about purchasing the sport product or service.

Organizational skills apply to planning and managing the sport product and service information in an efficient and effective manner. Sport salespeople often deal with multiple sport products and services. For example, ticket inventory can range from individual game tickets to group tickets, to partial plans to season tickets, and vary in costs based on quantity or location. The sport salesperson must have the ability to keep this information organized by offering it in an easy and usable format so that he or she can service the customer quickly and accurately.

Time management skills refer to the ability control time. In general, the salesperson spends a limited amount of time with a customer. The way in which that time is used is crucial to the decision-making process of the buyer. Earlier in the book we discussed the Pareto Principle, or the 80/20 rule, where 80 percent of a sport organization's business comes from 20 percent of its customers. Salespeople learn to spend more time with individuals to maintain the relationships; however, they cannot forget about the other 80 percent, as they represent future potential sales.

Knowledge skills are the collection, gathering, organizing, and sharing of information. The knowledgeable salesperson will be able to answer most of the questions from potential and existing sport customers. This knowledge includes knowing the sport product and service being sold, understanding the sport consumer, and having an intimate awareness of the industry, the competition, and the company itself.

Managing the sport sales force

The managing of a sales force for a sport organization is an elaborate process that starts with the recruitment, selection, and training of salespeople. When training salespeople, it is important that they have a significant knowledge about the company, their customers and products, the industry in which the company operates, and the competition present. In addition, training should focus on selling skills. New salespeople may have a range of selling skills – from none at all to expertise gained in previous employment. Regardless, the sales manager is responsible for ensuring that the salesperson has the selling skills required for the individual organization. These skills are most often taught through on-the-job training and job shadowing. Some organizations will also utilize classroom training, role playing, case studies, and experiential exercises to articulate the desired selling skills to salespeople.

It is important that the sales manager communicates a clear purpose for the selling methods utilized, and motivates them to succeed. Practice and repetition are the most important methods for improvement, and reinforcement provided by the sales manager helps keep the salesperson on task. The sales manager may also use incentives to entice salespeople to reach predetermined levels of productivity. However, it is important to remember that those sales goals need to be realistic, as setting the bar too high is a recipe for disaster and failure.

The sales manager is a crucial part of the evolution of the sales force by developing sales territories, forecasting the potential to sell sport products or services, and creating the resulting budgets and quota parameters for salespeople to work within. Throughout this process, the sales manager motivates and leads the sales force, and designs appropriate compensation programs based on their evaluation of salespeople.

One of the most challenging jobs for the sport sales manager is forecasting. The prediction of how sport consumers will make purchases in the future (whether tomorrow, next week, next month, or next year) is a function of a number of environmental factors. Obviously, changes in the level of competition within the target market will create change (either positive or negative) in sales opportunities (less competition = potential for increased sales; more competition = potential for a decrease in sales). The changes in the marketplace, both in consumer and industrial demand, will have a direct effect on sales. An increased demand has the potential to increase sales, while a decreased demand will probably result in a decrease in sales. In addition, there are leading business indicators published by the government and independent firms that state current market conditions, and estimate the future potential of that market. Examples of these business indicators used in sport business include reports published by the National Sporting Goods Association (www.nsga.org) and the Sport Business Research Network (www.sbrnet.com).

Planning, coordinating, and controlling the sales budget is also an important factor in managing a sales force. By estimating the costs of selling sport products and services, integrating that information with other important functions within the sport organization, and setting benchmarks that are achievable and cost-effective, the sales force can maximize their efforts. These benchmarks are often reported to the sales force in terms of quotas. A quota is a number or percentage that constitutes an upper limit (such as maximum inventory available), or in most cases for sales, a targeted minimum. The sales quota is utilized to provide goals for sales-persons, maintain control of sales activity and expenses, serve as an incentive for improved compensation for salespersons, and may also be utilized to evaluate the performance of salespersons. Sport sales quotas take many forms including sales volume, dollar vs. unit sales, financial quotas, and activity quotas. Sales volume refers to the amount of inventory sold. Dollars vs. unit sales deals with how much money has been brought in compared to the number of unit of inventory that has gone out. This is often used in ticket sales where there is an inventory of seats in an arena, but seats have different prices based on location, type of purchase (individual vs. season), and quantity (group discounts). Financial quotas require reaching certain dollar levels of sales. Activity quotas require reaching certain volumes of sales such as minimum numbers of sales calls, services calls, advertisement sales, or new accounts established. Regardless of the quota, it is important that the sales manager sets realistic quotas that salespersons can reach, and that the quotas are understood by all salespeople. If there is confusion, or if the quotas are perceived to be unachievable, the sales force will be resigned to failure.

This is where motivation and leadership become crucial components of managing a sales force. Motivation is the influence that initiates the drive to satisfy wants and needs. Motivating a sales force involves inspiring individual salespersons to move to action. Motivation can be intangible (praise, recognition) or tangible (bonus, salary raises). Leadership is the ability to influence a follower. The sales manager serves an important role in influencing salespeople to reach the specified goals. According to Sam Walton (Wal-Mart), "Outstanding leaders go out of their way to boost the self-esteem of their personnel. If people believe in themselves, it is amazing what they can accomplish."

In American culture, compensation is the single most important motivator for salespeople. Financial compensation in sales can be salary based, commission based, or a combination of the two. Other types of compensation can be additional benefits including medical, dental, sick and vacation time, and retirement accounts. The sales manager has the most control over the financial compensation of the sales force. While it is the goal of the salesperson to reach quotas and secure incentives, it is the job of the sales manager to motivate, lead, and evaluate the salesperson. The evaluation process usually includes such factors as quantity of sales, relationship with customers and colleagues within the company, and the sales skills possessed and utilized by the salesperson. The better the salesperson, the more salary, commission, and other incentives he or she will receive. In a way, sales are very much like sports in general – competition and cooperation. While the entire sales force is cooperating to sell on behalf of the sport organization to improve its place in the market, they are competing against each other and toward the quotas set to make additional compensation, gain recognition as a top salesperson, and in some cases retain their jobs.

THE SPORT BUYING PROCESS

The roles of the sales manager, the salesperson, and their cooperation in operating as a sales force are vital to the sport buying and selling processes. Many sport sales managers focus solely on the selling process without consideration for the buying process. However, sport marketing professionals understand that in order to be successful in sales, one must understand how consumers buy their products. The sport buying process is the steps involved in reaching a decision to make a purchase – including identifying the need, searching for products or services

166

which satisfied that need, evaluating options, making a decision, purchasing the product or service, and eventually re-evaluating the decision to determine whether to make the same purchase again or to change.

The way in which sport consumers make decisions was discussed in detail in Chapter 5 about sport consumer behavior. It is important to realize that the way in which the sport consumer makes a decision about a sport product or service will directly affect the way in which a sale is managed. For those decisions and needs that are simple in nature, all that needs to be accomplished by the salesperson is to make the sport consumers more aware of the sport product or service; build their confidence that the decision they are about to make is correct; supplement that with information that differentiates the sport product or service from others, and provides value to the sport consumer; and guide them through the purchase. For more complex decisions, the salesperson is increasing awareness, building relationships, educating the sport consumer, differentiating the product or service, resolving conflicts for the sport consumer, and customizing the purchasing process to make it as easy as possible (and impossible for the potential sport consumer to refuse!).

To understand the type of decision that is being made by the sport consumer, the salesperson must recognize the four main types of customers. The first is the perfect sport customer who already knows the sport product or services he or she wishes to purchase – right down to the features, brands, colors, and even model number. The job of the salesperson is to get that sport product or provide the sport service as quickly as possible because if it takes too long, the customer will move on to a competitor. Next is the sport shopper. These customers know that they need something, but they are still in the process of narrowing down their choices. The salesperson needs to provide important information about the sport product or service, articulate the benefits, and persuade the customer that this purchase is the logical choice. The sport browser is just looking around at the sport products and services available with no plan to purchase. However, these individuals tend to be impulse buyers – willing to make a purchase if they find something that interests them or are persuaded that they need the sport product or service. The salesperson needs to be more conversational and engaging, seeking to determine the interests of the customer, and finding those sport products and services that match the interest with the hopes of enticing that impulse purchase. The sport non-customer is lost or not interested in the sport products or services being offered. The salesperson needs to make an effort to engage these customers to determine if there is a possibility to convert them into buyers. If not, the salesperson needs to move on to potential buyers. In understanding the customers, the salesperson gets a view of the world from the buyer's point of view. Through this understanding, the sport salesperson can learn how to address that point of view within the selling process.

THE SPORT SALES PROCESS

The sport sales process focuses on taking the sport products and services available for sale, and developing the best methods for luring the sport consumer to make a purchase. Sport sales is a six-step process that includes prospecting for customers, developing the method for communicating with the sport consumer, making actual contact, sending the message through a "sales presentation," closing the sale, and servicing after the sale is complete.

Prospecting for customers

Prospecting is the process of identifying potential customers to purchase products and services. Probably the most difficult job for a salesperson is to find new customers. This is because it does not matter how well salespeople know their product or service, if they do not have a qualified prospect to sell it to, there is no sale. Prospecting involves two main components – identifying the needs and wants of potential customers, and determining those individuals who make the actual buying decisions. The second component is often more difficult as a result of individuals being in different life stages. Teenagers often influence and ultimately force the buying decisions of their parents, while in other family units the type of product or service will directly affect who makes the buying decision.

Prospecting requires practice. Those salespeople who prospect on a daily basis will get more leads. A good sports salesperson puts aside time every day to prospect via phone, email, and in person. Part of that practice is to be prepared. This will include having a script and reviewing that information so that it becomes second nature. Potential customers do not wish to hear a robot speaking in a monotone and delivering what is exactly on the paper. Potential customers also do not want to hear a person who is unprepared and fumbling their message. A quality script that is practiced and delivered clearly will result in the ability of the salesperson to engage and gather information from the potential customer. It is also important to remember that the salesperson should also be organized and take good mental or written notes once he or she engages a potential customer. By showing more intimate knowledge of sport consumers' needs, the salesperson will have a better chance of enticing them into a purchase.

Determining communication method

Once the customers have been identified, the salesperson must choose the type of communication method to use in order to build relationships with customers. Communication can be both verbal and non-verbal. Verbally, it can be part of asking open-ended questions, or part of stating a message about a sport product or service and seeking a response from the potential customer. Non-verbally, it can be the listening process, absorbing feedback from customers and using that information to develop more effective plans for selling the sport product or service.

It is important that when communicating with a potential customer, the salesperson must recognize that purchases are made for emotional reasons as related to the benefits perceived or received by the customer. Therefore it is conceivable that regardless of the sport products and services being sold, the manner in which salespersons sell themselves and the emotional reaction from the customer in relation to the salesperson is crucial in the communication process of sport sales management.

Therefore, a salesperson must be able to recognize the emotional needs of the sport consumer through this initial communication process. These emotional needs run the gambit, including saving money, saving time, increasing enjoyment, increasing social opportunities, satisfying a desire, or showing one's individualism and uniqueness. Through this filtering process, the salesperson must determine the emotional need that has to be addressed, and direct the consumer toward products and services that will meet his or her need.

Making contact and the pitch

Once the communication methods are understood, it is time to actually contact the potential customer. Prior to that contact, the salesperson should establish sales objectives that provide measurable, quantifiable, and understandable information to the potential customer. In conjunction with their prospecting efforts, salespeople develop objectives that will offer the greatest benefit to the potential customer. The actual engagement of a potential customer centers on three main concepts – professionalism, goodwill, and confidence. The result of understanding and effectively utilizing tactics that enhance these three concepts is crucial to increasing the probability of a sale.

Once a plan for the initial contact with a sport consumer is completed, it is time to make the pitch. A sales pitch is where the salesperson outlines and explains the benefits of a product or service to a potential customer in order to stimulate interest and motivate the customer to make a purchase. There are numerous different approaches a salesperson can take when pitching a sale to a potential or returning customer. Table 7.1 describes some approaches used to entice an individual to purchase season tickets.

Table 7.1 Approaches used to entice an individual to purchase season tickets

Approach	Example
Benefits	As a season ticket holder, you will also be eligible to attend special season ticket holder-only events such as after-game parties, team meet-and-greet sessions, and a pre-season kick-off dinner.
Compliment	Let me tell you why a person of your stature in the community will benefit from being a season ticket holder . . .
Introductory	Hi, I am Bob Smith from the Merrimack Marauders football team here for my 3 p.m. appointment to discuss a potential partnership between our organizations.
Product/service	Let me give you a tour of the arena and show you exactly where you would be sitting if you were to purchase these season tickets.
Question	What are the benefits you feel are important in association with purchasing season tickets with our organization?
Reference	Your friend John Smith has season tickets; we can sit you right next to him.
Sample	Be our guest at today's game so you can experience the excitement.

The method of delivery of the pitch may differ – from email to phone to mail to television or in person. The focus of the pitch may also vary based on the type of sport product or service being sold, the knowledge of the consumer, the benefits being offered, and the sales objectives of the organization. However, the attitude when approaching the sport consumer must be the same regardless. There is an expression, "You never get a second chance to make a first impression." This is especially true in sales management. A salesperson meeting a customer in person should be appropriately dressed, be neat and well-groomed, have an appearance of confidence without being cocky, and maintain eye contact. Those who communicate a sales pitch via telephone should speak clearly, use appropriate language that can be easily understood, and show confidence through practicing the pitch and delivering it in a conversational style. A sales pitch offered through email, mail, or other written means should be grammatically correct, without spelling errors, be concise, present pertinent information, and provide contact information so that the potential customer can contact the organization for more information.

Closing the sale

Once salespeople have made their pitch, their focus shifts to closing the sale. There are a number of factors that must be considered during this phase of the sales process. The potential customer will probably have questions and comments regarding the pitch and the product/service. The salesperson must learn to listen and read the individual, and often try to put him- or herself in the shoes of the customer. Since most salespeople have high sales goals, they should learn not to accept the first "no" from the customer. Try to clarify points from the sales pitch and provide any additional information that might complete the picture for customers and entice them to make a purchase. Regardless of the time this process takes or the resulting outcome, the salesperson must always maintain a positive attitude and be professional. Even if there is no sale, there is always the potential that customers will return if they are not satisfied elsewhere, or if they need another product or service offered by the organization.

As a result of the closing process, there are two main factors: handling objections, and the proper timing for closing the sale. Closing is when the customer has signed on the dotted line, or reached a final decision to make the purchase. However, it is not always this straight-forward. Another major factor a salesperson must deal with is handling objections. Some objections might include "I do not think this is right for me"; "I cannot afford this"; or "I am not familiar with that brand." The salesperson must not respond to objections too quickly. Providing misinformation, educated guesses, or too much information/too many answers can put off the potential customer. In addition, the salesperson should not get frustrated by arguing with the customer or displaying a doubt that the sale will never be completed. Patience and precise information are the main concepts that can overcome objections to a sale.

When timing the closing of a sale, there are a number of subtle comments that might be made by the prospect that sends a signal to the salesperson that customers are ready to make a decision one way or another. Some of these signals include the following:

- They make a positive comment such as "I really like this [product or service]!"
- They ask about the price.
- They ask about incentives.
- They physically handle the product, test or try the product, or ask for a pen when reading an order form for a product or service.
- They have a more positive tone than earlier in the conversation.

Servicing after the sale

Many would argue that servicing after the sale is the most important stage in the selling process. The concept of servicing involves providing work or a duty to a customer in response to a need or demand. Throughout the sales process, the salesperson is building a relationship and helping the buyer make a purchase decision. Once the purchase is made, the interaction is over unless there is adequate servicing after the sale. The majority of the sales process focuses on an individual sale. The servicing process seeks to persuade a repeat or additional purchase by those who made a purchase. It also serves to retain those who did not make an initial purchase in order to entice them into another purchase. Therefore, regardless of initial success or failure, the salesperson has a responsibility in servicing after the sale.

For those individuals who did make a purchase, there are a number of problems that may occur that are beyond the salesperson's control, and could turn a good sales experience into a bad one. Some examples would include: if the price goes down shortly after purchase; the delivery of the product or service is late; for an installation of a product, it is done incorrectly or with damage caused; or frustration because there was insufficient training provided to operate the product. When handling such issues, the salesperson should encourage the customer to provide as much information about the issue as possible. Then, the salesperson must often weed through the information provided to find out what information is fact, and what information is extraneous to the problem. Next, the salesperson should attempt to find a solution to the problem. Solutions to the above-mentioned problems could include: a store or company credit in the amount of the difference between the originally paid price and the new price (entices a repeat purchase); give a discount or credit back to the customer as an apology for the late delivery; pay for damage repairs and offer a discount on the customer's next purchase; or provide the training the salesperson needs on the sales floor.

The goal of servicing after the sale, and in fact throughout the sales process, is centered on overall customer service. Customer service is the behaviors exhibited by salespeople during their interactions with customers, including the general assistance provided before and after the sale. Salespeople who offer the best customer service do so because:

- They know their products and services and can answer any question posed by the customer.
- They know their customers so that service can be customized based on their needs and wants.
- They have a commitment to offering quality service by creating a positive experience for the customer, under-promising, and over-delivering.
- They have a positive attitude and treat people with courtesy and respect.
- They realize that the customer is the most important part of the selling process. Regardless of whether the salesperson feels that the customer is out of line or stretching the truth, he or she must never argue with the customer, never ignore the customer, and assume the customer is telling the truth.
- They always provide what is promised, or offer compensation if unable to deliver on the promise.
- They work to make the sales process as easy as possible.
- Most importantly, they focus on building a relationship with the customer, not just making money.

NON-STORE-BASED INVENTORIES FOR SALES IN SPORT

Electronic sport sales

The internet is the fastest growing conduit for connecting consumers to retailers. The purpose of electronic sport retailing is to generate additional sales by expanding the geographic reach from local → regional → national → international → global. The goal is also to create a presence and enhance the ever-increasing internet market. This is accomplished by providing information to consumers in a user-friendly manner through email and "point and click" links that are easy to follow.

The scope of electronic sales is growing exponentially around the globe, and sport retailing is right in the middle of that trend with the sale of merchandise and tickets, among many sport retail products. People use the internet to search for information about products they may not otherwise find in the retail outlet. Often while searching for that information, sport consumers are attracted to the selection available. In turn, because of the lower price (which is often discounted on the internet due to reduced infrastructure needed) and the convenience of ordering from his or her own home, the average person makes five internet purchases per year. The major fear in electronic sport sales is an issue of trust and security, especially in the areas of inputting financial data on the internet and shipping information not always being posted in the website. In general, these problems have been addressed adequately, but there are those who still will not purchase over the internet because they want to talk to a salesperson and/or see/touch/feel the sport product in their hands.

Direct sport marketing

Direct sport marketing is a variety of sport retailing in which the sport consumer is first exposed to a sport product through a non-personal medium such as a catalog, television commercial or infomercial, then orders the sport product by mail, phone, fax, or internet. As a result of this type of purchase behavior, direct sport marketers must initiate the contact with the sport consumer. Therefore, it is crucial that a comprehensive database be kept to collect relevant information about customers for use in future marketing efforts. The sport products offered through direct sport marketing may be specialized in nature, or may represent the entire gambit of sport product offerings.

Ticket sales

Ticket sales is not only the most prominent entry-level position for individuals entering the field of sport management, but it is the most important function within most professional sport organizations. The reason? It produces a significant percentage of revenue for the organization. Ticket prices are determined by a number of variables including: number of seats, socio-economics, media revenue, facility demographics, sponsorships, fan base, and opponents, to name a few. Offering a wide range of ticket prices and ticket packages will appeal to the greatest number of people.

CASE STUDY 7: SELLING TICKETS: ASKING QUESTIONS TO IDENTIFY NEEDS AND PRESENT MEANINGFUL SOLUTIONS

Authored and contributed by David Pierce and James Johnson, Ball State University

In traditional selling, products and services are sold as commodities. With similar products that can be purchased at a nearby competing retailer, salespeople utilize a product-focused sales approach emphasizing the product and its benefits, features, and quality. The unique nature of the sport product yields itself better to a customer-focused sales approach, focusing on the identification of the customers' needs and how the product will benefit or add value for them. The salesperson is an expert consultant helping customers to find a solution, rather than trying to convince them to buy something they may not need or want.

People make purchases in order to bridge the "gap" between where they are without the purchase and where they want to be after making the purchase. Sport marketing researchers have spent over 25 years attempting to identify these "gaps," which are the emotional, social, psychological, and financial reasons why people purchase the sport product. Effective salespeople ask probing questions to identify the reasons why the prospect purchases tickets and then mold their sales pitch around that reason, explaining how purchasing tickets can bridge the "gap." In the same way a doctor should not write a prescription for a patient prior to making a diagnosis, a salesperson should not pitch product features and benefits without asking questions in order to determine relevant facts, feelings, needs, and concerns. Most salespeople stay in probing mode for at least half of the sales call or appointment.

SALES SCENARIO

You are an account executive for an AA-level minor league baseball team responsible for selling season ticket packages to individuals. Packages include flexible packages of 12, 17, and 35 games, in addition to a full season package of 70 games. There are many promotional nights throughout the season, including Monday autograph days, thirsty Tuesdays where certain beers are US$1, Wednesday dollar nights where select concessions items are US$1, firework nights on weekends during the summer months, and a variety of promotional acts throughout the season. The stadium was built in 2010 and contains all modern amenities, including inflatable games for kids, batting cages, lawn seating, and picnic areas.

Questions for disscussion

1   List five possible reasons why people are motivated to purchase tickets and attend minor league baseball games.
2   Using your customer relationship management system, you learned that 25-year-old James lives one mile from the stadium and attended seven games on Tuesday last year. All purchases were made online at least two days in advance of the game.

173

While selling tickets is not in the spotlight as compared to other functions, the individual wishing to work his or her way up in sport marketing must usually start in ticket sales. This is because the sales function is viewed as the most fundamental function of marketing. If an individual can sell the organization, he or she will understand how to communicate with the customer. As a result, sport organizations will often take on individuals who have proven to be good salespeople, and then move them into other aspects of sport marketing.

The unfortunate part of ticket sales is that there is often a negative connotation attached to the position. Some of the comments often made about tickets sales include "It is beneath me"; "I do not like rejection"; "Sales is not a prestigious position as compared to marketing, community relations, or media relations"; and "Ticket sales is the worst position in a sport organization." All of these perceptions are untrue. Ticket sales is not beneath anyone; it is a foundation of marketing. Rejection is part of all aspects of marketing – it just has the potential of happening more often because the ticket salesperson deals with a larger number of people. By percentage, it is probably no different from the rejection percentage of a marketing professional trying to sell advertisements, a sponsorship coordinator trying to secure a potential business partner, or even a general manager trying to negotiate with a player. The only reason ticket sales are not viewed as a prestigious position is because it is often done behind the scenes with little external recognition. And as far as its being the worst position within the organization, the truth is that it is one of the most important from a revenue standpoint.

The other important aspect of ticket sales is the diverse inventory available for sale. While the salesperson often has a cap on how many seats are available for sale (there are only so many in the facility), the inventory is made up of a number of categories. The most prevalent ticket inventory is season ticket equivalencies, which make up approximately 50 percent of tickets sold. These are the combination of season tickets sold and partial season ticket packages. Another 25 percent of sales come from advanced ticket sales – individuals who purchase tickets prior to the day of the event. The remaining tickets come from group sales, walk-up sales on the day of the event, and specialty seating. Specialty seating includes:

1 Club seats with access to the private restaurant:

▪ Premium Club at the TD Garden in Boston: http://www.tdgarden.com/premium/index.html

2   Executive suites and club box luxury seats with catered food service:

- FedEx Forum in Memphis: http://www.fedexforum.com/pages/buy_tickets/premium_seats.aspx
- Manchester United Match Day VIP Europa Program: http://www.matchdayvip.manutd.com/en/MatchdayVIPPackages/Europa.aspx

There are four major strategies utilized in ticket sales management. The most basic is database management, where the ticket salesperson develops an organized collection of demographic, geographic, and other personal data (usually through a computerized program), and uses that information to maximize sales efforts. The sport salesperson uses this information to send direct mail and email, make phone calls, and during personal selling opportunities to generate sales.

Associated with database marketing is a concept called benefit sales. Data are often collected that show the reason why an individual does not wish to make a purchase. Benefit selling involves the creation of new opportunities, conditions, or perks that will counteract objections a potential customer may have about a product or service, and offer additional value to the consumer. An example of this is used in mini-ticket plans offered by most professional teams. There are always games that everyone wants to see because the opponent may be a rival or contender, or have a star player whom many want to see. There are other games where it would be difficult to sell out because of perceived inferior competition. So teams package a collection of "good" games and "bad games" to provide a benefit. Thus the Boston Red Sox might package an Oakland Athletics or Kansas City Royals game with a New York Yankees or Tampa Bay Rays. The fan might not purchase the Athletics or Royals game on its own, but the benefit of also being able to go to a Yankees or Rays game makes it a worthwhile purchase.

Upselling is directly associated with the "escalator concept" discussed in Chapter 2. The goal is to move customers from less profitable products or services in a specific category to either a more profitable one in the same category, or into another, more profitable category. One example of movement within a category would be moving a single game ticket holder to a mini-plan of 5, 10 or 20 games, depending on the sport and interest of the customer. An example of moving an individual into another, more profitable category would be a mini-plan ticket holder who has an interest in moving up into a shared corporate box and spending some money in advertising with the team. The key is to create a marketing plan or atmosphere for everyone from the US$8.00 sunburnt bleacher bum to the US$500,000 air-conditioned corporate box. Everyone wants to feel special in some shape or form.

Aftermarketing is a visionary sales process that encourages salespeople to communicate and service the sport ticket holders after the purchase is completed. Retaining a customer is significantly cheaper, easier, and less time consuming than starting from scratch. This is accomplished by the sport salesperson following consumer utilization and satisfaction periodically through regular communication. By addressing issues quickly, and showing genuine interest in the needs and wants of consumers throughout their involvement, the likelihood of continued association with the sport organization is greatly increased.

Sport ticket sales is a unique aspect of sport sales management because aspects such as team performance and awareness, weather, problems with facilities, and the economy are beyond the control of the salesperson. However, the number of contacts made, networks created, and relationships built are controllable and will have a direct effect on the level of success of a ticket salesperson. Referrals are crucial to initiating relationships; renewals are equally vital to continued relationships.

Sport ticket sales are a volume business – therefore the more one sells, the more one makes, and the happier sales managers and sport organizations are. It is also a frustrating business that involves a lot of rejection. It is important that the sport ticket salesperson be persistent, send a consistent message to all potential customers, and maximize the opportunities available. It is also important to remember that salespeople who strive to survive on making the "one big sale" might make a lot of money from the sale, but it is only one relationship. Multiple relationships equal success in ticket sales.

CONCLUSION

Sales are the backbone of sport organizations. As a result of the increase in competition, the creativity involved in sales management in sport has been considerable. Sport sales management is the process of directing and controlling the sales force to sell sport products and services, resulting in achieving a desired level of exchanges between the sport organization and sport consumers. Sales involve the multiple stages of the buying and selling processes, including directing and controlling the sales force, covering sales training, determining sales territories, forecasting sales, budgeting and setting quotas, and motivating, leading, evaluating, and compensating the sales force within ethical and legal boundaries.

The sport sales organization is made up of three components. Organizational design in sport sales focuses on how the buying and selling process is implemented. The sport buying process is the steps involved in reaching a decision to make a purchase – including identifying the need, searching for products or services that satisfied that need, evaluating options, making a decision, purchasing the product or service, and eventually re-evaluating the decision to determine whether to make the same purchase again or to change. The sport sales process focuses on taking the sport products and services available for sale, and developing the best methods for luring the sport consumer to make a purchase by prospecting for customers, communicating with the sport consumer, making contact and pitching the idea of a sale, closing the sale, and servicing after the sale is complete.

These functional processes focus on the other two components of the sport sales organization – sales managers and salespeople. A sales manager is responsible for many of the financial, economic, and managerial functions within the sales organization. Salespeople are the face of a sport organization, and must demonstrate excellent skills in communications, logic and critical thinking, organization, time management, and knowledge of sport products and services.

In sport, there are certain inventories, including advertising, naming rights, sponsorships, travel, and ticket sales that are unique because they do not adhere to the typical supply and demand model. There are only so many tickets to be sold, advertisement slots to be filled, naming rights to be applied, and sponsorship opportunities to be secured. Advertising inventories have evolved to include television, radio, and the internet, but still have involvement with traditional print advertising through game programs, media guides, and game tickets. Naming rights are often limited to that of the game facility, practice facility, or in some cases the team itself. Sponsorships require a lot of research, creativity, and time, as well as a significant financial commitment from the potential sponsor.

- Ticket sales are the major revenue stream for a sport organization, and offer a diverse inventory available for sale. This includes season ticket equivalents (season tickets plus partial season ticket plans), advanced ticket sales, group sales, walk-ups, and specialty seating. The four main strategies utilized in ticket sales management include database management, benefit selling, upselling, and aftermarketing. While there are many factors that are beyond the sport salesperson's control, the number of tickets sold is directly related to the number of contacts made, networks created, and relationships built through referrals and renewals.

FROM THEORY TO PRACTICE

MARK RODRIGUES, DIRECTOR OF TICKET SALES
Boston Bruins (NHL) Hockey Club,
Boston, Massachusetts

My role and experience in the world of professional sports has evolved over the past ten years. I started my career as many students do with a number of internships. Two internships in particular played a role in helping me find my passion for the industry. They were with the Nashua Pride Minor League Baseball team and the Manchester Wolves Arena Football team.

My responsibilities during the internships ranged from the usual daily office respon-sibilities to generating revenue through ticket sales. It was during this time that I found my true passion for not only the sport industry but also sales.

After achieving success with the Manchester Wolves as an intern I received two promotions within three years of being with the organization. I was promoted to Ticket Sales Manager during my sophomore year of college followed by my promotion to Director of Ticket Sales going into my junior year.

I was able to move up in a short period of time due to the strength of my work ethic and my ability to sell. I was able to establish myself as a valuable player within the organization. I produced in excess of US$120,000 in ticket sales revenue, which for a minor league team is a substantial amount of revenue. I was able to accomplish this while taking six credit courses in college and working part time.

There is no secret as to how to become successful in this industry. You must work hard, network, and wait your turn. I had been attempting to break into the "big leagues" since the first day I started my career. My opportunity finally came after winning a sales and marketing competition in Tempe, Arizona. I was then offered an entry-level ticket sales position with the Orlando Magic of the NBA.

During my time in Orlando in the entry-level position, I was the top-selling sales representative. Within a year I was promoted to Ticket Sales Account Executive where

I continued to sell and thrive in the industry. In Orlando I had the opportunity to receive management training and develop the next set of skills to move on to a management position.

One of the most important things to remember about the sport industry is that it is not always about what you know, rather who you know. In 2007 I received my break into a management role when Leigh Castergine, currently Vice-President of Ticket Sales and Service for the New York Mets, offered me the opportunity to join her in Boston to work for the Boston Bruins.

During my time in Boston as Ticket Sales Manager I was responsible for creating the organization's first Inside Sales Department. Under my leadership the department achieved record-breaking revenue for an entry-level sales department. Other responsibilities in this role included hiring, training, developing sales campaigns, and creating an environment for our sales staff to flourish.

After three years of managing the Inside Sales Department I received my opportunity to take the next step in my career. In 2010, I was promoted to my current role of Director of Ticket Sales for the Boston Bruins and TD Garden. In my current role, my responsibilities include overseeing a staff of 16, managing the sales and service efforts of the organization, all major sales campaigns, budget and financial responsibilities, staffing, recruiting, and much more.

I have been in the sport industry for about ten years, and yet I can say I still have a lot to learn. My advice to you when moving forward in your career is to find your passion right away. Ask questions, job shadow, do internships, listen, and work hard when given an opportunity.

And remember, "If you can sell, you will always have a job."

CHAPTER EIGHT

RETAIL MANAGEMENT IN SPORT

CHAPTER OUTLINE

- What is sport retail management?
- Retail value and relationship building
- Retail strategy
- Methods of planning a sport retail mix
- Targeting customers and gathering information
- Location, location, location
- Organizational structure
- Merchandise management
- Getting the message out: sport retailer communications
- Conclusion

CHAPTER OBJECTIVES

The reader will be able to:

- gain an understanding of sport retailing and sport retail management through a presentation of various retail strategies and a strategic approach to retailing in the sport field
- identify the major concepts inherent to strategic retail management
- recognize the factors and skills associated with situation analysis, targeting customers, and gathering information
- assess the concepts associated with choosing a retail location, managing a retail business, implementing pricing policies, and activating a merchandise management program
- compare and contrast the various ways of communicating with the customer.

WHAT IS SPORT RETAIL MANAGEMENT?

Sport retail management is the process of directing and controlling the business activities related to the sale of the sport product to consumers for their personal consumption. Sport retail management, as the end result of the distribution process, becomes an integral part of the entire sport marketing process – if there is no sale of the sport product then the previous sport marketing methods implemented have been useless. With the increased opportunities for sport product sales through the internet, and the growth of global sport marketing efforts, it would seem that sport retail sales in general are on an upward swing. However, the challenges faced by sport retailers are great due to a number of factors including the general population having less discretionary time and income, over-saturation in the competitive market leading to lower profit margins due to cost cutting, the high level of customer service expected in society, and the lack of knowledge by many sport retailers as to the proper use of the internet as a tool.

Retail in the United States is a significant part of the economy. As reported in January 2005 by one of the world's largest marketing information companies – AC Nielsen – annual retail sales in the United States topped US$4 trillion for the first time. Total sales of US$4.1 trillion in 2004 were up 8 percent from 2003, the biggest annual increase since 1999. The leisure goods sector of the retail industry, under which sport retail falls, grew almost 1 percent in 2011. Included in this sector are companies such as Sports Authority, Decathlon, Olympia Sports, and Dick's Sporting Goods.

As the final stage in the distribution process, sport retailers play an integral role as the primary contact between manufacturers and sport consumers. Sport retailers utilize the sorting process, whereby they assemble a variety of goods and services from various suppliers, buy them in large quantities, and sell them on to consumers. The goal is to maximize manufacturer efficiency while allowing consumers to have a choice when shopping at the sport retail outlet. In general, the goods and services sold by sport retail outlets are not owned and operated by the manufacturers. This allows a manufacturer to reach a wide range of consumers, while focusing on its area of expertise. The result of this is often reduced costs of producing the goods and services, which in turn will improve cash flow and increase sales.

Sport retail management can be quite a challenge because the average amount of a sales transaction for sport retailers is much less than for manufacturers. As a result, the sport retailer must control costs and inventory, while at the same time utilizing advertising and special promotions to maximize the number of customers coming through the door. Once the consumer is through the door, the sport retailer must increase the number of impulse sales by utilizing a very aggressive selling style. The reason for this is that final consumers often make many unplanned purchases. They may walk through the door to buy a T-shirt, but you as the sport retailer want the consumer to walk out of the door with that T-shirt, along with a pennant and a ball. Therefore, a major part of the aggressive selling style includes effective use of in-store displays, catalogs, and websites. In addition, stores must have an organized layout and be appealing to the consumer's eye. With the wide variety of sport retail outlets, the sport retailer must be able to draw consumers to their store location. Factors such as location, transportation, store opening hours, proximity of competitors, product selection, parking, and advertising need to be considered.

180

To make the process less challenging, it is important that a sport retail manager develop and utilize an effective sport retail strategic plan to guide the organization. All retailers should observe the following six steps when developing a retail strategic plan:

1 Define the type of business based on the goods or service category and the company's specific orientation.
2 Set short-term and long-term goals and objectives.
3 Determine the customer market on the basis of its characteristics, wants, and needs.
4 Devise an overall, long-run plan that provides a vision for the sport organization and its employees.
5 Implement an integrated strategy that combines store location, product diversity, pricing, and advertising to achieve goals and accomplish objectives.
6 Regularly evaluate performance, maintain or enhance strengths, and correct weaknesses and problems observed.

RETAIL VALUE AND RELATIONSHIP BUILDING

A sport retailer must understand and effectively apply the concepts of value and relationship from the perspective of the consumer, the manufacturer, and itself. The resulting goal is to have consumers believe that the sport retailer offers good value for the money being spent by the sport consumer, and to establish a positive relationship between the sport retailer and the sport consumer.

Value

Value is an amount of goods, services, or money that is a fair price or return for something of an equivalent amount. In sport retail management, the manufacturer and retailer represent value as a series of activities, exchanges, and processes that provides a set value for the consumer, known as a value chain. The goal of a value chain is to create a perception in the mind of the consumer as to the benefit of the sport product, and that the price being paid is worthwhile. Consumers must always believe they have got their money's worth. Sport retailers must understand that price is not the only consideration for value. Other considerations including location, parking, level of customer service, the variety of products, the quality of products, availability of products, and retailer's image, which are a significant part of value in the mind of the consumer.

The goal for the sport retail management is to ensure they are offering an optimal level of value to their consumers and hence maximizing the number of consumers entering their retail outlet. There are three levels of a value-oriented sport retail strategy. First, there are minimal expectations that all consumers desire. These expected value chain essentials include convenient hours, educated employees, quality service, a clean store, ample parking, having desired products in stock, and an acceptable return policy. Second is an expanded value chain, which is a sport retail strategy that offers additional elements to differentiate themselves from other sport retailers. These elements include offering exclusive brands, frequent shopper programs, delivery options, and superior salespeople and service. The third level is known as

181

a niche sport retail strategy. At this level, the sport retail outlet encompasses value chain elements that have not yet been addressed or refined by the competition.

Price/quality matrix

This relationship between price and value is often articulated in terms of the price/quality matrix, which articulates the relationship between price and quality in positioning the sport product as compared to others. Figure 8.1 illustrates the four quadrants of the price/quality matrix.

	QUALITY	
P R I C E	High price, low quality	High price, high quality
	Low price, high quality	Low price, low quality

Figure 8.1 Price/quality matrix

Successful sport retail businesses operate in as many quadrants as possible. The high-price/low-quality quadrant is one which all sport retailers avoid, as in most cases sport consumers will not pay top dollars for inferior products. However, the other three quadrants do offer opportunities for profitability albeit at different levels. Of the remaining quadrants, the least desirable for the sport retailer is the low-price/high-quality quadrant because of minimal profits (high cost to produce product vs. low selling price). However, most sport retailers must target this quadrant with many of their product because this is the most desirable for the sport consumer (getting the most for their money). High price/high quality is an advantageous quadrant for sport retailers because consumers are paying the most for the best, and there is always room to maximize profits. Low price/low quality does have its benefits, but it often requires large volumes of product to be in stock and sold to maximize profitability.

From the standpoint of specialized sport products, and based on the ever-changing perceptions of the sport consumer, price is often a more powerful tool than quality. With these types of sport products, the level of quality is often similar. Consumers often perceive products differently based on the price charged by the sport retailer. Therefore, sport products with a higher price often increase sales significantly as sport consumers may perceive the product to be better because it costs more. This concept only works if sport retailers understand their customers and can effectively determine whether their sport product fits in this category.

Relationships

This leads into the importance of building relationships with sport consumers. There are four critical factors to take into account when building those relationships – the market, customer service, customer satisfaction levels, and customer perks.

The market

The market is the fundamental concept of retail management. The market is what provides the opportunity to buy and sell based on the demand for goods and services. Inclusive of the market is the customer base, which is targeted based on the needs of segments such as population and lifestyle trends; reasons for shopping; the level of loyalty; and what kind of customer mix is desired between new and old customers. According to statistics from the United States Census Bureau, the population is aging, a quarter of all households have only one person, and one-sixth of the population moves annually. Most people live in urban or suburban areas. The number of working women continues to grow. Household income has been relatively stable for the past 25 years. In addition, minority and immigrant populations are expanding. Research shows that gender roles are changing, shoppers are more demanding, and market segments are more diverse in today's marketplace. In addition, there is less interest in shopping, and time-saving goods and services are desirable.

Therefore, in building consumer relationships, there are three major consumer-oriented factors that contribute to the success of sport retail businesses: (1) saving customers' time and energy; (2) the service and assortments offered; and (3) the uniqueness of the shopping experience. In addition, the sport retail business owner must realize that not all customers are equal. There are those who are worth cultivating long-term relationships with as they represent the core of the sport retailer's customers (80/20 rule). To maximize how sport retailers foster these relationships, they should analyze their customer base from three standpoints. First, the sport retailer should determine which customers are the most profitable and most loyal. This will define the customers who spend the most money and seem to prefer stable, long-term relationships. Second, analyze which customers place the greatest value on what sport retailers have to offer. As stated earlier in the chapter, consumers must always believe that they are getting their money's worth. Third, an evaluation must be completed by sport retail managers to determine which customers are worth more to them than to their competitors. A sport retail outlet cannot be everything to all people, but consumers who are worth more to a competitor will eventually go over to it.

Customer service

Customer service refers to the retail activities that increase the value consumers receive when they purchase goods and services. To service consumers in an effective manner, a sport retail firm must first understand how to take care of the consumer, and then outline a service strategy and plan for specific individual services.

To start, the sport retail firm must determine the most effective way to communicate with consumers about its goods and services. Once the consumer is "in the door," the sport retailer must get to know its customers so that it can predict their needs, wants, and desires. This knowledge differs based on the type of customer. For repeat and loyal customers, it is remaining trustworthy in the eyes of the consumer, and continuing to offer the products, services, and value essential to the consumer. For new customers, it starts by reading the consumers to determine not only what they need, want, and desire, but also what impulse items they might be apt to purchase. As the relationship grows, there is a shift to enhancing value and building trust, with the eventual goal of the new customer moving up the escalator to become a repeat or even loyal customer.

In all cases, the sport retailer needs to have a high level of product knowledge to better service the consumers. Often in mass merchandise stores such as Wal-Mart and Target, the individuals working in the sport department do not understand the products they are selling. In sport retail outlets, the consumer should know that employees have been trained to understand the products and services, and how to deal with a very knowledgeable customer – which many specialized product consumers are. When customers believe that the retailer cares about the individual and the product, they tend to continue their patronage of the retail firm.

In devising a strategy to take care of the consumer, a number of questions need to be asked. What customer services are expected? Do customers have a choice of services? Do we charge a fee for customer services (cost–benefit analysis)? What is the relationship of customer service to the sport retail firm's image? How long is customer service offered after the sale, and at what level?

Once these questions are answered, the sport retailer must choose the services it will offer. Some are basic, such as credit. Will you accept all major credit cards? Personal checks? Will you have your own credit card? Will you allow for corporate accounts that pay on a revolving basis? Other services might include delivery, installation and assembly, gift wrapping, gift certificates, return policies, special sales for repeat and loyal customers, and outside sales (orders via catalog, mail, phone, and/or the web).

Customer satisfaction levels

Customer satisfaction takes place when the value and customer service provided through a sport retail firm meet or exceed consumer expectations. As discussed in detail in Chapter 5, this is one of the most difficult areas for a sport retailer to understand because most consumers do not complain when they are dissatisfied. They just leave and go to purchase their goods and services from a competitor. Therefore, one of the most important tasks a sport retailer must perform to maintain a solid relationship is to make it easier for consumers to provide feedback. This can be done in simple ways by providing customer feedback opportunities at the register, or via the web. A more detailed way is to subsidize ongoing customer satisfaction surveys and track the ebbs and flows. Whatever methodology is utilized, one thing is abundantly clear: if consumers do not believe that their concerns are being met, they will no longer be customers. To retain customers, sport marketing professionals involved in retail management must utilize the marketing concept, which is a consumer-oriented philosophy which suggests that satisfaction of consumer needs should provide the focus for product development and marketing strategy, to enable the retail operation to meet its own organizational goals.

Customer perks

Customer perks reward those repeat and loyal customers for their long-term relationship with the sport retail outlet. Sport retailers spend time with these loyalty programs owing to the Pareto Principle (or 80/20 rule) – which states that 80 percent of business comes from the top 20 percent of customers. To implement a program, a sport retail firm must first devise a way to track shopping behavior – usually through a database created in conjunction with some type of buying card or tag. The sport retail firm must then find a way to personalize communications with those frequent consumers to make them feel special and to articulate the participation rules. Most importantly, the rewards have to be useful and appealing to the consumer. They must be reasonably attainable, have features unique to the retailer, and offer a range of rewards for short-term and long-term participation. An example of this is both Sports Authority and Dick's Sporting Goods email special offers and notification of sales to frequent shoppers. Retail operations also offer perks to their best customers in conjunction with the corporate sponsorship of sporting events, such as hospitality and participation opportunities at golf tournaments and auto races.

Channel relationships

Relationship building must also take place with other members of the distribution channel, specifically manufacturers, wholesalers, and potentially other retail outlets within a franchise. Each channel member is dependent on the other. However, due to contradictory goals, some channel members become difficult to deal with. The goal is to create positive relationships between the members of the sport retailer's channel so that they can better serve each other and the final consumer. This is often accomplished through category management – where all parts of the channel manage products in categories rather than individually. Category management allows all members of the channel to maximize their profit from the mix of brands in the category. This is often accomplished by allocating funds and marketing efforts according to the profit potential of each brand in the mix while deleting weak brands and adding new brands with higher profit potential.

Category management requires cooperation between all members of the channel. Sport retailers listen to customers and stock what they want. Profitability is improved because inventory follows demand closely. By being better focused, each department can become more desirable for shoppers. This data is then shared, usually through computerized means, to all levels of the channel so that they too can have efficient inventory management and stock what the customer wants. If the suppliers stock what the retailer needs, profitability will also be maximized.

Relationship-building differences between goods and service retailers

The move to the twenty-first century has seen a greater shift to service-based retailing. Therefore sport retail firms must not only understand the differences between goods retailing and service retailing, but also whether they are engaged in one, the other, or both. Goods retailing focuses on the sale of tangible products such as hockey pucks, sticks, helmets, and uniforms. Service retailing involves transactions in which consumers do not purchase or acquire ownership of tangible products, such as personal services, facility and equipment rental, and

185

recreational services. An example of this for the sport of hockey would be renting a hockey rink for practice or a birthday party, and hiring a coach for goalkeeper lessons.

Service retailing in the United States and worldwide continues to grow at a consistent rate, and represents a significant portion of overall retail trade. In the United States, consumers spend almost two-thirds of their income on services. Almost 80 percent of the labor force works in the services sector. A significant percentage of these services are in the fields of sport and recreation.

Service retailing is much more dependent on personal interactions and word-of-mouth communication than goods retailing. Therefore, the intangible nature of many services makes it more difficult for a sport retail firm to develop a clear consumer-oriented strategy owing to three main factors. First is the inseparability of the service provider from his or her services, which makes that individual indispensable. If the service provider ups and leaves, the sport retailer is left without the ability to service its customers. Second is the short life span of many services. This is especially true with technology-based products and services, where the average turnover is approximately six months. Third, the variability of services creates a situation where service quality may differ for each purchase, retail outlet, or service provider.

RETAIL STRATEGY

One of the major concepts discussed in the development of value and relationships is the development of a sport retail strategy. A sport retail strategy is the overall plan of action utilized to guide a sport retailer. This plan includes a situation analysis, goals and objectives of the organization, and an identification of customer's needs, wants, and desires. The creation of the overall strategy will include the specific tasks to be completed, how the work is to be controlled, and how feedback on the retail strategy will be collected and evaluated.

A well-implemented strategy results in the coordination of all aspects of the business, and helps the firm complete tasks and avoid disasters in a more efficient and effective manner. This involves variables the sport retail manager can control, such as store location, organizational structure, human resource management, operational management, merchandise management, and the ability to communicate directly with sport consumers to determine their needs, wants, and desires. In addition, there are other variables that cannot be controlled by the sport retail manager, which therefore require a modification to the retail strategy. These variables include the sport consumer itself, threats caused by competitive situations, and changes in economic, technological, and legal conditions.

To succeed, the sport retail strategy must be integrated throughout the organization. From an internal viewpoint, work is controlled via a sport retail audit. This periodical review involves analyzing the performance of the sport retailer with the goal of revealing the strengths and weaknesses of the organization. The goal is then to maintain and build on strengths, while improving upon and eliminating weaknesses. From an external standpoint, sport retailers must utilize tactical decisions to be responsive to the external aspects of the business – taking advantage of opportunities and avoiding threats to the organization. This is usually accomplished through a variety of retail tactics that are the basis of daily and short-term retail operations including: (1) the location of the sport retail outlet; (2) efficient and effective operating procedures; (3) efficient product management and pricing; (4) effective communication with customers/pleasant retail outlet atmosphere; (5) knowledge of sport retail products and services; and (6) implementation of effective promotional programs.

These elements of a strategic sport retail mix are utilized to help a sport firm become a destination retailer – one that sport consumers view as unique to the point of becoming loyal to the company and being willing to go out of their way to shop there. The largest sport destination retailer is Cabela's. With its internet department growing by leaps and bounds, Cabela's has seen tremendous online growth. Besides the thriving e-commerce side of www.cabelas.com, which went live in 1998, the website features a continuously updated content site, community pages, company information, and much more.

So how did they become the most successful sport destination retailers? According to www.cabelas.com:

> Cabela's retail division operates overwhelmingly popular stores throughout the U.S. As much wildlife museums and education centers as retail stores, Cabela's showrooms provide a truly unique shopping experience. True destination stores, Cabela's showrooms offer outdoor enthusiasts and their family an educational and entertaining shopping experience.

> To provide support for their co-branded credit card, which was started in 1995, Cabela's chartered the World's Foremost Bank, N.A., in 2001. The bank provides customer service, risk management and payment processing exclusively for Cabela's Visa cardholders. The Cabela's Visa card allows consumers to earn points back from all their purchases, which they can apply toward their next purchase at Cabela's.

> In 2001, the Cabela's Catalog was ranked as the fifth most popular catalog, behind such direct-mail giants as J.C. Penney and Sears, in a Consumer Shopping Survey administered by *Catalog Age* magazine. Other awards include: *Shot Business* magazine's Retailer of the Year; *Sporting Goods Business* magazine Specialty Retailer of the Year; BizRate.com Circle of Excellence Award for outstanding website performance over the holiday season. In 2006 Cabela's website was ranked No. 1 in the outdoor retailer industry and the company was named Company of the Year in *Sporting Classics* magazine's prestigious Awards of Excellence.

> Since 1961, Cabela's vision and willingness to adapt has placed them at the forefront of the outdoor recreation world. What started out as a mail order for fishing flies, grew into the fifth largest catalog business with the addition of bricks and mortar and then joined the World Wide Web. Cabela's has given the consumer multiple ways to view and purchase their products.

Goals and objectives

The goals and objectives of a sport retail organization reflect the short- and long-term targets a sport retailer hopes to reach. These goals and objectives must be clearly stated without ambiguity to ensure that the mission can be put into action. In sport retail management, goals and objectives are usually centered on sales, profit margin, customer satisfaction, and company image. Sales objectives focus on reaching specified volume goals such as increasing revenues, maintaining sales levels, maximizing percentage share in market, and attaining specified levels of units sold. Profit goals include dollars earned and increased operating efficiency (decreased operating expenses while increasing sales). Other profit goals may include reaching a specific level of return on investment (ROI) or return on equity (ROE), both of which are profitability measures which tell how effective investments and resources are utilized by the organization to make profits.

Customer satisfaction objectives go beyond meeting the needs, wants, and desires of valued constituents, but also maintaining good relations with them. Company image goals relate to the proper positioning of the sport retail organization so that it is perceived in the best light as compared to competitors. This image differentiation varies based on the type of retail outlet. Mass merchandise sport retail outlets strive to offer value, a maximal level of merchandise offerings, and substantial retail facilities, whereas niche retailers focus on specific segments and address the necessities of those segments.

If the goals and objectives can be achieved, the sport retail operation has a better opportunity to succeed. However, it is impossible to succeed without understanding and identifying the needs, wants, and desires of the sport consumer. A sport retailer utilizes three methods to reach its target market. Mass sport marketing is where goods and services are available for sale to an extensive group of sport consumers, such as Sports Authority or Dick's Sporting Goods. Concentrated sport marketing, or niche marketing, is concentrating on one specific group of sport consumers, such as Nevada Bob's Pro Shops (the world's largest chain of retail golf stores), Eastern Mountain Sports (focuses on hardcore, edgy, outdoor enthusiasts), and Pacific Sunwear (action sports lifestyle retailer of casual fashion apparel, footwear, and accessories for the chain's target customers – men and women aged between 12 and 24). Differentiated sport marketing focuses on two or more different sport consumer groups with divergent retailing approaches for each group. Examples include Aldila (high-performance graphite golf club shaft maker which also manufactures hockey sticks); and Brunswick (bowling and billiards products; fitness equipment including Life Fitness, ParaBody, and Hammer Strength; pleasure boats including SeaRay, Bayliner, Boston Whaler and Hatteras, and marine engines including Mercury and Mariner).

Situation analysis

A situation analysis looks at the current status of a business and examines which direction the business should head. In order to accomplish this, the sport retailer must complete a detailed evaluation of the opportunities available to capitalize on, and the threats facing the business from competitors and the environment. This becomes difficult, especially in retail operations, as the firm strives to identify trends at an early stage to satisfy customer wants and needs and to stay ahead of its competitors. However, if the retailer enters a new market too quickly, customers may not be ready for the change.

Mission

A situation analysis requires a comprehensive appraisal of the retail operation. This usually starts with an analysis of the organization's mission, which encompasses the goals and objectives of the firm. This mission should be in congruence with the firm's desired area of business, and the unique placement within the desired marketplace. The analysis of the organization mission includes: (1) evaluating the attitude of the business as related to its constituents; (2) the level to which consumers identify with the business entity; (3) how the retail business differentiates itself from its competitors; (4) whether business should be based on the goods and/or services sold by the entity, or based on consumers' needs, wants, and desires; (5) whether the sport retail outlet is to be an industry leader or follower; and (6) what the scope of the sport retail operation should be. As a result of this continual review, the organizational mission is often adjusted to reflect changes in the marketplace.

Ownership structure

There are numerous structures of ownership for a sport retail outlet depending on the marketplace niche. Some statistical background regarding the sport retail industry needs to be understood prior to discussing the structures. Currently, over 75 percent of all sport retailers own and manage a single retail outlet, and more than half employ two or fewer paid employees. On the other hand, according to Fortune 500, the top two sporting goods retailers since 2004 for sporting goods and toys continue to be Walmart and Target. In the direct sport retail industry itself, the top three companies (Dick's Sporting Goods, Cabela's, and Hibbett's Sporting Goods) accounted for nearly US$7.5 billion in sales for the year 2010.

The most basic of ownership structures is the independent sport retailer – your local small-town sporting goods store. The independent sport retailer usually owns only one outlet, and hence requires a limited investment to start. This type of ownership offers great flexibility as a result of the outlet's independent nature. Hence, the sport retailer can focus its offerings, have control over its own retail strategy, and project the image it desires for the organization. While this type of entrepreneurship does not provide for consistency, it does create a significant reliance on the ownership which often results in a decreased amount of time and resources to put into planning. In addition, an independent contractor has restricted bargaining power due to the limited quantities it purchases from manufacturers and wholesalers, which results in few economies of scale.

A sport retail chain runs multiple stores under one ownership group – such as Sports Authority and Dick's Sporting Goods. In this type of ownership, purchasing and decision making are not made at the retail store level but are usually centralized within the ownership. This centralized ownership often results in efficient levels of management throughout the organization because of multiple locations being run in the same manner. Another advantage of chains lies in bargaining power and cost-efficiency, increasing the number of economies of scale. While this reduction in costs is beneficial, it is often at the expense of flexibility, control, and independence at the local store level. In addition, from the corporate level, it requires purchasing large quantities of product that need to be delivered locally, regionally, nationally, and even internationally. These increased investments require high levels of cash flows and credit lines.

Many chains seek to reduce their liability while returning some levels of flexibility, control, and independence to the local retail store through franchising. Franchising involves a chain granting authority to an individual or business to distribute and sell products and service under the chain's established name. An example of this would be Golf USA (www.golfusa.com), where an individual who desires to open his or her own golf store would pay a fee and a percentage of sales to Golf USA in exchange for any number of benefits including exclusive selling rights, start-up practices and management training, negotiated buying programs, special buying opportunities, proprietary equipment, marketing and promotional programs, and business support. A franchisee is a middle ground in the retailer landscape – allowing an individual who may not have the ability to be an independent contractor due to a lack of resources to take advantage of the benefits of a chain.

Another option for a potential sport retail operation is to be a leased department. This is where a sport retail operator rents out a section of a larger store such as a department or specialty store. Usually rent is in the form of a negotiated monthly payment or a percentage of sales, whichever is more. An example of this would be a company like Ticketmaster having a retail location in places such as a department store of secondary retail outlet.

A final method of ownership structure is a consumer cooperative. One of the most successful sport retail consumer cooperative continues to be Recreational Equipment, Inc. (REI). According to www.rei.com:

> In 1938 mountain climbers Lloyd and Mary Anderson joined with 21 fellow Northwest climbers to found Recreational Equipment, Inc. (REI). The group structured REI as a consumer cooperative to purchase high-quality ice axes and climbing equipment from Europe because such gear could not be purchased locally. The word quickly spread, and soon many other outdoors people joined the co-op. As REI grew so too did the range of outdoor gear available to the co-op members.

> During the past six decades, REI has grown into a renowned supplier of specialty outdoor gear and clothing. We serve the needs of outdoors people through 78 retail stores in the U.S. and by direct sales via the internet (REI.com and REI-OUTLET.com), telephone and mail. Today, REI is the nation's largest consumer cooperative with more than 2 million members.

> Although the gear sold by REI looks much different now than it did in 1938, being a cooperative business remains central to REI. While non-members are welcome to shop at REI, only members enjoy special benefits, including an annual member refund on eligible purchases. REI's business success allowed the co-op to return member refunds to its 44 million active members. In 2010, REI's sales totaled $1.6 billion, and provide nearly $94.3 million in donations in support of the outdoors and outdoor recreation.

METHODS OF PLANNING A SPORT RETAIL MIX

To plan a sport retail strategy mix, one of three methodologies is used – the sport retail life cycle; scrambled sport merchandising; and the wheel of sport retailing.

The sport retail life cycle

This concept is similar to the product life cycle, and is documented in Figure 8.2. The first stage is the development stage, which determines the best techniques for entering the new sport

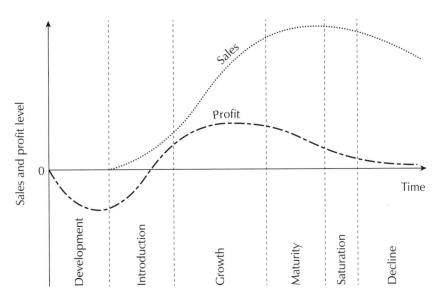

Figure 8.2 Sport retail life cycle

retail organization into the marketplace. Inclusive of this stage is the initial maintenance of the sport retail operation in an environment of controlled costs, limited but quality human resources, and selective product and service offering that the sport consumer desires. The goal is to provide optimal conditions for future growth and development of the business.

During the introduction stage of the sport retail life cycle, the goal is to find a niche in the marketplace and build a customer base. At this point the doors are open and the need is to attract customers. Therefore, advertising costs are often high to increase customer awareness. At the same time, sales are low in the beginning – at least until the sport retail outlet is accepted by the general public. As a result, the introductory stage is a time of negative profit at the beginning.

The goal of the growth stage is for sales and profits to increase as the business becomes more established. During this time, a sport retail firm expands its operations regionally, nationally, and perhaps even internationally. In turn, new retail firms enter the marketplace striving to take a percentage of the market. To remain in a strong market position, the costs of business to the sport retail firm often increase. The result is a negative effect to profit, either because the increased costs affect the bottom line, or a decrease in sales resulting from an increase in price to absorb the increase in expenses.

If the result is a decrease in sales, this signals that the sport retail firm is entering the maturity stage. The sport retail firm must reduce its profit margins to promote an increase in sales. Some of the reasons for the decrease in sales may also include a significant increase in competition, changes in the psychographic composition of the market, or the leadership of the sport retail firm may not be able to lead the sport retail organization to higher levels of profitability.

If changes are not made, the result for the sport retail firm will be the decline stage. This is where sales and profits continue to decline, and no matter what the sport retail manager does, the firm cannot recover from the tailspin. There are two decisions to be made: either reinvent the sport retail brand to encourage new growth, or have your "going out of business" clearance.

Scrambled sport merchandising

Scrambled sport merchandising is where a sport retailer offers goods and services that are dissimilar to the primary area of expertise of the firm. An example of this would be a golf store selling sunglasses. Although the expertise of the sport retailer is in golf products, it adds this item because golfers may need sunglasses, and may make an impulsive purchase while in the store. These additional items are usually highly sought after by customers, and can provide a high profit margin because of the convenience factor. Many consider superstores such as Sports Authority and Dicks to be scrambled merchandisers as they offer a wide variety of products, with limited expertise in the specific products. The goal of this is to reach a wider variety of target markets by attracting customers to this one-stop shopping opportunity. In addition, by offering a wide variety of products that change seasonally, the sport retail outlet becomes a year-round operation, and hence reduces the effects of targeted competitors and seasonality.

The wheel of sport retailing

In the wheel of sport retailing, the sport retail landscape is viewed as an ever-evolving system. Most sport retailers start as low-price options for the sport consumer. The sport retailer is strictly concerned with establishing itselfs in the market – it is less concerned with low profits, and makes every effort to keep costs down. As the sport retail outlet becomes more established in the marketplace, the sport retailer will upgrade the quality of the products offered; improve the facilities housing the sport retail operation, and offer additional services. All of this should work to increase sales, and if costs have been controlled, increase profit margin.

Since the wheel of sport retailing is based on the availability of discretionary income by the public, consumer who only care about price will not be loyal to the sport retail outlet. This provides an opportunity for competition to enter the market and fill in the void left in the market.

The wheel of sport retailing has three levels: low end/discount; middle of the road/general; and high end/luxury. Sport retailers must be careful when moving from one level to another, as the move will affect sales, the target market, and the image of the organization. The goal is to obviously improve on all levels. However, the sport retail firm must have a solid strategy to accomplish its goals.

TARGETING CUSTOMERS AND GATHERING INFORMATION

Once a sport retail strategy has been established, the sport retailer must develop a plan for targeting customers. The purpose of this is to identify the characteristics, needs, attitudes, and purchase behavior of sport consumers. Characteristics include demographics (the unique

192

qualities representative of human populations and population segments) and lifestyles (a manner of living that reflects the person's values and attitudes). Needs are an individual's basic shopping requirements. These needs often have a direct correlation to retail desire, which are the shopping goals that impact upon attitude and behavior. Attitude and purchase behaviors focus on the state of mind of the sport consumer. This state of mind often affects the way people shop, where they shop, how decisions are made, how purchases are made, and whether there will be repeat purchases.

With this target plan in mind, the sport retailer must then gather the information necessary to make informed retail decisions. Gathering data to make decisions is crucial to the decision-making process, and while this information gathering should be an ongoing process, it should also be constantly evaluated to determine whether the research is yielding the information needed.

A successful sport retail information-gathering operation involves not only the sport retailer, but also its suppliers and consumers. This coordinated effort keeps all parties on the same page. Sport retailers learn from suppliers about new models, sales forecasts, and reasons for price adjustments, while at the same time they learn about attitudes about styles and models, the extent of brand loyalty and the willingness of customers to pay a given price. Suppliers and consumers gather similar information from this collaborative process.

Unfortunately, many sport retailers feel that this cooperation will actually be used against them in favor of competitors. As a result, the sport retailer often uses non-systematic research to make retail decisions. Other reasons for using this methodology include lack of time, resources, and the ability to conduct solid research. While many feel this is an easy way out, having inadequate information may cause a sport retailer to implement a bad strategy.

In order to avoid this, sport retailers must implement a sport retail information system. This system, if implemented in an effective manner, will foresee the information needs of sport retail managers, store important data on an ongoing basis, and create a flow of information that will allow the sport retailer to make efficient operational decisions. Technology is a powerful tool that can be utilized as a framework for a sport retail information system. The two major technologies include database management and UPC/EDI technology.

Database management is the process of gathering and organizing information in a manner that allows the sport retailer to integrate and apply those data into the sport retail strategy. It also allows for storing the information for future evaluation and use. Database management may be internal or outsourced. Internal database management allows for better control of the information and instant access, while outsourcing to a database management company saves time and energy that could be utilized in other aspects of the sport retail operation. An example of this would be advertising through Facebook. Facebook has asked its customers for all of the information you are looking for, but it comes with a price.

The other technologies available to sport retailers are through information compiled through universal product codes (UPC) and electronic data interchange (EDI). Through UPC codes, the bar identification codes found on most retail products, sport retailers can record data on a number of product characteristics, including size, color, model, and brand. This can also help with inventory management, sales analyses, and purchase behaviors of consumers. As far as EDI is concerned, this process allows retailers and suppliers to share basic information with regard to inventory, delivery time, and unit sales, to name a few. In turn, this collaboration between supplier and retailer enhances the sport retailer's ability to make more effective decisions, control inventory more efficiently, and be responsive to sport consumer demand at a higher level.

In general, a sport retailer must understand its company, its consumers, and its competitors to target customers appropriately and utilize information properly. This also involves understanding the internal strengths and weaknesses of the sport retail operation, as well as its external opportunities and threats. This is then put into a plan that allows the sport retailer to: select its target markets; identify the characteristics, needs, and attitudes of sport consumers; gain an understanding of the purchase decision-making process of sport consumers; and implement an action plan for the sport retail operation.

LOCATION, LOCATION, LOCATION

Another significant part of the action and strategic plan is location. The placement of the store, whether as a traditional infrastructure or an e-store, is crucial to the success of the sport retail business. This is because a good location can often overcome shortcomings in strategy. In turn, no matter how good the strategy, a poor location cannot succeed.

CASE STUDY 8: THE YELLOW AND RED RETAIL STORE

Authored and contributed by David P. Hedlund, St. John's University, Queens, New York

As James, Director of Marketing Research, hung up the phone, he began to contemplate the questions posed to him and the challenges that lay ahead. Kris, the owner of Yellow and Red, a chain of two locally owned and operated retail stores that sold university-branded merchandise, had contacted James because he wanted to know more about consumers, the marketplace, and what types of issues he should consider when he created and implemented new marketing messages and strategies for his in-store and online retail businesses. Kris asked James to complete a marketing research study of the Yellow and Red store and its consumers, and report back to him within 90 days with his findings.

BACKGROUND ON THE LOCAL UNIVERSITY AND THE YELLOW AND RED STORE

The local university was a large state-sponsored university with an enrollment of approximately 40,000 students. The university had been educating students for more than 100 years. The university-sponsored sports teams played in Division I (NCAA). Every year, many of the men's and women's teams entered the NCAA championships in their respective sports, and the teams frequently brought home national championships.

For more than 30 years, Yellow and Red had been the pre-eminent non-university-owned retailer of university-branded merchandise in the city (population: 150,000). During the first 20 years, the only notable competitor was the university bookstore. Yellow and Red had two retail stores in the city. The primary and largest store was located on the main level of the largest and most popular shopping mall in a 50-mile radius. The second store was located a few blocks from the city's main multi-purpose arena and close to the university campus. Kris believed that both store locations were ideal and generated sufficient income to justify their existence.

Recently, however, nationally owned chain bookstores that focused on selling new and used books had begun to stock university-branded merchandise in their local stores. In addition, department stores and retail supercenters had entered the marketplace and had begun to sell university-branded merchandise. These bookstores and supercenters, in addition to online retailers, had cut into sales at Yellow and Red. During the past five years, in-store sales had dropped by more than 20 percent. To counteract the effect of the in-store drop in sales, Yellow and Red allocated more resources toward building what Kris termed the "largest online retail website for university-branded merchandise" in the area. The online retail website was considered a success, because despite the drop in in-store sales, the overall profits and revenues for Yellow and Red had increased at an average rate of 6 to 8 percent annually throughout this five-year period.

While profits and revenues had increased, during the previous four fiscal quarters, Kris had noticed that the increases were not as large as projected. He attributed these declines to a combination of an overall economic downturn that was affecting the entire country and the increased presence of a new online competitor. Recently, the university's athletics department had decided to begin selling sport- and team-based merchandise through its university-based athletics website.

As James considered the issues Kris had noted, several concerns dominated his thoughts. First, there were issues about the size and saturation of the marketplace. Could Yellow and Red continue to compete with more and more competition, especially with those that offered low-cost merchandise? What were the best ways to maintain Yellow and Red's marketplace position as the top retailer of university-branded merchandise both online and in-store? Moreover, how could Yellow and Red compete with university-owned and operated retailers that had more direct lines of communication with students and alumni? Second, James wondered about how consumers perceived Yellow and Red, the overall image of the store and its website, and consumers' perceptions of the merchandise it sold. Finally, James wondered about the composition of the marketplace; in other words, who was purchasing from Yellow and Red.

As James began to collect his thoughts, he also wondered if the research he was asked to undertake could also lead to the formulation of a new marketing message and strategies for the in-store and online retail businesses. As James started to write a list of the things he needed to complete during the 90 days, he also had to consider the timing and importance of each item.

The first step to choosing a location is completing a geographic trade-area analysis to determine the most appropriate place to set up the sport retail location. This trade-area analysis looks at the geographic and socioeconomic characteristics of the proposed site. The major characteristic to look at is the size and shape of the trade area. The best location has a primary trading area that encompasses the majority of the potential customers to the sport retail firm (75–80%). Another key feature of the trade area is the trend analysis, which involves projections for the future in an area (housing, population change, infrastructure) based on past data. This information can usually be obtained from governmental agencies or the local chamber of commerce.

Once a trade area has been determined, the sport retailer must examine the current attributes to determine minimum standards for moving forward with the chosen location. The major attributes to examine are population, economic base, and competition. For population, general demographics that may be obtained through the United States Census Bureau (www.census.gov) are important. However, more important is using the data to determine effective buying power in a trade area. This disposable income represents 50 percent of a formula called the buying power index (BPI). The formula, which takes into account retail sales and population size in a trade area, is used to determine the retail sales potential of an area. The formula is as follows:

BPI = .5 (DI) + .3 (%USRS) + .2 (%USP); where
- BPI = buying power index
- DI = disposable income for the area
- %USRS = percent of US retail sales for the trade area
- %USP = percent of US population representative of the trade area.

For the economic base of a trade area, the sport retailer is seeking one that offers the most stability and is not detrimentally affected by environmental changes. This is assessed by analyzing the labor force available in the trade area, the infrastructure available including transportation, banking and facilities, the stability of the economy in the trade area, and the growth potential of the trade area. Again much of this information may be obtained through local chamber of commerce offices, or via the internet.

As far as competition is concerned, the most important factor to consider within the trade area is the level of saturation within the industry. If a trade area is under-saturated, then there are not enough sport retail firms selling goods and services to satisfy the needs of the consumers.

When a trade area is over-saturated, then there are too many sport retail outlets, which in turn will lower the potential profit of the sport retailer due to the need to lower prices to compete. The ultimate aim for a sport retailer is a moderately saturated market where the addition of your firm will provide just enough sport retail operations to satisfy customers and maximize profit.

Once the trade-area analysis has been completed, the sport retail professional must determine the type of location. The three major types are as an isolated store, within a business district, or as a part of a planned shopping center. An isolated store is a stand-alone sport retail outlet. This is usually reserved for large sport retail outlets or discount stores. A business district may take numerous forms. A central business district (CBD) is the main retailing area of a city (downtown). A secondary business district (SBD) is located in a city or town at the intersection of two main streets. A neighborhood business district (NBD) serves the goods and service needs of a single residential area. A planned shopping center can take the form of a strip mall (group of a limited number of stores), a shopping mall (a larger group of stores with diverse offerings), or an outlet mall (group of stores offering discounted shopping).

Once the general location has been determined, an exhaustive analysis of the specific site must be completed. This rating is individual to each sport retail firm, as each outlet has its own needs based on its philosophy, mission, and vision. Some of the general areas of analysis include pedestrian and vehicular traffic, availability of parking and mass transportation, access of the facility to major highways to aid in smooth delivery of inventory and customers, and the quality and quantity of competition. Specific areas of analysis include visibility, store placement (corner vs. "middle of the block"), and infrastructural aesthetics including size and shape of the lot and building, and the condition and age of the building.

Another important consideration for location choice is whether the sport retailer plans on owning or leasing the facility. Most small operations are owned, and the major decision is whether to build from scratch or to buy an existing building. Sport retail outlets which lease usually have five options. A straight lease is the most simple as the sport retailer pays a fixed amount per month for the life of the lease. A percentage lease is where a minimum and maximum rent is set, and a sliding scale per month is charged based on a percentage of sales. A graduated lease is variable, with rent going up over a specified period of time during the life of the lease. A maintenance-increase-recoupment lease states that rent will go up if the expenses of the landlord rise beyond a predetermined point. A net lease is where the sport retailer pays rent plus all maintenance and utility costs.

ORGANIZATIONAL STRUCTURE

In the previous sections we have discussed sport consumer relationships, the development of sport retail strategy, and the location of the business. Now we move on to the people of the sport retail organization. In order to meet the needs, wants, and desires of the market, a sport retail firm must design an organizational structure that effectively and efficiently allocates tasks, resources, authority, and responsibilities. This is set in motion by creating a list of the tasks to be performed throughout the sport retail management process. The list below represents some of the typical tasks to be completed by a sport retail firm:

- purchasing merchandise from suppliers and wholesalers to be sold
- delivery of merchandise to the retailer
- receiving and checking incoming merchandise shipments
- setting prices and marking merchandise
- inventory management, including control and storage
- developing merchandise and window displays
- store maintenance (clean, working conditions)
- marketing and market research
- creating ease of flow for shoppers
- handling of complaints
- human resources management
- merchandise alterations, repairs, and returns
- billing customers
- maintaining financial records and credit operations
- sales forecasting and budgeting
- gift wrapping and other customer perks.

Once the list is developed, tasks are divided among organizational structure members. In dividing these tasks up, it is important to remember that a task should be carried out only if it is determined that the target market needs, wants, or desires it. If this is true, then management must choose the individual or group with the greatest competence to complete the task, and in a manner that is most economical to the sport retail firm. This is often accomplished by grouping the tasks within specific job responsibilities. These responsibilities are usually classified as functional tasks or product-based tasks, and are documented within the organizational chart. Usually within a small sport retail operation, there are few employees and limited specialization. This requires most employees to carry out multiple job requirements. In larger retail operations, the organization is usually divided between four tasks: publicity, financial control, store management, and merchandising. Publicity deals with the majority of the marketing function. Financial control deals with accounting, profit planning, asset management, and resource allocation. Store management deals with human resource management and operations management. Human resource management focuses on the recruitment, application process, interviewing, hiring, training, and retention of employees, as well as recurring evaluation of job descriptions, evaluation processes for jobs and employees, and compensation issues (salary, benefits, perks). Operations management focuses on setting goals and objectives, maintaining policies and procedures, space allocation in the store, scheduling of personnel, maintenance of the facility, security and crisis management, and inventory management. Merchandising deals with the buying and selling of merchandise.

MERCHANDISE MANAGEMENT

The buying and selling of merchandise focuses on having the proper assortment of inventory and selling those products in conjunction with the sport retail strategy. To be an effective merchandiser, sport retail managers must understand the planning aspects of merchandising, the manner in which merchandising is implemented, the maintenance of financial integrity, and the resulting development of merchandise pricing.

Merchandise planning

The planning aspect of merchandising centers on: the development of a merchandise philosophy; defining the procedures for buying and selling; the creation of merchandise plans; and the establishment of a management process for brand categories. A merchandise philosophy is the sport retail firm's values and beliefs. This philosophy centers on both buying and selling activities, and may be looked at as a collective pursuit or two separate efforts. Regardless of the focus, the philosophy acts as the framework for the organizational mission, goals, and objectives. In turn, the mission, goals, and objectives serve as a basis for the managerial processes of the sport retail organization. These processes include the level of formality, the degree of centralization, the scope of offerings of the sport retail organization, the manner in which personnel and resources are utilized, and the method by which general sport retail functions are performed.

The processes are utilized to develop the sport merchandising plan. This plan articulates the intended selection of merchandise, the management process of product categories and brands, the distinctiveness and innovativeness of the merchandise offered for sale, the timing of when merchandise is to be kept in inventory, the determination of how much inventory will be kept on the sales floor, and the resulting forecast of expected retail sales.

Implementation of merchandising

Implementation of the plan involves an eight-step process. First, the sport retail manager obtains information about the target market and potential suppliers by researching sources including consumers, suppliers, competitors, governmental agencies, commercial data, and the media. Next, the sport retailer will select multiple sources of merchandise and start a dialogue with them. During this discussion the sport retailer will be evaluating merchandise via inspection, sampling, and description buying – which is ordering in quantity based on the description of the product. At this point, the sport retailer will negotiate a purchasing contract with the supplier. Upon completion of the negotiation phase and signing of contracts, the ordering process is created. For larger sport retail operations, purchases are usually made through a computerized system. Smaller firms that do not have this capability usually process orders manually.

After orders are placed, the sport retail manager must plan for receiving and stocking the merchandise. This coordination of the movement of merchandise from the supplier to retailer, and ultimately to the consumer, is called logistics. Logistics, as previously discussed in Chapter 6, has external and internal aspects. Externally, logistics deals with supply chain management, order processing and fulfillment, transportation systems, and warehousing. Internally, the sport retailer deals with logistics related to customer transactions and customer service. This is when the sport retailer takes control of the merchandise and is responsible for inventory management, including receiving and stocking merchandise, paying the supplier for the merchandise, pricing the merchandise, setting up displays, completing sales, and processing returns and damaged goods.

Throughout this implementation process, reordering merchandise takes place to ensure that the sport retail outlet does not run out of stock. The process for this reordering involves understanding the process and time needed for ordering and delivering, the level of turnover for the specific inventory, the amount of money that must be paid, and ultimately whether keeping the merchandise in stock or ordering as needed is most effective and efficient.

In addition, the entire merchandising process is constantly evaluated. The purpose of this is to see what is working, what aspects can be improved, and what should be eliminated. The conclusions collected as a result of this evaluation process will be utilized, as the entire merchandising implementation process is ongoing and cyclical.

Merchandising and financial integrity

In order for the implementation process to go smoothly, there must be financial integrity within the sport retail organization. This involves controlling the products to be purchased, when they are to be purchased, and the quantity to be purchased. To maintain financial integrity within the merchandising function of the sport retail organization, there must be precise inventory control, accounting methodologies, and control of monetary outflows.

Inventory control

The two main inventory control systems utilized in sport retail management are perpetual inventory systems and physical inventory systems. The method utilized depends on the size of the sport retail firm and the desired outcomes of tracking inventory.

Perpetual inventory, also known as continuous inventory, is where the book inventory is always made to tally with the actual inventory through daily bookkeeping. Therefore cost of goods sold is determined each time inventory is sold. This inventory can be accomplished by hand, but this is extremely time consuming and would only be appropriate for sport retail operations with low inventory turnover. Most often, a point-of-sale system is used to process information via the scanning of barcodes. This information is immediately processed internally to tabulate profit, track inventory, and in some cases order new inventory from suppliers when stock on hand reaches a specific pre-set level.

In a physical inventory system, the cost of goods sold is determined at the end of the accounting period. The most effective means of managing a physical inventory system is by a stock-counting system. This involves the actual counting of units of merchandise, sometimes as often as on a daily basis. This system not only counts inventory in stock, but also purchases, sales volume, and shortages. This methods requires a lot of clerical work to maintain, and is not significantly effective unless the items are low-value and whose sales are predictable.

Accounting methodologies

Sport retail inventory accounting systems helps the sport retail manager keep track of sales, purchases, inventory value, quantity of merchandise, and the need to reorder merchandise. There are two major methods utilized in tracking these methods – the cost accounting method and the retail method.

The cost accounting method involves measuring, classifying, and recording costs of all merchandise. This method is used to identify and segment various production costs in terms

of the actual total cost of the merchandise purchased and the value of the inventory on hand. This information is used to assist the sport retail firm in making prudent operating decisions. This method is also most effective when utilized by a sport retail firm that has low inventory turnover (speedboats), limited assortment (a specific piece of workout equipment such as Bowflex), and high average prices (season tickets to the Boston Red Sox).

The retail method is more of an end-result method of accounting, and is utilized by most retailers in all industries because it is easier to use with larger and physical inventories. This retail accounting method involves a three-step process. First, the cost complement is determined by computing a ratio of the relationship between actual total cost and total retail value (CC=ATC / TRV). This is accomplished by putting a value on beginning inventory, determining net purchases, and adding shipping and handling costs from both an inventory valuation and retail valuation standpoint. Also included in retail valuation is the projected retail mark-up.

Next, the adjusted ending retail value is determined by examining the value of ending inventory and deducting mark-downs and discounts. The sport retailer then estimates any inventory shortages or overages, since physical inventory is taken infrequently due to the quantity of inventory and variation of products (however, once inventory is taken, the retail book value is corrected).

Finally, the cost of the ending inventory is estimated by multiplying the adjusted ending retail value by the cost complement (AERV * CC = CEI). This cost of ending inventory is also known as gross profit. While this method is very cumbersome and requires a lot of bookkeeping, and the numbers are not 100 percent accurate because it is based on average costs instead of actual costs, it does provide an average relationship between costs and selling price. This may then be used in general across the sport retail operation to make adjustments to increase profit on a total scale.

Controlling monetary outflows

Ultimately, all inventory control and accounting methodologies are utilized to develop the budget for the sport retail organization, as well as to forecast future financial operations. The combined functions of budgeting and forecasting are called the dollar-control process. The four steps of this process are selecting merchandise classification units, inventory and purchase planning, planning for profit margins, and forecasting for future sales.

Classification units for sport merchandise serve the purpose of categorizing selected sport products in order to control the inventory, target opportunities to sell more sport merchandise, and determine problems with any sport product lines. The most common way to categorize sport retail units is by department (golf, tennis, basketball, etc.) or price (budget items, general retail stock, high end and specialized merchandise).

Inventory planning takes two forms – level planning and reduction planning. Level planning strives to ensure that inventory on hand will be sufficient to meet sales projections. This can be accomplished in a number of ways such as stockpiling inventory and utilizing comparative ratios. The comparative ratios typically utilized in sport retail management differ depending on the classification unit, and may be researched via the National Sporting Goods Association (www.nsga.org) or the Sport Business Research Network (www.sbrnet.com). Reduction planning is represented by the following formula:

201

(Beginning inventory + Planned purchases) – (Projected sales + Ending inventory).

Profit margin planning is determining the percentage of earnings the sport retail firm would like to make collectively and on individual products. To determine this profit margin, an analysis is conducted on net sales, operating expenses, actual profit, and the aforementioned reductions. While profit margin may be generalized across the retail firm, individual items may be marked up further based on demand.

Sales forecasting is a sport retailer's projection for future revenues. Usually these forecasts are estimated across the sport retail organization, and then broken down for specific divisions or individual sport products. In general, sales forecasts for small sport retail firms are made by "best guess," whereas larger sport retailers will incorporate multiple types of statistical analyses, including consumer trends, time series factors, and regressions.

Development of merchandising pricing

As mentioned earlier, profit margin is a primary concern resulting from controlling monetary outflows. Sport retail products and services must be priced in a way that maximizes profitability for the retailer and satisfies customers. At the same time, the strategy employed to develop prices must be in congruence with the sport retailer's overall image, sales, profit, and ROI.

As defined earlier in the chapter, the wheel of sport retailing has three levels: low end/discount; middle of the road/general; and high end/luxury. The level at which a sport retail firm targets its customers will directly influence their place on the wheel, and hence direct its pricing options. For a low end/discount sport retail organization such as Play It Again Sports, prices will be low, especially since most of the merchandise sold is used. A middle-of-the-road/general sport retail such as Sports Authority or Dicks will price sport products at typical market price as determined by the overall industry. High end/luxury sport retailers tend to be specialty stores where the upscale client would shop and pay premium prices. An example of this would be a country club pro shop.

Pricing can be affected by a number of external sources, the most important of which is the consumer. From the point of view of a sport retail organization, elasticity of demand is the biggest influence on pricing. Elasticity of demand is the sensitivity sport consumers have to pricing changes, and the relationship to the quantity of sport product they will buy. When there is inelastic demand, changes in price do not significantly affect purchases. Elastic demand is where the percentage of change in purchases is significantly and inversely correlated to the change in price ($\uparrow$ price = $\downarrow$ sales; $\downarrow$ price = $\uparrow$ sales).

Other external factors ranging from manufacturers and suppliers to competitors and the government can directly affect a sport retailer's pricing strategy. Manufacturers and suppliers would prefer to control prices because they want to maintain their image, regardless of whether it is at the expense of the profit of the sport retailer. They try to control the eventual retail price by charging their selected price to the sport retailer. However, as the end-point of the sport retail channel, and the part of the channel most influenced by the sport consumer, the sport retailer will usually set the prices based on its own goals, vision, and image.

Competition has a significant effect on pricing. When there are large numbers of similar retailers in a target market, sport retailers have little control over price because consumers can shop around. As a result, market pricing occurs, which is very susceptible to elasticity of demand and competitive reactions. Consequently, some retail firms try to utilize administered pricing. This is when sport retailers seek to attract customers based on image, assortment, convenience, and service, thereby taking price out of the consideration process for the sport consumer.

The government also has a direct effect on pricing strategy. There are regulations set forth at the local, state, and federal level to control price fixing. Horizontal price fixing involves agreements between sport retailer and suppliers to set certain prices. This practice is against the law by way of the Federal Trade Commission Act and the Sherman Antitrust Act. Vertical price fixing occurs when suppliers seek to control the retail prices of their goods and services. As per the Consumer Goods Pricing Act, sport retailers cannot be forced to stick to retail prices guidelines set by suppliers. The goal of this is to support competition in the marketplace.

Sport retail pricing strategy

In order to develop a sport retail pricing strategy, the sport retailer must look back to the philosophy, mission, and goals of the organization. The sport retailer then uses this information to develop pricing objectives that support sales, profit, and ROI. Depending on the type of sport retail firm, either a market penetration or a market skimming strategy will be employed. A market penetration strategy is used when a sport retail firm seeks to gain greater market share in its existing market. This is accomplished by lowering prices to a point where profit is ultimately increased by the resulting increase in sales volume. This can only work if total retail costs do not significantly rise as a result of the increased volume. With a market skimming pricing strategy, a sport retail firm sets premium prices and attracts sport consumers who are less concerned with price. These individuals are influenced by service, assortment, and prestige. This strategy is appropriate when new competitors are unlikely to enter the market, and added sales will greatly increase retail cost.

Once the objectives have been set, a pricing policy must be implemented. This policy serves as the framework for applying the pricing objective within the sport retail organization. In general, sport retail firms employ a broad pricing policy so that short- and long-term objectives can be met. In addition, the sport retail firm must coordinate the pricing policy with the sport retail firm's image, the composition of the target market, and the elements of the sport retail mix discussed earlier in this chapter. Examples of pricing policies include: (1) discount pricing vs. market pricing vs. luxury pricing; (2) pricing leader in the market segment, or price follower; and (3) consistent pricing or changing pricing based on costs.

The creation of a pricing strategy comes as a result of the pricing policies, as well as from the understanding that the sport industry is demand-oriented. As a result, the sport retailer starts to develop its strategy by attempting to determine the maximum price the sport consumer will pay for a given sport product. The pricing is then adjusted based on the quantities purchased and feedback from sport consumers. This adjustment is referred to as mark-up pricing (which includes mark-downs). However, a major external factor may create an additional alteration to pricing. Competitor-oriented pricing is set in equivalence to that of a competitor to maintain an average market price, and allow the sport retailer to concentrate on other factors to differentiate its organization, including service, image, and convenience.

After the strategy is set, a plan for implementation must be instituted. The most common ways to implement a pricing strategy are via customary pricing or variable pricing. Customary pricing is when the sport retailer sets prices for goods and services, and seeks to maintain them for an extended period. The most common practice of customary pricing is "everyday low prices." Variable pricing is when a sport retailer changes its prices as a result of changes in costs or demand. This is especially true in the sport and recreational travel industry, where changes in costs and demand change based on environmental trends (seasons, weather, politics, societal issues).

There are a number of other implementations of pricing policies and strategies. A one-price policy is where all products are the same price (US$1 store). A flexible pricing policy is where consumers bargain over prices of products (eBay, Boston Whaler Boats). An odd-pricing strategy is a psychological pricing strategy where all products are priced slightly below the even dollar. For example, it is more likely that a person will spend US$44.99 on sneakers at one store than US$45.00 at another. A multiple-unit pricing strategy is where a sport consumer will receive a discount for purchasing in bulk. An example would be where a camp director could buy one basketball off the shelf for US$24.99, but will only pay US$22.49 for buying 100 basketballs (10 percent discount saves almost US$250).

GETTING THE MESSAGE OUT: SPORT RETAILER COMMUNICATIONS

Promotional tools utilized in sport marketing of sport retail operations include advertising, sales management, and public relations, to name a few. However, the major focus for sport retailers is image. Part of this image involves how the sport retail organization interacts with the community in which it is located. However, the sport retail firm does not have control of how those marketing and community relations efforts are viewed by the potential sport consumers. The one aspect over which a sport retailer has total control is atmosphere.

The sport retail atmosphere refers to the physical characteristics that project an image, attract customers, and keep them shopping. There is an expression: "You never get a second chance at a first impression." This is true in sport retail management – many customers form impressions of a retailer either just before or immediately after entering a store. Therefore, a sport retail manager must consider four major components of the sport retail atmosphere – the exterior, the interior, the layout, and displays.

The exterior of the sport retail facility is the physical exterior of the store, including signage, entrances, windows, lighting, and parking areas. Signage, including marquees and billboards, should display the name of the sport retail firm, advertise important information, and attract attention. The major issues regarding entrances include how many, what type (automatic, push-pull, revolving), and ease of flow. Windows serve three functions – to display merchandise, to show the interior of the store, and to brighten the interior with natural light. Abundant exterior lighting provides for ease of ingress and egress to and from the store. Parking facilities should be well lit, convenient, and uncongested.

The interior of a store will directly affect the mood of the customer and be a significant factor in the purchase decision-making process. Some of the most important factors to consider include the cleanliness of the store, adequate but non-distractive lighting, and store fixtures and shelving that are appropriate and easy for the customer to access. The interior also needs to be aesthetically pleasing, including the color of walls and ceilings, and comfortable floors to walk on. If the sport retail outlet is on more than one floor, there must be adequate transportation via elevators, escalators, and stairs.

The layout of the store should be in an organized manner with wide aisles, easy ingress and egress, and appropriate amenities such as rest-rooms and customer service areas. The typical floor space for a sport retail outlet is divided into selling space (displays, registers), merchandise space (storerooms), personnel space (break areas), and customer space (aisles, vending areas, wide aisles, vertical transportation). Throughout the design, easy traffic flow is crucial to a quality layout. A straight traffic flow has displays and aisles in a grid pattern, whereas a curving traffic pattern places displays and aisles in a free-flowing design.

Displays are the interior point-of-purchase efforts that provide the sport consumer with product information and promotional offerings. A traditional open display allows the sport consumer to look at, pick up, touch, feel, and even try out or on the sport product. A closed display is usually behind locked glass cabinets due to its higher value. However, the sport consumer can often touch and feel the sport product with the assistance of a customer representative. An ensemble display is utilized when products from different but associated product lines can be displayed together to complement each other and entice multiple purchases. A rack display is often used for sport clothing because it is hung and displayed on racks. The hardest problem with this type of display is to prevent items from being cluttered and misplaced. Regardless of the display, there are usually promotional peripherals such as posters, signs, and product description cards, which are used to further tempt the sport consumer to purchase the product.

Of course, these concepts differ if the sport retailer does not have a physical store, such as a company whose sales are mainly based on mail orders, catalogs, and the web. The exterior is the front page of the advertising pieces, catalogs, and web pages. The interior is the ease with which the sport retailer can navigate through the catalog or website. The layout aids with this ease, using indexes, tables of contents, forms, and links. The displays can be unlimited, but must avoid clutter and confusion.

One of the major difficulties for non-store retailers has to do with check-out points. Customers do not receive the product immediately in exchange for payment – they have to go through a longer process. Mail order is dependent on the efficiency of the mail service, and how swiftly orders are processed. Catalog orders are often made over the phone and are quicker, but again the time between ordering and receiving the product is not instantaneous. The same may be said for online orders, but there are still concerns regarding the security and privacy of orders as compared to purchasing in person. In addition, for all of these non-store options, there are often extra fees incurred for shipping and handling. Therefore, in order to entice the sport consumer to purchase sport products, the non-store-based organization must create both a positive tangible and intangible atmosphere.

CONCLUSION

In sport retail management, success is often measured by the amount of profit achieved. Sometimes numbers lie. It is equally important to coordinate policies and strategies, and to assess performance, to work toward reaching the goals of the sport retail organization. By incorporating and evaluating the overall organization, sport retail firms of any size or format can create a high-quality retail experience for the sport consumer.

As sport retail management continues to grow, its future is evolving into new areas. The sport industry continues to grow globally, which has opened new international and global markets to sport retailers. Changes in sport consumer lifestyles as a result of new sport segments (i.e., alternative sports) and the acceptance of marketing toward underrepresented markets (women, gay/lesbian) has opened up new market opportunities to sport retailers. As technology continues to grow, sport retail firms must decide whether they are going to become a multi-channeled retailer. This may become mandatory as competition among and between channel formats continues to be more prevalent.

Sport retail management is the end result of the distribution process, and is the focal point for the sale of the sport product to consumers for their personal consumption. Without sport retailers, there is no sale of the sport product, and sport marketing becomes useless. While there are many challenges, success in sport retail management is possible if a sport retail firm has a solid retail strategy, strong organization, sound application of the sport retail mix, and effective and efficient merchandise management.

FROM THEORY TO PRACTICE

MANDY CORMIER, FORMER MERCHANDISE MANAGER
Norfolk Tides Baseball Club,
Norfolk, Virginia

When I started in working in retail in 1998 for Lady Foot Locker I just considered it a job to make some money while in High School. After I decided where I was going to go to college my current manager wanted me to stay with the company and transferred me to the Pheasant Lane Mall in Nashua, New Hampshire. I continued to work throughout college and they were always understanding about basketball and school work. I became a shift manager, which allowed me to be the manager on duty if the Manager was not in the store. Soon after graduation in May I became Assistant Manager for the Nashua store; I could not believe that I was still with the company. After being Assistant Manager for only two months I was promoted to Manager in Cambridge, Massachusetts. This was an enormous step and a big accomplishment. Even though I was excited to be close to home the Boston cliental is completely different than New Hampshire.

My first week as Manager was really difficult. The staff at Cambridge were already set in their ways and most of my employees were the same age if not older. It was definitely a big change for me even though I had grown up right outside of Boston because their needs were different than what I was used to. In Nashua most of the customers were looking for technical sneakers for performance, whereas in Cambridge they were more looking for fashion styles. Since Lady Foot Locker is a corporate company I really did not have a say in what product I would receive. I could always give my input, but we (the managers) did not get to actually choose the items we would sell. With that said we would make the best of it by contacting other managers to either send them a style that had been sitting in the stockroom in our store, but they could have sold out of it. By doing this they in turn would send an item that we may have sold really well to replenish our stock. Basically the idea was to produce as much money at the end of the day as we could. We would be unable to do so if the trend remained that we are out of stock or out of sizes that had been repeatedly asked for.

In a corporate environment and for such a big company you have to listen to your customers. At Lady Foot Locker customer service was a big part of one's training; as managers we would constantly train our employees on customer service. I believe this to be an integral part of running a successful business, especially in the retail world. Up until the time that customers walk out of the door you are there to provide them with your knowledge, and that is why you work for a certain company. When customers leave, you want to make an impression on them to want to come back to your store and tell their friends to shop there too. Throughout this time as Manager I realized that I had been with the company for almost seven years and it was a great company to work for, but I felt as though I needed to move on.

A few months after I left Lady Foot Locker I sent my résumé to the Norfolk Tides Baseball Club in Norfolk, Virginia. At this time they were looking for a Director of Merchandise and, considering I had plenty of retail experience, I was confident that I could do a good job. Only about two days after I sent in my résumé, the General Manager called and asked to do a phone interview. We concluded our conversation after about an hour and he asked for a reference at Lady Foot Locker, considering that was all of my retail experience. About a week went by and he called me to ask if he could fly me down for a day to meet the front office, see the area, and to make sure I could see myself living there. This was all happening so fast that I could barely even talk to my parents about it; they just knew that they were dropping me off at the airport.

When I arrived in Virginia the General Manager was there waiting for me. We headed back to the stadium where the office was and everyone was very welcoming and hoping that I was going to join the staff. They took me out to lunch just to get a little background and what I thought I could bring to their novelty store. They must have been impressed because soon after we got back from lunch I was offered the position. I waited about four days to discuss it with my family; to me this was a pretty big move. After finally moving all of my stuff from New Hampshire to Virginia, I was ready to start work. This was what I had been waiting for since I graduated college.

Working for a sports team's novelty store is very different than the corporate world. Here at the Tides I actually get to decide which items to sell in the store. Part of this is that I also get to work with the art designers to figure out designs and colors to put on the items. One of the first things I had to do when I arrived here was to try to figure out the style in which people dressed and what my clientele was going to be like. Seeing that it is my first season here it was kind of difficult figuring out what was going to sell or not. By asking the office and doing my own research I tried to incorporate mainstream styles into the store. Once I can see the trends that come in and out I will be able to get more of a variety. The main goal is to have little inventory at the end of the season; you want to keep some because of your internet orders but you do not want to have a full stockroom. In a corporate environment if you are sitting on a certain item for a long period of time you can have sales or send the items back to the vendor. In a novelty store you are stuck with the leftovers, and having a sale will sell some of the items but not as many as you would think.

When you are thinking of what items to put into a store another main thing is that you want to make it look colorful and change displays often. Most minor league baseball fans are regulars or season ticket holders, so you do not want them to walk into the same store every home stand. At the beginning of the season you want to put your cold weather items toward the front of the store; blankets are a big seller at this time of year. Then you gradually want to push your T-shirts and tank tops toward the front. One thing that I instill in my game day employees is customer service; that is very important whether you work in corporate or not. After working the first exhibition game sales were really good, and so far all of the methods I learned from Lady Foot Locker have worked here at the Tides. I learn something new every day here as far as paperwork and talking with the vendors is concerned.

Overall this has been a great experience and I have learned a great deal about the retail industry. There are major differences as far as preparation, paperwork, and ordering items between corporate and sports novelty. Once all that is figured out it is the same as working at Lady Foot Locker and shining through with customer service. When working for a professional sports team you have to know the general clientele and how much you think the average baseball fan is going to spend. It is very important to watch the cost of items and realize what you can actually sell the item for. Of course you are going to have to take some risks with certain items or you will never know the outcome. In general keep the risks low and minimal; if a new idea sells, then the organization will be more open to new ideas. One of the most important things to also look for throughout the season is your inventory. Know what you have in stock and keep track of what was sold for two reasons; you never want to run out of a hot-selling item and you will know what trends to go with next season. Working in retail has been a great experience and I have met many people. There are many different aspects of retail other than just working in a mall, which most people do not know. The important thing is to get into the right environment like professional sports and let your ideas be heard. With that you can go to so many more places than you ever imagined.

CHAPTER NINE

E-MARKETING MANAGEMENT IN SPORT

CHAPTER OUTLINE

- What is e-marketing?
- Digital technologies utilized to manage sport e-business and e-commerce
- Conducting sport e-business and e-commerce
- Sport e-business and e-commerce in the new economy
- Conclusion

CHAPTER OBJECTIVES

The reader will be able to:

- understand the prevalence, importance, and continued growth of e-business and e-commerce in sport marketing and sport business
- know the categories of e-business and e-commerce, including B2B, B2C, C2B, and C2C
- appreciate the growth in digital technologies used to manage sport e-businesses, including the internet, the World Wide Web, intranets, and recent introductions of new technologies
- understand the factors that drive sport e-business in the new economy
- recognize how sport businesses utilize electronic means to overcome barriers of geographic boundaries to market, produce, and deliver sport products and services
- be cognizant of the latest technologies being utilized in the sport marketplace.

WHAT IS E-MARKETING?

In the twenty-first century, the use of electronic technologies to conduct business domestically, internationally, and globally is integral to growth and success. When we talk about the concept of "e" we are referring to electronic networks, including the internet, World Wide Web, and Intranet. These digital technologies make sport products and sport services more easily accessible to more people than ever. The two major areas that facilitate this accessibility are e-business and e-commerce.

Sport e-business

Sport e-business is an all-encompassing term that covers the internal information technology processes of a sport organization including human resources, finance, inventory management, product development, and risk management. The purpose of the e-business strategy is to streamline operations, reduce costs, and make productivity more efficient. This is accomplished by integrating business processes, information technology applications, and the infrastructure of the sport organization to facilitate business and marketing functions including communications, sales, and service.

A sport organization engaged in e-business will find numerous challenges when seeking to integrate with traditional business operations. Usually a combination of the following four strategies is employed to integrate the systems: Horizontal integration involves a number of the internal processes needed to bring sport products and services to market through an e-business structure. Sport consumer relationship management (to be discussed in greater detail in Chapter 15) is the use of various methodologies, information technologies, and internet capabilities to help sport entities organize and manage sport consumer relationships by developing a system that all members of the sport marketing effort can utilize to access information about sport products and strive toward meeting the needs and wants of sport consumers. Knowledge management involves the methods utilized by a sport organization to create, gather, classify, modify, and apply knowledge about sport consumers' values and beliefs to achieve goals and objectives. Sport organization resource planning involves assimilating all functions of the sport organization through information technology methods to become more efficient and effective in planning, manufacturing, marketing, and selling sport products and services. Supply chain management (Chapter 6) is the process of coordinating the movement of sport products, sport services, and other pertinent information from raw materials to manufacturer to wholesaler to retailer and eventually to the sport consumer.

Vertical integration is the speed with which information is delivered through internal and external information technology processes. Internal information technology includes the in-house servers and other automation utilized to take, process, and deliver orders, as well as track feedback from sport consumers. External information technologies are those utilized by the sport consumer where the sport consumer can view the sport product, possibly in some cases individually design the sport product, order the product, and track the order process.

Downward integration is the movement of information throughout the entire sport organization using information technology. Lateral integration is the movement of information between a sport organization and the sport consumer or business partners. All of these sport e-business integration strategies are difficult to implement owing to the complexity of and need for significant knowledge of information technology. However, sport e-business has a greater possibility of revenues and profits as a result of more efficient and effective processes, and the overall lower costs of conducting business.

Sport e-commerce

Sport e-commerce entails the external information technology processes of a sport organization including the marketing and sales functions. More specifically, sport e-commerce involves the buying and selling of sport products and services through the World Wide Web (www) and the internet. It also involves Intranet functions such as electronic funds transfers (EFT), smart cards (card with a chip that holds customer information and money available), and fan-loyalty reward programs. Sport e-commerce also includes the internal function of the organization that facilitates these external exchanges.

From an integration standpoint, e-commerce specifically coordinates the vertical integration function of e-business. E-commerce also integrates with traditional sport business operations in two additional ways. First, there is cross-business integration where the sport organization must coordinate the information technologies of suppliers, sport consumers (personal web-sites), and web-based marketplaces (such as eBay). Second, there is technology integration. This involves modifying the traditional processes of order handling, purchasing and customer services with the specific needs of the sport consumers, and the unique abilities of the sport organization in mind.

In the twenty-first century, sport marketers must understand e-commerce strategy if they are to be successful. Most organizations, especially as a result of the expansion from domestic markets to international and global markets, are engaged in e-commerce, and utilize this function as a primary method for interacting with sport consumers, suppliers, and distributors. The major challenge for the sport marketing professional is that the electronic environment changes even more rapidly than the traditional marketplace. Therefore, the ability to shift resources, update content, and modify revenue models is crucial to success in sport e-commerce.

There are two major strategies that are utilized by sport marketing professionals to react to this quickly changing electronic environment. The KISS (keep it simple) approach is just that – have simple rules within the sport marketing strategy to allow for easy reactions to changes in the environment. This makes it easy for the sport marketing professional to adapt to change, which will help the organization reduce overall time in creating and/or modifying products and services desired by the sport consumer, and in turn will reduce overall costs in the long term.

The sense-and-respond approach is another method utilized to respond quickly to changes in the sport market. The premise is that strategic thinking is intuitive, reactionary, and simple. This adaptive sport marketing approach means that the sport marketing professional must utilize the e-commerce structure to allow sport consumers to tell the professional who they are, what they value, why they have an interest in a sport product or service, and how they want to consume it.

This approach is a significant departure from traditional market approaches where there is a collection of information, the information is over-analyzed, coming up with a number of options, further analyzing the pros and cons of each solution, and eventually choosing a course of action. By the time this entire process is completed, the e-commerce environment may have changed again, and the sport organization will have missed out. The sense-and-respond approach encourages sport marketing professionals and sport organization management to be more proactive in their decision-making and problem-solving processes. This is accomplished by taking the information collected, realizing that those who take their time providing feedback via e-commerce communication methods are most likely those with a vested interest in the sport product or service, and reacting to that information by experimenting with solutions that will satisfy the needs, wants, and desires of the sport consumer.

In general, the evolution of sport e-commerce has introduced two significant concepts into the sport marketing vocabulary. The first is individualization which takes personalizing and customizing sport products and services to another level by allowing for personalized communications between the sport consumer and the company (usually via a website or social networking sites). Sport consumers can also customize the interface with the sport organization to suit their needs. An example of this ability to customize is the website www.trophy central.com. On this website, customers can start with a basic uniform or trophy and customize their order by designing the product to their specifications. The customer can choose color, style, graphics (either uploaded by the customer or selected from a catalog), text (font and size), material, and much more. The customer can then review the order, make changes as necessary, select quantity, delivery and payment methods, and complete the order.

The other main concept that has evolved as a result of sport e-commerce is interactivity. This is the ability of the sport consumer to have more two-way communication with sport organizations and sport marketers. In traditional marketing, most marketing communication is one-way through television, radio, and print advertising. There are also sport marketing communication efforts that are one-to-one, where methods such as direct mail and telemarketing create one-time, one-way contact. In interactive marketing communications, these efforts may be in real time (instant feedback via email) or asynchronous (discussion and message boards). This allows the customer to be in control of the communication, and increases the likelihood of a positive interaction between the sport organization and the consumer.

The sport marketing professional who manages an e-commerce strategy must be able to coordinate technology, capital, media, political, and legal issues. Therefore, the sport marketer must take a cross-discipline, integrative position to be able to make strategic decisions quickly and with the proper authority. As a result, the sport marketing professional must be able to create a vision for e-commerce, develop the methods for setting objectives and accomplishing goals, be the central figure in driving the implementation of processes, and be ultimately accountable for the performance of the strategy.

Sport e-commerce is a relatively new concept that requires the sport marketing professional to understand the evolution of consumer behavior and technology, balance the changes that are inevitable in the sport marketplace, and integrate traditional business operations with online activities. The sport marketer who can effectively integrate these concepts can design plans that will react to environmental changes, maintain a competitive advantage, and create new value chains in the sport marketplace.

Categories of e-business and e-commerce in sport marketing

The concepts of sport e-business and sport e-commerce involve the various interactions between businesses and consumers through digital communications. In the traditional communication process, the sender uses a channel to send a message to a receiver, who then provides a response and feedback. In the digital communication process, the type of interaction is directly related to who the sender is and who the receiver is. For sport e-business and e-commerce, there are four categories: business-to-business (B2B), business-to-consumer (B2C), consumer-to-business (C2B), and consumer-to-consumer (C2C):

- Business-to-Business (B2B) refers to the transactions, collaborations, and business interactions that occur between two organizations. For sport organizations, this can include a multitude of functions including management of inventory, channels, and sales, as well as service and support operations. In the sporting goods industry, Sport Supply Group (www.sportsupplygroup.com) is one of the leading B2B e-commerce suppliers of equipment for institutions and the youth sports marketplace. Sport Supply Group acts as an intermediary in online sales of sports equipment from selected manufacturers to primary and secondary schools, colleges and universities, camps, youth organizations, and governmental agencies.
- Business-to-Consumer (B2C) focuses on the transactions between businesses and consumers. For the sport organization, these transactions are usually plentiful, but smaller in scope than those transacted through B2B. Ticketmaster (www.ticketmaster.com) is one of the most popular B2C websites, offering to the consumer tickets to sport events, concerts, show, and other leisure activities across the United States and the world.
- Consumer-to-Business (C2B) is where the consumer initiates the transaction process by soliciting organizations to compete for the individual's business. While this is not widely used directly in sport business, an example of C2B would be www.priceline.com. Priceline.com is a travel service that allows consumers to name their own price, and airlines, hotels, travel packages and rental car agencies will respond to the consumers and potentially meet their demand.
- Consumer-to-Consumer (C2C) involves transactions between customers. Many of these transactions will involve an online third party business, such as eBay (www.ebay.com). One customer can sell directly to another customer an assortment of items ranging from sport memorabilia to event tickets. This may also be referred to as peer-to-peer (P2P).

DIGITAL TECHNOLOGIES UTILIZED TO MANAGE SPORT E-BUSINESS AND E-COMMERCE

Digital technologies are the centerpiece of sport e-business and commerce, as they are used to manage the exchange of sport products and services. The internet is the collection of computer networks interconnected by wires, fiber optics, and cables. This is very different from the World Wide Web (www), which is a collection of interconnected documents that are connected by uniform resource locators (URLs) and hyperlinks. Uniform resource locators, more commonly known as main web addresses, are the actual location of an internet item that an individual would like to see, such as www.atomicdog.com. Every page on the web has a unique URL. Hyperlinks refer to text or graphics placed on a web page to provide cross-referenced materials for the user. For example, www.oursportscentral.com is one of the leading minor league and independent league news websites. It would be impossible for them to put every piece of news onto one page; therefore they create separate pages for each news item, and put hyperlinks on the main page to connect with each story.

As far as the exchange of sport products and services via e-business and e-commerce is concerned, the main method is through sport company websites. This allows for interaction between the buyer and the sport company 24 hours a day, 7 days a week, 365 days a year, regardless of the location of the company.

In addition, there are three other types of websites that are utilized for the exchange of sport products and services. Brokering sites act as an intermediary between one sport business wanting a sport product or service, and another sport business seeking to provide such a product (see Sport Supply Group above under B2B).

Infomediaries publish trade and industry standards about an industry for those who operate in that industry. An example for the sport industry is F+W Publishing (www.fwpublishing.com), which publishes special interest magazines and books for a variety of consumer enthusiast categories, including sport collectibles. Some of their publications include "Sports Collectors Digest" and "Card Trade."

E-procurement, also known as product supply and procurement exchanges, is where the purchasing function is often outsourced to a third party. That company acts as an agent to shop for supplies, request proposals, and bid on making purchases on behalf of their client. It is also used occasionally for the storage of items, as the e-business rarely pays for that kind of storage space. An example of an e-procurement site would be www.bidnet.com, where buyers can streamline their purchasing processes, and vendors are connected with the ability to bid on government contracts. Specifically, their e-procurement department was established to create and manage websites so that purchasing agencies could register their vendors and deliver bid information directly to them.

CONDUCTING SPORT E-BUSINESS AND E-COMMERCE

Operating in sport e-business and e-commerce shares some similarities with traditional sport retail management. While a traditional sport retail store is a physical setting, a sport e-business or e-commerce store is virtual. While the e-business or e-commerce manager will be mainly focused on functions related to payment collection, delivery of orders, and security issues, the sport marketing professional will be concerned with three main areas: placement, size of "location," and presentation.

Placement

Placement refers to the actual location from where sales will be conducted. In traditional sport retail management, the major concerns regarding location include the competition in the area, the geographic attractiveness, adequate floor space, and a convenient locale for customers. For those sport organizations involved in e-business and e-commerce, location is in terms of a highly visible website that is easily found. Traffic to an e-commerce website is determined by the placement of links in prominent locations, or the placement of advertisements on the websites of business partners or collaborators. On the website of the organization, hyperlinks need to be clear and easy to find, and cannot require the user to go to more than three additional hyperlinks to find information. In addition, organizations will pay search engines such as Google and Yahoo to make sure that when a search is done on their category their organization comes up early in the search. There are also Search Engine Optimization (SEO) firms; these firms may start calling themselves inbound marketing firms in the future, and they will optimize the website to show up on top of the most used search engines.

Size of location

The size of the location is traditionally dependent on how much inventory and merchandise needs to be kept on hand, and the potential number of customers that will enter the establishment. Size of the location also covers associated facility needs, including adequate parking, rest-rooms, and entrances/exits. A sport organization engaged in e-business and e-commerce is concerned with digital size in the forms of bandwidth, data storage capacity, and processing power.

Bandwidth is the amount of information that may be passed through a communication channel at any one time. General standards in e-business and e-commerce state that average bandwidth utilization should not exceed 30 percent of the maximum available, and during peak usage should not exceed 70 percent. It is also important to realize that if a sport organization needs a website that requires high-resolution graphics, streaming audio or video, or provides downloadable files, it must spend more on digital infrastructure to accommodate larger servers. If not, the website will provide information at a significantly slower rate, which in turn will likely result in lost sales.

Processing power is the amount of information that can be handled by a website at any given time. This includes being able to show the breadth of sport products and services available, handle the number of transactions in proportion to the size of the sport business, and the level of interactivity the sport organization plans to have with customers – including email, discussion boards, social networking sites, and real-time assistance.

Data-storage capacity is also important to sport e-business and e-commerce. Working in an online environment provides the sport organization with the ability to collect large amounts of information, including demographics, billing and payment histories, and customer purchase patterns. In addition, a valuable tool for the sport marketing professional is click streams, which track the sequence of pages visited by a customer after the initial interaction.

Presentation

Presentation involves how the sport product or service is viewed by consumers. In traditional sport retail management, as well as e-business and e-commerce, the two main concerns about presentation are store layout and customer service.

Store layout in a traditional sport retail management operation focuses on the image a store wants to portray, in addition to the types of customers it wishes to retain. In e-business and e-commerce, the store layout is better known as user interface. User interface involves the ability to create a digital representation of the theme of the store, the ease with which the consumer can navigate around the website, and the provision of a pleasurable experience for the consumer. This requires the sport marketing professional working with the information technology specialists to ensure that the sport consumers are seeing everything that the sport organization wants them to see. This goes back to the earlier discussion of having the appropriate size of bandwidth, processors, and data-storage capacity. It also means having the appropriate hardware and software to maintain the desired effect.

Customer service in a physical setting involves creating a positive image for the sport organization, and offering a significant positive experience for the consumer. This includes physical interactions between salespeople and the customer, as well as intangible interaction created by advertising, promotions, and publicity. Online customer service differs because there is no direct physical interaction with the customers, and the customers do not experience the purchasing environment. This requires the sport marketing professional to be savvy when it comes to being able to communicate with customers via the World Wide Web and internet, especially utilizing tools including email, chat rooms, social networking sites, and discussion boards.

CASE STUDY 9: ETHICS IN E-MARKETING: SUSTAINABLE KNOWLEDGE

In the 1950s, retail automation was exemplified by polished copper containers and an elegant system of vacuum tubes into which any salesperson could insert a copper container from anywhere on the sales floor. The copper containers traveled quickly to the accounting department upstairs, to be returned just as quickly with the correct change, and the sales receipt. I particularly remember the customer gossip when the new system was installed as everyone in our neighborhood heralded "a new age in retail sales."

Fast-forward 40 years to the late 1990s into the early 2000s, the rise and fall of the dot.coms was the focal point of business in the media. Regardless, it is to recognize the long-lasting benefits of the technology that was created and implemented during that decade. Major corporations discovered new revenue channels and new ways of reaching existing customers. Hundreds of new technologies emerged to assist in the trans-formation. One example: as the Director of Internet Applications in 1996, [the author Robbins] was responsible for building a single method for searching all corporate information. The cost, in staffing and software licenses, exceeded US$1 million and required ten months to implement. Today one can purchase the Google Server for under US$50,000 and it only takes six minutes to install. That is the contribution afforded to everyone during the technology boom, benefits that are only now coming to light.

Now into the twenty-first century (2005), every type of American business is dependent on some form of information technology – credit card transactions, supply chain, inventory control. Most adults conduct some manner of transactions via the internet for travel, hotels, little league registration, birthday wishes, and charitable donations. It has recently been suggested that eBay has become the largest employer in the world, with its ecosystem of buyers and sellers providing products via that portal.

With the ubiquity of technology enabling business transactions for even the smallest stores and markets, when all business has become an e-business, how can we specifically distinguish the term "e-business" today? The term remains useful to help us understand our evolving information economy by means of a more distinct definition: in an information economy, e-business is that form of financially related exchange that is accompanied by aggregated information – information about the customer, the supplier, and the product. For example, according to this definition, a small site providing handcrafted stationery via an online web form may not be an e-business. It may simply be a modern version of retail automation reminiscent of the vacuum tubes – a more efficient method for buying and selling product. To be an "e-business" by the above definition, the transaction must also be founded upon a secure gathering of pertinent information that can be usefully reviewed and utilized to further understand the exchange. In other words, as a part of the financial transaction, there must be a transfer of knowledge.

In its simplest form, it may be the provision of basic contact information, so that the next time the customer visits the site, his or her shipping address and billing information is already provided by the underlying system. In more complex transactional systems, this information becomes a valuable repository of customer preferences, allowing for additional sales – of similar items, additional software licenses, etc. Value increases (to the buyer and the seller) as our knowledge of the transactions increases, allowing for in-depth analysis of patterns and trends.

A basic diagram (Figure 9.1) demonstrates this definition of e-business. This circular aspect of successful e-business ventures is wholly dependent on the capability of the provider to capture, analyze, and utilize knowledge about the interaction for the benefit of all parties involved. This sustainable knowledge becomes an essential component of an institution's ability to leverage a single event's information in multiple dimensions; indeed, the knowledge about the initial transaction may prove to the more valuable than the actual profit margin of that transaction over time.

As with previous historical phases when we were challenged to adjust to the influence of new technologies, we are once again faced with the obligation to reconsider aspects of our institutional cultures. There is an explicit responsibility, as we gather knowledge about ourselves and others in our business systems, to review our use of this information, and that remains the challenge of e-business in the coming decade: to not only capture and utilize the knowledge that adds value to our businesses, but to intelligently consider the broader social consequences and their impact on our industry, to ask and to answer the difficult questions about ethics and intellectual property and, in doing so, to elevate the discussion beyond the simple equations of profit and loss.

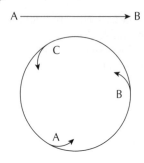

A ────────────► B   The straight line, moving from A to B
                    is the old way of doing things. The
                    circle, encompassing A through B to
                    C and back to A, is the "new way."

The circle epitomizes an exchange of
value in an information-based economy,
wherein each transaction adds value,
provides new opportunities, increases
understanding, and creates a sustaining
advantage for both the customer and
the supplier.

Figure 9.1 Definition of e-business

Source: Robbins, S. (1996). The system is a mirror. *ACM-SIGDOC Proceedings*.

Source: Adapted from Robbins, S. (2005). In e-business, the value of every transaction increases. *Information Systems Management* 22(3): 85–86.

Questions for discsussion

1   By definition, e-business is that form of financially related exchange that is accompanied by aggregated information – information about the customer, the supplier, and the product. An e-business customer is often willing to transmit valuable personal information (address, credit card number, social security number, etc.) over the internet to purchase the product or service being offered by a sport organization. From an ethical standpoint, what types of issues could arise to create an aura of distrust for the sport consumer? What steps would you take, as the Director of Sport Marketing for an online sporting goods firm, to ensure that these issues are prevented, and that the image of the sport e-business organization is maintained at the highest level possible?
2   From an ethical standpoint, how much information should a sport e-business be allowed to collect? What types of information gathering would be considered ethically correct? What types would not?

SPORT E-BUSINESS AND E-COMMERCE IN THE NEW ECONOMY

The concept of the new economy has changed over the years. In its original form, it referred to an economy without business cycles or inflation. It evolved during the dot.com era into an industry that produced computers and other related products and services, and an industry of accelerated rate of productivity and growth. After the crash of many internet-based businesses, the definition has been modified to reflect the influx of e-business and e-commerce throughout all industries. For the purpose of this chapter, the new economy is the use of information, communication, and digital technologies for manufacturing, selling, and distributing products and services.

The new economy as related to the sport industry is continuing to grow at a rapid pace. As a result, the sport marketing professional must understand the effects of the new economy on the sport organization as a whole, and more specifically how to utilize sport e-business and e-commerce to enhance sport marketing efforts. In assessing the strengths and weaknesses of the sport organization when it comes to e-business and e-commerce, the professional will look to the digital technology infrastructure discussed earlier in this chapter. From an external standpoint, the sport marketing professional must evaluate the sport marketing opportunities available as a result of the e-business and e-commerce infrastructure. In addition, sport marketers must be concerned with sport business development, sport consumer relations, integrated sport communications, sport marketing metrics, and strategic sport management, through e-business and e-commerce.

Sport market opportunities

There are numerous market opportunities that are unique to sport e-business and e-commerce. This is especially true when it comes to dealing with competition. First, competition moves beyond industry boundaries as a result of products and services being offered virtually. As a result, sport organizations can create value based on the perspectives of a wider range of sport consumers. Second, competition is not one-on-one in sport e-business and e-commerce; it is team-on-team. There is a significant reliance on additional complementary products (computers, servers, operating systems software, etc.). Therefore, sport marketing professionals and the management of the sport organization must evaluate those collaborators in business in order to determine the feasibility of accomplishing specified goals and competing in the marketplace. Finally, competition in sport e-business and e-commerce changes rapidly due to the speed with which changes in trends, events, and opportunities can be addressed. This requires the sport marketing professional to continually assess the environment and effectively react with speed and efficiency.

In addition to competition, the manner in which consumer behavior is evaluated has changed significantly with the introduction of e-business and e-commerce. Sport marketing professionals must listen even closer to the needs, wants, and desires of the sport consumer. This is because the opportunity to meet those needs will be short-lived, and those sport organizations that try to only meet sport consumer expectations will be ignored as a result of more choice. As a result, sport marketing professionals must be visionary, determining the experiences that sport customers will want in the future as a result of their actions now.

Involvement in sport e-business and e-commerce also creates a need for sport organizations to reorganize their value chain – those activities that add value directly to the consumer while adding indirect value through the support of other organizational operations. There is more direct contact between sport consumers and sport organizations through e-business and e-commerce as a result of the increased amount of information that can be made available at lower cost through e-value chains.

The sport market opportunity analysis framework is utilized by sport marketers to identify and evaluate the attractiveness of an opportunity in the sport marketplace. The premise of this framework centers on four environmental factors: the sport consumer, the sport organization (and its collaborators), the technology available, and the competition within the marketplace. Figure 9.2 identifies the steps a sport marketing professional would follow in assessing the sport market opportunity.

1. Identify the unfulfilled need of the sport consumer

⇩

2. Identify the specific sport consumers the sport organization will target

⇩

3. Assess the advantages the sport organization has over its competition

⇩

4. Determine the availability of adequate resources to meet the needs of the sport consumer

⇩

5. Gauge the market readiness of the e-business and e-commerce technology to be utilized

⇩

6. Detail the sport opportunity in terms of value to the sport consumer and the sport organization

⇩

7. Consider the attractiveness of the opportunity

⇩

8. Act

Figure 9.2 Steps to assess a sport e-market opportunity

Sport business development

As with any business, a sport organization engaged in e-business and e-commerce must have a business model. There are four components that are necessary in the development, implementation, and management of such a business model. The first is value propositions, which describe how a sport organization will differentiate itself to sport consumers in terms of the value offered. Value propositions require choosing the appropriate target segments, customer benefits, and resources.

The choice of the sport consumer target segment focuses on the attractiveness of the market chosen, and the ability of the sport organization to compete in that chosen market segment. This attempt at operational excellence is a function of a number of variables including market size, growth rate of the market, needs of the sport consumer in the segment, and the level of competition within the segment.

The choice of customer benefits to be delivered to the target segment requires an understanding of digital supply and demand. From the supply standpoint, the sport organization must employ the appropriate digital systems to deliver those benefits. From the demand end, the sport organization must ensure the message is clear and singular, as multiple messages will often confuse the sport consumer.

The choice of unique, differentiated resources is what separates one sport organization from another. By becoming a leader in the specific sport product or service market, the sport marketer seeks to show that the benefits of association with his or her sport organization is more beneficial than that of a competitor. Leadership in the marketplace comes from having better core abilities, business strengths, and unique capabilities.

The second component of the business model is the online offering, which is the determination of the sport products, services, or information that will be placed on the internet and the World Wide Web. To accomplish this, the sport organization must first decide on the scope of the categories of sport products or services to be offered online, and whether it will be offering these within their specific category, or across multiple categories. Next is the need to identify the decision-making process of the sport consumer, from pre-purchase through the actual purchase and afterwards into post-purchase. Once this process is understood, the sport marketing professional will design a plan to enter into the purchase cycle and return often.

The third component is the resource system, which is the process of selecting and utilizing resources to provide the benefits valued by the sport consumer. The activities of a digital resource system involve utilizing virtual assets to offer a wide range of benefits through strategic alliances with collaborators based on the demand of the sport consumer. This is accomplished by identifying the most important benefits valued by the sport consumer, determining the resources that can be used to offer the benefit, establishing a plan for delivering those benefits, and secure strategic partnerships that will help to offer them.

The final component is revenue models, which focus on the method of securing earnings for the sport organization. The sport marketing professional will work with the e-business and e-commerce staff to secure revenue through advertising, sport product and service sales, subscriptions to website content, and the licensing of content on the website.

Sport consumer relations

Sport consumer relations in e-business and e-commerce focus on the use of various methodologies, information technologies, and internet capabilities that help sport entities organize and manage the interaction between the sport consumer and the sport organization. Sport marketing professionals need to manage these relationships very differently in the virtual world through their involvement in designing an effective website. Figure 9.3 articulates the framework of this online relationship with sport consumers.

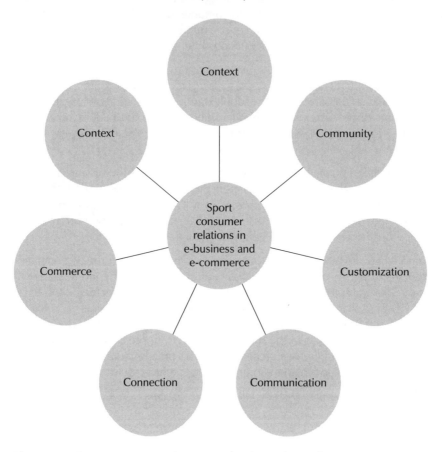

Figure 9.3 Sport consumer relations and online relationships

Content is the actual text, pictures, graphics, audio, and video found on a website that provide information to the user. Context refers to functionality and the aesthetically pleasing look of a website, including the ease of navigation, and the use of appropriate graphics, colors, and design features. Commerce involves an organization's ability to sell products and services using their website, including the collecting of items in a "shopping cart," and payment through secure websites. Communication involves an ongoing dialogue between users and the website (the organization managing the website), including customer service requests, email notifications of specials and opportunities, and instant messaging. Community is the ability to interact with other users including email, chat rooms, social networking sites, and discussion boards. Connection is the ability for websites to link to other websites or to be connected to what is called the social graph (Facebook Connect). Customization is the ability of a website to adapt and modify itself based on the wants, needs, and desires of the user.

Integrated sport communications

Integrated communication in sport e-business and e-commerce, as in traditional marketing communication, focuses on branding. However, the importance of integrated sport communication to the online medium cannot be overstated. It is integral to the interaction between sport consumers and sport organizations, utilizing: general online communications (banner ads, emails, online transactions); personalized online communications (building individual relationships through specialized services); traditional mass media communications (utilizing radio, print, and television advertising to market online capabilities); and direct communications (using sales representatives, direct marketers, and telecommunications to market online capabilities).

Branding, just as in traditional sport marketing efforts, is the process of seeking to provide a clear message to the sport consumer for the purpose of building organizational image. The sport organization seeks to build this brand equity by increasing brand awareness to, and brand association with, the sport consumer. This is not only an internal process conducted by the sport marketing professional, but it is also accomplished by partnering with collaborating organizations that aid in the delivery of the sport product or service. In sport e-business and e-commerce, the process of branding has evolved. In the introductory phase of the internet and World Wide Web, brands were categorized as either offline or online. Offline brands were traditional bricks and mortar stores such as Foot Locker, Sports Authority, and the merchandise stand or pro shop at an arena or stadium. Early online brands focused on the sport industry, such as Online Sports (www.onlinesports.com). Since 1995, Online Sports has stayed focused on keeping its niche market. With the growth of the online environment, and the opportunity to grow into other markets, most traditional offline sport organizations now brand themselves in both mediums.

Therefore, these sport organizations have had to learn to rebrand themselves utilizing these new digital technologies. The five methods utilized for e-branding an offline product in the online environment includes brand reinforcement, e-brand creation, virtual sport product and service trials, sales leads, and e-store traffic. Brand reinforcement is using the online environment to strengthen a brand that is already in the traditional sport marketplace. E-brand creation is the development and introduction of a new brand via the online environment. Usually this focuses more on building awareness rather than loyalty, as the digital environment changes rapidly. Virtual sport product and service trials through online branding provide the sport consumer with an opportunity for free access to the sport product and service. The goal of the sport organization is to entice the sport consumer to become a new and eventually repeat customer. Sales leads via e-business and e-commerce involve the sport marketing professional deciding that the online environment will be utilized to attract new customers. E-store traffic is used to determine whether the online sport marketing efforts are working. These are measured through e-business and e-commerce sport marketing metrics.

Sport marketing metrics

Sport marketing metrics are the indicators that a sport marketing professional utilizes to evaluate the sport organization's impact on the environment, and the sport organization's level of progress and success. Metrics are used for a range of activities including determining financial success, the level of relationships with sport consumers, the quality of internal operations, and the growth potential of the sport organization. The sport marketer focuses on metrics that will evaluate market opportunities, enhance marketing communications, and build brand awareness.

In sport e-business and e-commerce, metrics would normally change on an ongoing basis in conjunction with rapid changes in strategy. However, this change can be very costly to a sport organization because change requires a significant strain on resources.

The most basic of metrics used was number of hits on a website. Hits are the number of times an individual goes to a web page. Eventually this metric was deemed to be unreliable because if a page had a graphic this was made up of multiple elements. Therefore, the more graphics on a page, the more hits were registered. Sport marketers could not easily track whether a page with all text (one hit) was truly more popular than one with graphics that registered multiple hits.

Metrics evolved to utilize a counter to determine the number of times a web page was viewed within a specific period of time. While better than hits, this method was also deemed imperfect because it did not account for individuals who came back to the page multiple times. For example, every time a screen refreshed while an individual was watching the scoreboard during a game on nfl.com this was marked as a page viewed. There was no way to truly determine how many individuals were viewing the web page.

Then, a metric called conversion rates was developed. Conversion rates are measurements utilized to calculate how many viewers of a web page actually do what the organization wants. This is a two-step process. It starts with micro-conversion, which tracks the specific behavior a sport marketer would like the sport consumer to do to become more involved with the sport product or service being offered. Examples include going to a selected number of different pages on the website, signing up for an e-newsletter, or providing feedback on a question provided on the web page. This is followed by the main conversion, which is enticing the sport consumer to take action, including making a purchase or contacting the sport organization for more information. A metric utilized in conjunction with conversion rates is an impression. An impression is the number of times a banner or static advertisement is viewed on the web. The goal of the sport marketing professional is that a specific number of impressions will translate to a set amount of sales.

Strategic e-management

Sport marketing professionals must have an appropriate e-strategy when working in an e-business and e-commerce setting. This sport marketing strategy focuses on three areas – technology, the media, and resources. Technology drives e-business and e-commerce, and the sport marketing professional must understand how the internet and websites drive change for the sport organization. This not only includes understanding the methods that are most effective to communicate through technology; it also includes understanding the infrastructure, the available software and programs, and how to make the appropriate choices to drive aware-ness, loyalty, and eventual growth of the specific sport products, services, and organization.

Since the online environment is a convergence of mass communication, the media play a crucial role in the marketing of sport products and services, as well as the awareness and image of the sport organization. The external media still provide a third-party presentation about the sport organization and its products and services. However, since there are thousands of opportunities to place information external to the website of the sport organization, a major task of the sport marketing professional in e-business and e-commerce is as a publisher of information. The sport marketer must basically also become an e-journalist – including deciding on what design programs to use, styles to use, where to publish editorial pieces, and especially what content to include or exclude.

Managing the resources available to the sport marketing professional is another crucial factor in the implementation of a sport e-business and e-commerce strategy. Building a resources system that will endure the ebbs and flows of sport e-business and e-commerce will be an important step in making certain online sport marketing efforts successful. The resource system starts with quality leadership, including the management structure of the sport organization, and especially the sport marketing manager. It involves all aspects of the sport organization, including organization structure, human capital, efficient processes for task accomplishment, and a culture that provides a sense of meaning and belonging to its employees. The resource system also needs quality internal systems including supply chain management and technological infrastructure, as well as effective external partnerships and collaborations to create, promote, and sell the sport products and services.

The implementation of the sport e-business and e-commerce strategy brings a new set of challenges for the sport marketer and the management of the sport organization. A primary concern is the high visibility of errors as a result of the expanded number of potential customers who can view the sport organization through digital technologies. In addition, with the ever increasing number of services and websites that provide a forum for customer feedback on sport products and services, the effect of any error may be multiplied. It is also important to remember that errors may decrease the customer base because the cost of switching to another company is nil for the sport consumer. In the offline world, if a person is not happy with sport products and services, it is not as easy to switch because there may be additional costs associated with the switch, including increased travel time, costs (gas, wear and tear on a vehicle), and learning about a new company. In the online world, it is as quick as a click of the mouse!

Another challenge to implementing a sport e-business and e-commerce strategy comes from the complexity of transactions. With the need for partnerships and collaborations, the communication processes that need to take place between all parties involved can be difficult and messages may be misinterpreted more easily. The result is that the boundaries dividing the sport organization and partners/collaborators become more blurred, which in turn may cause confusion in the marketplace.

CONCLUSION

The use of electronic networks for mass communication is an integral part of sport marketing in the twenty-first century. Sport e-business, the internal information technology processes, focuses on integrating all the systems within the sport organization to ensure that the business functions of communications, sales, and service can be offered in an online environment. This is accomplished through a combination of horizontal, vertical, downward, and lateral integration. Sport e-commerce focuses on the external information processes through the World Wide Web and the internet. Sport marketers today operate most often in this area of digital technology, working to conduct cross-business and technology integration with traditional marketing functions to build brand equity, image, and awareness. The goal is to provide individualization and interactivity for the potential and returning sport consumer.

E-business and e-commerce have four major types of relationships. Business-to-Business (B2B) refers to the transactions, collaborations, and business interactions that occur between two organizations. Business-to-Consumer (B2C) focuses on the transactions between businesses and consumers. Consumer-to-Business (C2B) is where the consumer initiates the transaction process by soliciting organizations to compete for the individual's business. Consumer-to-Consumer (C2C) involves transactions between customers, many of which will involve an online third-party business.

Digital technologies are the centerpiece of sport e-business and commerce, as they are used to manage the exchange of sport products and services. The two major digital technologies utilized are the internet and the World Wide Web. The internet is a worldwide system of publicly accessible computer networks that transmit data by a process called packet switching to standardized Internet Protocol (IP) addresses. The World Wide Web is a collection of interconnected documents that are connected by uniform resource locators (URLs) and hyperlinks. The sport product and service exchanges take place through sport company websites, brokering sites, infomediaries, and e-procurement.

When conducting sport e-business and e-commerce, the store is virtual – no bricks and mortar. The sport marketing professional must focus on the actual locations where sales will be conducted from (placement); the size of the virtual location in terms of bandwidth, processing power, and data capacity; and how the sport product or service will be viewed by the sport consumer online (presentation).

In the twenty-first century, the sport business is operating in the new economy – where information, communication, and digital technologies are widely used in the manufacturing, selling, and distribution of sport products and services. This has a direct effect on how a sport marketing professional manages sport marketing opportunities, sport business development, sport consumer relations, integrated sport communications, sport marketing metrics, and strategic sport management, through e-business and e-commerce.

The sport e-business and e-commerce marketplace is a dynamic, changing, and competitive environment that places a sizeable set of responsibilities on sport marketers and the management of sport organizations. However, those firms which choose to ignore the online environment are sure to be left behind. With the complexity of the online marketplace, sport marketing professionals must adopt a hands-on approach to ensuring quality and success. They must hold all members of the sport marketing team accountable for reaching goals in line with the metrics set, and ensure that the guidelines, processes, and rules are followed. In addition, because the online environment is continuously changing, there is always a need for constant improvement. Finally, as with all types of marketing, it is important to remember that regardless of whatever strategic plan is decided upon, the customer is still the most important factor. Everything to be accomplished must be completed with building image and awareness in the mind of the sport consumer at the forefront of the sport e-business and e-commerce strategy.

FROM THEORY TO PRACTICE

BUFFY FILIPPELL, FOUNDER
TeamWork Consulting and TeamWork Online,
Cleveland, Ohio

As the first woman sports agent for Mark McCormack's IMG, I had no role models. In fact, Mr. McCormack often booked our senior staff meetings at the Union Club in Cleveland, Ohio, and I would have to take the back elevator and the men would walk up the front stairs. So when I left IMG, got married and moved to Italy, and returned a year later there was no Women in Sports and Events mentor group, no online recruiting system, and a few but growing number of sports management programs, so I was alone, unconnected, and had competition.

In my search for my own job, I found not only my need but perhaps the need of many graduates of these sports management programs – how do you find a job in sports? If I struggled so will you. I found out that there were such people as "headhunters." They put people into companies when the companies needed a head. Making only US$37,000, I wasn't a head. But could I help others find jobs? If sports did not have headhunters, I'd be the first! So I created an executive recruiting firm, a search firm for sports "headhunting," and called it TeamWork Consulting. For about 11 years I was the only firm hunting "sports heads" and I racked up some impressive searches for the President of the Toronto Maple Leafs, Calgary Flames, San Jose Sharks; Commissioner of MLS, then the entire marketing and sales staffs of the Memphis Grizzlies, New Orleans Hornets, and Houston Texans, catapulting to recruiting the entire 112 team business executives for the short-lived XFL.

It was while recruiting for the Houston Texans that I realized the dot.com world could be putting employer and job applicant together faster than I could. Instead of defending my personal recruiting business, I decided to cannibalize it and lead everyone into the digital recruiting age, and I called that business TeamWork Online.

Being first to market has its advantages and although I was first in sports, I was not first in digital recruiting, but I made some lucky strategic decisions, different from the norm in 1999, that positioned us for later success as the internet exploded.

I allowed candidates to enter their information for free. I charged the employer a nominal flat fee, and gave them unlimited rights to post jobs. The employers had to subscribe for 12 months, not just post a job. That encouraged them to post internships and internships helped students get the right work experience which bought me adoption with the younger generation. And I created community systems for the leagues and individual

227

e-marketing management in sport

ones when the team wanted more personal branding. I had my programmer create a recruiting system, which I learned was an applicant tracking system, and made every employer required to link it on their website and my website, a portal page or "aggregated site" of my systems, which helped grow both of our web traffic. Then, within the past four years during the recession, we overhauled the system, created the candidate's universal application across all systems, then matched the candidate application in four ways to an employer's job posting – location, salary, skills, and name of employer. Then we connected these employers' databases together, though no employer can see anything unless the candidate applies. We kept statistics and made everyone record their successes. We marketed statistics before data analytics became popular. An intern suggested the scoreboard and it's become "hope" for the candidates and the traffic driver to our website which led to a #1 ranking on Google for "sports jobs."

TeamWork Online is a model of efficiency. We have corralled all of the candidates in the past 12 years who have applied for over 43,000 sports and live events jobs, put them in a database, invited more in daily, and have successfully matched over 80 percent of the jobs posted to hires in the last 12 years, and 92 percent in the past 12 months.

Thus, my need for a job turned into a business to help you find yours.

PART IV

PROMOTIONAL ASPECTS
OF SPORT MARKETING

CHAPTER TEN

COMMUNICATION MANAGEMENT AND PROMOTIONS IN SPORT

CHAPTER OUTLINE

- What is communication management?
- The communication process
- Sport organizational image
- Sport promotions
- Conclusion

CHAPTER OBJECTIVES

The reader will be able to:

- appreciate the role of communications in the sport marketing process
- identify the internal and external elements of organizational image in sport marketing, including internal marketing communications, corporate image, logos, and publicity campaigns
- understand the various elements of the sport promotion mix, including public relations, licensing, personal contact, incentives, and atmospherics
- recognize the incorporation of sport promotion activities with integrated communications plans, event planning, pricing development, and location and distribution strategies
- identify the various elements for each of the promotion mix components
- know the various indirect (word-of-mouth) and direct (sales) promotional strategies in relationship to positioning, building brand equity, increasing credibility, and enhancing image transfer and association.

231

WHAT IS COMMUNICATION MANAGEMENT?

Communication management involves the planning, implementing, supervising, evaluation, and modification of the various methods of communication both internal and external to a sport organization. Effective and efficient communication management is crucial to success in sport marketing because it is the conduit by which information between employees and organizations is exchanged, and ensures that all parties have access to the same information. Communication management also seeks to create continuity in the decision-making process by ensuring that all parties are involved in goals setting and attainment in a coordinated and organized manner.

The sport marketing professional is involved in a number of roles to make sure that effective and efficient communication takes place throughout the organization in terms of the marketing process. These include:

- developing organizational communication strategies including the structure of the internal and external communication processes, the goals and objectives of organizational communication, and the policies and procedures to follow related to communication of information regarding the sport organization
- planning, implementing, managing, and evaluating the flow of information in and out of the sport organization through verbal, written, and online communication methods
- managing all sport organizational images in terms of presentation to the public, the media, and the online environment
- developing, implementing, managing, and evaluating the organizational crisis communication plan
- providing training to all staff in the organization about appropriate communication methodology.

In order to effectively and efficiently manage communication for a sport organization, the sport marketing professional must focus on having a full understanding of three main areas: the communication process, sport organization images, and sport promotions.

THE COMMUNICATION PROCESS

Communication is critical to the success of a sport marketing professional. Communication helps to establish and maintain relationships with the sport consumer by providing a conduit for listening and reacting to the sport consumer. The key components of the communication process are documented in Figure 10.1.

The source starts with an idea of how to communicate information about the sport product or organization. As the source continues developing the idea, it is encoded into a message. The encoding process involves giving the idea a personality. A representation of the idea and the sport entity is created in print, verbal, and/or visual form. This representation may range from a simple photograph to the use of sport personalities to endorse the sport product. Depending on the choice of representation, the message may be delivered as an auto-biographical sketch, a narrative, or a drama. The autobiography is where the message about the sport product is directly from the sport entity to the sport consumer. The narrative is where

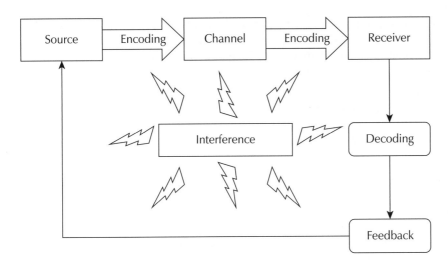

Figure 10.1 The communication process

a third party (such as an athlete endorsement) tells the sport consumer about the sport product. The goal is to entice the sport consumer to be involved with that product as a result of the reputation of the endorser. Sport products may also be advertised in a dramatic form, where "characters" act out events in front of an imaginary audience, and the act is reproduced in print, verbal, and/or visual form to persuade the sport consumer to purchase the specific sport product.

Once the message is encoded, it is then sent through marketing channels to the receiver. Marketing channels include many different forms of media, including print, radio, television, and the internet. The receiver then decodes the message and provides feedback to the source. The goal is to establish effective and efficient communication between the source and the receiver. Effective communication occurs when the intended meaning of the sender is identical to the interpreted meaning of the receiver. One of the major reasons why communication is not effective and efficient is due to interference with the process. This interference can come from a number of sources, including poor choices in communication channels, poor expression of the message, and environmental distractions.

SPORT ORGANIZATIONAL IMAGE

One of the most significant issues faced by sport marketing professionals in terms of communication management is the sport organization's image. Organizational image is the combination of how the internal organization believes others view the organization, and the beliefs and perceptions the external organization actually has of the organization. Based on these beliefs and perceptions, sport consumers either wish to be associated with or avoid the organization. It is a major role of the sport marketing professional to control communications to maximize the public image of the sport organization. One method used to control the outflow of information from the organization is through internal marketing communications.

Internal marketing involves the perceptions of individuals from inside an organization about how they view that organization. As a result, the sport marketing professional treats individuals within the sport organization as customers, with the goal of using principles of leadership and motivation to help shape the organization's image.

Sport marketing professionals also seek to control external organizational images, which involves the perceptions of individuals from outside an organization and how they view that sport organization. This is a significant challenge because external organizational images seek to control the beliefs and perceptions of potential customers – a challenge that is easier said than done.

There are a number of methods utilized by sport marketing professionals to articulate the organizational image to external constituencies, including brand image, publicity campaigns, crisis communications, and sport promotions. As discussed in Chapter 6, branding and brand image is one of the most powerful external organizational images. Branding involves using a name, term, design, symbol, or feature to identify one sport product, service, or organization as being different from another. The mixture of attributes may be tangible or intangible, are usually symbolized in a trademark, and if managed properly, create value and influence for the sport organization.

Another method utilized to convey external organizational image is the publicity campaign. A publicity campaign is the use of communications, activities, and media coverage to convey specific information to a targeted market over a specific period of time. The development of this type of focused effort to communicate the sport organization's image involves a number of steps, as listed below:

▪ *Internal audit*: the sport marketing professional must conduct an appraisal of the internal operations and systems of the sport organization to observe and evaluate their efficiency and effectiveness in quality delivery of products and services, appropriate risk management practices, and financial control
▪ *Identification of weaknesses*: identification of deficiencies within the sport organization and how they will adversely affect the sport organization's image
▪ *External research*: an investigation of the opportunities and threats that may result in a change to the sport organizational image
▪ *Target audience*: the process of determining the best method for getting the sport organization's image into the minds of specific consumers
▪ *Message structure*: developing a specific communication that has a specific goal, is aimed at a specific group of individuals (target audience), and has a measurable component to determine effectiveness
▪ *Methods for outreach*: a plan of action to communicate the message to the external environment
▪ *Post-campaign evaluation*: an assessment of the overall campaign to determine whether the message was clear, understood, and had a positive influence on the organizational image.

Also integral to controlling the external organizational image is crisis communications. Crisis communications involve the development of a contingency plan that is based on existing communication resources and operational capabilities, and allows sport marketing professionals to effectively respond to a crisis related to the sport organization. This plan is crucial

234

to maintaining a positive organizational image during times of public scrutiny. Crises can come in numerous forms for a sport organization, which requires the sport marketing professional to forecast potential crises and have a method of dealing with said crises from a communication point of view. This will often include having a plan for articulating the organization's response to all internal members of the sport organization, a policy for external communication regarding the situation (often by directing inquiries to a designated spokesperson), and a targeted channel for disseminating information regarding the crisis. By maintaining control of the information, the sport marketing professional can help to minimize the damage a crisis has on the organizational image of the sport entity. However, at the same time, since the new millennial generation expects information in an instant as a result of the explosion of information available at their fingertips via the internet, and the speculation that often occurs when accurate information does not get disseminated quickly enough, maintaining control can become quite a challenge.

The most extensive and significant methods for communicating external organizational image is through sport promotion. Sport promotion is defined as the procedure of communicating information about the sport product or service to consumers. The sport marketing professional entices consumers to make a purchase by managing the sport promotional mix. As a significant part of the sport marketing because sport promotions is an integral part of the sport marketing mix, the remainder of this chapter will focus on the elements of sport promotions.

CASE STUDY 10: MULLET NIGHT

The Manchester Monarchs of the American Hockey League have administered a promotion called "Mullet Night." Prior to offering this promotion for the first time in 2003, the front office of the organization contemplated numerous promotions to offer during the season. According to Jeff Eisenberg, General Manager of the Manchester Monarchs, "The Monarchs have the same goals for other promotions: sell tickets, add value, and build brand. While the organization may have slightly different goals for individual promotions . . . the ultimate goal is to use promotions to get to a sell-out." The organization's goal is not to have promotions on the dates they call "dog dates" – those dates that will be low capacity due to a game being midweek or on a holiday, or the game is against a non-rival opponent – as the promotion will do little to help attendance. The Monarchs gauge whether a promotion was successful or not by getting a game that was not going to be a sell-out to reach sell-out. The result of this will be that the more sell-outs, the "hotter" the ticket becomes.

According to Eisenberg, the Manchester Monarchs use promotions to "help keep the Monarchs on the minds of the fans," and that the promotions are used so that "the fans always have fun." They do this in a number of ways to maintain their visibility in the public eye. They begin this by being "promotion heavy" during the first 20 games, which is traditionally the time of year when fans are not thinking about hockey yet – especially with the Major League Baseball post-season, and the National Football League being in mid-season. As Jeff Eisenberg stated, "The goal with every promotion is to 'under promise

235

and over deliver,' as this will enhance the experience of the fans, entice them to come back, and promote the team further through word of mouth."

To measure the success of the Mullet Night promotion, the Monarchs had three key benchmarks. The first would be an increase in ticket sales. Second is if the promotion enhanced the game experience. Finally, did the promotion create brand awareness and exposure, both before and after the event? In pre-event planning, the Manchester Monarchs felt that the promotion had a chance of success for a number of reasons. Mullet Night was unique, as it had never been done before by anyone. The number of people anticipated to participate in the promotion would be large (5,000 wigs were to be given out). Not only is the hairstyle funny, but it also has a cult following in hockey. Finally, and most importantly, the promotion was geared to "make fun of themselves," hence not taking themselves too seriously.

For a promotion to work, the front office staff of the Manchester Monarchs had to get information out about the event. This was accomplished in a number of ways, including involving the media (including the largest radio and television media outlets in the state) by providing the media with material to "pre-sell." They also promoted a contest for the best mullet, and hyped the event as "a part of the American lifestyle."

The first year, the event was a tremendous success. Why? According to Jeff Eisenberg, General Manager of the team, there were a number of reasons:

- Putting hair on people (5,000) is funny.
- Players wore the hair during warm-ups.
- Kids wore the hair for the entire game.
- There was a subculture that appeared at the game – people made their own T-shirts and wore fake teeth (ugly green teeth, buck teeth).
- The interviews conducted brought people into it – they became part of it; they took the interviews "seriously" and gave appropriate answers.
- They were able to get Barry Melrose involved, which gave the event credibility – he is a hockey icon, the "hockey guy" on ESPN – and this also helped to get in on ESPN.
- "It was still funny in the third period".
- A certain "mood" had been created from the pre-event publicity: "You could feel the excitement".
- Fans were the ones who made the event so successful.
- Security wore mullets.
- A Hall of Fame made it even more of an event – where famous people who had real-life mullets were "inducted" into the Mullet Hall of Fame.

In the case of Mullet Night, all three benchmarks were achieved, and after two years the promotion exited in a "big" way, especially in the area of brand awareness and exposure. The promotion received coverage on ESPN (courtesy of Barry Melrose), CNN, TNN, and Hockey Night in Canada. In addition, over 80 local television and radio affiliates ran the story. Charlie Sherman, the Sport Director for WMUR TV in Manchester, New Hampshire, was critical in getting national exposure. Before the game was complete, Sherman went to the office and edited highlights, uploaded it to the satellite, and sent the corresponding satellite numbers for the networks to download. This allowed all media outlets to download footage and put it on TV. While the first Mullet Night received a short mention the first year, the second Mullet Night received approximately four minutes of coverage on ESPN. In expanding their reach nationally, the *Los Angeles Times* (the home city of the parent organization, the Los Angeles Kings) ran an article on the second page of the sports section that discussed the event. According to Eisenberg, "It was great to have the exposure in Los Angeles with the parent company, as it adds credibility to the Monarch's organization." From a local perspective, this exposure was well received and accepted by sponsors and fans. The ticket was the "hottest" ticket in town, with season ticket holders being "proud" to have a ticket to the game. The post-game coverage added to the "allure" of the event.

Source: Adapted from Schwarz, E. C. and Blais, D. (2005). How to get a minor league promotion major league publicity. In *Where Sport Marketing Theory Meets Practice: Selected Papers from the Second Annual Conference of the Sport Marketing Association*, edited by B. G. Pitts (pp. 227–230). Morgantown, WV: Fitness Information Technology.

Questions for discsussion

1 Is it ethical to use promotional techniques that might be deemed derogatory to a subcultural group? Why or why not?
2 Outside of specific promotions, one of the major ethical issues currently being dealt with in college athletics is the use of Native American names as the namesake of their athletic teams (such as the Florida State Seminoles, the North Dakota Fighting Sioux, and the Utah Utes). You are Director of Marketing for an athletics department that uses a Native American name to represent its teams. You have two choices – prove to the NCAA that the use of the name is not derogatory (as Florida State and Utah did); or start a plan for changing the name of the school's teams (which North Dakota was forced to do).
  a In the interest of time, cost, tradition, and notoriety – you choose the first option. Outline the marketing efforts that will ensure that the Native American name is treated and used with respect, and is acceptable to all parties (the school, the NCAA, and the Native American community).
  b In the interest of respecting the wishes of the local tribe to remove the name, and creating a new brand identity – you choose the second option. How would you go about the process of re-branding and marketing your entire athletic program?

SPORT PROMOTIONS

The elements of sport promotions (also known as the sport promotional mix) include advertising, sponsorship, public relations, licensing, personal contact, incentives, and atmospherics. Advertising involves paid, non-personal communications about a sport product or service through the print, broadcast, or electronic media that are designed to attract public attention and subsequent purchase. In sport marketing, advertising may include broadcast commercials, direct mailings, facility signage, and manufactured media. Sponsorship refers to the relationship between a corporation and a sport organization as a tool to develop brand image and customer loyalty as a result of the association. Public relations is the collection of activities, communications, and media coverage that convey who the sport organization is and what it has to offer, all in the effort to enhance the organization's image and prestige. Licensing is one of the fastest growing components of sport promotions, and involves the creation of a strategic alliance in which the manufacturer of a sport product gives permission to a second party to manufacture that product in return for specific royalties or payments. Personal contact involves one-on-one communication between a representative of the sport organization and the sport consumer that should result in achieving promotional objectives ranging from providing information about products and services, to generating sales. Incentives are the benefits or reduced costs that are offered to motivate a sport consumer to purchase the specified sport product or service. Atmospherics utilizes the design of visual communications in an environment, such as lighting, colors, music, to entice the sport consumer's perceptual and emotional responses to purchase the sport product or service.

There are a number of generalizations that can be made about promotion. Promotions temporarily increase sales substantially; promotion in one product category may affect sales of brands in complementary and competitive categories; and promotions can result in increased traffic. Most of the generalizations are true; however, it is important to understand how to utilize these elements in order to ensure that the results are longer lasting, and lead to maintaining current and attracting new customers.

Advertising

Advertising is one of the primary elements of the promotional mix. It is the process of attracting public attention to a sport product or sport business through paid announcements in the print, broadcast, or electronic media. Sport advertising is the communication process utilized most often in sport marketing – sending paid messages through communication channels to the sport consumers with the goal of persuading them to make a purchase.

There are three distinctions within advertising: advertisements, advertising campaigns, and integrated brand promotion. Advertisements are paid public announcements about a product or service through the print, broadcast, or electronic media that are designed to attract public attention and subsequent purchase. Advertising campaigns are a series of advertisement messages with a single mission and theme that are promoted through a variety of media options during a specified time frame. Integrated brand promotion (IBP) is the use of multiple promotional tools in a coordinated manner to build and maintain overall awareness, identify, and preference for sport products, services, and the associated brands. These methods, to be discussed in greater detail in Chapter 11, are crucial to getting the message out to the target audience. As a result, understanding the basic communication process is a natural first step in understanding the entire advertising process.

Sponsorship

Sport sponsorship involves acquiring the rights to be affiliated with a sport product or event in order to obtain benefits from that association. Sport sponsorship is another significant element of the promotional mix as the main goal is to promote a product or services through a third party (sport product or event). Sport sponsorship is seen at multiple levels within the sport business landscape, including with governing bodies, teams, athletes, facilities, events, and the broadcast media. Through the articulation of corporate and brand goals, the sport marketing professional creates various criteria for sport sponsorship, and then utilizes those criteria to choose the companies the sport organization should partner with. The sport marketing professional is involved at all levels from developing sport sponsorship packages to engaging in sponsorship negotiations. This will be covered in more detail in Chapter 12.

Public relations

In sport marketing, this element of promotions is so significant that it is broken down into the fifth "P" of the sport marketing mix, and is often referred to as publicity. Publicity focuses on the use of unpaid, non-personal promotion of a sport product or service through a third party that publishes print media or presents information through radio, television, or the internet. The goal of any good publicity is that it is viewed as coming from an unbiased, neutral source.

As a sport marketing professional, understanding and utilizing public relations is critical to success, as it is the management function that helps to evaluate public attitudes, articulate policies and procedures of an organization that may be of public interest, and execute programs of action to acquire public understanding and approval. Three aspects of public relations utilized in sport marketing efforts are media relations, sports information, and sport journalism.

Media relations

Media relations are the activities that involve working directly with individuals responsible for the production of mass media including news, features, public service announcements, and sponsored programming. Effective media relations maximize coverage and placement of messages and information in the mass media without paying for it directly through advertising.

Most media relations activities are designed to get free media coverage for programs and issues. The major advantage of this effort is in the appearance of neutrality. There is usually a significant level of cynicism toward paid advertising because it is viewed as a first-person account of a message. Publicity through media outlets is viewed as second party accounts, and is therefore regarded in a more positive light.

Getting free media coverage is not easy because there is a lot of competition for a limited amount of air time or print space. Therefore, in order to entice the media to cover your story, event, product, or service, it is imperative that the sport marketing department in coordination with the communications department cover the issues fully, and present an attractive and complete picture of what needs to be covered. This will entice the media to be more receptive to coverage, mainly because they will need to invest less work in printing or broadcasting the information. However, it is important that the organization will have no control over the end result of the publicity – it is all in the hands of the media outlets. If your message is not clear to the media, they may place their own interpretation on the meaning, and this may result in the intent of the organizational message becoming blurred or skewed.

From the internal sport organization's point of view, the sport marketing professional and/or separate sport media relations coordinator must provide to the mass media information that maximizes the communication of ideas, images, and information that supports the philosophy, mission, and vision of the sport organization. At the same time, the professional will seek to minimize the negative or incorrect impressions of the sport organization that appear in the mass media. While the latter are more difficult to control, building awareness through maximizing communication efforts is key to the successful integration of internal media relations efforts and external mass media production. This is most easily accomplished by knowing what the mass media are looking to cover and assisting the mass media in presenting all information as clearly and fairly as possible.

The best media relations pieces:

- include different, expanded, or new information about the organization or a product/ service
- follow the KISS principle, stating information in a simple and clear format that will be interesting to the reader
- include quotes or research from credible or well-respected sources
- have information that is relevant to the local community where the information will be published or broadcast
- provide information in a timely manner (in many cases, stories more than 24 hours old will not be covered).

Sports information

A specialized area of media relations is sports information. Sports information involves gathering results and other pertinent sporting information on individuals, teams, departments, and leagues. Once the information has been gathered, it is the responsibility of the sports information director to shape the message and disseminate this information to all media outlets. This latter aspect is where a sports information director or department differs from sports journalism.

The largest entity in sports information dissemination is ESPN. Now a subsidiary of ABC, ESPN started as an alternative to standard television news broadcasts and the information found in "Sports" sections of newspapers. It began as a fairly small operation and often had to broadcast unorthodox sporting events, such as the World's Strongest Man Competition; international sports relatively unknown in the United States, such as Australian Rules Football, as well as the short-lived United States Football League (USFL), to attract viewers. In 1987, ESPN landed a contract to show National Football League games on Sunday evenings, an event which marked a turning point in its development from a smaller cable TV network to a marketing empire, a cornerstone to the enthusiastic "sports culture" it largely helped to create.

Sport journalism

Sport journalism encompasses all types of reportage and media coverage of current events in the world of sport. All forms of media are included: press, magazines, television, radio, and electronic media. The various disciplines practiced include: writing, commentary, reporting, interviewing, and photography. Sport journalism is highly specialized and requires specialist knowledge, but the disciplines and practices employed by a sport journalist do not differ greatly from those of a standard journalist.

Licensing

The licensing process gives sport organizations the opportunity to establish a presence in a specified marketplace while also creating a new source of revenue. This is most often accomplished through the creation of licensed merchandise, such as hats, shirts, uniforms, and other apparel. The goal of licensing is to enhance brand awareness and appeal, especially in new markets.

The licensing process involves protecting an intellectual property such as a logo or mark. The intellectual property may be registered publicly, for example, in the form of a patent or trademark, as a means of establishing ownership rights. It may also be retained within the firm. Commonly referred to as know-how, this intellectual property is generally based on operational experience.

The licensee usually makes a lump sum (front-end) payment. In addition, there is normally a royalty rate which tends to vary around a rule of thumb of 5 percent, depending on the type of industry and rate of technological change. A minimum performance (payment) clause is considered essential and some firms allow the licensee a "period of grace" to get production and marketing started. There are also some companies that agree on a cross-licensing deal, whereby they just swap licenses instead of paying.

Royalty management and distribution

Licensing, as a promotional tool, is a business arrangement in which the manufacturer of a product (or a firm with proprietary rights over certain technology, trademarks, etc.) grants permission to some other group or individual to manufacture that product (or make use of that proprietary material) in return for specified royalties or other payment.

Royalties are a share of income, in accordance with the terms of a license agreement, paid by a licensor for the right to make, use, or sell a product or service. Royalty management and distribution of funds is usually handled by a third party who will advise and make recommendations during contract negotiations.

The benefits of a third party royalty management firm are:

- an assessment of risks to the license portfolio
- the development of strategies to manage, monitor, and control those portfolios
- the establishment of compliance programs for licensing, distribution, pricing, and other contractual agreements

- forensic-based royalty examinations
- commercial reviews of royalty and financial provisions in agreements
- advice on royalty rates and licensing fees
- acting as expert witness.

Personal contact

One of the most effective ways to promote products and services is through one-on-one communication between a representative of the sport organization and the sport consumer. The goal of personal contact is to provide additional information about products and services in a manner that is not sales based or visibly targeted. The sport marketing professional seeks to build awareness of the organization and its products and services through goodwill in the community, and social involvement with members of the population. This is accomplished either via community relations, or as a result of "giving back" efforts through socialization.

Community relations

Community relations is the process of the sport organization interacting and connecting with a target population within a specific area. Community relations is an integral part of any sports organization whether the relationship is player, team, or league initiated. The main goal of community relations and sport organization is to foster goodwill in the community and develop a long-term relationship with individuals and the community as a whole. This type of effort is a monumental and fragile undertaking, as it only takes one negative comment or action to erode years of goodwill.

There are a number of community relations projects in the sporting world. Community relations efforts can be league initiated, team initiated, player initiated, or event initiated. The National Football League has a long-standing community relations effort (32 years) with the United Way to strengthen America's communities. The league also has an ongoing fight against childhood obesity with the Play60 community relations campaign. The campaign creates a movement where it promotes activity for at least 60 minutes a day. In addition, a part of the campaign is to give a community the chance to meet players from a local team for 60 minutes of play.

Almost every professional team has a community relations department for involvement in its area. The Boston Red Sox work with an organization known as the Jimmy Fund. Since 1953, the Red Sox have worked to raise money and awareness in the fight against cancer in New England and around the world.

Individual players have also engaged in their own community relations efforts. One example is the 2011 Roberto Clemente Award Winner David Ortiz of the Boston Red Sox. This award is given to the MLB player who has made positive contributions both on and off the field of play. In 2005, Ortiz founded the David Ortiz Children's Fund to raise money to assist families to access critical pediatric care for children in the United States and his native Dominican Republic through a partnership with Massachusetts General Hospital in Boston. Over the past year, his foundation has raised over US$1.5 million and provided funding for more than 200 heart operations and other critical care for children. Another arm of his foundation, Papi's Pals (named after his nickname Big Papi), purchases and donates blocks of Red Sox tickets to patients at the hospital, as well as to other Boston Red Sox and Boston-area charities.

The same is true for major sport events around the world. For example, most tournaments for the Professional Golfers Association (PGA) are linked with a charity. THE PLAYERS Championship in Ponte Vedra Beach, Florida has contributed more US$46 million since 1973 for charities in Northeast Florida. The tournament's goal for the next ten years is to generate US$50 million for youth-related charities in Northeast Florida. This is just one of many charitable contributions provided by PGA tournaments, and the PGA itself. The overall program is called "Together. Anything's Possible" (together.pgatour.com). This initiative brings together tournaments, players, charities, sponsors, partners, volunteers, and even fans to be socially responsible by providing a positive social investment in communities where tournaments are held and players live. Through their contributions of multiple millions of dollars to over 3,000 charities in local communities across the United States, the beneficiaries are wide reaching and provide a better tomorrow for individuals in need.

Socialization

Socialization is usually arranged by an individual or team to demonstrate commitment to a community or city. This is a type of "giving back" to the community. Some players will not give their hard-earned money to foster community relations; they prefer to give their time. A historic example that has been recounted in baseball lore for centuries is Babe Ruth, who regularly visited children's hospitals to boost patients' spirits, telling one child that he was going to hit a home run for him that afternoon . . . which he often did. Today, professional athletes work in soup kitchens on holidays, bring Thanksgiving or Christmas turkeys to homes of the needy, and even run free sports clinics, all in the name of giving back to the community.

During the 2005 season, the head coach of Notre Dame at that time, Charlie Weis, visited a very sick child who was a huge Notre Dame Football fan. During their conversation, Coach Weis ask the child if there was anything that he could do for him; the child said he would like to call the first offensive play against the number one ranked University of Southern California. The child passed away the day before the game, but Coach Weis honored his request.

These acts of socialization are what solidify personal relationships and make differences in individual lives, as well as the community. It also allows the viewing public to gain a glimpse into what they perceive to be the human side of being a celebrity in professional sports.

Incentives

Incentives are the benefits or reduced costs that are offered to motivate a sport consumer to purchase the specified sport product or service. This may include price deals, premiums, contests, free samples, and a number of other benefits that will encourage the sport consumer to purchase a product of service. Incentives are mainly used during the later stages of the promotional process, as the customer is already aware of the sport product or service, and often needs the extra push of an incentive to make a purchase. In sport marketing and promotions, there are three main categories of incentives: price-based incentives, sales incentives, and behavioral incentives.

Price-based incentives are benefits derived from lowering the retail price of a product or service. Some of the most common types of price-based incentives include discount pricing, coupon redemption, and free trials. While this method may be good to attract customers who would otherwise not purchase the product or services, the sport marketing professional and sport organization that becomes too reliant on such an effort is doomed to failure. Offering too many price breaks may decrease the image of the brand, and cause problems with those customers who had to pay full price for the product or service.

Sales incentives offer a premium to attract first-time or bulk buyers of products and/or services, but are more often used to reward those repeat customers. It is important to make similar sales incentives available to all customers. An example would be the comparison between a season ticket holder who needs four extra tickets to a game, and an individual who is buying tickets for a group of 100. The season ticket holder has more revenue potential in the short term because of the price of the season ticket. Therefore, you may offer a 10 percent discount on the additional tickets. The group bringing 100 fans to the game is considered a solid customer who may repeat this buying behavior in the future, or any of the 100 fans might be a future customer. However, if that group leader did not get a discount equal to 10 percent, and he or she were to find out about the deal with the season ticket holder, he or she may be discouraged and not make this purchase or any future purchases. In turn, if the group gets a 20 percent discount on the 100 tickets and the season ticket holder finds out, the season ticket holder might be put off by the organization and potentially cancel his or her season ticket subscription.

Behavioral incentives are inducements offered to consumers to entice them to purchase a product or service based on a perceptual relationship created between the consumer and the product or service. One of the most significant behavioral incentives is achievement. This achievement may be in the form of a participation opportunity, a desire to gain intellectual knowledge, or the desire to reach a certain level of recognition. Another major behavioral incentive involves affiliation. Human beings in general have a sense of needing to belong. Sport products and services offer that opportunity of involvement; for example, the singing and camaraderie seen at a home soccer match in England, where singing takes place during the game, often with someone fans have never met. Behavioral incentives also serve as an opportunity to be part of a group. In fact, studies have shown that fewer than 2 percent of Americans attend a sporting event by themselves. In Australia, they have taken this sense of belonging a step further by offering Australian Rules Football fans the opportunity to become a "member" of the club for a fee. This customer-to-organization affiliation is very strong and deep rooted, and can be utilized by sport marketers to offer additional products and services.

Atmospherics

Atmospherics is the intentional control and structure based on environmental cues. Sport businesses must direct considerable attention to the way in which the atmosphere of their consumption environment can promote the desired relationship with clientele. Atmospherics represents the collection of all elements in a brand's marketing mix that facilitate exchanges by targeting the brand to a group of customers, positioning the brand as somehow distinct from other brands. Examples of this are sports drinks. Gatorade, Red Bull, PowerAde, SoBe, and Double Shot are all targeted primarily at teens. Companies have positioned the brand as standing for fun, exhilaration, and energy; and communicated the brand using a diversity of promotional media and sponsorships. By maintaining a consistent message over time the brands will achieve their goal.

Managing atmospherics starts with gaining an understanding of the target market. Once defined, the sport marketing professional will develop a theme that will be attractive to the market and meaningful to the sport consumer. This includes choosing those elements of the physical setting to which the target market will be able to relate. To enhance the message, the delivery will also include specific sensory elements to ensure the message is received and remembered.

A perfect example of this process can be seen in Gatorade's commercials. A Gatorade commercial from 2006 depicts professional basketball player Kevin Garnett bursting out of a basketball at center court of a fenced-in blacktop basketball court, just like millions of recreational courts across America. With sweat dripping off him, the first thing he does is drink Gatorade. Now, no one in the world is bursting out of a basketball; however, the notion that arguably one of the best players in the games at that time attributes his success to drinking Gatorade all his life and playing on a blacktop court in the middle of a neighborhood will resonate with many fans of Kevin Garnett, and will result in fans around the globe purchasing Gatorade.

Sport promotion strategies

The purpose of a sport promotional strategy is to build brand loyalty and product credibility, develop image, and position the brand. A promotional strategy is similar to a marketing strategy, but a promotional strategy seeks short-term objectives, both direct and indirect. Promotional objectives usually include increased sales, stimulate impulse buying, raise customer traffic, and present and reinforce image. The strategy also provides information about products and services, publicizes new stores or websites, and creates and enhances customer satisfaction.

A sport marketing professional must understand the various parts of promotional integration, which is usually viewed as one of the final stages of the entire sport marketing process. Promotional integration is the actual creation and delivery of the promotional message that involves defining how the message is to reach the consumer, ensuring that the promotional message will be received and understood, and that the promotional message will lead to the purchase of a product or service. This process starts with building awareness, which is the measurement of the percentage of the target market that knows about the organization's products and/or services, including customer recall as related to brand recognition, brand features, or brand positioning.

This is followed by a series of integrations that will lead to the overall strategic promotional implementation. Image integration is the relationship between the opinion of consumers and the promotion of the sport product, service, and/or organization. Functional integration is how the design or operation of the product, service, and/or organization can be utilized to effectively promote it. Coordinated integration is how all operational aspects of the organization work together to promote the products, services, and/or the organization itself. Consumer-based integration is the involvement of the buyers and users of products and services as an integral part of the promotional process. Stakeholder-based integration is how the ownership and employees of the organization have a vested interest in the efficient promotion of the product, service, and/or organization. Relationship management integration is how all aspects discussed above work cooperatively with each other to effectively and efficiently promote the product, service, or organization.

Direct promotional strategy involves the actual process of identifying customers, connecting with them, increasing their awareness and interest in the product or service being offered, and persuading them to make a purchase. Direct promotional strategy is centered on the concept of sales management. The promotional strategy employed by the sport marketer must involve initiating contact with the sport consumer. This often involves creating exposure through a non-personal medium such as a catalog, television commercial, or infomercial. The sport consumer then enters into the decision-making process, which may result in either ordering a sport product by mail, phone, fax, or internet, or choosing to find out more information about the sport organization.

Indirect promotional strategy refers to all the methods whereby an individual or organization can create, convey, and place messages in the mind of the prospective customer. There are four motives for an indirect promotional strategy:

1 positioning the product
2 enhancing the brand and building brand equity
3 providing credibility
4 using image transfer and association positioning.

Unfortunately, with so much information provided, the promoter must be concise and clear in designing a message to win "space" in the consumer's mind. The consumer must believe in the product or service and in the company providing that product or service. The relationship between the company and the consumer must be based on the product's usefulness, prestige, durability, attractiveness, and/or perceived attributes.

The most common method of indirect promotions is word of mouth, defined as spoken communication that does not come from the primary party. Examples of this include testimonials, referrals, endorsements, and impressions through promotions. Testimonials consist of the words and experiences of past users of the products or services being promoted. Individuals who offer testimonials send a message to potential and repeat customers about the positive interaction they have had with the product, service, and/or organization, including the quality of customer service, and the plan to continue involvement with the product. Testimonials are often found on the websites or marketing materials of companies. While some testimonials come from famous people, the most beneficial often come from the general public, since the potential consumer has a better chance of relating to that testimonial. The following are two examples of testimonials from Warrior Custom Golf (www.warriorcustom golf.com), a custom golf club company:

> Thank you for inviting me to try your new golf clubs. After seventy years searching I have found the perfect golf clubs. The natural feel; the solid hit makes the club feel like it is part of me. I am getting 10 to 20 yards more distance with the woods and the control with the irons in unbelievable. I LIKE THEM !!!

> These clubs and service meet and exceed my expectations . . . Thank you Warrior Custom Golf, your product speaks for itself, "outstanding"!

Referrals are recommendations made by one individual to another about a specific product, service, or organization. Most referrals come from friends, but may also come from everyday people. Most referral programs are combined with incentives. If one individual refers another, and that person makes a purchase, then the referee will receive a thank-you gift, a discount on a future purchase, a gift certificate, or some other benefit as a reward.

Endorsements usually use high-profile individuals such as athletes, actors, and prominent businesspersons to exploit their notoriety or position to assist an organization in promoting or selling their products or services, with the result being an enhanced image because of the association. A good example of a product endorsement would be the Miami Heat's Dwayne Wade's endorsement of Court Grip by Mission Athlete Care. Court Grip is a product that helps the basketball player gain traction on the basketball court. The commercial is of Wade on a court talking about how this will be the last time you will ever slip on a basketball court and allow court conditions to dictate your play. The commercial then shows Wade using the product and moving around on the court.

Impressions refer to the sport organization receiving third-party exposure through the media to create an association between the product or service being promoted and the reader (print or internet), listener (radio and TV), or viewer (TV or live). Impressions are tracked by sport marketing professionals to determine whether the marketing effort being employed is beneficial and profitable to the organization.

CONCLUSION

Communication management involves the planning, implementing, supervising, evaluation, and modification of the various methods of communication both internal and external to a sport organization. The sport marketing professional is involved in a number of roles to make sure that effective and efficient communication takes place throughout the organization in terms of the marketing process. These include developing organizational communication, controlling the flow of information in and out of the sport organization through various communication methods, managing sport organizational images, administering the organizational crisis communication plan, and providing communication training to all organizational staff.

In order to achieve total quality communication management, the sport marketing professional must focus on achieving a full understanding of the communication process, the sport organization's image, crisis sport communications, and sport promotions. Understanding the communication process helps to establish and maintain relationships with the sport consumer by providing a conduit for listening and reacting to the sport consumer. Managing the sport organization's image includes the role the brand, the logo, and publicity play in communication information to the external environment. Crisis sport communication planning allows the sport organization to control the quantity, flow, and type of information being released to the public and the media.

Promotions is a very involved communications process that aids in providing information about the sport product, service, or organization to consumers through the promotional mix.

The elements of the sport promotional mix include advertising, sponsorship, public relations, licensing, personal contact, incentives, and atmospherics. Advertising involves paid, non-personal communications about a sport product or service through the print, broadcast, or electronic media that are designed to attract public attention and subsequent purchase. Sponsorship refers to the relationship between a corporation and a sport organization as a tool to develop brand image and customer loyalty as a result of the association. Public relations is the collection of activities, communications, and media coverage that convey what the sport organization is and what it has to offer, all in the effort to enhance its image and prestige. Media relations, sports information, and sport journalism are all significant components of public relations.

Licensing is the creation of a strategic alliance in which the manufacturer of a sport product gives permission to a second party to manufacture that product in return for specific royalties or payments. Personal contact involves one-on-one communication between a representative of the sport organization and the sport consumer that should result in achieving promotional objectives ranging from providing information about products and services, to generating sales. Community relations and giving back to the community through socialization efforts are critical elements of personal contact.

Incentives are the benefits or reduced costs that are offered to motivate a sport consumer to purchase the specified sport product or service. Incentives are categorized as price-based incentives, sales incentives, and behavioral incentives. Atmospherics utilizes the design of visual communications in an environment, such as lighting, colors, or music, to entice the sport consumer's perceptual and emotional responses to purchase the sport product or service.

To coordinate the interaction between the elements of the sport promotional mix, a strategy must be developed that focuses on building brand loyalty and product credibility, developing image, and positioning the brand. The strategic process involves promotional integration, which is the actual creation and delivery of the promotional message that involves defining how the message is to reach the consumer, ensuring that the promotional message will be received and understood, and that the promotional message will lead to the purchase of a product or service.

This process starts with building awareness, and is followed by a series of integrations (image, functional, coordinated, consumer based, stakeholder based, and relationship management) that will lead to the overall strategic promotional implementation. This implementation will be either indirect or direct in nature. Much of indirect promotional strategy focuses on word of mouth, including testimonials, referrals, endorsements, and impressions through promotions. In contrast, direct promotional strategy is centered on sales management, which involves the actual process of identifying customers, connecting with them, increasing their awareness and interest in the product or service being offered, and persuading them to make a purchase.

FROM THEORY TO PRACTICE

MATT LAWRENCE, MINOR LEAGUE VIDEO COORDINATOR
Los Angeles Dodgers,
Los Angeles, California

Ever since high school I knew that I wanted to pursue a career in baseball. Having a college degree in sport management has certainly complemented my career search, but the degree alone was not enough to land a job in one of the most attractive and competitive industries. Rather, it was what I took away from my business, marketing, and sport courses and the experience I gained from applying their concepts into practice that got me to where I am today.

Example I: My most impressionable moment came in my sophomore year at my first job fair. I was overwhelmed by the amount of jobseekers that flooded the hall – my competition. I overheard a student from an Ivy League school boasting about his grades and academic accomplishments, while bragging about how many interviews he was sure to get. Being from a small college I was concerned. However, in seeking advice from a potential employer I was informed that being a good student is only the starting point, but that being involved on campus and showing initiative outside of the classroom were equal to if not more important than classroom accolades; in short, he wanted someone who was more than just a student. Having already been involved on campus and with several events under my belt, I snagged 11 interviews and was offered my first internship; I knew I could do better the following year.

Experience, experience, experience; the three most important words one will hear when beginning a career search in the sports world. The biggest challenge is how do you gain experience with no previous experience? Masquerading as a bad riddle, this is actually a challenge that most college students will face. A college degree is a great foundation, and without it it is hard for one to stand one's ground, but it is the structure that one builds from that foundation that opens doors for interview opportunities. So how does one become more than just a student and build on that academic foundation?

Example II, Extracurricular activities: I applied what I was learning in the classroom by getting involved with student organizations/clubs and student government. These student-based opportunities provided me with an extension of the classroom that allowed me to explore and sharpen my skills in a friendly environment while also boosting my résumé. I became interested in using video as a tool in sports, and thus started my own video club. However, I would not have known anything about clubs if I had not been a part of student government and several other organizations. I was able to utilize the club to complement my study of sport, since my major did not offer video instruction.

Example III, Volunteer events: Working volunteer events was another way I applied my studies to the sports world. During the school year I volunteered for the Boston Marathon, NASCAR races, the NBA All-Star Event, the NHL All-Star Event, and a NCAA Division III basketball tournament. While most of the work was not glamorous, the experiences were invaluable, and the basketball tournament gave me the opportunity to plan and work with video during the event, which I found very appealing. All of the events provided me with more insight into the operations of the sports world and the experience needed to help my résumé stand out.

Example IV, Internships: The most valuable part of my study of sport management was the two summer baseball internships I completed with the New Jersey Cardinals and the Pawtucket Red Sox. These opportunities allowed me to experience the business of baseball first hand, while also giving me the chance to realize which areas of the game I wanted to stay away from and which areas I wanted to further explore. My college studies combined with experiences allowed me to land both internships; in return, both internships guided my levels of interest and areas of study. When the PawSox learned of my initiative with my school's video club they made me their in-game cameraman – which, unbeknownst to me at the time, provided me with the practical experience I needed to land a job with the Red Sox three years later.

While a college degree is important, especially when compared with someone with no college experience, it does not put one significantly higher on the qualified applicant list. The fact that there are college grads everywhere looking to get their foot in the door in the sports world, coupled with the idea that working in sports is easy time with great compensation, causes the applicant pool for jobs in sports to be severely over-saturated. Employers are looking for experience. Anyone can be just a college student.

The questions are then: who was more than just a student; and who exceeded what was asked or expected of them? This is where experience weighs in. Any experience in sports, no matter how trivial it may seem, is a major advantage.

Example V: I attended four job fairs over five years at baseball's Winter Meetings as a jobseeker. Each year I received multiple interviews and job offers. With each interview employers were getting to the same point: how did I apply what I had learned from my degree and different experiences to the career path I was pursuing? I was able to point to and expand on my experiences and internships. I quickly found myself interviewing for many positions each year, while many of my counterparts without experience struggled.

Example VI: In my current position, I have attended the past four Winter Meetings as an employer interviewing candidates for entry-level positions. I am flooded with résumés of jobseekers. Grades and coursework are important, but how did the applicant take those lessons learned and apply them outside the classroom? Which candidates took the initiatives to go above and beyond what was required; which provided them with valuable experience and the ability to transcend from the classroom to the stadium? With so many applicants each year, and with so few job openings, it is the candidates who stand out from the pack that are going to get the first look.

The reason the experience in sports is so highly touted by employers is because the reality of working in sports is far from the idealistic view most college grads have of well-paid positions and a glamorous work environment. Employers know that those who have some experience in sports, no matter at what level, will have a more grounded understanding of what it is like to work in the sports industry; long hours, low pay, and many responsibilities.

Experience does not have to come from sports. I had many experiences in sports which led me to two internships in minor league baseball, a four-year job in Video Productions with the Boston Red Sox, and a full-time job as the Director of Video Operations with the Carolina Mudcats, but it was my dedication to continued learning and applying those lessons to new experiences in sports, the same as I did in college, which led me to my current position with the LA Dodgers.

Example VII: I knew that I wanted to get into Baseball Operations, perhaps the most coveted department within most baseball organizations. With no clear path in any textbook about how to get into baseball ops, each year the competition becomes fiercer as more applicants enter the pool. Some candidates submerge themselves with statistical research while others hope that law school will open some doors. I saw video coaching as a niche and decided to pursue it. Until that opportunity became available, I proceeded to gain baseball video experience by working in video production for the Mudcats and Red Sox; I began working for video production firms and freelancing my skills outside of sports to gain more technical experience; and began coaching college and summer baseball to better understand the coaching side of the game. The Dodgers saw what I was doing, and when they made the move to start a minor league video department, they brought me onboard to run it.

My position title is Minor League Video Coordinator, but like most jobs in baseball, my job description covers many aspects.

Minor league video is relatively new to major league organizations. The Dodgers were one of the first teams to go all in and provide coaches' video at each minor league affiliate. Overseeing a staff of six interns and video at six affiliates, I work directly for the front office as well as working with our coaches and players at both the major and minor league levels. My job is extremely demanding and requires long hours throughout the year: weekends and holidays are almost non-existent. Dedication and sacrifices are a must, but I was well prepared for this step in my career.

Baseball is a fiercely competitive industry, and each year more major league organizations are starting their own minor league video departments. Trying to remain on the leading edge of my field, it falls on me to keep my organization ahead of the curve in technology, policy, and business. Though it is tempting to sit back sometimes and say "I have made it" (getting a full-time job in baseball operations), my path is far from over. I still find myself continuing to learn and applying those lessons in practice, the same as I did throughout college.

CHAPTER ELEVEN

SPORT ADVERTISING

CHAPTER OUTLINE

- What is sport advertising?
- Advertising for sport teams and sport retail businesses
- Sport advertising and image
- Social, ethical, and regulatory aspects of sport advertising
- Sport advertising and consumer behavior
- Creating sport advertisements and commercials
- Ambush marketing in sport advertising
- Sport advertising and integrated brand promotion
- Conclusion

CHAPTER OBJECTIVES

The reader will be able to:

- appreciate the role of sport advertising for sport team, sport retail business, and the overall business process
- know the structure of the sport advertising industry including advertisers, agencies, and support organizations
- recognize the various social, ethical, and regulatory aspects of sport advertising, including the role of consumer behavior, business ethics concepts, and ambush marketing
- realize the complexity of creating sport advertisements and commercials

- understand the integration of the field of sport and the engagement of inter-disciplinary thinking as it relates to audiovisual communications, development communications, telecommunications, and mass communications
- be familiar with the relationship between sport marketing and integrated brand promotion.

WHAT IS SPORT ADVERTISING?

As discussed in the previous chapter, sport advertising is the process of attracting public attention to a sport product or sport business through paid announcements in the print, broadcast, or electronic media. Traditionally, advertising was viewed as an artistic profession that was simply used to articulate product benefits and image. However, advertising has evolved to become one of the critical elements of business. This is especially true in sport advertising, where these efforts are used as an integral tool of marketing as related to brand development and management, segmentation, differentiation, and positioning.

Consumers are increasingly "bombarded" with advertising messages and information. As a consequence of this information overkill, a brand has become the abbreviation of all of its positive and negative rational and emotional associations. The brand strategy has a direct impact on the brand's corporate value – success in the market, growth, market share, price, margins, and earnings – and thus in market capitalization and corporate value.

A brand strategy must result in a conclusive, focused, and efficient marketing mix, and must be economically viable. This strategy would involve looking at the following:

- What is the "actual" position of a brand from the consumer's perspective? What are the Actual Value Perception (AVP), Projection (PVP), Actual Consumer Base, and competitive environment?
- What "ideal" target position should the brand take in the competitive environment? The Target Value Proposition (TVP) should be strategically differentiated from the competition.
- What is the optimal brand strategy from the "actual" to the "ideal" brand position? A road-map including milestones from actual to target position of a brand.
- What are the corresponding measurements for the entire marketing mix? Things such as an action plan, or Future Execution (FX), that are consistent across the entire marketing mix.
- What are the costs involved and what is the impact on the business plan? Cost of repositioning, consequences for turnover, margin, and profitability in the short, mid, and long term.

This strategy then flows into the branding process. The results of this process should provide the sport consumer with a clear understanding of the attributes and values of the brand. The process starts by completing an analysis of the target market, including identifying the brand audience, understanding target consumers, determining key customer leverage points and behaviors, and monitoring the actions of direct and indirect competitors. Once this is enacted, the development of brand architecture should ensue. This involves managing the relationship

254

structures between the various levels within the organization, as well as with sub-brands and other products and services being offered by the organization. As these relationships are solidified, communication with potential and existing consumers must be developed to provide a clear description of how they should view and value the product or service. This message should not only be clear, but also articulate the quality and usefulness of the product or service, come from a trustworthy source, and be consistent over time. The final step is the establishment of feedback systems, so that consumers have an avenue to respond with their perceptions of the product or service. This is crucial to determine whether the advertising and branding processes are working, and if there are other opportunities that could be targeted. It also provides significant information about problems with the entire process, which in turn requires the sport marketing professional to re-evaluate and retool the entire advertising and branding process.

Today's markets are more volatile than before and possibly the traditional "mass media" advertising focus is no longer appropriate. One option is to focus on different niches of the market where we are able to satisfy their needs and wants. This is possible with market segmentation – dividing the market into groups of potential clients with similar needs and profiles and which present similar buying habits.

Market segmentation is the basis of other marketing actions. It will require a major management effort to direct the strategy to each market niche and also the necessary investigation, implementation, and control for realizing a correct segmentation. The main objective of the segmentation is to improve the position of the company and better serve the needs of consumers. We will also be able to increase sales, improve our market share, and enhance our image.

How many segments should we consider? The answer is logical; we should act in as many segments as our business capacity allows. To get a product or service to the right person or company, a marketer would first segment the market, then target a single segment or series of segments, and finally position within the segment(s).

Segmentation is essentially the identification of subsets of buyers within a market who share similar needs and who demonstrate similar buyer behavior. The world is made up of many buyers with their own sets of needs and behaviors. Segmentation aims to match groups of purchasers with the same set of needs and buyer behavior. Such a group is known as a "segment." Market segmentation allows product differentiation by preparing appropriate marketing mixes for each market segment, organized distribution according to buying characteristics, and more focused media advertising according to habits and lifestyles.

Targeting strategies can usually be categorized as concentrated, differentiated, product-specialized, market-specialized, or full coverage. Concentrated strategy is a single-segment strategy where one market segment is served with one marketing mix. A single-segment approach is often the strategy of choice for smaller companies with limited resources. Differentiated strategy is a selective specialization or multiple-segment strategy where different marketing mixes are offered to different segments. The product itself may or may not be different – in many cases only the promotional message or distribution channels vary. Product specialization involves an organization specializing in a particular product or service, and tailoring it to different market segments. Market specialization differs in that the organization specializes in serving a particular market segment, and offers that segment an array of different products. Full market coverage is the organization's attempt to serve the entire market. This coverage can be achieved by means of either a mass market strategy in which a single undifferentiated marketing mix is offered to the entire market, or by a differentiated strategy in which a separate marketing mix is offered to each segment.

Positioning is the process of designing a company's offer and image so that it occupies a distinct and valued place in the mind of the consumer. Positioning a product consists in gaining a benign meaning in the customer's mind as to where the product sits in the market segment to which it belongs. This may be achieved by the product's own attributes or through the influence of advertising. The objective of positioning a product is to make sure that it occupies a certain place in the mind of the consumer, differentiating it from the competition.

Positioning is about how the product or service is differentiated in the mind of a prospective customer. It is an organized system for finding a window in the mind of your prospect in order to position your product – merchandise, a service, a company, or a person – effectively against its main competitors. This system is based on the concept that communication can only take place at the right time and under the right circumstances. The mind accepts only that new information which matches its current state. It filters out everything else. In other words, positioning is a process by which a psychological "anchor" (any stimulus which evokes a consistent response) has been placed into the minds of prospects so that they come to choose one specific person or company over another.

ADVERTISING FOR SPORT TEAMS AND SPORT RETAIL BUSINESSES

The real lesson seems to be that the advertising rules which apply to most traditional consumer brands do not apply to sport teams. Consumers looking to purchase sporting goods usually search for the best price and or the quickest service. The get-it-and-forget-it attitude applies in most cases, but loyal fans have an emotional bond that is virtually impossible to break. The Cubs make a good counterpoint to the Yankees; the team's fans are just as loyal despite not having won a championship since 1908. You could argue that the Cubs are consistent losers, that they deliver on what has become an unfortunate brand promise. So ball clubs may have little to learn from brand marketers. But perhaps brands can learn from the sports teams' ability to develop ties with their consumers that are strong enough to withstand the toughest challenges.

In 2001, Manchester United, one of England's best-known soccer clubs, joined forces with Major League Baseball team the New York Yankees in a merger that sought to raise the profile of both clubs across the globe. Under the marketing alliance, Manchester United explored sponsorship, television, and other cross-promotional opportunities with YankeeNets LLC, the parent company of the New York Yankees, which also owned at that time the New Jersey Nets NBA basketball team and the New Jersey Devils of the National Hockey League. The agreement resulted in Manchester United's own television channel, MUTV, broadcasting Yankee game highlights, for example, and Manchester United replica kits sharing boutique space with Yankee pinstripes.

In this example, the brand extensions for team loyalty and image sought to gain footholds in the American market for soccer, and in Great Britain, Asia, and the Far East for baseball. Both

256

clubs hoped to use their fan base to promote each other's products. This marked a fundamental change in brand loyalty, with the introduction of cross-cultural marketing of dissimilar sports. The long-term benefits of mergers such as this could significantly distance the organizations from their peers financially, giving them another advantage on game day. While this partnership dissolved due in part to the breakup of YankeeNets LLC, the concept has now led to the discussion of similar partnerships between European Premier League Clubs and MLS clubs, including Arsenal and the Colorado Rapids, and Chelsea with DC United.

Is there too much promotion? It is more likely that there is not enough. When it comes to the down time of professional sports, the "in-game entertainment" has become part of the show through various gimmicks, pyrotechnics, and promotions. These special events have blurred the line between sport and entertainment. Teams pay more attention to the food, free T-shirts being sling-shot into the crowd, blimps that circle over the crowd and drop items into the customers' laps, exotic laser light shows, and various events that take place at half-time or between the periods. It is all done with the intent to make games into events, and to help the consumer justify the cost of the ticket.

Consumer communications are crucial for a retailer to position itself in customers' minds. Various physical and symbolic cues may be used, such as store location, merchandise assortment, price levels, physical facilities, mass advertising and public relations, personal selling, and sales promotion. A retail image requires a multifaceted, ongoing process. For chains, it is essential that there be a consistent image among branches.

The retailer's interior and exterior of a store encompasses its parking, display windows, flooring, colors, lighting, scents and sounds, temperature, width of aisles, dressing facilities, personnel, self-service, merchandise, price displays, cash register placement, technology and modernization, and cleanliness. All of these features are designed to elicit a specific response while promoting the corporate message to consumers.

To persuade customers to devote more time in the store, some of the most common retail tactics include experiential merchandising, solutions selling, retailer co-branding, and wish list programs. Customers react favorably to retailers involved in such activities as establishing stores that are barrier-free for disabled persons, supporting charities, and running special sales for senior citizens. The more positive or pleasant feelings a retailer can provide the consumer, the more favorable feeling will be placed on the franchise or brand.

Advertising in pro shops can help a company (such as golf pro shops) transform their bottom lines in a number of different ways. Because the consumer has already entered the place of business, a company can focus its advertising dollars on making the consumer's experience a pleasant and memorable one. The company can also solicit sponsorship because the pro shop has already created a target rich-environment in the golfing industry.

A pro shop can generate revenue by companies sponsoring a hole, tee box, fairway, green, club house, or naming rights for the course. Self-promotion in the pro shop can bolster corporate functions such as a golf tournament or inventory blow out. In some cases, golf pro shops offer touch-screen GPS locators that help their consumers range each green. In the down time for this technology, companies can advertise their products on the LCD screen or place an order at the snack bar to be picked up at the turn.

Brand loyalty is a consumer's preference to buy a particular brand in a product category. It occurs because consumers perceive that the brand offers the needed product features, images, or level of quality at the right price. This perception becomes the foundation for a new buying habit. Consumers will initially make a trial purchase of the brand and, after satisfaction, tend to form habits and continue purchasing the same brand because the product works well or is familiar.

Consumers must like the product in order to develop loyalty toward it. In order to convert occasional purchasers into brand loyalists, habits must be reinforced. Consumers must be reminded of the value of their purchase and encouraged to continue purchasing the product in the future.

To encourage repeat purchases, advertising before and after the sale is critical. In addition to creating awareness and promoting initial purchases, advertising shapes and reinforces consumer attitudes so that these attitudes mature into beliefs, which need to be reinforced until they develop into loyalty.

SPORT ADVERTISING AND IMAGE

Sport is one of the most important social concepts. Many companies use sport as a tool to create brand loyalty. The companies using professional athletes produce the image that their equipment is the reason why the athlete is successful. As a result, the equipment produced by the company sells very well.

Advertisements make sports more popular. All the organizations hoping for profit use concepts like arts and sports to introduce or re-create themselves. This is the basic factor in sport image. Sport image can be used in various types in society. The basic objective of advertisements is to link the product with the success, and for the consumer to transfer that image of success to the product.

The case for advertising is traditionally based on its economic role, but a case can also be made for the psychological and social value of advertising. Advertising is everywhere, and people everywhere are united by it. Perhaps for the first time, young people of all ethnic and geographic origins share images and experiences, thanks in large measure to mass media and mass advertising.

More than 90 percent of the revenues from television advertising directed at children are reinvested into children's programs. Successful children's programs on Nickelodeon rely on advertising techniques to teach children all manner of things. Advertising has been doing this for years. If a company can create brand loyalty at an early age, maintaining that loyalty is less costly as an adult. As stated earlier, it is more cost-effective to foster the consumer–supplier relationship than it is to reinvent that relationship every time a purchase is made.

SOCIAL, ETHICAL, AND REGULATORY ASPECTS OF SPORT ADVERTISING

Since it is so visible, advertising gets criticized frequently, for both what it is and what it is not. Many of the criticisms focus on the style of advertising, saying it is deceptive or manipulative.

Collectively it might refer to these as short-term manipulative arguments. Other criticisms focus on the social or environmental impact of advertising. These are long-term macro arguments. Discussion of the economic impact of advertising focuses primarily on the first two principles of free-market economics: self-interest, and many buyers and sellers. The social aspect of advertising typically involves the last two principles: complete information and absence of externalities.

Social issue debates may be seen as instances where advertising tends to violate one or more of these basic economic principles. Some of the most important aspects of these principles are deception and manipulation in advertising, the effect of advertising on our value system, commercial clutter, stereotypes, and offensiveness. By examining these common criticisms of advertising, consumers can debunk some misconceptions, and examine the problems that do exist.

One of the most common short-term arguments about advertising is that it is so frequently deceptive. Anything that detracts from the satisfaction of the transaction produces a loss of activity that ultimately hurts both parties. If a product does not live up to its ads, dissatisfaction occurs – and in the long term that is as harmful to the advertiser as to the buyer.

For advertising to be effective, consumers must have confidence in it. Thus any kind of deception not only detracts from the complete information principle of free enterprise but also risks being self-defeating. Even meaningless embellishment (puffery) might be taken literally and therefore become deceptive. Puffery refers to exaggerated, subjective claims that cannot be proven true or false, such as "the best," "premier," or "the only way to fly." Under current advertising law, the only product claims, explicit or implied, that are considered deceptive are those that are factually false or convey a false impression and therefore have the potential to deceive or mislead reasonable people. But puffery is excluded from this requirement because regulators maintain that reasonable people do not believe in it anyway. Since advertisers regularly use puffery and non-product facts to enhance the image of their products, they must think consumers do believe in it. Non-product facts are not about the brand but about the consumer or the social context in which the consumer uses the brand.

An example is "Pepsi – The choice of a new generation." The fact is that advertising, by its very nature, is not complete information. It is biased in favor of the advertiser and the brand. People expect advertisers to be proud of their products and probably do not mind if they puff them a little. But when advertisers cross the line between simply giving their point of view and creating false expectations, that is when people begin to object. One problem is the difficulty of seeing the line, which may be drawn differently by different people. These kinds of problems can be avoided if marketers simply improve the kind of information they give in their advertising. Companies require advertisers to have a reasonable basis for any claims they make, whether or not those claims are facts about the product. This would contribute positively to a free market system.

Advertising to children presents different challenges. Kids are not sophisticated consumers. Their conceptions of self, time, and money are immature. As a result, they know very little about their desires, needs, and preference, or how to use economic resources rationally to satisfy them. The nature of children's conceptual ability makes it likely that child-oriented advertising can lead to false beliefs or highly improbable product expectations.

While most children and parents are still joint consumers, more and more children are becoming sole decision makers. To protect them, and their parents, both critics and defenders agree that advertisers should not intentionally deceive children. The central issue is how far advertisers should go to ensure that children are not misled by their ads. To promote responsible children's advertising and to respond to public concerns, the Council of Better Business Bureaus established the Children's Advertising Review Unit (CARU). CARU provides a general advisory service for advertisers and agencies and also offers informational material for children, parents, and educators. For more than 20 years, CARU's *Self-Regulatory Guidelines for Children's Advertising* has guided marketers in the development of child-directed advertising for all traditional media.

In 1997, CARU published its updated *Guidelines* to include new directions for marketing to children via online media. The basic activity of CARU is the review and evaluation of child-directed advertising in all media. When children's advertising is found to be misleading, inaccurate, or inconsistent with the *Guidelines*, CARU seeks changes through voluntary cooperation of the advertisers.

In the developed world, other countries are far stricter than the United States about advertising to children. Sweden and Norway, for example, do not permit any television advertising to be directed toward children under 12, and no advertisements at all are allowed during children's programs. Germany and Holland prohibit sponsorship of children's shows, and the Flemish region of Belgium permits no ads five minutes before or after any programs for children.

In the area of television advertising, the government and consumer groups play an important role at both the national and international level to ensure that adequate consumer protection for children is maintained and strengthened where necessary.

The "Truth in Advertising Creed" was developed because corporations wanted to gain market share. In the absence of information, consumers will listen and believe the loudest voice. If that voice is promoting fiction, or partial truths, how would the consumer know the difference? There are a number of non-governmental organizations whose sole purpose is to educate the consumer, such as the Better Business Bureau and Consumer Reports.

The Better Business Bureau keeps records of improprieties and of proper ethical standards on every business in the United States. Consumer Reports continually tests products to provide the consumer with the most current, safest, quality products in the marketplace. Both of these organizations can be accessed at no cost using the World Wide Web.

Every day, advertisers from the local mom and pop shop to international corporation marketers have to deal with the actions and decisions of all branches of government, state and federal, and the laws they pass that affect advertisers.

In today's society, a major regulatory issue facing advertisers is privacy. Today, most advertisers know it is illegal to use a person's likeness in an ad without the individual's permission. Since 1987, even using a celebrity look-alike or sound-alike can violate that person's rights. The courts have also ruled that people's privacy rights continue even after their death.

Now, with the increased use of fax machines, mobile devices, and the internet, all of which can be used for advertising directly to prospects, the issue of privacy rights is again in the news. This time it is over people's right to protect their personal information. Privacy is an ethical issue as well as a legal one. It is also a practical issue. Prospective customers who find advertising faxes, telemarketing calls, and emails annoying and intrusive are not likely to buy the offending company's products. Internet users worry about people they do not know, and even businesses they do know, getting personal information about them. This concern is not without reason since many websites create profiles of their visitors to obtain data such as email addresses, clothing sizes, or favorite books. Some sites also track users' hobbies, usually without their knowledge, to better target ads for products.

To create these user profiles, websites use tiny software programs, called cookies, that keep a log of where people click, allowing sites to track customers' web-surfing habits on that particular site. The cookies are placed on people's computers when they first visit a site or use some feature like a personalized news service or a shopping cart. Internet companies argue that such tracking is not personal; it is typically performed anonymously and helps them customize sites and content to match users' interests.

Fortunately, consumers are not completely helpless. Consumers can disable the cookies on their computers. But this may limit their internet access, because some websites actually require that cookies be implanted. Internet surfers also have the option to "opt-in." This feature allows users to set the terms for which they give personal information. Also available is the "opt-out" feature, which allows sites to continuously gather information about visitors unless they specifically inform the site not to do so by clicking on a button.

SPORT ADVERTISING AND CONSUMER BEHAVIOR

Marketing communicators direct their efforts toward influencing consumers' brand-related beliefs, attitudes, emotional reactions, and choices. Ultimately, the objective is to encourage consumers to choose their brand rather than the competitor. To accomplish this goal, marketers design advertising messages, promotions, packaging cues, brand names, sales presentations, and commercials.

Supply and demand makes the economic world go round, and creates the foundation for competition. Although the media usually portray owners in pursuit of dollars, this is a two-way street. Just like any other product, sports fans demand team output and are willing to pay for it. What makes sports consumers demand team output? The answer is all the characteristics of the sport product: the beauty of athletic prowess, absolute and relative team quality, and the thrill of victory or the agony of defeat.

The quality of teams is a commodity that generates the competition that fans enjoy. In most cases the level of quality is directly related to the willingness of an organization to purchase high-quality players. In order for a league such as the NFL to gain dominance and maintain their consumer base, the league must ensure that none of the teams get too strong or too weak. The more opportunity for parity, the more consumers believe their team will win and the more those fans are willing to pay to see it happen.

Consumers are systematic decision makers. Consumers would not be responsive to advertising unless there was something in it for them, and there is. All advertising and promotions techniques provide consumers with rewards (benefits, incentives, or inducements) that encourage certain forms of behavior desired by brand managers. Consumers also obtain nonfunctional benefits when taking advantage of advertising and promotional offers, such as the sense of being a wise shopper, the stimulation of trying different brands, or in entertainment value.

When establishing symbolic relations, advertisers often use non-literal language. Nike has made famous the "swoosh" symbol to identify its brand and impart the notion of speed. This is a key in conveying a performance attribute, especially when this brand was introduced in the heyday of jogging and road-racing.

Consumers are also an integral part of the overall decision-making process for advertising. Once people have decided on what goods to consume, advertisements clearly present the array of possible choices for a particular good. Ads may help consumers make brand choices. The typical viewer of any sport is male between the ages of 25 and 52. It is not by coincidence that consumers are bombarded by beer, cars, and tools. Consumers identify with being in a particular consumer base such as Pepsi drinkers or Coke drinkers, or Red Sox fans or Yankee fans. These ads solidify brand loyalty and, once brand loyalty is solidified, it is very difficult to make a new first impression.

CREATING SPORT ADVERTISEMENTS AND COMMERCIALS

In the first-ever televised World Series, Major League Baseball Commissioner Happy Chandler said, "It would not be good public relations for baseball to have the Series sponsored by the producer of an alcoholic beverage." Sport advertising has come so far since then. Advertising messages can be developed with little thought for a systematic approach. To appreciate the role of an advertising plan, imagine a soccer team approaching an upcoming game without any idea of how it is going to execute its offense or defense. Without a game plan, the team would have to play in the same spontaneous fashion as do players in a pick-up game. Advertising strategy is the formulation of an advertising message that communicates the brand's value proposition, its primary benefit, or how it can solve the consumer's problem.

A systematic approach to creative advertising makes sense in theory but ultimately the people who write the advertising copy must create a visually pleasing concept. Even though research has shown that advertising copy is based on copy-writers' own implicit theories of how advertising works for consumers, they do not have the luxury to create for the mere sake of engaging in a creative pursuit.

In many advertising agencies, the work of copy-writers is directed by a framework known as a creative brief. This is a document designed to inspire copy-writers by channeling their creative efforts toward a solution that will serve the interest of the client. The creative brief is an informal pact between client and advertising agency that represents agreement on what an advertising campaign is intended to accomplish. Once this agreement has been reached, production can begin.

Advertising productions can take many forms such as newspapers, magazines, billboards, and direct and indirect mail. In addition to print, electronic and digital media have opened many doors. The use of websites' banner ads, pop-ups, and site sponsorships has assisted the advertising world both locally and globally. Digital media have allowed different programming segments, syndication, networking, cable, and pay-per-view to reach more consumers than ever.

AMBUSH MARKETING IN SPORT ADVERTISING

Ambush marketing is a method utilized by organizations to create an illusion that their products or services are associated with a specific sport endeavor. This association is without the permission of the sport endeavor or its official partner(s), and the desire is to deceive the sport consumer into believing that there is an official association.

CASE STUDY 11: PEPSI VS. COCA-COLA: IS IT ADVERTISING OR AMBUSH MARKETING?

While football fans have been enjoying the World Cup, off the pitch FIFA has been cracking down on companies and individuals attempting to "ambush" the FIFA World Cup through various activities infringing its intellectual property rights.

Since the conclusion of the 1998 World Cup in France, FIFA has been using a specialized "anti-ambush" team, comprising trademark specialists, commercial lawyers, and sports marketing specialists. Its strategy for this World Cup began with a worldwide trademark registration program of "FIFA World Cup," the official mascots, the official emblem, and the FIFA World Cup Trophy. These measures were taken to ensure that FIFA is in a strong position to protect and enforce its intellectual property rights and the rights of the official partners, the official suppliers, and the licensees.

One of the highest profile examples of FIFA's enforcement activities involves the soft drink manufacturer PepsiCo. Although Coca-Cola is one of the FIFA World Cup's official partners, rival PepsiCo has produced advertisements that suggest a sponsorship relationship between it and the FIFA World Cup.

In 2002, an Argentinian court ordered PepsiCo to immediately cease the use of an advertisement. The court found that the prohibited advertisement would cause confusion among consumers as it suggested a "presumed sponsorship relationship" between PepsiCo and the FIFA World Cup. The advertisement in question combined the use of the phrase "Tokyo 2002," famous footballers, and other football imagery in association with the logo of PepsiCo. The court ordered PepsiCo not to use the advertisement on TV, in printed media, or by any other means. Had FIFA decided not to act, its inactivity would have diminished the value of its trademarks as well as the exclusivity of agreements with official partners such as Coca-Cola.

The Argentinian court order comes on the heels of PepsiCo's claims earlier in the week that its advertising will not mention the FIFA World Cup. However, this is not the only promotion related to the FIFA World Cup which has caused PepsiCo to be in hot water with FIFA: in Ecuador, FIFA has also instructed counsel to initiate legal proceedings against PepsiCo as a result of similar TV commercials; and in Mexico, PepsiCo is in the midst of negotiations with FIFA to settle a case involving the unauthorized use of FIFA's trademark-protected emblem of "2002 FIFA World Cup."

Businesses spend considerable time and substantial sums of money devising brands and marketing their products or services. This investment should be protected whenever possible by registering trade names, logos, strap-lines, and other trademarks. If a trademark is registered, the registration gives the owner a monopoly right in that country to use the mark in respect of the goods or services in which it is registered and provides protection against infringement.

Source: Adapted from Meikle, E. (2002). *Lawless Branding – Recent Developments in Trademark Law . . . FIFA Defends World Cup Against Pepsi Ambush Marketing.* Retrieved March 3, 2006 from http://www.brandchannel.com/features_effect.asp?pf_id=103.

Questions for discssussion

1   Even if PepsiCo does not use any official logos, player likenesses, or wording that implied direct association with the World Cup, can the company create advertising that still could imply to the consumer that it is directly associated with the World Cup? Give at least three examples.
2   Come up with at least three examples of how you would use integrated brand promotions to advertise PepsiCo at the World Cup without fear of legal recourse from FIFA and Coca-Cola. Explain in detail how you would place these advertisements.
3   Examine the evolution of anti-ambush marketing laws for the 2006 (Germany), 2010 (South Africa), and 2014 (Brazil) FIFA World Cups, as well as for hallmark sporting events around the world over the past decade in numerous countries including the United States, Canada, England, Australia, New Zealand, and India.

Companies hire marketing firms to find creative ways to crash the event without having to pay the high sponsorship fees. They will do this in a number of ways, including signage near the event, buying television commercial time during the event, and offering promotions in conjunction with the sales of products that are related to the event. Four of the more classic advertising efforts that involved ambush marketing occurred during the 1994 Winter Olympics in Lillehammer, Norway; the 1996 Summer Olympics in Atlanta, Georgia; the 1996 International Cricket Council (ICC) World Cup in India; and the 2002 Super Bowl in New Orleans, Louisiana.

■   In 1994, when American Express was replaced by Visa as the official credit card sponsor for the Winter Olympics, American Express came up with an advertising campaign centered on the slogan "If you are traveling to Lillehammer, you will need a passport but you do not need a Visa."
■   In 1996, at the height of the "cola wars," and the desire to be the most recognized soft drink company globally, Coca-Cola paid a significant amount of money to be the official soft drink of the Cricket World Cup. Pepsi, not to be outdone, countered with an advertising campaign centered on the slogan "Nothing Official About It." In addition, Pepsi sought to get further association with the event by flying hot-air balloons near the venues with the Pepsi logo on them, and also encouraging players who had endorsement deals with Pepsi not to go near Coke drink carts.

264

- Also in 1996, although Nike was not an official sponsor, it plastered its logo on billboards around the city, and on banners and merchandise handed out to people leaving public transportation headed to the Olympics. The images, captured in photographs and on worldwide television, created the impression that Nike was an official sponsor when it was not.
- In 2002, Proctor and Gamble wanted to get its laundry detergent recognized in conjunction with the Super Bowl. Since it could not use the words "Super Bowl," it decided to have signage placed near the Louisiana Superdome that said "Because there are more than XXXVI [the roman numerals for that year's Super Bowl] ways to ruin your clothes. Enjoy the Big Game."

These ambush marketing efforts have resulted in many changes to laws and policies. One example in Detroit, Michigan is an anti-ambush marketing law that has created a no-ad zone around stadiums. While the original proposal was for one mile, the law was modified by the request of MLB and the NFL when bringing hallmark events to the city (the All-Star Game and Super Bowl respectively). In response to the Pepsi scenario in 1996, the International Cricket Council (ICC) has instituted ambush marketing protection contracts with sponsors, and has encouraged individual Boards to have their players follow the approved agreement for tournaments. In addition, New Zealand, the host of the 2015 World Cup (who also hosted the 2011 Rugby World Cup), enacted laws to combat ambush marketing.

SPORT ADVERTISING AND INTEGRATED BRAND PROMOTION

As previously defined, integrated brand promotion (IBP) is the use of various promotional tools in a coordinated manner to build and maintain brand awareness, identity, and preference. The goal of integrated brand promotion includes the coordination of all verbal and visual communication efforts for the purpose of reaching all members of the target market at a minimum, and with aspirations of reaching the entire population. In integrated brand promotion, the sport organization incorporates its logo with advertising and other efforts that include support media, point-of-purchase (P-O-P) displays, sales promotions, direct marketing, sponsorship, and promotions.

Support media are the use of non-traditional media efforts to connect with members of the target audience who have not been reached through traditional media (print, radio, television). The goal is to reinforce and support the original advertising messages. Examples of support media include aerial advertising (blimps, sky banners, sky writing), mobile billboards (trailers, truck, vans), transit advertising (buses, subways, taxi-cabs, trains), in-store media (kiosks, signs, video screens), promotional products, and the Yellow Pages.

Point-of-purchase displays are special exhibits involving a product or service at the point of sale. Examples of traditional P-O-P displays include cardboard cut-outs, end caps, kiosks, and signage. As the digital age has become more infused in all aspects of advertising, digital signage has become a very popular method for delivering messages to potential customers because it can be more easily customized for the target audience. These displays are considered one of the most important aspects of advertising (and merchandising) because of the concept of impulse buying, which is the act of making a spontaneous, unplanned purchase. P-O-P displays help to entice consumers to make a purchase at the most critical point – when they are in the store and have money available.

Directly associated with this aspect is sales promotion. Sales promotion is a unique promotional method that is utilized to generate immediate interest in a product or service. Some of the most common methods utilized include contests and sweepstakes, and coupons and discounts. Direct marketing shares some similarities with sales promotion, in that the goal is to generate immediate interest in a product or service. However, where sales promotions are usually directly connected to a store (whether retail or online), direct marketing seeks to deliver promotional materials such as brochures, catalogs, leaflets, or print ads straight to the current or potential consumer. Some of the most common methods are through direct mail, door-to-door selling, and telemarketing.

CONCLUSION

Sport advertising is the process of attracting public attention to a sport product or sport business through paid announcements in the print, broadcast, or electronic media. As a primary element of the sport promotions mix, it is the communication process utilized most often in sport marketing. Through advertisements, advertising campaigns, and integrated brand promotion, advertising helps establish and maintain relationships with the sport consumer by providing a conduit for listening and reacting to the sport consumer.

Advertising has evolved from being viewed simply as an artistic profession utilized to articulate product benefits and image to being one of the critical elements of business. This is especially true in sport advertising, where these efforts are used as an integral tool of marketing as related to brand development and management, segmentation, differentiation, and positioning. As a result, the sport advertising efforts need to be in congruence with the brand strategy and the branding process. The brand strategy has a direct impact on the brand's corporate value – success in the market, growth, market share, price, margins, and earnings – and thus on market capitalization and corporate value. The branding process provides the sport consumer with a clear understanding of the attributes and values of the brand. Regardless of whether sport advertising focuses on sport teams, sport retail businesses, or sport brand associations, advertising efforts will be unique to the products and services being offered. The two areas of continuity across all sport advertising efforts are creating brand loyalty and building image.

There are numerous social, ethical, and regulatory issues important to sport advertising efforts. When violated, social and ethical issues arise, and the government may take corrective measures. Society determines what is offensive, excessive, and irresponsible; government bodies determine what is deceptive and unfair. Advertising gets criticized frequently, both for what it is and what it is not. Many of the criticisms and social debate focus on the style of advertising, saying it is deceptive or manipulative. This in turn brings about questions of the effect of advertising on our value system, commercial clutter, stereotypes, and offensiveness. This is especially true with advertising focused on children, where they are not yet sophisticated consumers who truly understand the decision-making process. Therefore by creating sport advertising and commercials that stay within appropriate social, ethical, and legal constraints, and in conjunction with understanding the behaviors of sport consumers, sport marketing professionals can build the brand image and entice the sport consumer to be brand loyal.

This is most often accomplished through integrated brand promotion, which is the use of various promotional tools in a coordinated manner to build and maintain brand awareness,

266

identity, and preference. This is accomplished by incorporating the sport organization's logo with sponsorships and promotions (to be discussed in the next two chapters), as well as with advertising efforts enacted through support media, point-of-purchase displays, and sales promotions. Support media are the use of non-traditional media efforts to connect with members of the target audience who have not been reached through traditional media (print, radio, television). Point-of-purchase displays are special exhibits involving a product or service at the point of sale. Sales promotion is a unique promotional method that is utilized to generate immediate interest in a product or service. Some of the most common methods utilized include contests and sweepstakes, and coupons and discounts.

FROM THEORY TO PRACTICE

KRISTOPHER M. LULL, MARKETPLACE MANAGER
Baseball America,
Durham, North Carolina

There is not always a direct road that will put you in a position for success in sports. My career has taken me down many paths to get me to the place I am in now. For me, I knew that Sales, Marketing, and Advertising were where I needed to be; however, finding experience to go with my educational knowledge was difficult. My road starts with school and ends with a job in advertising sales with the leading baseball magazine. But believe me when I say I had to fight for everything!

I started college in 2000 ready to take on the world. I had a love of sports and a passion for baseball. I will be the first to say that, for me, my view of college was to graduate just to show potential employers that I had the ability to finish something I started. Over the nine years it took me to complete school, that idea changed dramatically.

In 2001 my situation had changed and I was forced to take over my student loan payments while still in school. I had to get a full-time job and finish school. For me I took this as an opportunity to start my sales career. It also delayed my graduation date, but added experience, so that I was able to compare the real world to the book world.

I began working in the retail market, selling cell phones in a mall in New Hampshire. When they talk about "location, location, location" that was not the place to sell a lot of phones. We needed to change the standard way of drawing in potential clients. The biggest tool I used to grow and succeed in that market was the SWOT analysis. Our SWOT analysis looked like this:

- *Strengths:* we had a strong sales force, a lot of opportunity for sales, and a superior product.
- *Weaknesses*: slow foot traffic, people were still skeptical of their needs for a cell phone.
- *Opportunities*: in 2001 only 12 percent of Americans had a cell phone. There were plenty of new customers.

■ *Threats*: we were an authorized retailer of AT&T and SunCom. So we competed against every company, even the ones that we sold.

As a small company with just a few locations in New England, we did not have the luxury of running on our name alone. We also had to find a way to draw customers into our kiosk. I had to develop a sales process that would allow us to succeed in that market. At the time all cell phone companies waited for walk-up traffic. With a market that did not find a need for your product why would you wait for a walk-up? We developed an approach where we would stop customers and draw them into our location. At the time this was unheard of; however, we knew that we had the sales force that could make this successful. It was: within two months we outsold the Beverly Center Mall in Los Angeles. A small mall in Nashua, New Hampshire outsold a mall in Los Angeles; think about that. The company overall adopted our sales training process and by 2004 we outsold every other AT&T dealer and direct store combined. So if you have ever been stopped and asked about your cell phone plan, Sorry!

For me this was the stepping stone that gave me the background I wanted to get my career started. I did know that I needed to diversify my sales skills, so I took a 6 percent pay cut to take a job in telesales. I had learned in my Leadership in Sports class that to be successful in your career you need to take time to step back and evaluate your abilities and goals. For me my goals were to work in baseball, and sales. Taking this new job gave me a new skill-set to allow me to grow in my career.

That same year I also started to work in baseball by taking an operations internship with the Nashua Pride, an independent league baseball team. That summer I worked in my full-time telesales job, game days with the Pride, and took four classes. In 2009 I took my last internship with the Carolina Mudcats as a food and beverage intern. The Mudcats were, at the time, the double-A affiliate of the Cincinnati Reds. For the first time in my career I was working outside of sales. This was an important season for me, because food and beverage was the one area at the ballpark in which I did not have any experience. I cannot stress this enough: you need to continuously add to your skill-set. You can always do this in the working world; however, college is the best place to add to your knowledge base and skill-set.

After graduation I finally took my "first" job in baseball. I always say that I was drafted first round in the 2010 draft, as I started on June 7, 2010, which happens to be draft day. Working for a publication that is the leading resource on prospect baseball it was a pretty special day. Since then I have had the opportunity to do some awesome things in the sport. I have attended the Winter Meetings, gone to the last College World Series at Rosenblatt, the Home Run Derby, the All-Star game, the Hall of Fame indications, and the Cape League All-Star game. I have worked with one of my clients to create an award for the Minor League Catcher of the Year, called the All-Star Captain's Award. I came up with the idea of naming the award after the face of the clients' business, Jason Varitek. I had the opportunity to meet him in the locker room at Fenway during the interview for the announcement of the launch of the award.

Now, looking back at the road that got me here in the middle of the business of baseball, I review my past and how I got my start selling cell phones in a mall in New Hampshire and think how crazy it really is. Many college students look at the retail world as a place to pass time and make some money on the side. Remember that many of us in the sport got our start in the retail industry. If you can take anything out of this, remember three things:

1 Persistence breeds success. Make a goal and stick to it no matter what gets in your way.
2 Work hard at everything you do, and every job you take; you never know where it will lead you.
3 Do not be afraid to take a step back if it allows you to build a skill-set that will help you in the future.

CHAPTER TWELVE

SPORT SPONSORSHIP

CHAPTER OUTLINE

- History of sport sponsorship
- Areas of sport sponsorship
- Corporate and brand goals for sport sponsorship
- Sport sponsorship agreements
- Conclusion

CHAPTER OBJECTIVES

The reader will be able to:

- gain an appreciation of the significant role sponsorship plays in the sport promotional mix
- understand the history and growth of sport sponsorship over the past 20 years
- recognize the various areas of sport sponsorship, including governing body sponsorship, team sponsorship, athlete sponsorship, broadcast sponsorship, facility sponsorship, and event sponsorship
- appreciate the corporate and brand goals of sport sponsorship
- understand the various criteria for sponsorship, and how they are utilized in choosing the companies to partner with, developing sponsorship agreements, and engaging in sponsorship negotiations
- know how to identify components within the sport organization that are available for sponsorship
- recognize the role advanced research plays in sponsorship acquisition, including the corporate decision-making process regarding sponsorship spending
- understand the processes for developing, selling, managing, and evaluating sport sponsorships.

HISTORY OF SPORT SPONSORSHIP

Sponsorship has been a significant part of sport promotions for well over 2,700 years. The first sport sponsorships have been recorded back to the period of Antiquity. This period of history ran from 3000 BC until the fall of the Roman Empire around 476 (this is the period prior to the Middle Ages). Classical Antiquity started during the seventh century BC, during the time of growth in Europe, the Middle East, and North Africa, starting with the poetry of Homer, running through the rise of Christianity, and ending at the fall of the Roman Empire. During the early days of classical Antiquity, the Ancient Greeks developed a concept called "ekecheiria," which roughly translated means "Olympic Truce." In 776 BC, the first celebration of the "Olympic Games" took place as a celebration of the achievements of the human body. It was during this and subsequent events that the first sport sponsorships were seen. Prominent Greek citizens and local governments gave financial support to the organization of the Olympics. This desire to improve standing and reputation (awareness and image) for their cities made the Olympics a commercial event. These sport sponsorships ranged from minor financial contributions to show involvement and improve political aspirations, to the level of sponsorship of one Irodis Attikos, who individually incurred the entire expense of the Kalimarmaro stadium.

Over the years, sport sponsorship has ebbed and flowed. However, there is one marked event in sports that changed the way sport sponsorship would be conducted forever. The 1984 Olympics in Los Angeles was an interesting time in the world of sport. The end of the 1970s and the early 1980s were some tumultuous times. The former Soviet Union invaded Afghanistan in 1979, and the United States in protest boycotted the 1980 Summer Olympics held in Moscow. In response, the Soviet Union almost decided not to show up at the 1980 Winter Olympics in Lake Placid (which would have resulted in no "Miracle on Ice"). Many countries followed suit in the boycott of the Summer Games in Moscow. In 1984, with the Summer Games coming to the United States, the Soviet Union among 14 other countries including East Germany and Cuba boycotted the Games. There were significant concerns that a number of events (especially boxing, and track and field) would be of a lesser quality, and hence that people might not come. There were also concerns that this would yet again create a situation where the Olympic Games would be a losing business venture, as no Olympics has turned a profit with the exception of the 1932 Summer Olympics also in Los Angeles (however, this was during the Great Depression; no other city in the world even bid on the Games, and less than half the usual number of athletes and nations competed because they could not afford the trip to Los Angeles).

Enter Peter Ueberroth, President of the Los Angeles Olympic Committee, who had anticipated the possibility of a boycott, and at the same time viewed the Olympics as an event that should be profitable. He had a vision of creating a financially successful Olympic Games that would be in total contrast to the deficit spending most host cities engaged in. He worked with the USOC and IOC to allow use of the Olympic symbols by corporations in their advertisements in exchange for financial support. A total of 43 major sponsors stepped forward for the opportunity to be the official Olympic sponsor. Sponsorships at the time cost a minimum of US$4 million each, with the television network ABC paying slightly over US$200 million. This first effort into sport sponsorship was successful, with the Olympic Games making a profit of US$225 million.

This subsequently led to the International Olympic Committee's (IOC) creation of The Olympic Partner (TOP) Program. As the only sponsorship vehicle that offers exclusive worldwide marketing rights to both the Winter and Summer Olympic Games, TOP also provides technical and product support for the International Olympic Committee, Organizing Committees (OCOGs), and National Olympic Committees (NOCs). This in turn trickles down to provide benefits to athletes, coaches, and spectators. As the most successful brand name in worldwide sports, the Olympics and the TOP Program provides the most exclusive global sport marketing platform in the world.

Peter Ueberroth was also a key figure in increasing the amount of sponsorship for professional sport leagues. Ueberroth succeeded Bowie Kuhn as Commissioner of Major League Baseball in 1984. In the subsequent five years, he was the driving force behind increasing owners' revenues through television contract sponsorship negotiations, as well as sport marketing programs that enticed large corporations to spend significant amounts of money on promotional opportunities and sponsorships. This model serves as a framework not only for Major League Baseball, but moving forward to all sport organizations in the future.

The growth across the board, both domestically and globally, is historic. The growth of commercialization of sport through sponsorship has reached a projected value of US$12 billion per year in the United States, and according to the International Events Group (IEG), the leading sponsorship research and consulting company in the world, the value of worldwide global sponsorship reached US$33 billion in 2011. It is also projected that with prominent worldwide events such as the Winter Olympics in Sochi, Russia (2014) and Pyongchang, South Korea (2018); the Summer Olympics in London, England (2012) and Rio de Janiero, Brazil (2016); and the FIFA World Cup in Brazil (2014), Russia (2018), and Qatar (2022), the probability of substantial growth in sponsorship dollars spent is inevitable. Table 12.1 shows

Table 12.1 Top United States sport sponsors in 2010

2010 Rank	Company	Amount (US millions)	Projection for 2011 (US millions)
1	General Motors	$388.4	$410.9
2	Anheuser-Busch InBev	$309.2	$327.3
3	Miller Coors	$272.0	$287.8
4	Toyota	$245.5	$259.7
5	Verizon	$228.2	$241.4
6	AT&T	$226.7	$239.8
7	Yum!	$210.0	$222.2
8	Sprint	$205.0	$216.9
9	Ford	$197.3	$208.7
10	Geico	$171.3	$181.2
11	McDonald's	$155.4	$164.4
12	Southwest Airlines	$126.5	$133.8
13	State Farm	$117.1	$123.9
14	Chrysler Group	$115.4	$122.1
15	Subway	$98.6	$104.3
16	Proctor and Gamble	$95.4	$100.9

the top 16 sport sponsors in the United States in terms of their advertising spending in 2010 – each is projected to have spent over US$100 million in 2011.

AREAS OF SPORT SPONSORSHIP

Sport sponsorship has grown for a number of reasons, ranging from increased media attention in sport to the desire for companies to target consumers of the sport lifestyle through non-advertising efforts. In contrast to other industries, the majority of sport sponsors are not sport corporations. In fact, none of the top-ten corporations engaged in sport sponsorship is from the sport industry. Most sponsorship comes from the automotive industry (three: General Motors, Toyota, Ford); the food and beverage industry (three: Anheuser-Busch, InBev, MillerCoors); and the telecommunications industry (three: Verizon, AT&T, Sprint).

As mentioned earlier, sport sponsorship is divided into six categories: sport governing body sponsorship, sport team sponsorship, athlete sponsorship, broadcast and media sponsorship, sport facility sponsorship, and sport event sponsorship. Each of these distinct areas makes up the majority of a US$12 billion sport sponsorship industry in the United States.

Sport governing body sponsorship

Sport governing bodies are sport organizations that are responsible for developing the rule structure for the specific activity as well as organizing competitions at levels from local youth to international. At various levels, the sport governing body is also responsible for selecting teams, raising and distributing funding, providing coaching and other administrative and technical services, and promoting and developing the individual sport.

All sport activities have governing bodies. They range from national governing bodies such as the National Football League (NFL) and the National Collegiate Athletics Association (NCAA); to international governing bodies such as the International Olympic Committee (IOC) and the Fédération Internationale de Football Association (FIFA).

From a sponsorship standpoint, these associations between corporations and the sport organization tend to relate to receiving "official sponsor" status. "Official sponsor" status refers to the sport organization's public acknowledgment of the association between the sponsor and the organization. Official sponsors are often promised exclusivity, which is the guarantee that the products or services of the sponsoring organization will be the only type in that category to have an association with the sport organization. Official sponsors also receive additional benefits as a result of the sponsorship, including inclusion in all sport organization marketing efforts, the ability to use the sport organization's logo in their own marketing efforts, and hospitality opportunities to entertain subsidiaries, clients, and customers.

The corporations that enter into sponsorship with governing bodies tend to be larger, national, or multinational companies, mainly due to the large financial investment required with these sponsorships. An example of a national governing body sponsorship would be Nextel/Sprint's sponsorship agreement with NASCAR. On June 19, 2003, NASCAR ended its 33-year relationship with RJ Reynolds (RJR) Tobacco Company to take on Nextel (and eventually Sprint) as its title sponsor. At the time, the ten-year contract was the largest sponsorship deal in the history of professional sports, at a staggering cost of over US$700 million.

Many wondered how Nextel could expect to turn a profit with such a high-priced sponsorship affecting its bottom line. Nextel countered by stating that if it were to secure 1 percent of the NASCAR viewing market per year, which is estimated to be approximately 75 million fans, the 750,000 new customers would translate to US$600 million in revenue. Nextel also hedged its bets on NASCAR continuing to be the number one spectator sport in the United States. It further recognized that a number of other factors would also count as positive to their bottom line:

- It is only second behind the NFL in television viewership.
- Approximately 15 percent of Forbes' 500 companies are involved in NASCAR.
- NASCAR fans are the most loyal of any sport fan when it comes to purchasing products and services from companies that sponsor NASCAR. More than twice the rate of baseball and basketball fans; more than three times the level of football fans; and five times more likely than fans of the Olympics.

The result for Nextel? The company was bought out by Sprint . . . who chose to continue the sponsorship. The result for Sprint? It has had such valuable brand relationship, brand awareness enhancement, and entitlement partnership with NASCAR that in 2011 it extended the deal through 2016.

An international governing body with significant sponsorship partnerships is FIFA. The organization's sponsorship opportunities range from grass-roots initiatives to signage at World Cup events. Its partners, called commercial affiliates, originally fell under three categories. Official sponsors have global marketing rights. Official suppliers have marketing rights in the host country of the individual event only. They also have licensees who have association, but are not able to associate their corporate brand with licensed products.

However, in 2007, the company's sponsorship program changed to create three new levels of sponsorship. A FIFA Partner enjoys full association with all FIFA operations, including competitions, special events, development programs, and exclusive marketing assets. The first company to become a FIFA Partner was Adidas, followed shortly thereafter by Hyundai, Sony, and Coca-Cola. A FIFA World Cup sponsor received global rights to category exclusivity, brand association, specific marketing assets, and secondary media exposure for the 2010 and 2014 World Cups. A National Supporter allows local companies to promote their category exclusivity, association, local marketing opportunities, and domestic media exposure within the host country of the 2010 (South Africa), 2014 (Brazil), 2018 (Russia), and 2022 (Qatar) World Cups.

Sport team sponsorship

Traditional team sponsorships are usually more appropriate for local or regional companies that have smaller marketing budgets but have a desire to become the official sponsor of a team.

CASE STUDY 12: THE ERIE OTTERS VS. BIG AL'S USED CARS: AMBUSH MARKETING OR FREEDOM OF SPEECH?

Authored and contributed by Jordan I. Kobritz, SUNY Cortland; and Matt Kastel, Manager of Baseball Operations and Events for Maryland Stadium Authority

Stu Mulligan, owner of the Erie Otters, an indoor soccer team playing at a city-owned facility, had a problem, one which required the assistance of the team's legal counsel, Marie Walling.

Marie was a sports fan at heart and had been representing the Otters basically for free throughout their ten-year existence, in part because she knew the team struggled to break even. After Marie ushered Stu into her office, she grabbed a pen in one hand, a legal pad in the other, and said, "Tell me about Allen Anderson."

"You mean Big Al, owner of Big Al's Used Cars," Stu responded. Big Al was a local personality famous for his outrageous car commercials, starring Big Al himself, offering to match any competitor's prices. "I am not sure where to start," sighed Stu.

"Start at the beginning," said Marie.

"Believe it or not, our relationship got off to a great start. When we started the Otters, Al was one of our first season ticket holders and sponsors. Individually he bought eight season tickets, and in addition, Big Al's Used Cars purchased a sponsorship package."

"So what went wrong?" asked Marie.

"Over time, Al became more of a problem than he was worth. His over-the-top TV persona is not an act; he is also that way in person. Each year he insisted on getting more exposure than what he was paying for, and during games he would walk around the arena like he owned the place. Honestly, when he told us he was dropping his sponsorship last year, despite the loss in revenue, which we need, I was relieved. I thought it would be one less headache to deal with. But in my heart I knew he would still be a problem."

"How so," asked Marie?

"Big Al renewed his season tickets. He has eight seats in total, four over each goal in prime locations. When games are televised, his seats are in direct line with the TV cameras. You cannot help but see whoever is sitting in those seats. Anticipating that Big Al was going to pull some sort of stunt, I updated our ticket policy, stating ticket holders could not promote or market other events or businesses inside the arena without our written consent."

"How did you communicate this new policy to your ticket holders?"

"By including the policy on the back of the tickets," said Stu. "I also sent Big Al an email informing him of the new policy."

275

sport sponsorship

When Marie asked if all the season ticket holders were sent an email regarding the new policy, Stu shook his head. Marie couldn't help but cringe. "What is Al doing now that is causing such a ruckus?"

"At every game he makes sure the people sitting in his seats are wearing Big Al's Used Cars T-shirts, in large letters and bright colors. He knows this will get him free advertising on TV. In addition, Big Al has one of those snappy jingles that once you hear it, you cannot get it out of your head. During breaks in the action, the people in Al's seats will start singing the jingle from opposite sides of the arena. The fans pick up on it and soon the entire arena sings along.

"The worst part is I have a sponsorship with another company that is paying us to pick a child out of the stands at half-time to sing its company's jingle. The owner is furious that while he is paying, another company is getting its jingle sung for free. Additionally, I replaced Big Al's sponsorship with another used car company and he is none too happy with Big Al, or us."

Marie closed her eyes for a moment and thought about her options.

Questions for discsussion

1   Was Big Al engaging in ambush marketing? Explain the various ways he engaged in this behavior.
2   If the Otters revoked Big Al's season tickets, would they be in breach of contract?
3   Can the Otters have Big Al and his friends removed from the arena? Or would such action violate Big Al's and his guests' First Amendment right to free speech?

The goal of most team sponsorships is to create long-term and mutually beneficial relationships between the team and a corporation. The resulting objectives include: building awareness of the company's products and services; enhancing opportunities for new customer relationships; the ability to offer internal benefit programs such as employee rewards, hospitality areas, and sales incentive programs; and brand association with the sport team. Sponsorship opportunities range from signage on the field/court or boundaries to association with special events (home team introductions, half-time/intermission/time out contests). It may also offer other opportunities, including sponsorships of the cheerleading and dance team, or promotional packages given away on game days.

However, large corporations will be involved with team sponsorship based on the market or the ability to significantly expand awareness. Some of the most prominent team sponsorship deals take place in soccer, especially in Europe. The largest at the time of writing is Manchester City of the English Premier League, whose ten-year sponsorship agreement with Abu Dhabi-based (UAE) Etihad Airways is reportedly worth US$642.2 million. This far exceeds Manchester United's 13-year, US$486 million deal with Nike. Other major deals outside the English Premier League include Juventus in Italy (ten-year/US$265 million with Tamoil); Barcelona in Spain (Five-year/US$265 million with the Qatar Foundation, and five-year/US$210 million with Nike); and Bayern Munich in Germany (Three-year/US$115 million with Deutsche Telekom).

Another example of team sponsorship that includes both national and multinational corporations, as well as local and regional companies, is individual NASCAR teams. Teams can bring in anywhere between US$15–US$40 million, and in some cases more, just from sponsorship of the car alone. Figure 12.1 illustrates the price breakdown of NASCAR team sponsorship of automobiles per season.

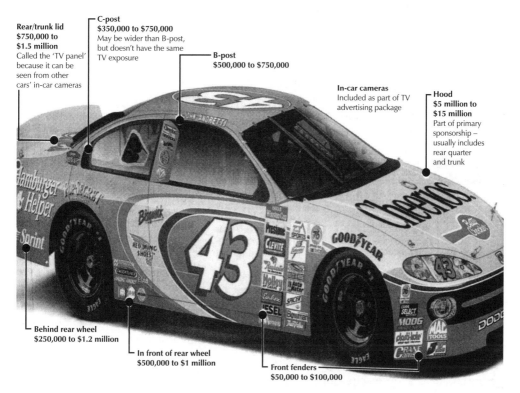

Figure 12.1 Example of NASCAR car sponsorship inventory values

Athlete sponsorship

There is often confusion between athlete sponsorship and athlete endorsements. They are often used as interchangeable terms, but they are two different concepts. An athlete sponsorship is where a corporation seeks to become affiliated with an athlete to secure the rights to market the association and reap the benefits of that association. An athlete endorsement is a type of athlete sponsorship where the athlete is describing his or her personal association with the product or service.

Athlete sponsorship tends to work better in individual sports than in team sports, simply because the sponsor can focus its efforts and generate significant numbers of visible impressions for the consumer. For example, golf and tennis players can have logos on hats or shirts, and can easily be focused on.

The superstar athlete in most team sports can overcome this desire of corporations to focus their athlete sponsorships on individual athletes. Some of the most prominent athletes who currently have significant sponsorship deals are basketball players in the NBA. This is mainly due to the "Michael Jordan" effect. In 1997, Michael Jordan earned US$47 million from sponsorships with companies ranging from Nike to McDonald's to Gatorade to Wheaties. After his retirement, a number of NBA players have reaped the benefits left behind by Michael Jordan, such as LeBron James' seven-year, US$90 million deal with Nike.

In light of this, if an athlete is a superstar in an individual sport, the sponsorship dollars come rolling in. For example, golfer Tiger Woods in 2006 pulled in more than US$80 million in endorsement and sponsorship agreements, and followed that with over US$100 million in 2007. Even after Tiger Woods had marital problems and his play was less than stellar, he pulled in US$60 million in endorsement dollars in 2011. Phil Mickelson, another perennial top-ten golfer, pulled in US$57 million in sponsorship dollars in 2011 from companies such as Callaway, Rolex, Barclays, and ExxonMobil – to name a few. Dale Earnhardt Jr., NASCAR's most popular driver over the past ten years, raked in approximately US$22 million in sponsorships and endorsements in 2011. This is not only true on the American sport sponsorship landscape – tennis player Roger Federer brought in over US$30 million in sponsorships and endorsements in 2011, with Rafael Nadal not too far behind at US$21 million. Michael Schumacher in Formula 1 Racing is their sport's top sponsorship earner, garnering nearly US$27 million – and that was in his first year after coming out of retirement!

Sport broadcast sponsorship

Broadcast sponsorships involve corporations that purchase an association with specific sport programming either via the radio or television. Broadcast sponsorships can range from a basic sponsorship of a local radio broadcast to being some of the most lucrative associations in all of sport sponsorship.

Before broadcast sponsorships can even be considered, there must be an association between a sport organization and the media outlet. This usually involves a broadcasting rights contract. These broadcasting rights contracts are the single largest revenue source for sport organizations. These contracts happen at two levels – local and national. Local broadcasting contracts usually cover events of and games played by the individual sport organization. Local agreements are usually for multiple years, and may include such additional broadcasts as pre-game and post-game shows. Many local broadcasting contracts also include team sponsorship in the form of "the official team station" or the "official broadcasting partner of the sport organization." For example, the Los Angeles Lakers are in the midst of a 25-year contract with Time Warner Cable that is believed to be worth as much as US$200 million annually. The Boston Celtics have signed a similar deal with CSN New England.

However, even the landscape of local broadcast contracts is changing, with national broadcasters helping to fund the creation of local and regional sport broadcast stations. In 2011, FoxSportsNet had 19 regional sport networks across the United States broadcasting local, regional, and national sporting events. College sports conferences have started creating their own broadcasting networks to highlight sports from their conference. They include the

278

Big Ten Network, SECTV, and the Pac 12 TV Network. Even individual schools are starting to create their own network. Most notable is the University of Texas' Longhorn Network, created by ESPN at a cost to the University of US$300 million for 20 years.

National broadcasting contracts are usually multiple-year deals with a series of local radio or television networks that are part of a national syndicated broadcast network to air the games of leagues. Usually, the broadcasting dollars are split evenly across all teams within a league, and are of significant cost to the broadcasters over a specified time period. Broadcast agreements are justified by networks because they are able to recoup some of that expense by selling broadcast sponsorship agreements for significant sums – up to Super Bowl advertisements that in 2011 went for approximately US$3 million for a 30-second advertisement. Table 12.2 provides examples of the current broadcast deals across various sports leagues and events.

Sport facility sponsorship

Facility sponsorships are naming rights agreements for stadiums, arenas, and other sport facilities. Since 2000, this has been the fastest growing area of sport sponsorship, as many sport facilities across the country have sold their naming rights to sport corporations. These deals are usually long term and significant in value. In addition, the value of the sponsorship will vary with the size of the market, the level of competition playing, and the assortment of events scheduled by the facility. Tables 12.3, 12.4, and 12.5 document some of the sport facility sponsorship deals in place in 2011.

One benefit of the sport organization or the sport facility owner is the out clause for the sponsorship. Should the corporate sponsor go out of business or miss a required payment the facility reacquires the naming rights of the facility and may resell the sponsorship. Some of the prominent facilities where this has happened are documented in Table 12.6.

Sport event sponsorship

Sport event sponsorship provides a way for corporations to create an association with a sport event. Most relationships of this type are with hallmark events, such as tournaments (golf, tennis), championships (college football bowl games), and others, ranging from the horse racing Triple Crown (made up of the Kentucky Derby, the Preakness, and the Belmont Stakes) to the New York City Marathon.

However, there are questions as to whether sponsorship of an event is beneficial to the corporate sponsor as compared to those sponsorships that offer more benefits over a longer period of time, such as naming rights being on a facility 365 days a year, or being associated with a league or sport that promotes the association over the numerous months of prime operations. The answer is yes: event sponsorship is lucrative as a result of the significant media and advertising exposure related to the event, whether categorized as a regular event or a hallmark event. To put this into perspective, take a look at the media exposure values for the 2010 NBA Draft. According to Front Row Marketing, the one-night event, broadcast on a Thursday evening, garnered the sponsor exposure values shown in Table 12.7.

Table 12.2 Current sport broadcast deals

League	Network	Event	Agreement (US$)
MLB	Fox	26 Saturday afternoon games; All Star Game; Alternate AL/NL League Championship Series each year; all World Series	1.8 billion (2007–2013)
	Turner	26 Saturday afternoon games; any regular season tiebreaker games; Alternate AL/NL League Championship Series each year; all AL and NL Division Series	1.19 billion (2006–2013)
NASCAR (Sprint Cup)	Fox	Races 1–13 (including Daytona 500)	1.76 billion (2006–2014)
	Turner	Races 14–19	660 million (2006–2014)
	ESPN/ABC	Races 20–36	2.16 billion (2006–2014)
NBA	ABC	15 regular season games; 9 playoff games; NBA Finals	Individual numbers not available, but entire contract reported by NBA to be worth a total of 7.44 billion (2009–2016)
	Turner	52 regular season games; All-Star Weekend; playoff games including one Conference Final	
	ESPN	73 regular season games; playoff games including one Conference Final	
NCAA	CBS/Turner	Men's Basketball Tournament	10.8 billion (2011–2024)
	ESPN	Football BCS (4 games)	495 million (2011–2014)
NFL	CBS	AFC Games/Super Bowl in 2013, 2016, 2019, and 2022	5.65 billion (2014–2022)
	ESPN	Monday night Football and NFL Draft	13.33 billion (2014–2022)
	Fox	NFC Games/Super Bowl in 2014, 2017, and 2020	6.47 billion (2014–2022)
	NBC	Thursday night opener; Sunday nights; Super Bowl in 2012, 2015, 2018, and 2021	5.45 billion (2012–2021)
Olympics	NBC	2012 Summer Olympics (London, England)	1.18 billion
		2014 Winter Olympics (Sochi, Russia)	775 million
		2016 Summer Olympics (Rio de Janeiro, Brazil)	1.23 billion
		2018 Winter Olympics (Pyeongchang, South Korea)	963 million
		2020 Summer Olympics (not available at press time – to be announced in 2013)	1.42 billion

promotional aspects of sport marketing

Table 12.3 Major professional sport facility sponsorship deals in 2011

Name of facility	Location	Sponsor	Terms of agreement (US$ millions)
Farmers Field	Los Angeles, CA	Farmers Insurance	$700 for 30 years
MetLife Stadium	East Rutherford, NJ	Met Life Insurance	$400 for 25 years
Citi Field	Queens, NY	Citi Bank	$400 for 20 years
Reliant Stadium	Houston, TX	Reliant Energy	$320 for 32 years
FedEx Field	Washington, DC	Federal Express	$205 for 27 years
Barclays Center	Brooklyn, NY	Barclays Bank	$200 for 20 years
American Airlines Center	Dallas, TX	American Airlines	$195 for 30 years
Philips Arena	Atlanta, GA	Royal Philips Electronics	$182 for 20 years
Minute Maid Park	Houston, TX	Minute Maid OJ	$178 for 28 years

Table 12.4 Independent, minor league, and minor professional sport facility sponsorship deals in 2011

Name of facility	Location	Sponsor	Terms of agreement (US$ millions)
Chukchansi Park	Fresno, CA	Chukchansi Casino	$16 for 15 years
Raley Field	Sacramento, CA	Raley's and Bel-Air Markets	$15 for 20 years
CenturyLink Center	Omaha, NB	CenturyLink Telecom	$14 for 15 years
KFC Yum! Center	Louisville, KY	Yum! Brands (Food)	$13.5 for 10 years
Wells Fargo Arena	Des Moines, IA	Wells Fargo Financial	$11.5 for 20 years
Verizon Wireless Arena	Manchester, NH	Verizon Wireless	$11.4 for 15 years
Keyspan Park	Brooklyn, NY	Keyspan Energy	$10 for 20 years

Table 12.5 College sport facility sponsorship deals in 2011

Name of facility	Location	School	Terms of agreement (US$ million)
Save Mart Center	Fresno, CA	Fresno State University	$40 for 20 years
TCF Bank Stadium	Minneapolis, MN	University of Minnesota	$35 for 25 years
Comcast Center	College Park, MD	University of Maryland	$25 for 25 years
AT&T Stadium	Lubbock, TX	Texas Tech University	$20 for 25 years
Brighthouse Stadium	Orlando, FL	University of Central Florida	$15 for 20 years
Papa John's Cardinal Stadium	Louisville, KY	University of Louisville	$15 for 32 years

Table 12.6 Recent sport facility sponsorships renaming

Location	Former name of facility	Current name of facility	Reason for change
Foxboro, MA	CMGI Field	Gillette Stadium	Rights bought by Gillette as a result of the dot.com bust that started in 2001
Houston, TX	Enron Field	Minute Maid Park	Bankruptcy of Enron
Indianapolis, IN	Conseco Fieldhouse	BankersLife Fieldhouse	Bankruptcy of Conseco
Nashville, TN	Adelphia Coliseum	The Coliseum	Missed payment by Adelphia
Phoenix, AZ	AmericaWest Arena	US Airways Arena	US Airways bought AmericaWest

Table 12.7 Media exposure values for the 2010 NBA draft

Sponsor	Total estimated value (by Front Row, US$)
EA Sports	1.85 million
Hewlett Packard (HP)	315,000
Kia	303,000
T-Mobile	237,000
GlowPoint	108,000
Total	2,813,000

These seem to be quite good for a one-night event; but again, the scope of the event makes the difference. Now let us take a look at a study by Image Impact Inc., which reported numbers produced by the American Broadcasting Company (ABC) of the profitability of being a sponsor of one of the four Bowl Championship Series games in 2005, simply from the media image exposure during the television broadcasts of those games (Table 12.8).

Table 12.8 Profitability of sponsorship of one of the four Bowl Championship Series Games in 2005

Sponsor	Event	Location	Total estimated value (by ABCUS$)
Federal Express	Orange Bowl	Miami, FL	29,599,506
Nokia	Sugar Bowl	Atlanta, GA*	20,911,958
Tostitos	Fiesta Bowl	Tempe, AZ	30,376,683
Citi	Rose Bowl	Pasadena, CA	25,466,643
Total			106,354,790

* The Sugar Bowl is usually hosted in New Orleans, LA, but following the devastation of Hurricane Katrina in 2005, the game was moved for 2005 to Atlanta, GA.

Hence, based on the scope of the event, the exposure value can be significant, and the return on investment of paying for a sport event sponsorship can also be significant in comparison to the outlay of money. Each of the sponsors paid approximately US$12 million per year to be the title sponsor of the game, and probably spent another US$20 to 24 million on related advertising and promotions. Based on the numbers above, they got a significant ROI just from the broadcasts; and for FedEx, it was calculated by Front Row Marketing that the company received a total ROI of US$50 million from its sponsorship of the Orange Bowl that year.

CORPORATE AND BRAND GOALS FOR SPORT SPONSORSHIP

The reason for entering into a sport sponsorship agreement varies from organization to organization. It also differs as to whether it is the corporation becoming involved with a sport entity, or the desire of the sport brand to engage in a partnership with specified corporate entities. Regardless, it is important that any entity determine what they desire to achieve through the sponsorship. This will involve the sport marketing professionals and management from each entity creating a list of desired outcomes that will serve as a framework for determining the appropriateness of the partnership.

Corporations have numerous goals as a result of sport sponsorship. The most logical are to increase public awareness and enhance their company image. Most promotional efforts do that. From a business standpoint, corporations use sport sponsorship to build business and trade relationships with other sponsoring organizations. In the public relations area, corporations use sport sponsorship to change or improve public perception of their company. They can use the usually positive relationship to alter the opinion of the consumer as related to the corporation. This is also accomplished through community relations, where the sport sponsorship may be used to increase community involvement in that target area. This is often achieved through goodwill efforts. Finally, corporations often use sport sponsorship to enhance personnel relations by offering opportunities for employees to attend sponsored events, including attendance at hospitality areas. The company hopes to use the relationship created by the sport sponsorships, especially when significantly positive, to increase the morale of employees through the perceived association with that brand.

Sport brands also have numerous goals as a result of sponsorship other than the obvious ones of taking in additional revenue from the agreement, and increasing target market awareness and image. The sport brand is also seeking to use the relationship with the corporation to increase its own sales. Associations often bring about more interest from the general public, and especially from those connected with the sponsoring corporation. The goal is to market this new association to get more people in the seats. As a result, there is a hope that the sponsorship will increase the market share for the brand, which in turn will prevent competition from getting the upper hand in the marketplace.

SPORT SPONSORSHIP AGREEMENTS

Sport sponsorship relationships enable the corporate sponsor and the sport brand to project their image, increase their audience, and amplify the number and quality of media opportunities. With this in mind, the potential corporate sponsor and the sport organization should have similar target markets, and have a mutual understanding about the mission, goals, objectives, and vision for each other. This information is then utilized to develop sport sponsorship proposals and negotiate sport sponsorship agreements. Sport sponsorships are designed to articulate the benefits derived from the agreement for all parties involved.

In a sport sponsorship, the corporation is referred to as the "sponsor," and the sport brand is called the "sponsee." One of the main benefits that a sponsor will often pay a premium for is exclusivity, to guarantee that all other competitors, their products, and their services will be prohibited from entering into sponsorship agreement with the sponsee. Other benefits derived from the sponsorship will usually include the right to use the logo of the sponsee, advertising support, signage and announcements at events, and tickets to events. Other than the rights fee, the sponsee benefits from an agreement with a corporate sponsor due to the guaranteed advertising and promotional commitments that are a part of the sponsorship. In addition, sponsees seek to have multiple year commitment to ensure continuity in those advertising and promotional efforts.

Identifying components available for sponsorship

The process of developing sponsorship agreements involves a number of stages. The initial stage is for a sport organization to identify every element that could be available for sponsorship. While a sport organization could maximize revenue by putting sponsorship on everything it owns, this would be unwise, as the organization would become a walking billboard for other corporations, and would most likely overshadow the sport organization's brand and purpose. As a result, sport organizations seek to optimize their sponsorship programs by determining what components are sponsorable without adversely affecting the visibility of the sport organization.

In identifying those components available for sponsorship, the sport organization must fully detail the extent of benefits that can be offered for each individual element. This information is crucial to the overall sponsorship process, as it would be unwise to develop sponsorship agreements without knowing what is to be offered. Benefits can range from building brand awareness from the association between the sport organization and the sponsor, to perks such as free tickets, merchandise, and other promotional opportunities.

The role of advanced research in sponsorship acquisition

Once the sport organization understands what it has to offer, it needs to conduct significant research to match potential sponsors to the sponsorship opportunity. This research starts with an internal evaluation of the strengths and weaknesses of the sport organization, as this information will be crucial in articulating benefits to sponsors. Information that is important for the sport organizations to understand include: the consumer demographics, psychographics, and geographics; the successes and failures of the organization; the growth or decline in popularity, participation, and/or attendance; current and past sponsors; relevant public relations/media relations/community relations; and financial status.

Once this information is collected and disseminated, the research process moves to an analysis of potential sponsors. There are two major stages in this research process – prospecting for sponsors, and determining the needs of potential sponsors.

Prospecting for sponsors

The prospecting process involves identifying potential sponsors and investigating whether a partnership would be mutually beneficial. If both the sport organization and the potential sponsor cannot reap rewards from a relationship, then the sponsorship should not be pursued. However, the information should be kept on file for future sponsorship opportunities where a relationship has the potential to be mutually beneficial.

When identifying potential sponsors, the following should be considered:

- List potential sponsors that have similar target markets and demographics of the sport organization. In addition, identify sponsors of competitors, and find direct competitors of those sponsors.
- Divide the list based on the category of product offered by potential sponsors.
- Establish whether the potential sponsor has an interest or the financial ability to enter into a sport sponsorship agreement.
- Determine if there are any natural links with the potential sponsor – including but not limited to: geographic region; similar demographic and psychographic target markets; historical associations; similarities in values, beliefs, and/or vision; products and/or services of mutual benefit; etc.
- Evaluate the status of the potential sponsor in its industry segment, including: the success of its marketing approaches; its success in its industry segment as compared to direct competitors; and its previous involvement with sport organizations, including positive and negative experiences.
- Determine the value of a potential sponsorship and the projected results.
- Prioritize and determine the needs of the potential sponsors from the top down.
- Finalize a list of those potential sponsors that offer the best probability of mutual success through a sponsorship partnership.

Determining the needs of the sponsors

Prior to finalizing a list of potential sponsors to approach, a crucial stage in the research is to determine the needs of the sponsor. All the advanced research may point to a partnership that has the potential of being mutually beneficial. However, when further detailed research into the needs of the potential sponsor is conducted, the sponsorship may no longer be mutually beneficial.

Major corporate goals for sponsorship agreements may include some or all of the following:

- Increase the market awareness of the corporation and its products and services.
- Either improve image (usually when the corporation is viewed in a positive light) or modify perceptions (usually when the corporation is viewed in a negative light).
- Position products and services in a manner that will result in increased sales and market share.

- Increase visibility in a community by building relationships, developing programs of goodwill, and other avenues to become more involved with the community.
- Create a profit for the corporation – considering both tangible and intangible benefits.

Developing sponsorship proposals

In developing a sport sponsorship proposal, there are four main features that should be considered as a framework for the agreement – goals and objectives; characteristics of the sport organization; compatibility between the potential sponsor and the sport organization; and maximizing exposure for the potential sponsor.

Goals and objectives

The first feature is the goals and objectives of the parties entering into the sponsorship agreement. This provides an opening mechanism to present the values, beliefs, and position of the sport organization. It also allows the sport organization to articulate what it would like to accomplish as a result of the sponsorship, and how they proposes to do it. In addition, by articulating the perceived benefits to the sponsor in terms of the advanced research, the sport organization can convey an understanding of the needs of the potential sponsor (provided that the research conducted was reliable, valid, and evaluated properly).

Characteristics of the sport organization

The second feature of the sponsorship proposal should comprise the characteristics of the sport organization. This section includes three main components – a full description of the sport organization; a description of the specific aspect to be sponsored; and an overview of the sponsor's industry in terms of sport sponsorships in place. A sport marketing professional cannot make the assumption that a potential sponsor knows about the sport organization or about sport in general. Thus the initial task is to provide a complete overview of the sport organization to educate the potential sponsor. Once this overview is complete, then the proposal should target the specific aspect of the sponsorship. This section is often the meat of the proposal, since it will serve as the introduction to the remaining structure of the sponsorship proposal. Included here will be the components of the agreement, the products or services to be sponsored, and the main people who will be involved in implementing and managing the sponsorship. Finally, the sport marketing professional will provide an overview of the potential sponsor's industry in terms of similar sponsorship agreements in place. The goal here is to show the potential sponsor that there are already competitors using this type of promotion for their company, or that there is an opportunity to be the leader in their industry by becoming involved in sport sponsorship.

Compatibility

The third feature involves showing the compatibility between the sport organization and the potential sponsor. This often starts with a comparison of goals and objectives from the initial research to show the similarities in mission between the two organizations. The most important factors to be analyzed in this comparison are as follows:

- the correlation between corporate images
- the similarities in target markets and customers
- the likelihood of a successful relationship between brands, associated products and services, and related activities in terms of building awareness and increasing sales
- the ability of the relationship to offer additional perks to the sponsor that will increase employee motivation (e.g., free tickets, merchandise, priority seating) and customer importance (hospitality opportunities).

This section needs to conclude with an illustration of how the price being paid for the sponsorship translates into value for the potential sponsor. The goal of the sport organization is to prove that although the cost of a sport sponsorship may be high, the value received in return has the potential of being significantly higher. This is especially important to communicate to the potential sponsor, as one of its main goals is to determine if the overall performance of the sponsorship agreement will be a profitable venture.

Exposure

The final feature of the sponsorship proposal is an explanation of how the sponsorship will maximize exposure for the potential sponsor. There is a wide range of opportunities for increasing exposure for a potential sponsor, but this usually falls into one of two categories – attendance and participation, and exposure. Attendance and participation involves individuals from outside the sport organization utilizing the offerings that have been made available. These offerings include membership in a club, attending an event at a facility, and a player for a team. Exposure would include signage, product sampling, announcements through public address systems, and any other method utilized to increase visibility.

A second area that is important to increasing exposure for the potential sponsor is through the media. There are two distinct areas where media exposure can come from – broadcasting and media coverage. Broadcasting allows the sport organization to control the level of exposure a sponsor receives. Whether it is television, radio, or the internet, the sport organization has greater control of promoting its loyalty to sponsors by maximizing sponsor exposure within the broadcast. This can be as simple as a mention at the beginning or end of the broadcast of the list of sponsors, to maximum exposure via the exclusive sponsorship of a segment during the broadcast. On the other hand, media coverage is independent of the sport organization and hence cannot be controlled. However, the sport organization will attempt to maximize exposure for sponsors through public relations, media relations, and communication relations efforts.

The final area utilized to offer exposure for the potential sponsor is through promotions and advertising. While these areas are different from the sponsorship itself, they are utilized in conjunction with the sponsorship to increase value.

Selling sponsorship opportunities

Now that the proposal has been designed, it is time to approach the potential sponsor. The sales process involves five stages: prospecting for customers, determining communication methods, making contact and the pitch, closing the sale, and servicing after the sale. This process is slightly modified for the sport sponsorship process, but generally follows the same methodology.

Communication and the corporate decision-making process

Corporations receive many sponsorship proposals over the course of a fiscal year, and have to make shrewd decisions regarding which would be most beneficial to them. In order to have the greatest chance of the sponsorship proposal being read, the sport organization must create two very important documents – the cover letter and the executive summary.

The cover letter is the introduction to the sport organization and the proposal. It will cover the essential elements of the sponsorship proposal and the enthusiasm the sport organization has for the potential partnership. The letter needs to be well written, grammatically correct, and professional. If not, there is very little chance of the sponsorship proposal being read. In addition, the letter should be personalized to target the special relationship that is possible, and hopefully create enough interest for the reader to continue reading.

The executive summary is placed at the beginning of the sponsorship proposal, although it is the last document created as part of the sponsorship proposal development process. This short document (usually fewer than two pages) would include everything that would be covered if the potential sponsor conducted a five-minute interview with the sport organization. The executive summary would include the fundamentals of sponsorship opportunities with the sport organization, the specific aspect of the sponsorship to be considered in the proposal, the anticipated benefits from the partnership, the main people to be involved with the sponsorship, and a vision for what the sponsorship can bring to the business in the future. Again, this document should be professional and enthusiastic, but also complete and concise. The executive summary serves as an introduction to the sponsorship proposal, and if written correctly will encourage the corporate sponsorship decision makers to continued reading the details of the proposal.

At this point, the sport organization will have done everything possible to get the sponsorship proposal into the hands of a potential sponsor. Should the sponsorship proposal get through the cover letter and executive summary phases, it will then be reviewed by the major decision makers within the marketing or sponsorship department of the corporation. During the decision-making process, the potential sponsor will balance the sponsorship proposal against its benchmarks and goals to determine a level of best fit. It will also determine how the sponsorship can be amalgamated within its overall integrated marketing communications plan. Ultimately, regardless of best fit, the potential sponsors will determine whether their investment into the sponsorship agreement would bring about a positive return on investment. Should the results of these issues be viewed as positive to the corporation, the proposal will be moved forward for further consideration.

Presentation, modification, and closing the deal

Should the sponsorship proposal move forward for further consideration, the sport organization will be brought in for a presentation and discussion about the potential partnership. The presentation should not only include verbal discussion; it should also contain visual aides including a PowerPoint presentation, copies of all relevant documentation, and related merchandise and collateral materials as applicable. As a result, it is important to know how many people are going to be at the presentation, and bring more than the required quantity of materials (some for important people who could not be at the presentation, and/or people who show up unplanned).

During this presentation, the sport organization is effectively making a sales pitch to the potential sponsor. As previously discussed in sales management (Chapter 7), the focus of the pitch should be on the sponsorship proposal, especially targeting the benefits to the corporation. The attitude of the presenters is crucial during this stage, and they become the face of the sport organization. In this sense, they will not get a second chance to make a first impression. Therefore, the presenter should be appropriately dressed, be neat and well groomed, have an appearance of confidence without being cocky, and maintain eye contact.

After the presentation, there will often be a question-and-answer session to clarify points from the presentation or proposal, and to ask ancillary questions that may be of interest to the corporation. During this time, the representatives from the sport organization must listen and read the individuals asking the questions. They must make every effort to clarify points from the proposal and/or presentation, and provide any additional information that might complete the picture for the potential sponsor and entice them to enter into an agreement. This process may take a long time, and a number of meetings. Regardless, the sport organization must always maintain a positive attitude and be professional. Even if there is no agreement, it is important to leave the door open for possible future sponsorship agreement.

Assuming that the presentation goes well and there is interest in creating this mutual agreement, the tactics change to closing the sale. This is often conducted through negotiation, which is a type of alternative dispute resolution utilized by two parties to complete transactions. Prior to entering the negotiation forum, the sport organization will usually review its initial meeting with the potential sponsor, determine if any modification needs to be made to the sponsorship proposal based on feedback received, and modify and resend the updated proposal prior to the negotiation session.

While negotiations may differ slightly because of cultural issues, the types of discussions to be negotiated, or the parties involved, the generic process is as follows:

- *Non-task sounding*: The first five to ten minutes is used to introduce all the participants and briefly talk about topics other than the business at hand, including family, sports, news, and the economy.
- *Information exchange*: This is the point where all the cards are laid on the table and information is provided by both parties and feedback exchanged.
- *The first offer*: This is the offer made by the sport organization, and is usually fairly close to what it wants to get for the sponsorship agreement.
- *Consideration*: The sponsor mulls over the offer, asks additional questions, and considers tactics to discuss modifications.

- *Counter-offer*: This is where the potential sponsor articulates what it wants and/or is willing to pay for the sponsorship.
- *Persuasion stage*: Each side is seeking to gain some ground on issues, answer questions, clarify positions, and often argue over points.
- *Making concessions*: Each side will make concessions in order to reach a mutually beneficial and agreeable point. It is important to realize that this point is not always reached, and without agreement, the partnership opportunity may terminate at this point.
- *Reaching an agreement*: However, should there be agreement on the terms of the proposal, they are laid out in contracts. The contracts will spell out the terms of the contract including the rights of each party, the parameters of the sponsorship (broadcasting, signage, advertising, promotions, collaterals, merchandise, hospitality, public relations, community relations, etc.), the price to be paid and over what time period, whether this is a contract of exclusivity, the liability of all parties, the protection of intellectual properties for both parties, confidentiality statements, contingencies, termination clauses, and any additional errors and omissions. These contracts are then read over by legal counsels, and signed by the proper authorities for each organization.

Managing the sponsorship

In addition to ensuring that the terms and conditions of the sponsorship contract have been met, the sport marketing professional has other responsibilities regarding the management of the sponsorship. First and foremost is the creation of a yearly sponsorship report. This document is effectively an annual report on how the sponsorship was implemented, and details the tangible and intangible benefits that the sponsor received. This report often includes a sample of advertising and promotional materials, PowerPoint slides with pictures and/or CDs/DVDs with videos showing commercials, broadcasts, and game action which incorporate elements of the sponsorship agreement. The goal is to list all of the contractual elements, describe how they were fulfilled, and provide a measure for the sponsor to determine whether it received value and a result on investment for its sponsorship dollars.

Evaluation of the effectiveness of sport sponsorships

The evaluation process involves investigating the performance of the sponsorship and determining whether the marketing efforts associated with the sponsorship are working. This evaluation process is also crucial as a part of the sport marketing professional's responsibility for entering into renegotiations and renewals of sponsorship agreements.

Many of the qualitative and quantitative research methods from market research are effective means to evaluate sponsorships. Focus groups, interviews, and surveys may be used to collect primary data regarding sponsor awareness and association to the sport organization. Secondary data including sales reports, advertising effectiveness reports through media outlets, and sponsorship effectiveness reports from companies such as IEG also serve an integral role in evaluating sponsorships.

290

When sponsors evaluate the effectiveness of their sponsorship contracts, they are specifically looking at measurable increases in exposure, awareness, media coverage, and sales. In addition, the sponsor also evaluates whether the goals of the sponsorship and an acceptable level of ROI were met. Should the results show that objectives were not met, value or an appropriate level of ROI was not attained, or other concerns arose (direction of the sport organization or company, budgetary issues, increase in costs, insufficient execution of contracts, or other conflicts), the marketing professionals from the sport organization need to work to rectify those issues and assure the sponsors that terms will be met in the future.

CONCLUSION

Sport sponsorship involves acquiring the rights to be affiliated with a sport product or event in order to obtain benefits from that association. Sport sponsorships play a significant role in the sport promotional mix, and take place at multiple levels of the sport business landscape. The history of sport sponsorships has its roots in Ancient Greece during the Olympic Games, but entered the modern era of sport business during the 1984 Summer Olympics in Los Angeles. The profitability of these Olympic Games as a result of significant corporate sponsorship, and the subsequent move of Los Angles Olympic Committee President Peter Ueberroth to Major League Baseball, has led to an age of growth and prosperity in sport created by these partnerships.

Sport sponsorship is a global multi-industry concept. Industries such as food and beverage, automotive, electronics, and mobile industries are engaged in sport sponsorship. These companies have options in six main sport sponsorship categories: sport governing body sponsorship, sport team sponsorship, athlete sponsorship, broadcast and media sponsorship, sport facility sponsorship, and sport event sponsorship.

Sport sponsorship agreements are usually documented within a sponsorship proposal. These packages are designed to articulate the benefits derived from the agreement for all parties involved. The reason for entering into a sport sponsorship agreement varies from organization to organization. Corporations have numerous goals as a result of sport sponsorship, including increasing public awareness, enhancing their company image, building business and trade relationships with other sponsoring organizations, changing or improving public perceptions of their company, increasing community involvement in the target area, and enhancing personnel relations by offering opportunities for employees to attend sponsored events, including attendance at hospitality areas. The goals of sport brands as a result of sponsorship include taking in additional revenue from the agreement, and increasing target market awareness, image sales, and market share.

FROM THEORY TO PRACTICE

KATIE COX, DIRECTOR OF MARKETING
Gator Bowl Association,
Jacksonville, Florida

I work year round, full-time planning and marketing a post-season college football bowl game, the TaxSlayer.com Gator Bowl. The scope of my job as Director of Marketing for the Gator Bowl Association is quite diverse and includes inside and outside sales, sponsorship activation, web-based marketing initiatives, advertising, promotion, volunteer management, and grass-roots marketing programs. This diversity affords me the opportunity to work with a wide array of people which allows me to continually learn, grow, and perfect my craft.

I was never an athlete, but was always fascinated with the behind-the-scenes operations of athletic events. Call it what you may: a coincidence, fortunate stroke of luck, or preparedness, but one phone call while enrolled in an introductory-level sport management class laid the pathway to a successful career in athletics. That phone call transformed my entire life by facilitating a move half-way across the country and out of my comfort zone. The individual on the other end of the phone became my mentor and continues to be a fixture at every fork in the road helping to nurture my dream.

Throughout the education process in the classroom, in volunteer experiences, and during internships, I found that hard work and positive networking were common traits for successful athletic professionals. I also learned an important adage, "It is not who you know, it is who knows you." Those attributes and that saying have been and continue to be foundational in a successful career in college athletics. I apply them to everything that I do.

My hard work, diligence, and attention to detail in my internships first with the City of Jacksonville Special Events (Super Bowl XXXIX) and then with Denver Broncos allowed me to create lasting relationships with my supervisors which subsequently turned into a full-time job. I was hired at the Gator Bowl in 2006 as the Marketing Manager albeit, with no face-to-face interview and marketing experience, but because I came highly recommended by my previous employer at the City of Jacksonville. While it was a leap of faith for both the Bowl and myself, it was one from which we have both benefited. My career path has been unique simply because the leadership at the Gator Bowl Association believes in education and mentoring. I have worked and continue to work with the same diligence and desire that I had on my first day and, as a result, they have invested their time to nurture and educate me in their business. From my initial position as Marketing Manager, I have worked my way up to now hold the Director of Marketing position at the Bowl.

The functionality of the Marketing Department is instrumental to the success of every other element necessary to execute the TaxSlayer.com Gator Bowl and ancillary events.

As I mentioned previously, my day-to-day tasks are quite diverse and unique, but all are grounded in brand image and revenue generation. The core of my job and the success of revenue generation lie in corporate support, or sponsorships. To best highlight the importance of sponsorships, one can look at the marquee sponsor of any bowl game: the entitlement sponsor.

In my personal opinion, the most important element in successful activation and branding of a sponsor is learning the fundamentals of their business and what their goals and objectives of being a sponsor are. Once these items have been addressed, we can then begin to formulate and execute a plan to meet the needs. Any sponsor, but specifically the entitlement sponsor, is entrusting its brand into my hands – I must protect it as if it were my own. Our entire staff work to manage the positive view of the Gator Bowl brand, but I specifically pay close attention to the integration of TaxSlayer.com into our branding effort and all advertising and web-based messaging. I also oversee the successful execution of all other elements of their contract from tickets to hospitality to client entertainment.

Because of this, I must communicate openly and effectively with our entire staff so that all contractual elements are successfully executed and that the brand is being promoted consistently. While every department is affected by any sponsorship, large or small, the ticketing and events departments are impacted most frequently.

For instance, while protection and promotion of the brand and subsequent events are overseen and monitored by me, they are actually implemented by the Events Department, so open communication is a *must* at all times. From a ticketing standpoint, each partner receives a ticket and hospitality package as part of their contribution. I must communicate their requests to ticketing so that the appropriate amounts of game tickets and event tickets are reserved on the partners' behalf.

In all activation of sponsorships, whether it is tickets, exposure, or hospitality, it is incredibly important to under-promise and over-deliver. This will help drive a higher return on investment and show that you are fully vested in the sponsorship.

The work ethic and drive that was instilled into me in my youth have proven to be the most valuable assets that I have. My job is not 8 a.m. to 5 p.m. Monday through Friday; it is 24 hours a day, seven days a week. I search in everything that I do to find new and unique ways to secure new sponsors, more successfully activate partnerships, and brand our Bowl. Marketing is a consumer-driven field, and thus we must react to the ever-changing environment that our consumers create.

As you begin your career in sports it is important that you capitalize on *every* opportunity that presents itself to you. You never know when someone whom you encounter in that opportunity will be instrumental in the long-term success of your career. Do not become frustrated by the exorbitant hours, and lack of acknowledgment and pay for the effort that you are putting forth – people are watching and it will pay off in the end!

CHAPTER THIRTEEN

SOCIAL MEDIA AND NETWORKING IN THE SPORT INDUSTRY

CHAPTER OUTLINE

- What are sport social media?
- A short history on social networking
- Modern social networking and media
- Social networks
- Geolocation social media
- Future of social media
- Conclusion

CHAPTER OBJECTIVES

The reader will be able to:

- understand what social media and social networking are
- understand the inner workings of a Facebook page
- understand how to effectively use Twitter for sport marketing
- acknowledge the analytics of Twitter and Facebook
- recognize the networking and sales opportunities with LinkedIn
- realize the power of new media like geolocation social media and other mobile applications have
- appreciate just how little potential social media has actually reached.

WHAT ARE SPORT SOCIAL MEDIA?

Social media or social networking have been defined as websites that allow the user to construct a public or semi-public profile within a bounded system, articulate a list of other users with whom they share a connection, and view and traverse their list of connections and those made by others within the system. The nature and nomenclature of these connections may vary from site to site. This definition is fantastic but it would be good to break this down into more casual terms. Social media allow the user to connect with people they may have never connected with before. No longer does a person who moved away from their hometown have to wait until a high school reunion to see what his or her classmates ended up doing with their lives.

Social media are not just about connecting people, however. When people put their lives online on Facebook, Twitter, LinkedIn, or whatever social network they like to use, they leave a huge trail of data for a sport marketer to use. This data may be a typical address and phone number or it could tell the marketer what other brands their customers like, and that will enable the marketer to see what else interests the consumer.

A SHORT HISTORY ON SOCIAL NETWORKING

The first social network that allowed the user to create a profile and list friends was called SixDegrees. SixDegrees lasted for only a few years but it paved the way for future networks. By definition, the first social networks were anything from Classmates.com to dating websites that allowed users to browse profiles of other users.

The modern-day social networks emerged in the early 2000s with Friendster trailblazing a path for LinkedIn, Facebook, Twitter, MySpace, YouTube, and more. There has also been a strong showing from the lesser known niche networks like Dogster, Couchsurfing, deviantART, Goodreads, and in the sports world there are sites like FanNation that is now partnered with CNN and Sports Illustrated.

MODERN SOCIAL NETWORKING AND MEDIA

Thus, in the present day, the internet is graced with more social networks than we know what to do with. There are still the giants such as Twitter, Facebook, and YouTube but there are more and more networks being created every day for whatever niche exists. At the end of 2007 sport social media expert Jason Peck posted 50 sports social networking websites and the number has only increased in the past four years.

So how does the sport marketer use social media to their advantage? In Figure 13.1, you will see that everything revolves around the sport organization or player's website or blog. Content is created and placed on the website. After content is created, it should be shared on the different social networks where your fans take part, so it is important for the sport marketer to do research to find out what social networks their demographic is highly engaged in. The content shared on social networks should be shared in a way that promotes conversation and keeps the reader or watcher on the Facebook page or website so that he or she will continue to engage.

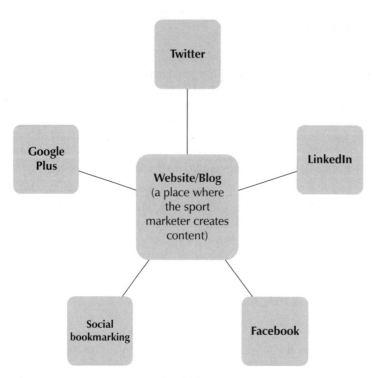

Figure 13.1 How content should be created and shared

Social networking is best used by organizations that engage their fans. So what exactly is engagement? This is best described as an example from the New York Jets Facebook page. The Jets use contests to enhance the fan experience. The organization also posts pictures of fans from the game and allows other fans to comment; this creates a feeling of fan envy and may lead to a person looking at the pictures and then buying a ticket because the atmosphere looks like something that they cannot miss. This is just on Facebook; on Twitter the organization engages fans in short conversations. It also has a Twitter List (more about this later) where it promotes players with Twitter accounts. A few of its players – Dustin Keller and Darrelle Revis – will respond to fans that tweet @ them. This enhances the fan experience and will continue to move fans up the escalator.

Social media are a very cost-effective way for small market teams and leagues to promote themselves. For instance, the WNBA does a good job of producing content that its fans want to share with their peers. The WNBA content also has the fans engaging with other fans on the WNBA Facebook page. In another example of smaller league capitalizing on social media, the Arena Football League utilizes good content that people want to share. The AFL also uses humor to engage its fans; for instance, in the 2011 Bowl Season the league commented on how the high-scoring Alamo Bowl between Washington and Baylor was just like an AFL game and how the season must have come early. The comment got a lot of "likes" which helped promote the league to the friends of the people who "liked" the comment.

SOCIAL NETWORKS

As already noted, there are many different social networks but this textbook will only cover four: Facebook, Twitter, LinkedIn, and Google Plus.

Facebook

The mission statement of Facebook is "to give people the power to share and make the world more open and connected." Experts would declare this Mission Accomplished for Facebook. Statistics taken from the network's website show that they have 800 million active users, and that figure will only grow; the average user has 130 friends, the site is available in more than 70 languages, and more than 75 percent of the users are from outside the United States. So the user base is large but the connectivity is also impressive. Every month, more than 500 million people use a Facebook application on Facebook.com or experience the Facebook platform on other websites. More than 350 million active users currently access Facebook on the go with their mobile devices and that number will only rise as smartphones continue to gain more market share. So at the current state in 2012, Facebook can account for around 11 percent of the world's population.

Facebook pages

The first thing a sport marketer needs to know about Facebook is how to use a Facebook page. The page is how brands interact with their fans on Facebook. So where do you start with a Facebook page if you are trying to develop your organization's presence on Facebook? It is best to start with a three-part strategy:

1   What types of goals does the sport organization have for its Facebook page? Does the organization want to use the page to sell more tickets? Engage the fans? Use the page for sheer marketing of ticket deals and community events?
2   Who is the organization trying to reach?
3   Figure out the content that will be shared. If the page is being used for ticket sales, then the content will be mainly used to promote ticket packages. If engagement, then it will be pictures, videos, news pieces, and any type of content that will get conversation going among the fans and the page owners.

Now that the sport marketer has developed a strategy, the page can now be created. We will not go into detail on how to create a page because it changes and it is self-explanatory. One of the first things that the sport marketer will need to do is create a landing page. Some examples of good landing pages are shown in Figure 13.2.

These landing pages are good because they have a call to action to like the page and they tell potential fans why they should like the page. A call to action is necessary because otherwise a potential fan might just browse over the organization's page, not hit the "like" button, and not have content delivered straight to his or her Facebook news stream. It is important that content is delivered to the news stream because if the content is good fans will like/share/comment on the content, thus spreading the reach of the content to their friends on Facebook.

Figure 13.2 Examples of Facebook landing pages

In addition, these two examples are polar opposites when it comes to marketing budgets but look at how the Texas Stars are able to have a design that is just as inviting as the big budget Phoenix Suns; this goes to show that social media are all about content and not about big marketing and advertising budgets.

Once the organization has developed a landing page and has all the information about the organization filled out, it needs to start spreading the word about the page. The best way to do this is to include some sort of Facebook plug-in on its website and to include its Facebook page in its traditional advertising. However, it is important to tell people why they should like the page and not just post a Facebook logo at the bottom of a commercial.

Facebook insights

Once the organization's page is running, content is starting to be shared, and fans are beginning to converse, it is time to start paying attention to the built-in analytics called Facebook insights. As of writing, the analytics will inform the organization of their:

1   total likes
2   friends of fans – how far the organization's reach extends on Facebook
3   talking about this:
   - likes your page
   - likes, comments on, or shares your page post

- answers a question you have asked
- responds to your event
- mentions your page
- tags your page in a photo
- checks in or recommends your place

4   total reach – The number of unique people who have seen content associated with the page.

The analytics for a page post are:

1   reach:
- number of unique people who have seen the post

2   engaged users:
- number of unique people who have clicked on the post

3   talking about this:
- number of people that have created a story from the post. Stories include:
   - sharing, liking, or commenting on your post
   - answering a question
   - responding to an event

4   virality:
- percentage that have created a story from all the people who have seen the post.

There are also demographic data that break down the organization's page fans by gender, age, country, city, and language.

Facebook ads

Facebook ads are a very powerful way for a sport organization to reach the 800 million people on the social network. The reason the ads platform is so powerful is because it allows the advertiser to pinpoint certain demographics that will see the advertisement. As the advertiser selects the different targeting criterion Facebook shows an approximate number of users who are being targeted.

The different targeting criteria for Facebook ads are as follows:

- location
- age
- sex
- personal interests, which help to precisely target people in a certain region who are interested in the organization's sport – for example, if you are a baseball organization, you would include baseball in the personal interests
- connections, which allow the advertiser to target people connected to pages, events, or groups of which the advertiser is an administrator
- sexual orientation
- relationship status: married, single, engaged, or in a relationship
- languages
- education
- workplaces.

As you can see, it is possible for an advertiser to only target people within a 50-mile radius of the stadium who are married, engaged, and in a relationship for their Valentine's Day ticket special. It is possible to only target the LGBT community for a LGBT Pride Community Night. This type of target has been extremely difficult to achieve in a traditional advertising space but it is achieved easily through Facebook.

Twitter

Twitter is a micro-blogging platform where users can post 140-character updates. Each user has a personal stream where he or she sees "tweets" from every user he or she follows. *Tweets* are the updates, and they can be (1) an original message, (2) a retweet – a repeat of what someone else has tweeted, (3) a direct message to a user who follows you. Tweets can include mentions and hashtags that allow users to target their message more easily. A mention – @user targets specific individuals so that it shows up in their mention stream which does not have as much activity as their personal stream, unless they are really popular and attract a lot of mentions. A hashtag allows a user to target a specific Twitter search; for instance, during the AFC Championship the hashtag was #afcchampionship and everyone who tweeted about the AFC Championship could include that hashtag in their tweet to be shown in the Twitter search result which can be seen by people who do not follow them. A hashtag could eventually become a trending topic either locally, nationally, or worldwide. A trending topic is seen on every Twitter user's home page.

Organizations have used Twitter to promote content, engage fans, customer service, and whatever type of promotional strategy will fit into a 140-character tweet. Some of the best uses of Twitter by the sport industry have been professional athletes interacting with fans. For example, current NFL player Larry Fitzgerald uses Twitter to respond to his fans along with posting news and inspirational quotes. Twitter is able to reach into an athlete on a personal level. Twitter allows for there to be a press conference 24 hours a day, seven days a week, and the people asking the questions are not journalists, they are fans. It is up to the athlete to answer the question but answering it could create a fan for a lifetime that could transcend trade and free agency moves.

Twitter moves fast and a good sport organization will have tools in place to catch things that are being said about its organization. There are tools devised by various companies that use algorithms to track how a brand is being portrayed on Twitter through searching keywords. These tweets are put through a sentiment analysis that tracks whether the tweet is positive, negative, or neutral. Those individuals measuring their brand on social networks have to know if the systems are taking account of sarcasm and how that could skew their numbers. In addition, if a trend like #ILoveTheJets is used with a tweet that says, "Why is #ILoveTheJets trending, I hate that team! #GoGiants!," that tweet might skew the results of the person measuring Twitter sentiment about The New York Jets. Automatic measuring needs to be done carefully and the organization needs to understand what it is measuring.

At the time of writing, Twitter has released a beta of an advertising system through promoted content. A user can promote a tweet on a cost-per-engagement (CPE) which means that the promoter only pays when someone retweets, replies to, clicks, or favorites the promoted tweet. A user can also promote a trend for a fee that has not yet been officially disclosed. The promoted trend is featured on the trending topics list and is clearly marked as promoted. A promoted trend allows for a brand to quickly get conversation started on a time-sensitive topic but it can be confusing for some users since it is new, and a lot of the Twitter user base does not understand how it works.

The sport marketer needs to make certain that the Twitter platform is being used to listen to its customers. This means responding to tweets about the sport organization, especially if a person is complaining about the organization. An organization's Twitter and Facebook page is its home turf, and if someone is going to complain about your organization let it happen there.

LinkedIn

LinkedIn is a social network for business and professional networking. The network at the time of writing has more than 135 million members in over 200 countries and territories, so this network is very global, with members representing business leaders from every industry.

LinkedIn allows users to build a profile that showcases their business experience. The profile shows the user's current and past positions, education, recommendations from other users, number of connections, links to the user's website and other social networks. The users are also allowed to write out a summary of their business skills and experience.

LinkedIn caters for different ways of messaging people on the network. The network allows connections to message back and forth freely. InMails, messages that are bought on the website, allow a user to send a message to a person even if they are not connected with them. Introductions are not necessarily messages but they are a way to get someone from your network to introduce you to a second- or third-level connection.

How does a sport marketer utilize LinkedIn to increase sales for the sport organization? The network allows the sport marketer to target companies and individuals that can afford and would be interested in season tickets. LinkedIn Answers allow people in the sport industry to ask questions relevant to the sport industry or to answer questions that are asked. For example, a sport organization is looking to develop a mobile application and has questions about the viability and the process of creating the application; the organization could ask other professionals who have had experiences with mobile applications. It creates a give-and-take relationship with people who could become future clients. LinkedIn groups are a great way for the sport marketer to create a networking group that could end up producing leads for the sales team.

GEOLOCATION SOCIAL MEDIA

Geolocation social media are platforms that use the global position system (GPS) on a smartphone to check into a service. The service will then show the connection where the user is located. Some services are mixing in competitions with their service, while others are using it as a way to give out discounts. All geolocation services have one thing in common: exploring the world around you and being rewarded for it.

Foursquare

Foursquare operates like a game. Users of the application can explore their neighborhoods and find discounts, earn badges, or become the mayor of an establishment, and there are many other ways in which people use Foursquare. Foursquare has tools for business owners that they can use to engage customers. According to the Foursquare website, the seven tools are:

1 *mayor specials*: unlocked only by the mayor of your venue. Who's the mayor? It is your single most loyal customer! (the user who has checked in the most in the past 60 days).
   ■ "Foursquare has deemed you the mayor! Enjoy a free order of French fries!"

2 *check-in specials*: unlocked when a user checks into your venue a certain number of times.
   ■ "Foursquare says you have been here 10 times! That is a free drink for you!"

3 *loyalty specials*: unlocked every X check-ins.
   ■ "Foursquare users get 20 percent off any entree every fifth check-in!"

4 *swarm specials*: set a minimum number to check in for a three-hour period and if the minimum is reached, the special is unlocked.
   ■ "1,000 people have checked in, you have unlocked a special!"

5 *friends specials*: set a number of Foursquare friends a user needs to check in with to unlock a special.
   ■ "Check in with eight of your friends at the same time to unlock this special!"

6 *flash specials*: a first-come-first-served type of special with a set limit on the number of specials available.
   ■ "Check in fast to get this special because there are only 200 available today!"

7 *newbie specials*: a special for the person who is new to your venue.
   ■ "First time checking in? Here is a special deal for you!"

Facebook Places

If this chapter had been written in the early part of 2011, this section would have been about Gowalla and how it was the other location-based service that was competing with Foursquare. However, that changed when Facebook bought the development team of Gowalla.

CASE STUDY 13: CREATING VALUE FOR AN ORGANIZATION USING GEOLOCATION SOCIAL MEDIA

Authored and contributed by A. J. Vaynerchuk and Sam Taggart from VaynerMedia LLC, New York, New York

When you are the sport marketer for the worst team in the league, you have to think outside the box because no matter what, it is your job to put people in the stands. So

---

how do you bring in fans with a very small budget? One way is to turn to new media and develop a partnership with a new technology platform to test the waters because at this stage it is nothing ventured, nothing gained.

So when the New Jersey Nets needed to put people in the stands they turned to VaynerMedia and Gowalla. The Nets needed people in the stands and the other two organizations needed to see if geolocation could actually move people into the stands because it was untested. The key to this marketing initiative was to use word-of-mouth instead of any traditional or internet marketing.

The campaign was focused around "dropping" virtual goods at various locations that could be found by people checking in at these locations. Gowalla dropped 250 pairs of tickets for the last regular season home game. The tickets were dropped at sports-themed and outdoor locations within 75 miles of the Izod Center, the Nets' home arena. To extend the experience, virtual goods would be redeemable for memorabilia during the game.

The campaign started with Gowalla posting a blog about its partnership with the Nets. The NBA team then released a press release the following week. Twitter was buzzing about the marketing initiative creating a positive brand sentiment for both the Nets and Gowalla. The buzz continued for over a week, and not only from Nets fans but from fans all of over, even including fans of teams in other sports.

Of the 500 seats that were available for the campaign, 76 were filled. Therefore, 15.2 percent of the Gowalla ticket finders redeemed their tickets at the event. This was considered a success because the event was on a Monday night and the venue is not easily accessible from New York City, where a lot of the fans would come from.

Gowalla and the Nets did not stop engaging the fans once they gave them tickets. Instead they continued to increase the experience for the ticket finders at the game. When the Gowalla winners arrived at the game they were directed to a Gowalla branded table that gave out their tickets, T-shirts, and stickers. The winners were instructed to check in on Gowalla to be entered into a draw for a chance to win one of the several jerseys provided by the Nets.

The fans continued to be engaged by Gowalla and the Nets during half-time with people being reminded to check in on Gowalla to win the jerseys, which not only reminded the free ticket finders but also made it apparent that everyone could check in to win free memorabilia. So 89.5 percent of the ticket finders checked in upon arrival at the event.

The buzz continued on Twitter during the game with people posting pictures of the event exclaiming how their kids were having a blast and how it was the closest they had ever sat at a NBA game. The reason the buzz was happening across all networks was because the users of Gowalla are the social media power users and if they use a check-in service the chances are they use every service and have followers on every service.

After the event was over, people continued to post pictures on Twitter and talk about how great the promotion was for them. There were tweets such as "Great seats, my 6 year old had 'the best day of my life, ever' particularly mini-sly."

A key takeaway was the fact that the Nets were able to use a geolocation service to fill seats that would otherwise not have been filled. In those seats, people were talking about the organization, thus increasing brand recognition for not only the Nets but also Gowalla and VaynerMedia. Those people also bought merchandise and concessions, which generated more revenue than the Nets expected for that night. Most important though was the fact that the three organizations helped improve fan loyalty with all of the Gowalla winners, which is priceless.

Source: Adapted from Taggert, S. and Vaynerchuk, A. J. (2010). Early proof that geolocation marketing will succeed [Web log message]. Retrieved from http://vaynermedia.com/2010/04/early-proof-that-geolocation-marketing-will-succeed/.

Questions for discsussion

1   The Gowalla and New Jersey Nets campaign showed that geolocation social media can help get rid of expiring tickets while still creating value for the organization. Give two examples of how else an organization could use geolocation social media.

2   The Nets and Gowalla decided to use word-of-mouth to promote this campaign instead of using traditional marketing or internet marketing. Give at least three examples of how you could use traditional marketing or internet marketing to promote a geolocation social media marketing campaign.

Facebook Places works a lot like Foursquare does – users check into different places as they journey throughout the world around them. They check in through going to Facebook on their smartphone either in an app or their web browser. Just like Foursquare, Facebook Places gives brick-and-mortar businesses the ability to create check-in deals.

The service offers four types of check-in deals: (1) individual, (2) friend, (3) loyalty, and (4) charity. The individual deal is offered to both new and existing customers. The friend deal allows a business to offer a deal to groups of up to eight people when they check in together. The loyalty deal rewards loyal customers by offering a reward after a certain number of check-ins. The charity deal allows customers to make a donation to a charity of their choice.

The Golden State Warriors have had success in using Facebook deals with their special Golden State Warriors Home Game Facebook page. They have offered check-in deals like "First 200 – Shoot Postgame Free Throws On The Court" and "Exclusive Post-Game Q&A."

Facebook Places is bound to break through to the mainstream of check-in services because of the over 200 million people already using Facebook on their mobile devices. It will be up to the sport marketer to tap into this service to reward new and old customers who like to explore the world around them.

SCVNGR

SCVNGR is a mobile gaming platform that allows the user to "Go places. Do challenges. Earn points!" The game allows brands and institutions to create treks that send their users on what is basically a scavenger hunt. The challenges that players face while they are exploring the world around them can also lead to real world rewards.

The Boston Celtics partnered with SCVNGR in 2010 to do a trek that had fans going around the city confronting challenges at places marked with a Celtics logo. The fan who accumulated the most points by the deadline won a pair of season tickets for the 2010 to 2011 season. The trek included such challenges as going to the TD Garden Pro Shop and taking a photo wearing a green foam finger for two points in the contest. One of the other challenges was to check out the Massachusetts Bay Transportation Authority (MBTA) map and counting the Rondos' jersey number in stops from the South Station. The campaign was able to successfully accomplish the use of new media in a clever way and allowed fans to become deeply engaged in the Celtics brand.

Location-based services will come and go, and will evolve to offer more and more interactivity. The sport marketer needs to include these services to reach a demographic that are becoming increasingly mobile in their computing and consumption.

FUTURE OF SOCIAL MEDIA

The future of media is interesting and constantly evolving. The surface has only been scratched with what a smartphone and tablet can actually do. As a society, we have gotten more social and comfortable with sharing our lives online. So what does the likely near future of social media entail?

First off, mobile will continue to grow and will become more interactive with augmented reality. Augmented reality (AR) is already being developed and a number of applications are already in the marketplace, but they have not yet been adopted by the masses. AR allows users to see a different reality through their viewport on their smartphone. An example of this would be going to the Olympics and having a competition where the users search for Olympic rings that are hidden in different places and the person that has the most rings at the end of the competition gets rewarded. Think of AR as graffiti that does not blemish the landscape around us.

Some more uses in sport marketing for AR would be for fans of an organization to hold their phone up to a team store and see pictures of specials and featured items without going into the store. Another good example would be for bar patrons to hold their phones up to the outside of the bar to see what the schedule of games is for the upcoming weekend along with drink specials. AR basically makes it a simple, easy, and effective way of reaching a customer. If you would like to learn more about augmented reality a good source is Augmented Planet (www.augmentedplanet.com).

The second trend for social and new media is social currency. Empire Avenue is basically a stock-market for social people where you can invest a fictional currency called Eaves in people who are influential in their industry. This type of thinking could lead to some interesting innovation in currency and the global social web. We could possibly see a social currency that is given out to fans of brands that share content, extending the reach of a brand. The currency could then buy items with the brand. For example, a sport organization could gift tickets to its top team ambassadors. The possibilities are endless.

Micropayments would be great for a major ticketing business to develop. A micropayment could allow for individuals to buy a ticket directly from Twitter or Facebook and have it deducted from their bank account or online wallet. For example, a game starts in three hours but is not sold out; the organization could tweet or post on Facebook with a discount ticket that could be bought directly from Twitter or Facebook and have the ticket go to a special card or will call.

The third evolution of sport marketing should be in the category of content marketing, which is becoming more and more important, as targeted demographics spend their life on the internet. The content marketing in this case is using live streaming to engage a fan base. The infrastructure is already there with services like Livestream, Ustream.tv, and Justin.tv. The phenomenon that is live streaming can already be seen in a niche sport called eSports, competitive video games. In 2011, Twitch.tv – a gaming spinoff of Justin.tv – told gamers in so many words to quit their day job by introducing their partner program which allowed streamers to run advertisements during their broadcast. At any given moment you could see thousands of viewers watching popular gamers playing games. Twitch.tv is also a service for eSports tournaments to stream their events to a large number of people while keeping costs down and allowing them to bring in revenue from advertising and also channel subscriptions.

So how could live streaming break into more traditional sports? Live streaming gives sport organizations the opportunity to connect with their fan base on an extremely personal level; for example, exclusive post-game press conferences specifically for subscribers. Another example could be a streamed scrimmage during the pre-season. As there are increasing numbers of people who have the internet bandwidth to stream video and those same people are dropping their cable television packages, it will be in a sport organization's best interest to use internet video to interact with its fan base.

CONCLUSION

Social media allow people to be connected in ways that they have never been connected before. The information which people store online not only connects people with their past but also creates a lot of data that may be used by a sport marketer.

Social media have come a long way since the early days of the internet. Now social giants like Facebook, Twitter, and LinkedIn pave the way for the future of the internet. Facebook has made it easy for sport organizations to have an online presence that connects their fans not only with the organization but also with other fans. Twitter has created a platform where fans can engage with their favorite athletes and organizations in 140 characters or less. LinkedIn is the world's best networking group that allows sport professionals, especially salespeople, to connect with other industry professionals and future clients.

Facebook pages and ads come with loads of data called Facebook insights. Insights allow owners of a page to see how far their content has reached, the number of likes on their page, how many people are talking about the organization on Facebook, and the virality of a post on their page. Insights allow sport marketers to gauge just how successful is their content. Facebook ads can target by age, location, relationship status, sex, interests, sexual orientation, education, and workplace. It is easy to say that Facebook ads allow sport marketers to pinpoint exactly the demographic that their organization is attempting to reach.

Twitter is a service that allows a sport marketer to engage a following in 140 characters or fewer. The service also allows the sport marketer to promote certain tweets or trends to the top of relevant feeds. Twitter also allows for an account to be promoted so that other users see the sport organization in their "Who to Follow" section on the user's Twitter home page.

Geolocation social media are services that help individuals explore the world around them. The media merge the online digital world with the real, tangible world that everyone lives and walks in every day. Services like Foursquare, Facebook Places, and SCVNGR allow brands to use this medium to offer fun challenges, great deals, and priceless engagement for their fans, and will promote the brand to the fan's circle of friends and followers since the service is attached to the rest of the fan's social media life.

The future of social media is exciting to look at because the possibilities are pretty much endless. The sport industry should start to utilize augmented reality applications to advertise its brands in new and exciting ways. The sport industry should also look into the ability of using social currency to help promote brands and micropayments to pay for tickets and merchandise in an easier fashion. The sport industry would also be wise to start utilizing online live streaming to help engage the demographic that has gone to strictly online media.

FROM THEORY TO PRACTICE

DANIEL P. SMITH, SENIOR VICE-PRESIDENT OF MARKETING
ClickSquared, Inc.,
Boston, Massachusetts

Professional sports are not all fun and games – it is a business, one where winning and keeping fans can be a real challenge; sports fans can be fickle. Based on the team's win-loss record, it can be a struggle to keep the fans' attention (if not their allegiance) – and ultimately fill seats. Throw in a troubled economy, uncertain weather, and the ongoing competition for the fans' entertainment dollar, and the sports marketer's task can be daunting indeed.

Like many people in the sports marketing industry, it has been a circuitous route to my present role as CMO of ClickSquared. I grew up in Orchard Park, NY – home of the Buffalo Bills and Ralph Wilson Stadium. After a season-ending injury in high school, my coach asked me if I would be interested in working in the Buffalo Bills' scouting department: no pay, but I would get two 50-yard line seats to every home game and have my pick of the equipment room on away weeks – typically taking home a football, T-shirt, or sweatshirt. It was an interesting experience: I compiled college player statistics for the scouts – height, weight, 40 time, injury notes, bench-press and squat weights, tackles, completions, etc. – on paper spreadsheets and giant whiteboards (this was before PCs). The internet did not yet exist either, so I scoured 40 to 50 newspapers a week looking for feature articles on players that might otherwise slip below the scouts' radar – dutifully clipping the article and adding the player's data to the "other" whiteboard dedicated to identifying undrafted players.

I had the good fortune to go on to play college football, and witnessed the other side of the equation as a few of my teammates were drafted into the NFL and the then-fledgling USFL. I graduated from college with a degree in industrial engineering, and entered the world of banking just as the use of computing was exploding. In my very first job, I was part of a Chemical Bank (now Chase) team that built the fraud intercept system for MasterCard – basically by tracking individual cardholder purchase behavior (purchase amounts/frequency of use/merchant-categories/locations) and identifying statistical anomalies that suggested unauthorized use. If you have ever had a cashier hand you the phone to talk to your bank to confirm your identity, you know first hand what we did.

Spin forward 25 years – a happy marriage, three children, 27 seasons as a youth coach, and senior positions at a handful of marketing software companies – and I now find myself merging my early experience working with the Bills and the behavior analysis techniques we developed for MasterCard with my understanding of the day-to-day needs of marketers. Instead of trying to identify players, we are now trying to identify fans; instead of identifying fraud, we are now looking to identify attrition risk or the unmet needs of a fan; instead of interrupting the fan's purchase with an embarrassing phone call, we are trying to speak with him or her using his or her preferred communication channel.

Sports franchises are intensely focused on collecting fan data to create a personalized experience for each and every fan. Capturing data such as favorite player, fan birthdays, ticket-purchasing preferences, favorite opponents, game attendance history, and more can become the key to securing and keeping a loyal fan. Armed with this data, franchises can communicate with fans using highly relevant cross-channel marketing programs that include reaching out to fans, when, where, and how they want to hear from their team.

Of course, getting fans to give you this information can be a challenge. Here is where sports franchises, and their technology partners like ClickSquared, have gotten creative. With the increasing popularity of social media, many teams are leveraging its ubiquitous presence to reach and engage sports fans. Whether it is an app hosted on a team's Facebook page (share your name and email address to play), an in-bowl mobile sweepstake (opt-in to win), or branded fan forums like The Boston Celtics' *Banner Moments* that encourage the sharing of memories, pictures, and video, fans are usually willing to share detailed information when they are reassured that the team will use the data in a responsible manner.

At ClickSquared, we work with sports franchises to help them acquire and keep those sometimes fickle fans. The Boston Celtics, New England Patriots, Miami Dolphins, Philadelphia Eagles, Houston Rockets, and Oklahoma Thunder (to name a few) all rely on ClickSquared to help them develop acquisition- and behavior-based communication strategies that include highly personalized, relevant, and targeted messages for their fans.

Our Software-as-a-Service platform, the Cross-Channel Marketing Hub ("The Hub") brings together enterprise-class campaign management, social media apps, marketing database management, customer intelligence tools, and predictive models with delivery and execution across email, print, web, mobile, and social channels. This means that we can now help sports franchises provide exactly what fans want – fun ways to engage with the team and highly tailored, relevant communications; when, where, and how they like it – without the need to install and integrate multiple marketing applications or manage databases and servers.

One valued client of ours is the Kraft Sports Group (KSG), best known as the owners of the New England Patriots. This is a complex organization, with multiple business touching over 2.5 million fans and customers. In the past, the organization had its customer data spread across multiple databases, with little or no understanding of a how a particular customer interacted with other parts of the Group. Those individual databases included season ticket holders, premium seating members, fans on the waiting list for season tickets, and single-ticket buyers.

Other siloed data sources included clients of the events business, *Patriots Football Weekly* (the team's newspaper) recipients, Patriots Extra Points (the loyalty credit card program) members, Patriots Place (the restaurants and shops at the stadium) patrons, The Pro Shop customers, as well as fans and ticket holders of the New England Revolution, a professional (MLS) soccer team.

Working with ClickSquared, KSG was able to link, clean up, and consolidate its databases. This allowed the organization to see the overlap in fans across its teams and businesses, and pinpoint unmet needs. Using this insight, KSG was then able to leverage fan preferences and behavioral information to create highly impactful communications tuned to the fans' specific interests and needs.

From a preference center that enabled the Patriots to capture critical fan information, to tracking ticket use for the purpose of reaching out to season ticket holders who had missed a game, or the development of "onboarding" communications to ensure that every new season ticket holder has a positive and memorable experience, all efforts are directed toward making sure that each communication meets the needs of the individual fan. One-size-fits-all marketing is not part of the repertoire.

As a result of the team's behavioral modeling and tailored marketing efforts, customer open rates are up 15 percent over 2011 and email click-through rates score even higher. The organization is sending more relevant information in a much more targeted manner, dramatically impacting upon fan engagement and ultimately the bottom line. These efforts also translated into the Patriots achieving a season ticket renewal rate of 97 percent for the 2011 season – an achievement that is envied across the league.

What I love most about this story is that the Patriots have a ten-year waiting list for season tickets; it would be easy to just sell the seats to the next person in line. Instead the team puts enormous energy into making sure that its season ticket holders are happily renewing. I think this approach speaks volumes to the team's desire to engage with its fans and create lasting loyalty. It is a great example of how a sports franchise can use analytics and intelligent cross-channel marketing to create lifelong (and even multi-generational) bonds with its fans.

PART V

THE EVOLUTION OF SPORT MARKETING

CHAPTER FOURTEEN

INTERNATIONAL AND GLOBAL MARKETING IN SPORT

CHAPTER OUTLINE

- Introduction to international and global sport marketing
- The relationship between culture and the international/global sport marketplace
- International and global sport market opportunities
- International and global sport marketing strategies
- Conclusion

CHAPTER OBJECTIVES

The reader will be able to:

- understand the ever-growing and ever-changing internationalization and globalization of marketing in and through sport
- appreciate the historical, cultural, political, and legal dynamics that are evident in international and global sport marketing and cultural environments
- understand the complexity of negotiation, mediation, and arbitration with international and global sport markets
- identify the numerous international and global sport marketing opportunities available in established and emerging sport markets
- gain an insight into the differences between international strategic sport marketing strategies and global strategic sport marketing strategies.

313

INTRODUCTION TO INTERNATIONAL AND GLOBAL SPORT MARKETING

Many have seen the documentary *Do You Believe in Miracles* and the movie *Miracle*, the story of the 1980 U.S. Olympic Hockey Team who against all odds beat the mighty Russians and eventually went on to win the gold medal. The time was very different – fear as a result of the Cold War, a hostage crisis in Iran, and an overall turbulent political and social environment. Business and sport was a very competitive arena, but its focus is generally on the domestic market.

How things have changed in a quarter of a century. While there are still many issues facing the world today, including terrorism and assorted political and social issues, the world has fundamentally changed. It is a smaller place owing to innovations in travel and technology. Changes in trade agreements have made the movement of goods and services easier on an international and global scale.

These changes are not lost on the continuous growth of sport marketing and management. Numerous companies have overseas offices and factories to conduct business in emerging markets. The training and recruiting of athletes from other countries is increasingly evident in the United States. More international sport figures have chosen to play in the United States. Examples in 2011 include 28 percent of Major League Baseball players being born overseas; 20 percent of NBA players coming from 40 different countries; and many European soccer stars, including David Beckham and Thierry Henry, signing contracts to play in Major League Soccer (MLS). The internationalization and globalization of sport is an integral part of the growth of sport business, and hence it is a crucial aspect of sport marketing. But what is international and global sport marketing?

International and global sport marketing defined

To understand the implementation and existence of sport marketing outside of a domestic context opens a new door to significant opportunities for sport businesses. International refers to those efforts that extend beyond national boundaries and involve two or more nations. In the twenty-first century, opportunities in sport cross international borders on a regular basis, and it requires sport marketing professionals to capitalize on these opportunities, especially as a result of advances in technologies. As this growth has continued, another term, "global," has become important to sport marketing. Global is a more comprehensive term that refers to worldwide involvement. As a result, the definition of international has been modified, and for the purpose of this text the following definitions will apply:

- *Domestic*: sport marketing efforts focused internally (one country).
- *International*: sport marketing efforts that involve at least two countries up to a maximum of ten. Usually the countries are within one or two continents.
- *Global*: sport marketing efforts that involve more than ten countries and usually a minimum of three continents.

These definitions are generic in nature, and may have some fluctuation based on the make-up of the association. For example, if a sporting goods distributor focuses its business on the United States, Canada, Australia, and England, by definition it would be global. However, since the business effort is not truly global (North America, one country in Europe, and a country that is for the most part a continent unto itself), this business would most likely be referred to as an international company. However, if this company were to expand its business efforts to China and France, it would most likely be referred to as a global company since even though it only operates in five countries, it operates in more than 50 percent of the continents in the world.

Determinants of international and/or global sport business involvement

A sport business can be involved in sport marketing efforts in one of five stages. The most basic is where a sport organization is not involved in marketing efforts outside its own country, or has no direct foreign sport marketing. For those sport organizations that dabble in foreign markets as a result of a surplus of products or a temporary increase in demand, this is referred to as infrequent foreign sport marketing. Regular foreign sport marketing is where a sport organization has a permanent presence outside national borders, but its primary market (50 percent or above) is domestic. This level of involvement necessitates a domestic sport market extension orientation, where domestic business is the priority, and the manner in which business is oriented at home will work anywhere in the world. If it works – great; if not – minimal effort will be made to make adjustments, or else the sport marketing mix of these products and services will be modified to entice purchases domestically.

International sport marketing, in addition to the definition discussed above, actively engages in marketing in the various markets. Those sport firms involved in international sport marketing will develop a multi-domestic sport market orientation. In this model, the sport marketing professional develops an individual sport marketing strategy and program for each country.

Global sport marketing takes the international distribution of products and services to more of a worldwide level. This global sport market orientation differs in that countries are usually grouped into marketing units based on similar economics, political environments, legal structures, or cultural compositions, and sport marketing strategies and plans are developed for each unit. This is done especially with sport organizations that are involved in a significant number of countries. For example, it would be almost impossible to manage 50 different marketing strategies and plans for a sport organization involved with that many countries. They instead might have ten plans that encompass five countries each.

Therefore the major difference between international and global is the scope and spread of the sport business. As a result the terms will be used concurrently throughout the remainder of this chapter.

The mission of international and global sport marketing

A mission for a sport marketing effort involves understanding the philosophy of the sport organization (its values and beliefs) and developing appropriate goals and objectives under which to operate. As we defined earlier (in Chapter 1), sport marketers segment, target, position, and deliver to the chosen market. Our decision factors regarding product, price, place, promotion, publicity, and people (the six Ps) are generally internally based and are able to be controlled. The difficulty in domestic sport marketing as generally discussed in this text comes from opportunities and threats within the environment. Those major opportunities and threats come as a result of competition, political and governmental policies, and the economy. International sport marketing is even more complicated because there are additional situations that directly affect the ability to effectively market the sport product or service. These situations are even more complex when a global sport marketing effort is undertaken.

Competition is greater due to the expansion of sport business operations. Political and governmental policies will differ because not all countries in the world are constitutionally based federal republics with democratic and capitalistic traditions like the United States. Economics will also differ owing to the numerous currencies around the world with variable values. The level of technology is not the same in all countries – while some are more technologically advanced than the United States, most are less so. This is also true of the ability to distribute sport products and services. Often this is as a result of the geographic terrain of a country, and the infrastructure present. Most of the understanding of these opportunities and threats stems from one key aspect that all international and global sport marketing professionals must understand – culture.

THE RELATIONSHIP BETWEEN CULTURE AND THE INTERNATIONAL/ GLOBAL SPORT MARKETPLACE

As defined earlier, culture is the principal attitudes, behaviors, values, beliefs, and customs that typify the functioning of a society. The difficulty for sport marketing professionals is that, when working in an international or global context, they must be able to comprehend how culture will affect the desires and outcomes of the sport marketing effort. To understand the international and global sport market, sport marketers must understand the principle of marketing relativism. This principle focuses on the realization that sport marketing efforts are usually based on strategies, values, and beliefs formulated from experience. The result is that sport marketing professionals develop their plans and outcomes based on their own past experiences and knowledge. When entering an international or global market, sport marketing professionals must often ignore a significant part of this relativistic thinking, and enter the marketplace with an open mind, willing to learn about and understand the culture they will be targeting.

So how do sport marketing professionals avoid making decisions based on their self-reference criteria? First, they must define the marketing goals in terms based on their own experiences. Next, the sport marketer must also define the marketing goals in terms of the culture of the place in which the effort will be applied. This requires a clear understanding of the cultural habits, norms, and values. Once the two definitions are made, the sport marketing professional must compare the two "lists" to gain an understanding of the similarities and differences between the two marketplaces. The sport marketer may be able to use past experiences to reach outcomes in the area of the similarities. On the other hand, the sport marketing professional will have to understand the differences, redefine the problem statement in terms of the cultural differences, and create a plan to accomplish the goals in consideration of the different culture.

316

In order to achieve success in accomplishing goals and reaching outcomes, the sport marketing professional must be able to work under three guiding principles. First, when working outside cultural norms, the sport marketing professional must be unbiased. This objectivity will allow the sport marketing professional to assess the opportunities within the international or global market. Second, the sport marketer must be open-minded. One of the most difficult concepts for humans is respect for individual differences. Sport marketing professionals must especially have tolerance for and acceptance of cultural differences if they wish to succeed. Third, sport marketers must be educated and well versed in the various markets they will be working with. In addition to understanding the history of the culture, sport marketing professionals engaged in international and global sport marketing must also be able to assess the international and global sport marketplace in terms of worldwide market opportunities, international and global economic conditions, and the variations in international and global business customs, politics, and the law.

Understanding and assessing cultures

Culture is a significant part of all human existence. As such, the sport marketing professional must understand all aspects of that culture when trying to communicate information to that culture. Culture is a philosophically based concept that directly relates to that culture's individual value and belief systems. These value and belief systems are often centered on religious beliefs, but often go much deeper into social tradition. The most basic of these is language. The ability to communicate appropriately with members of different cultures is central to the entire sport marketing effort. By communicating in their language, the sport marketer can get messages across more clearly, and it often shows the members of that culture that the sport organization has respect for their individual culture by making the effort to communicate with them in their language. Too often sport marketing professionals assume that the English language is universal. This is untrue. Understanding and using language appropriately allows sport marketers to show respect for the culture and the individuals within it.

In addition, understanding the history and social make-up of a culture is integral to success in sport marketing. Knowledge regarding the humanities and social sciences of a culture allows the sport marketing professional a deeper understanding of symbols, meanings, and practices within the culture. Awareness of the social make-up, including education, politics, legal issues, and social organization, allows the sport marketer an insight into how members of a population interact with each other. In addition, the technological and economic structures and abilities are instruments utilized to determine the extent of engagement in specific sport marketing efforts, and the likelihood of success or failure.

To gain knowledge about a culture, one must be very careful to understand the difference between factual knowledge and interpretive knowledge. Factual knowledge is information that can be easily researched through secondary resources – an example would be that the most popular sport in England is soccer, and that can be found through any number of websites, periodicals, and literature. Interpretive knowledge is the meaning of those facts with the society in mind. In the scenario described above, one cannot get a true flavor of the popularity of soccer, especially how fans live and die with their teams, without being immersed in the culture (primary research). This is why so many leagues, teams, and marketing organizations have offices across the globe – to place individuals in the culture to better understand how to communicate with them through sport marketing efforts. This immersion also serves to gain greater cultural sensitivity, as well as providing an opportunity to articulate that information to the domestic public with the goal of increasing cultural tolerance.

International and global sport business customs

Culture also serves as a framework for the business customs within that country. Therefore, the sport marketing professional must understand how culture affects sport business practices, attitudes, and motivation. An example of this was when Yao Ming was selected to become the #1 pick in the National Basketball Association draft in 2002 for the Houston Rockets. Usually, when a player is drafted, a team would be negotiating with the player's agent, the player, and potentially the parents. However, in China, it is done very differently. First, the Houston Rockets had to deal with an intermediary between them and China. That person was Erick Zhang, a distance cousin of Yao Ming, and two professors from the University of Chicago who had family ties. This is because personal relationships are very important in Chinese culture and business. In addition, negotiations not only took place between the agents and team, but the Houston Rockets also negotiated with the Shanghai Sharks (Yao Ming's team in China), the Chinese Basketball Association, the Chinese National Team, and the Chinese government (which asked for half his salary and endorsement contract money to be sent to them).

In general, there are four main concepts that a sport marketing professional must keep in mind when entering a foreign market. The first is the ability to adapt. Adaptation (the ability to make change or modification) may in some cases be imperative to maintain successful relationships. For example, in the scenario with Yao Ming, if at any time the Houston Rockets or the NBA created a situation where the Chinese "lost face," Yao Ming would not have been in the NBA because negotiations would have ended. At other times, adaptation may offer the option of involvement – if the action is not engaged in, it will not hurt the relationship; however, involvement may enhance the relationship. For example, if an American does not bow when meeting a Japanese businessperson, it will not hamper negotiations. However, if the American does bow, it is a sign of respect and goodwill, and will often go far to enhance negotiations. It is also important to remember that there are certain practices that are exclusive to a culture, and involvement may be unacceptable or a sign of disrespect. For example, it would be inappropriate and disrespectful to act like a Muslim by bowing and praying to Mecca if undertaken by an Arab businessman during negotiations.

Second, the sport marketing professional must realize the various methods of doing business in different countries. People in each country have different goals and objectives as related to the purpose of business. Some make decisions based on their own personal goals (Arab countries), while others make decisions that will offer them additional security or mobility (industrialized European Union countries such as England, France, and Italy). In Japan, personal life is business life, and the decisions made must often correlate with either business identity or social acceptance. In other countries, especially in South America, social and political power is directly related to any business decision.

318

It is also important to remember that concepts such as methods of communication, formality, time, gender biases, and speed of decisions will vary greatly from country to country. In addition, sport marketing professionals must understand business ethics in each country they deal with, as what is right in one country may be very wrong in another.

Third is the effect of politics on international and global sport marketing efforts. There are arguments that sports and politics should not mix. Whether that is true or not, business and politics have always had a relationship. In fact, the structure of the political environment in a country will have a direct effect on the success or failure of sport marketing efforts in that country. Issues including the stability of the government, the political parties and structure in power, and the relationship of nationalism to the sport marketing effort must be understood by sport marketing professionals prior to engaging in business with foreign lands.

Fourth are the legal issues affecting international and global sport marketing. International and global sport marketing can bring about conflicts of law as a result of the differences in law between the home country of the company and the place of business. There are four ways for determining what law should be applied:

1   *Center of gravity approach*: the law of the country that has the most significant relationship to a given situation has jurisdiction.
2   *Grouping of contacts approach*: the law of the country that is most concerned with the outcome of the case has jurisdiction.
3   *Lex Fori Theory (Law of the Forum)*: the law of the court in which a situation is brought has jurisdiction.
4   *Renvoi*: where a court utilizes its own laws, and has the option of adopting the center of gravity laws from another country.

Alternative dispute resolution in the international and global sport marketplace

As in the United States, many countries around the world utilize alternative dispute resolution, which is the collection of methods employed to hear disagreements and determine an appropriate ruling about a situation. Negotiations are utilized by two parties to resolve disputes or to complete transactions. If the two parties cannot agree, they bring in an independent person to hear both sides. The independent person is a mediator, and the process is called mediation. The mediator is neutral, and has no legal standing to make a decision on behalf of the facts. The mediator simply assists the parties in reaching a mutually agreeable solution. If the parties still cannot agree, the process moves to arbitration. This is where an arbitrator oversees a hearing to determine the facts of the situation. The arbitrator is authorized and given the power by all parties involved to make a decision that is final and binding.

Challenges to alternative dispute resolutions

Alternative dispute resolution takes on a challenging role in international and global sport marketing. The most basic of these challenges is the ability to communicate – both verbally and non-verbally. Language was alluded to earlier in the chapter. Research shows that

American culture, as well as Australian culture, lacks multiple language skills and prefers to conduct all business in English. This has a direct effect on alternative dispute resolution in two ways. First, there is room for misinterpretation. For example, if you were doing business on the Dutch island of Aruba and you suggested (in English) going out to lunch for sushi, an English-speaking person would think lunch was raw fish. However, a native of Aruba who may only speak Dutch or Papiamento (although most do also speak English and Spanish) would ask why you were going to eat garbage for lunch (sushi=garbage in Aruba). Second, during negotiations, people will often have side conversations in their native tongue to clarify points or explain a concept further. However, the message often comes across to the other party very differently. Some of the assumptions that are often made include "they are talking behind our back"; "they are plotting something"; "they are keeping something from us"; or "how disrespectful is that."

Communications issues are also non-verbal in nature. Depending on the culture, there are certain tactics that are used as a normal function of bargaining behavior. Silent periods of ten seconds or more are commonly used in Japanese and Russian cultures to think about what has been said, attempt to draw out additional information, and seek to control the room. Conversational overlap, or the number of times conversations are interrupted because of hand or facial gestures, is a tactic used by the Germans, French, and Spanish to control a conversation. These cultures are also adept at using facial glazing, which is extended time looking directly into the face of a speaker. In Latin and South American culture, touching during negotiations (pat of the hand, tap on the shoulder) is commonplace.

A more serious challenge regarding the effectiveness of alternative dispute resolution in both international and global sport marketing is the significant differences in values and beliefs. Concepts including competitiveness, equality, objectivity, and time vary widely from culture to culture. The American business culture tends to make decision based on facts, what will make the most money for the organization, and the notion that "business is business." However, in most countries around the world (with the exception of some European Union countries), these notions will not work. This is especially true with the concept of time, where in many cultures the time to complete negotiations is often slower, either because they have a "just make them wait" attitude (typical in Russian negotiations), or that time just tends to go slower because of the pace of life in those cultures (typical in Latin and South American cultures).

The most significant challenge to alternative dispute resolution in international and global sport marketing is the considerable difference in decision-making processes. We understand in American culture that each individual or group has a different thought process as a result of that individual's education, experiences, and environment. Now multiply that by thousands of different cultures around the world that sport marketing professionals might engage with as a result of their involvement in international and global sport marketing efforts. This is a challenge, and requires the sport marketing professional to take a holistic approach to negotiations. This approach includes being prepared to discuss multiple concepts simultaneously, and must often defer to an unorganized, disorderly process. This is as a result of negotiations not taking place in the step-by-step process to which Americans are usually accustomed.

There are a number of tell-tale signs that can help the sport marketing professional to recognize whether negotiations are progressing, and decisions are nearing their conclusion. In most foreign countries, as more high-level executives join in the conversations, a decision is closer to being reached. As a result, questions about the situation become more direct, whereas most questions at the beginning of negotiations tend to be broad and generic in nature. Another sign of success in negotiations is that attitudes become softer and more reasonable, and often result in the parties taking more time to study the issues at hand. A final sign that the decision-making process is nearing its conclusion is that the language used becomes less formal and more personal.

Succeeding in alternative dispute resolutions

To succeed in alternative dispute resolutions on the international and global stage takes a lot of preparation and patience. To start with, the sport organization must select the most appropriate individuals to be on the negotiating team. While this does include members of the sport marketing department, there is often a need to secure outside consultants experienced in negotiations with the specific country or region.

Once the team is selected, negotiation preliminaries must be addressed. From an internal sport organization standpoint, this includes assessing the situation and the individuals involved in the negotiation, reviewing the facts involved in the negotiation, and creating an agenda. In addition, the sport organization must consider alternative solutions and concessions willing to be made. From an external viewpoint, there are a number of aspects that must be agreed upon prior to the start of the negotiations. These include the location and physical arrangements, the number of individuals or groups to be involved, whether the meeting will be open to the public or closed door, the level of confidentiality required, and limitations on time per session.

Once all the rules have been put into place, the time has come to "sit at the table." One can think of the negotiation table like a football game – four quarters. The first quarter involves non-task sounding, where the first five to ten minutes are used to welcome the participants and briefly talk about topics other than the business at hand, including family, sports, news, and the economy. It is important to understand the background of the other parties involved in case certain topics would be inappropriate because of their culture. Also important is the time spent on non-task discussions, as the time Americans spend in this area domestically is considered too short as compared to most places around the world. In fact, in cultures ranging from Japan to Brazil, the time spent on non-task sounding is crucial to the overall success of the negotiations, and these cultures will not do business with a salesperson – they will want to do business with someone they know, feel comfortable with, and may even consider to be a friend at the end of the negotiation process.

The end of the first quarter, depending on the culture, could take a significant amount of time. From an American perspective, this may seem to be wasted time. However from an international and global perspective, it is often viewed as being time well spent. At an appropriate time that can only be judged being at the negotiation table, the second quarter would start with information exchange. This is the point where all the cards are laid out on the table. Information is provided by both parties and feedback exchanged. One thing to remember is that negative feedback is usually impossible to gauge during this process, as most cultures view this as being inappropriate during the initial stages of negotiation. Therefore, it is important for the sport marketing professional to view the material presented in a neutral manner, not make negative comments or connotations when not in agreement, and not to expect to get much information back.

At the two-minute warning (near the end of this segment of negotiation), a first offer is usually made. It is important to remember that the first offer made by an American negotiator tends to be pretty close to what he or she wants. In most international and global cultures, the first offer is usually significantly inflated to encourage longer periods of bargaining. Half-time comes with the initial offer being considered and tactics being modified and re-created.

The third quarter of the negotiation game is a true persuasion stage. Each side is seeking to gain some ground on issues, answer questions, clarify positions, and often argue over points. In American culture, we often seek to get objections out on the table, provide more information, and handle the situation. Often, when the negotiation does not go in the desired direction, frustration and anger often enter the equation. This may sometimes result in making threats and issuing ultimatums, and even sometimes leaving the table ("taking their ball and going home"). While these tactics may work domestically, internationally and globally is a different study. Many cultures will just let you walk out of the door and never open that door again. This is true in Japan and China, where threats and ultimatums may be viewed as creating a loss of face. In France and Germany, it will elicit an attitude of "typical Americans," and they will make the negotiations even more difficult. In other countries, the tactics may be viewed as being childish, taunting, or barbaric.

We finally reach the fourth quarter of the negotiation game – making concessions and coming to an agreement. Americans tend to make concessions during the negotiation process and expect reciprocation from the other party. However, in most international and global negotiations, concessions are not made until the persuasion process is complete. Again this is very frustrating, as it is a different manner of thinking to the American way of negotiating.

Probably the most important stage occurs once negotiations are finished and an agreement is reached. It is important to understand how the agreement will be viewed by the other culture. For example, American companies have no problem sending contracts through the mail for signature, or signing contracts behind closed doors. Other countries often require much "pomp and circumstance" with a formal signing ceremony including the highest level of authority from the organization (usually the CEO). Another difference is the way in which the contract is viewed. While in America a contract is a legal and binding agreement, in China it is viewed as a guideline for business operations, and is renegotiable at any time. In all cases, follow-up communications and the continued building of personal relationships will allow continued success in the sport marketing efforts agreed upon in the negotiation process.

INTERNATIONAL AND GLOBAL SPORT MARKET OPPORTUNITIES

Developing relationships with international and global sport markets serves as a foundation for entry into those markets. With the continued growth of international and global trade as a result of improvements in technology and transportation, sport organizations must create a vision for this involvement. This vision will differ depending on whether the sport organization wishes to enter an existing sport market, or try its hand at entering an emerging sport market.

322

CASE STUDY 14: NBA GOING GLOBAL: BASKETBALL WITHOUT BORDERS

Authored and contributed by Chiyoung Kim and Bob Heere, University of
Texas at Austin; and Matthew Walker, University of Southern Mississippi

INTRODUCTION

After David Stern became League Commissioner in 1984, he led the league to
unparalleled growth. During his tenure, the NBA added seven franchises, enjoyed a 15-
fold increase in league-wide revenues, launched both the Women's National Basketball
Association (WNBA) and the NBA development league, in addition to raising the
popularity of basketball through cutting-edge marketing and promotional campaigns.
Currently, NBA games are televised in 215 countries in 43 languages, and their own
network (i.e. NBA TV), is available in 73 countries around the globe. The league's website
attracts more than three million visitors each day, more than half of them from outside
the U.S. And yet, David Stern has many challenges to face.

After NBA superstar Michael Jordan retired, the domestic growth of the NBA slowed,
and its popularity in the U.S. market lagged behind that of other professional sports.
Moreover, the Harris Poll, a yearly barometer of American sport interests, found that
college football had moved ahead of the NBA as America's third favorite sport. In fact,
during the 1990s, TV ratings for both the NBA playoffs and finals were in double
digits, while so far this century the NBA finals have struggled to receive double-digit
ratings. Over recent years, many NBA teams have been caught in the recession,
making it difficult for them to complete their day-to-day operations. Some NBA
owners have lost millions, further enflamed by the recent negotiation issues between
the players' union and the owners, resulting in the shortened 2011 to 2012 NBA
season.

BACKGROUND TO THE NBA'S STRATEGY

Stern's strategy for the league rests on three pillars: (1) Take advantage of the emergence
of cable TV. Thus, he split the TV rights between public networks (ABC) and a cable
network (TNT). In addition, both ABC and ESPN are involved with NBA TV, which has
further extended the scope of NBA programming. (2) Maximize arena income through
a corporate focus. Under his reign, professional arenas were transformed from basic
facilities, oriented toward families and regular sport fans, to modern facilities focused
on corporations. These modern facilities are laden with luxury suites and corporate
seats, which allowed NBA teams to maximize arena-related income. As a case in point,
Forbes reports yearly on the most profitable stadiums in the U.S. (i.e. on a per-seat basis)
and lists basketball/hockey arenas in nine of the top ten spots. However, the majority
of revenue still originates from the seats. An average ticket for an LA Lakers game goes
for US$100. As such, arena revenue is still heavily dependent on ticket sales, and
(collectively) gate receipts and concessions account for more than 60 percent of the

overall annual revenue for an arena. Despite these increasing prices, attendance for NBA teams has remained stable at around approximately 17,000 spectators per game.

The first two pillars set the stage for the third pillar: (3) Selling the league to an international market. At the beginning of the 2011 to 2012 season, NBA teams featured 186 international players on their rosters. Irrespective of their multi-million-dollar international corporate contracts, this international push has been the best way for the NBA to strike it rich abroad. The importance of selling the league worldwide is likely best expressed in aggregate merchandise sales – the NBA was able to double its sales after the international push had taken root. In 2002, for example, the NBA sold US$1.8 billion in merchandise; in 2006, it sold US$3 billion. Most of this growth is driven by foreign sales. In 2010, it was estimated that 30 percent of all merchandise sales were overseas, with an annual growth rate of 10 percent.

FROM SPRINGFIELD TO SHANGHAI

Basketball has a long history in China. In the 1890s the first YMCA missionaries arrived in the city of Tianjin carrying "The Thirteen Rules of Basketball," along with their Bibles. These missionaries believed that salvation would come through the collective efforts of God and hoops (Larmer, 2005). More than a century later, another wave of Western preachers began to permeate the Chinese market with the different symbols of faith. The Nike swoosh, NBA logo, and highlight films of the "air man" Michael Jordan became new symbols for a changing Chinese society. When the NBA was first introduced to China, Nike was the official partner for the NBA teams' apparel and footwear (Dayal-Gulati & Lee, 2004). According to Nike, basketball was more effective than any other sport in attracting Nike's target Chinese consumer (i.e. the teenage, trend-setting, outgoing male). The Nike brand, coupled with the NBA's arrival in China, was a strong and powerful movement with enough inertia to drive Chinese masses to their televisions. Since that time, Nike has constructed a basketball complex in Shanghai where it sponsors three-on-three basketball tournaments, as well as several high school basketball programs.

Among the international players who partly comprise the NBA, it was Yao Ming, a 7-foot-6-inch (2.29m) center from Shanghai, who further ignited the Chinese passion for basketball. Larmer (2005) described the moment when Yao scored his first basket in Houston: "millions of his compatriots celebrated him as a patriotic icon who smashes the stereotype of the weak and diminutive Chinese and shows how China can compete against the best in the world" (p. 69). The world's largest multinational corporations (e.g. Pepsi, Reebok, Visa, and McDonald's) saw Yao's entry into the league as a tipping point for basketball globalization and seized the opportunity to offer multi-million-dollar endorsement contracts. Corporate executives fell over themselves for Yao because he was tall, talented, and had a winning (and quite likable) personality. Due to the "Yao effect," basketball surpassed football as the most popular sport in China, which contributed to around 300 million Chinese basketball enthusiasts. Recent data show that nearly 75 percent of Chinese males aged 15 to 24 identify themselves as NBA fans

(Janoff, 2005). Executive Vice-President and Managing Director of ESPN International, Russell Wolff, said that "having big stars is like an invitation to be interested in the NBA, and then it's a membership in the club. People say, 'I am going to be a Rockets fan because of Yao.' And then they get interested in other players." This sentiment is not too far from reality, as Chinese fans have expanded their view of the NBA by becoming interested in other players. For example, in 2006, shortly after the Yao effect took hold, the jerseys of Allen Iverson and Tracy McGrady were sold more often in China than Yao's. In 2008, Kobe Bryant was the No.1 selling jersey in China, and the Yao jersey was the tenth most popular. It appeared that the love of the Chinese fans for the NBA was more than just supporting their fellow countryman; they cared about the NBA in general.

Based on the emerging popularity, the NBA has explored the possibility of Chinese expansion. In 2008, the NBA created a new legal entity, the "NBA China." Since its inception, the new organization has attracted US$253 million of private investment through partnerships with such notable companies as Disney, Bank of China Group Investment, Legend Holdings Limited, Li Ka Shing Foundation, and China Merchants Investments (Lombardo, 2008). Recently, the NBA China announced its plan to build 12 basketball arenas throughout the country in partnership with the American Entertainment Group (AEG). The first facility was the 18,000-seat basketball arena Wukesong Indoor stadium in Beijing, used during the Olympics, which was exemplary to arenas that would be built in cities like Nanjing (6 million people), and Guangzhou (10 million people). A new arena in Shanghai (13 million people) was finished in 2010 and seats 18,000 people.

THE CURRENT STATE OF THE GLOBAL NBA BRAND

As the NBA is slowly becoming one of the largest and most popular sport entities in the world, expansion to China seems inevitable. NBA China has developed partnerships with global behemoths including McDonald's, Budweiser, Coca-Cola, Eastman Kodak Company, Reebok, and The Walt Disney Company. Although dealings with the Chinese government are deemed to be complicated, the enthusiasm of the Chinese consumer makes expansion to China impossible to pass up. The bottleneck resides with the possible creation of facilities which are able to generate revenue to American standards. If the Chinese basketball teams want to be competitive with the American franchises, their new arenas would have to generate approximately US$150 million a year, a number that few sport franchises outside the U.S. reach, including many European football teams.

David Stern knew that in the current economic recession he could not afford to make any mistakes internationally. The NBA could not afford to spend (and potentially lose) the same amount of money the NFL did with its expansion into Europe. The NBA was about to approach a tipping point in its international strategy, and a careful implementation of the marketing strategies, as well as the establishment of new "American-style" facilities would have to be thoroughly planned and operationalized.

International and global trade in sport business

As stated above, the continued development of digital, satellite, and internet technologies has been an integral part of the evolution of international and global trade. This, combined with the decrease of barriers to international and global trade, has resulted in many corporations beginning to develop an international and global marketing strategy. This has not been lost on the sport industry. The ability to transmit visual images related to sport has broadened the scope in which fans can view sport across the globe. This has also increased the ability to market products, services, and related peripherals around the world, with the eventual goal of generating the same demand as in the domestic market.

International and global sports used to be exclusively associated with the Olympics, international federations, and continental tournaments. Now, professional sports leagues from the United States and corporate involvement in sport on an international and global stage has evolved at an astronomical rate, especially due to the aforementioned development of technologies and reduction in trade barriers.

There are a number of reasons why sport firms, and indeed non-sport firms, have become involved in the international and global marketplace. One is that there has been an over-saturation of products and services in the American market. Much of this has been caused by the relationship of too much competition in comparison to the maximum level of discretionary income being spent by Americans on sport products and services. Therefore, many corporations have sought to extend their product and service distribution to an international and global audience. Sport marketing professionals must seek ways to understand those foreign markets, and communicate with those markets about the image and components of their sport products and services. Just as with traditional sport marketing domestically, the goal is to increase awareness and sales in the international and global market. The most common method utilized by sport businesses to expand the awareness, and hopefully resulting sales, in international and global markets is by sponsoring non-American athletes in their home countries, marketing popular American athletes on a global scale, and enhancing their sponsorships of prominent events such as the Olympics and World Championships.

Aside from sport corporations, professional sport organizations such as Major League Baseball (MLB) and the National Basketball Association (NBA) have sought to increase their popularity around the world. All three of these leagues have created international divisions to guide sport marketing efforts and manage offices overseas. The international and global sport marketing efforts have focused on the marketing of foreign athletes, broadcasting and multimedia efforts, licensing and merchandising, and the growth of sports through various grass-roots efforts. Table 14.1 shows how these leagues have expanded their offices in order to effectively market their leagues on an international and global basis.

Table 14.1 International offices of United States professional leagues

League	Offices in:
MLB International	Central Office in New York City Australia and Oceania Office in Sydney China Office in Beijing Japan Office in Tokyo Europe, Middle East and Africa Office in London
NBA Global	Central Office in New York; other offices in: ■ Beijing, China ■ Hong Kong, China ■ Istanbul, Turkey ■ Johannesburg, South Africa ■ London, England ■ Madrid, Spain ■ Mexico City, Mexico ■ Milan, Italy ■ Moscow, Russia ■ Seoul, South Korea ■ Shanghai, China ■ Taipei, Taiwan ■ Toronto, Canada

Additional examples that show the expansion of these international and global efforts, including other leagues such as the National Football League (NFL), National Hockey League (NHL), and MLS (Major League Soccer), are as follows:

■ Major League Baseball (MLB) is co-sponsor of the World Baseball Classic. The 2013 tournament will be played with 28 eligible teams. Non-automatic qualifiers (new teams and teams that did not win a game in the 2009 tournament) will play for a place in the tournament in November 2012 in Taiwan. Then, the remaining 16 teams will play games in multiple locations around the globe (in 2009, they were played in the United States, Puerto Rico, and Japan) during February 2013. Teams represent all six continents where baseball is played (not Antarctica).
■ The National Basketball Association (NBA) has regularly sent teams to play in Europe since 1988. These teams have also played exhibition games in Russia, China, and Japan.
■ NBA.com has separate websites for Africa, Brazil, China, France, Germany, Greece, India, Italy, Japan, Korea, the Philippines, and Spain. In addition, it has NBA.com Español for Spanish-speaking countries.
■ The National Football League, in addition to having a pre-season game outside the United States every year since 1986, had its first regular season game outside the United States

in 2005 (Arizona Cardinals vs. San Francisco 49ers in Mexico City). The League now plays one regular season game each year at Wembley Stadium in London, and is even considering a Super Bowl in London in the future.

■ International and global grass-roots efforts focused on increasing participation and educating people about the specifics of the individual sport are offered by MLB (Pitch, Hit, and Run; Let's Play Ball!; Envoy Program; Equipment Donation Program; MLB International Academy Program); and the NBA (Basketball without Borders).

Creating a vision for the international and global sport marketplace

The concept of developing a vision for the international and global marketplace is a significantly more difficult task as the scope of the vision is greater because of the expansiveness of the research needed to be undertaken. In domestic sport marketing, the scope usually focuses on developing a marketing plan that addresses the elements of the sport marketing mix – product, price, place, promotion, publicity, and people. In international and global sport marketing, the research necessary for establishing an appropriate vision also includes collecting information about the country, the region, and the foreign market. In addition, the sport marketing researcher must have a grasp of the trends apparent in the overseas marketplace, and how to forecast the needs of that marketplace in terms of sport consumers, potential economic growth, sport industry trends, the political and sociological climates, and growth opportunities in technology.

While many of the same domestic sport marketing research tactics are utilized in completing international and global sport marketing research, one of the unique challenges involves multicultural research. Multicultural research is dealing with international or global sport markets that have different attitudes and beliefs, economic and social structures, and language. There is a challenge, as a result of these differences, in being able to compare data across cultures, and therefore it is difficult to find correlations between results. It is also difficult to guarantee reliability and validity in the research, as the research design of surveys and questionnaires will vary from culture to culture. For example, the Japanese culture usually does not respond to mail surveys – they will usually need to be distributed from a known source and face to face.

INTERNATIONAL AND GLOBAL SPORT MARKETING STRATEGIES

Throughout this chapter, the concept of international sport marketing and global sport marketing has gone hand-in-hand. However, when it comes to developing sport marketing strategies, the definitions become somewhat differentiated. International sport marketing strategy, also sometimes called multinational sport marketing strategy, focuses on cross-cultural differences, and the fact that each individual culture requires a separate sport marketing strategy adapted to that particular culture. In contrast, global sport marketing strategy views the world as one big market, and the sport marketing strategy seeks to define and target similarities between various cultures around the world. The eventual goal is to create a diversified marketing strategy that will allow the sport organization to compete in any market in the world.

328

An international sport marketing strategy is a direct approach of sport marketing, where the plan is individualized for the specific sport market. The global sport marketing strategy is more of an indirect approach, where a sport marketing strategy that has worked in one country may be used and slightly modified in another owing to similarities in culture and perceived product and service benefits. This ability to transfer experience from one culture to another allows sport organizations to enter new markets in a faster and more efficient manner. It also makes it easier to coordinate and control strategic operations. In addition, the economies of scale, especially in the area of advertising, are a great benefit. For example, by only having to create a few television commercials that can be used globally and targeted to similar markets, it becomes significantly less expensive as compared to developing dozens of individual television commercials for each country. By determining common themes among various countries' value sets, generic television commercials can be developed and only voice overlay would have to be added for the specific language of a country. As a result, a sport organization can also more easily control its global image. This is especially important in new and emerging markets, where reputational value carries a significant amount of weight owing to the lack of personal experience and contact with the products and services of the sport organizations.

CONCLUSION

There are similarities and differences between sport marketing efforts in domestic sport business as compared to international sport business and global sport business. As a result of the disparity between cultures in the international and global sport marketplace, the sport marketing professional must be well versed in being able to assess these cultures. One of the common misconceptions is that as long as someone can speak the language, business can be conducted. This chapter shows that it is much deeper – including differences in verbal and non-verbal communication, history and social issues, and business customs. This requires the sport marketing professional to be able to adapt to various situations, appreciate different value and belief systems, be able to understand many different methods of doing business, and to be aware of political and legal dynamics entangled throughout the international and global sport marketing processes. These situations will often be discussed through various methods of alternative dispute resolution – most often negotiations, but also potentially including mediation and arbitration.

There are numerous opportunities in the international and global sport market. Many professional leagues and sport businesses have already taken advantage of entering foreign markets, and have also created visions of entering emerging markets. All of these plans are centered on the strategic sport marketing process. Strategic sport marketing planning is utilized in matching the sport organization to a specific country or region. This is orchestrated by adapting the sport marketing mix to the specific target markets, developing a targeted sport marketing plan, and arranging for the best methods for implementing and controlling that plan. This is especially important in the areas of product and services management, channel and logistics management, integrated communications systems, and financial management. These concepts and more will be discussed in more detail in the next and final chapter. All the concepts from this book will be tied together from a domestic, international, and global perspective, and will explain how to develop, implement, manage, and evaluate all aspects of strategic sport marketing plans to the advantage of a sport organization regardless of location or environment.

FROM THEORY TO PRACTICE

MICHAEL JOHNSTONE, MARKETING MANAGER
National Rugby League,
Sydney, New South Wales, Australia

The high point of my sports marketing career to date has been my involvement with the National Rugby League (NRL) All Stars. A team of indigenous players are chosen by public vote to form the Indigenous All Stars, and then one non-indigenous player from each of the 16 NRL teams is chosen by the public to form the NRL All Stars. All money raised from the game is distributed back to the 16 NRL Clubs to run programs benefiting the indigenous community. My role is to ensure that as many tickets as possible are sold through marketing programs targeting rugby league fans throughout New South Wales and Queensland. All three games played so far have sold to 99 percent capacity.

The first All Stars game was played on February 13, 2009, the first anniversary of the Australian government's "apology" to indigenous Australians. In three years the All Stars week has become so much more than a game of football. It is now a week of community activities, a celebration of Australia's indigenous culture, and has become a flagship event for indigenous Australians. The depth of feeling shown by the many indigenous supporters and players during the week truly is something in which I am so proud to be involved. In the words of Smiley Johnstone (Chairperson of the Australian Rugby League Indigenous Council), "there is no greater example of reconciliation in action." It is fair to say that this is not something I had envisaged being involved in when I started my sports marketing career.

Working in sport not only provides the thrills of being closely involved in huge sporting events, the personal satisfaction of selling record numbers of tickets, or memberships, but it has allowed me to make a real contribution to the welfare of the entire community.

The number one objective of my role as Marketing Manager of the National Rugby League is quite simple: help the 16 NRL clubs to increase their game day attendances by providing marketing support.

Quite soon after starting this role it became apparent that one of the most effective ways to support clubs was to provide marketing support to their membership (season ticket) programs. We moved quickly to appoint a full-time Membership Manager to work with the clubs on their membership programs. The results since 2007 have been very encouraging, with game-wide membership increasing from 60,000 to 200,000 between 2007 and 2012. Average game-wide attendances have also grown by 5 percent since 2007.

The NRL Marketing Manager's role also encompasses the promotion and advertising of Representative games – State of Origin in Sydney and Melbourne, Test Matches played in Australia, the All Stars game, and Finals series matches including the Grand Final.

Like many who end up in the world of sports administration I grew up participating in a number of leisure activities, particularly the sports of rugby league, rugby union, and cricket. Being raised in New Zealand was the perfect environment to develop a passion for sport with access to great recreational facilities and attending schools that encouraged participation in swimming, athletics, cross-country, and winter and summer sports.

By the time I got to university, and it had become obvious I was not going to have a career playing sport, my long-term ambition was to become a professional sports administrator. I had no idea how to get there, however. At my university (University of Canterbury) there were no sports marketing or administration courses. My rough plan was to get a university education, then find a "real" job that would give me enough experience to one day get a job in sports. At the University of Canterbury I took a wide range of courses before settling into Bachelor's degrees in law and business administration majoring in marketing.

Fortunately my career in sports marketing started much sooner than I had thought possible. A couple of years after graduating, I landed my first role. Eighteen months earlier I had read in the local newspaper that NZ Cricket were restructuring its marketing department, so I wrote a letter to the Marketing Manager of NZ Cricket, Neil Maxwell, and said that "I would be perfect for a new role, should one come up, and despite having degrees in marketing and law I would be very happy to work from the bottom, 'sweeping floors' if that is what it took."

Fortunately, when NZ Cricket did indeed decide to hire a new Marketing Assistant, Neil Maxwell had kept the letter on file and made contact to see if I was interested in interviewing for the role. After I had taken the job I asked Neil why he had got in touch with me, and I remember him saying that he was impressed with my willingness to start from the bottom and work my way up.

The things that I believe have contributed most to the development of my career so far are:

- reading as widely as possible so that I could continue to learn about new marketing techniques and keep evolving my skill base
- attending conferences and meeting other sports marketers to share ideas and experiences
- attending as many sporting and cultural events as possible to see what people love about those events and how they have been promoted
- striving to understand the big picture about sports organizations' revenue streams so that I have been able to prioritize my efforts accordingly
- taking time to understand market research techniques so that I have been able to use research to understand what is important for consumers and how consumers make their decisions
- tracking and staying within budget.

While Australian marketers have been able to learn so much about sports marketing by looking at U.S. sports organizations, there are some salient differences in our marketplace.

From my understanding of U.S. sports organizations the major differences are:

- Australian sports organizations are relatively under-resourced with personnel. This means that the sports marketer must have a wide range of skills and knowledge, including sponsorship sales and account management, membership (season ticket) sales and operations, database management, event management, and game day ticket sales promotion.
- Australian markets are very crowded. For instance, within two hours' drive of Sydney (population: 4 million), there are ten NRL teams, two AFL teams, one Super Rugby team, three A-League (soccer) teams, two NBL (basketball) teams and a Women's netball team all competing for the sports consumer's dollar. Sports entertainment also competes with the amazing natural beauty and great climate of Australia, where it is not uncommon in the middle of winter for fans to choose to go to the beach rather than attend a home game.
- Generally, ticket sales are generated through a mixture of PR, social media and advertising. Outbound call centers selling tickets have not been used extensively in the Australian market, although increasingly teams are using outbound telemarketing to sell memberships (season tickets).
- Social media and the emergence of Pay TV in Australia over the past 15 years have radically changed the way Australians consume sport. While there is a market and thirst for fans to watch more sport, Australia's small population of 20 million makes it difficult to convert that high level of interest into revenue.

One thing our markets do have in common has been the emergence of social media channels as a communication and sales tool. Because of the interest and passion for sports brands, database development has been reasonably simple and inexpensive. Social media have also enabled fan groups to communicate easily with each other and with sports organizations, which is leading to a much closer relationship between the organization and fans.

Sport marketing was always the dream career – I am now living the dream. The hours are crazy but I feel blessed having such a fulfilling career.

CHAPTER FIFTEEN

EMERGING SOCIOLOGICAL SPORT MARKETING CONCEPTS

CHAPTER OUTLINE

- Introduction
- Relationship and experience sport marketing
- Recovery sport marketing
- Social sport marketing
- Conclusion

CHAPTER OBJECTIVES

The reader will be able to:

- evaluate the role of relationship and experience sport marketing as applied in the sport industry
- assess the importance of recovery sport marketing during and after a negative situation, and how to recapture a market
- interpret the role social sport marketing plays in expanding the role of sport businesses beyond profit-making operations to include offering intangible social benefits.

INTRODUCTION

Sociology is the study of the origin, evolution, organization, and functioning of people and societies. More specifically, it looks at the social behavior of individuals, groups, organizations, institutions, communities, and the overall society. Sport sociology looks specifically at the relationship of sport and society and how it influences behavior. This has a direct relationship to sport marketing as we analyze the behaviors of our consumers to develop products and services that meet their needs and wants. As such, in order to advance the body of knowledge in sport marketing, we must look to the evolution of sport sociology concepts and how they will directly influence sport marketing efforts. While it would be impossible to analyze all sociological concepts that have a direct effect on sport marketing, there are a few that seem to be integral to successful sport marketing over the next decade. They include relationship and experience sport marketing, recovery sport marketing, and social sport marketing.

RELATIONSHIP AND EXPERIENCE SPORT MARKETING

Relationship marketing is a concept that extends the marketing communication process beyond basic advertising and sales promotional techniques to building long-term value with customers through continued interactions. The importance of creating these ongoing relationships is the foundation of consumer retention plans and increasing the number of repeat customers, as well as the basis for customer satisfaction analysis. The concept of relationship marketing started with the concepts of creating quality customer service and building good face-to-face relationships with customers. As society has evolved from just being a product-based society to a service-based economy, combined with the evolution of internet and mobile electronic platforms, relationship marketing has evolved into becoming more collaborative through social networking and communication channels. Much of relationship marketing started with mainly outbound efforts that focused on market research demographic and customer service data. Relationship marketing now includes inbound data obtained through public relations, social media, and other internet communication platforms. Another result of these marketing efforts is the evolution of customer experience marketing. This allows consumers to engage and interact with the brand, products, and services through personal interactions. In a way, this is an extension of the concept of endorsements discussed in Chapter 12 on sponsorship, where an endorser (such as an athlete or media star) talks about his or her personal experience with a product to help entice consumers to buy the product. Through experience marketing, sport organizations seek to drive sales, increase brand awareness, and improve brand image by encouraging their customers to describe the features of the product through their personal experiences with it.

Both sport consumer relationship marketing and consumer experience marketing are integral sport marketing tools in the twenty-first century. Understanding the historical foundations and current applications of each will provide the sport marketer with an advantage when trying to reach customers in this evolving marketplace when information is disseminated from multiple platforms and utilized in multiple ways.

Sport consumer relationship marketing

As the growth of internet technologies continues, as well as the need for advanced customer services, sport marketing has entered the twenty-first century through the use of sport consumer relationship marketing (SCRM). SCRM is the use of various methodologies, information technologies, and internet capabilities that help sport entities organize and manage sport consumer relationships. The goal of SCRM is to develop a system that all members of the sport marketing effort (management, sport marketers, salespeople, service providers, and consumers themselves) can utilize to access information about sport products and strive toward meeting the needs and wants of sport consumers.

The objectives of SCRM include the following:

- Helping a sport entity enable sport marketing professionals to identify and target their best customers, manage sport marketing campaigns with clear goals and objectives, and generate sales.
- Assisting the sport entity to improve telesales, consumer account management, and sales management by optimizing information shared by multiple employees, and making existing information-sharing processes more efficient and effective. An example of this would be taking orders via the internet or through mobile devices.
- Allowing the formation of individualized relationships with sport consumers. By identifying the most profitable sport consumers and providing them with the highest level of service, sport entities will improve sport consumer satisfaction. The result of this will be the optimization of profits.
- Providing sport marketers with the information and processes necessary to know the sport entity's customers, understand their needs, and effectively build relationships between the sport organization, its customer base, and distribution partners.

The Nashville Predators (NHL) and the San Diego Padres (MLB) were two of the first sport organizations to extensively utilize sport consumer relationship management as a cornerstone of their sport marketing effort for the future. Now, dozens of sports teams in Major League Baseball (MLB), the National Basketball Association (NBA), the National Football League (NFL), the National Hockey League (NHL), and minor league hockey and baseball teams have followed suit.

The Nashville Predators initiated a customer relationship management technology provided by AIM Technologies to collect information about the demographics and psychographics of its fans. The Predators use that information and in turn run a fan-loyalty reward card program. They use this program to market to their fans by enticing them to attend more events. This in turn increases secondary revenue from sales of merchandise and concessions. The Predators also use the information about their fans to attract advertisers and other sponsors. In addition, by tracking the number of times fans are attending, sport marketing professionals can get a better idea of where their fans are on the "escalator," and can target market to fans based on their level by understanding which fans will more likely buy season or ticket packages in advance.

The San Diego Padres had similar success with EDCS's Top Prospect system. Their program, called the Compadre Club, provide fans with a membership card that may be used at kiosks around the stadium, as well as when purchasing tickets, merchandise, and concessions. It has been described as a "frequent flyer program" for the baseball fan. The more fans use their cards, the more points they get and the more benefits they will receive. They also marketed promotions and other specials through the card. The overriding goal is to get these fans to attend at least one more game per year. To put that in perspective, if a team had 150,000 card members who attended just one more game per year at $20 per ticket, there would be additional revenue in the amount of $3 million for the organization!

Fast forwarding to the current marketplace, customer relationship marketing or management programs (commonly referred to as CRMs) are embedded in practically every type of marketing software being used by sport teams, leagues, and companies. The goal is to provide sport marketing managers with a complete view of the sport business, ranging from sales to buyer history to internal reports to how staff are interacting with customers. In fact, many CRM programs are now directly connected to prospecting databases to expand and enhance sales efforts. One company, Glitner Ticketing (www.glitner.com), services many minor league franchises in the United States. Through its CRM program, built into the overall ticketing system, it can:

- track attendance on an event-by-event basis and target those who attended to gather their feedback or inform about future events
- integrate with the prospecting system to track renewals, help manage calling campaigns, and organize work flow based on real data
- manage internal data based on the types of customers – for example, full season, partial season, special event, group sales, etc.
- coordinate with marketing campaigns (email, social media, snail mail, etc.) to promote future events
- work in coordination with all other aspects of the internal reports system of the organization including ticketing, sales and marketing, scheduling, concessions, contracts and legal, accounting, and much more.

CASE STUDY 15: NEW WORLD TRANSACTIONS, TECHNOLOGY, AND THE HISTORY OF CUSTOMER RELATIONSHIP MANAGEMENT

Ticket sales are still a key indicator of a club's popularity despite the fact that they represent a declining share of total revenue for many clubs in the top European football leagues and major league sports in North America. Sponsors and TV companies buy into teams and sports that can sell out stadiums and arenas, while secondary event day income from merchandise and food and beverage relies on a ticket first being sold to the fan inside the venue. However, while the value of media rights and sponsorship packages appears to have peaked, many teams are suffering from a decline in live audiences.

The market for ticket sales benefited from the scheduling of two global events in 2006, when the Torino 2006 Organizing Committee expected one million spectators to be watching 63 different competitions during the Olympic Winter Games in February, and FIFA managed the distribution of seven million tickets for the 64 matches of the 2006 World Cup in Germany. Both organizations relied on electronic ticketing systems to automate the process of distributing massive volumes of tickets – of different types and for multiple events – to customers who use different languages and currency.

NEW WORLD TRANSACTIONS

Methods of purchasing tickets have evolved from the simple cash payment at the turnstile or box office. The first development was telephone sales, which is still a popular method of booking a ticket having been enhanced by Interactive Voice Response (IVR) and call centers. However, the internet has quickly become the most popular sales and distribution channel for many events. The development of new hardware and software has enabled the introduction of seamless integration with box offices, call centers, and fulfillment houses. This technology has subsequently evolved into other forms of electronic ticketing, such as kiosks, countertop units, and even personalized applications on computers and Smartphones.

More venue operators are now using the additional functionality and reduced costs of ticketing software to enhance traditional paper-based systems, while some clubs and franchises have taken the opportunity to install new information systems when they have either relocated, rebuilt, or refurbished their stadium. In 2004, English Premier League club Fulham decided to install Venue Solutions' VenueCast system at its Craven Cottage football stadium when it returned to its venue. The club used the relocation as an opportunity to integrate its ticketing function with its business operations system. Matthew McGrory, head of IT at Fulham FC, says: "The applications have enabled us to operate our business more effectively saving both time and enhancing our internal business processes."

Venue operators have been able to use e-ticketing to reduce box office operating costs and offer a better quality of service to customers. Fans can select their preferred seat, ticket type, and payment choice at a time and place that is convenient for their lifestyle. Box offices are limited by manpower and the number of customer points, such as box office windows or telephone lines, whereas ticketing systems are able to cope with peak demand and process transactions much quicker. This now means that some events can literally sell out in minutes.

Numerous companies have further developed electronic ticketing by creating a product that integrates with venue and business management systems. Dominic Berger, Managing Director of Venue Solutions, believes that ticketing data are essential to sports organizations for business planning: "Trends can be identified, ROI on marketing campaigns can be analyzed and new programs can be developed. By cross-referencing across multiple information sources, this adds value across all business departments."

FULFILLMENT AND ACCESS CONTROL

Technology has revolutionized the channels via which consumers can purchase tickets as well as the ways in which transactions can be fulfilled and how sports fans enter a venue.

The traditional paper ticket is still a popular and versatile medium and has benefited from enhancements such as special inks and barcodes. This has not only improved venue safety and security by reducing opportunities for counterfeit tickets and providing more efficient access control, but it has also enhanced customer service.

Some venues have introduced kiosks to supplement the box office. The kiosks are able to read credit or debit cards and instantly print tickets, thereby reducing queues at box office windows. They are particularly suited for ticket collections from the box office and also generate incremental sales from walk-ups and by reducing walk-aways. Major League Baseball's Atlanta Braves were one of the first organizations to introduce kiosks and can process 2,000 tickets per game from the units located at their Turner Field stadium. Kiosk technology has further evolved and can now be integrated with a turnstile so that customers no longer have to queue separately to first purchase a ticket only to then queue again to access the venue.

Barcodes have also enabled print-at-home ticketing and have been applied to media such as smart cards and mobile phones. More sports fans are now printing their own tickets and Ticketmaster reports that more than 50 percent of tickets for NFL Seattle Seahawks games are printed by fans using its ticketFast service.

But it is arguably the introduction of smart cards that has revolutionized ticketing more than any other medium. These cards are personalized using a barcode, magnetic strip, or chip to record data about a customer and his or her transactional history, and to allow access to a stadium or arena. Cards are now being introduced by a number of sports clubs and franchises for season tickets, membership schemes, and VIP areas.

Philips and Sony championed the development of contactless smart cards that do not have to be swiped in a reader. These cards can be produced in a variety of sizes or shapes and the technology has even been integrated into watches, key fobs, and mobile phones in order to provide a virtually a cashless environment with smart cards being used by fans as electronic cash to purchase merchandise or food and beverages from concessions.

In August 2005, Roda JC and Philips commenced a trial in which 50 season ticket holders were supplied with a Nokia mobile phone that also acts as a ticket and e-cash device. Fans are able to check their balance on the phone's screen and can top-up their account by holding the handset to a credit-loading terminal. That trial showed how well mobile ticketing would be accepted and what challenges were to be faced as a result of full-scale implementation. The initial feedback from fans was very positive, and it led to it being possible to add the functionality that enabled customers to use the phone to purchase tickets and pay for credits, and has evolved into Smartphones becoming one of the most common mediums for ticketing by providing the capability to integrate ticket booking, payment, fulfillment, and access control.

CUSTOMER RELATIONSHIP MANAGEMENT

Electronic ticketing has enabled venue operators to capture more data about their customers and, through the use of customer relationship management (CRM), has allowed them to foster more sophisticated marketing relationships with fans. This has become increasingly important as sport faces more intense competition from other leisure and entertainment brands. A number of sports organizations have used CRM systems to analyze data about each fan and then adapt their communications, products, and services to each individual's preferences.

With an effective CRM system, every transaction a customer completes is recorded wherever possible. In the case of sports venues, this may include purchases at concessions and retail outlets as well as tickets, membership schemes, or other affiliated products and services. The venue can then profile customers by the recency, frequency, and value of their transaction history, and also segment the database using geo-demographics metrics such as age, gender, family status, and income.

CRM facilitates the production of targeted and personalized marketing communication and the opportunity to up-sell and cross-sell. For example, an organization may target fans who have attended more than 75 percent of matches with a promotion for season tickets or perhaps an offer of an inclusive travel, accommodation, and ticket package to occasional visitors who live more than 100 miles from the venue. By profiling the data contained within the CRM database, it is possible to implement marketing campaigns targeting the acquisition of new fans and the retention of existing customers.

Although many professional sports clubs and franchises now have access to CRM tools, even years into integration there are still some doubts about whether the associated technology has generated a positive ROI. Some venues have experienced difficulties in procuring an appropriate system. The CRM market is complex with a range of options on offer, including off-the-shelf, customizable, and modular systems, plus the option for systems to be developed in-house or outsourced. Managers have reported problems with implementation, which may be attributable to an overcomplicated user interface or inadequate staff training.

The capture of quality of data is paramount, since CRM can only be as good as the information that is recorded. Sports organizations may have to commit more time and resources to data management because so many transactions at sports venues are completed in a hurry.

INTEGRATION

Venue operators may also not be extracting maximum value from CRM but instead treating their customer records as a homogeneous database. Matthew McGrory of Fulham FC highlights the benefits of targeted and personalized communication: "We now have information on our fans and corporate clients in a central system which enables us to more effectively communicate with our customers and increase our revenue." It is therefore essential that CRM coordinates with all customer "touch points" and not just the ticketing and box office function. This includes websites, direct and email communication, mobile phone services, food and beverage concessions, retail, media, and membership schemes.

Suppliers of CRM systems are now integrating systems with other management functions, including marketing, operations, finance, digital signage, CCTV, access, and temperature control as well as general management systems to improve business efficiency.

Ticketing and CRM systems will continue to be used for the sale and distribution of millions of tickets for mega events such as the Winter Olympic Games and FIFA World Cup Finals, but have also been successfully adopted by clubs and franchises of all sizes to acquire and retain customers.

With some professional sports suffering from declining attendances as well as a stagnating market for media and sponsorship rights, it seems likely that the effective application of CRM will become increasingly important for those venues seeking to generate sustainable revenue streams.

Source: Modified from Stevens, A. (2006). Standing out for the crowd. Reprinted with permission by *SportBusiness International*.

Questions for discsussion

1   Based on your understanding of customer relationship management and integration from this case study and the chapter, as well as the evolution of CRM technology over the past decade, outline how you would go about designing and integrating a CRM program for a minor league baseball team in a large city where there is competition from professional sport organizations. Include in your outline a discussion of the reason you selected specific elements of the plan, the timeline for implementation, and your strategy for managing and evaluating the plan.
2   How would you integrate your CRM plan with a customer experience management plan? Discuss how the two plans can work together to maximize the experience of the sport consumer.

More than just relationships: offering sport consumer experiences

Sport consumer relationship marketing is often not enough to entice the sport consumer to purchase the sport product. No longer is the sport event just a game. Depending on the event or the sport, it may be viewed as either an entertainment spectacle or an integral part of a lifestyle. Traditional sports such as baseball, basketball, and football have been looking for ways to continue to attract fans to events, but offer them a little more to enhance the value placed on the price paid for the ticket. Alternative sports such as skateboarding, snowboarding, and BMX racing have gone down a different avenue. They want to be more than just an activity or event; they want to be an integral part of the lifestyle and culture of the consumer.

"Traditional" sports: more bang for the buck

As stated above, the sport consumer wants more, especially as related to the sport event. In general, Americans have less discretionary time. Therefore, they want to maximize their participation opportunities while minimizing the money and time necessary for participation. To address this need, sport enterprises are doing exactly that – offering event amenities to attract the sport consumer through the door.

340

Event amenities go beyond just the typical event promotions and giveaways – they expand the experience beyond the core sport event. At many sporting events today, there are pre-game and post-game events such as musical entertainment, live spots by radio and television broadcasters, interactive events such as climbing walls and video games, and autograph signings by former players, current players, cheerleaders, and mascots.

These mini-fan festivals are a product of the larger interactive fan festivals that have developed since the early 1990s. At this time, professional sport leagues in the United States recognized that maintaining and strengthening their fan bases would require innovative tactics that focused primarily on creating experiences and building relationships with fans rather than generating short-term revenues. As a result, leagues started a marketing trend with the development of interactive fan "festivals" which they produced at existing premier competitions such as all-star games and championships. These interactive fan festivals included various forms of entertainment, food, and sport attractions that gave fans of all ages the opportunity to participate, interact, and experience the sport product first hand. Table 15.1 lists the current interactive fan festivals in professional and amateur sport.

Table 15.1 Interactive fan festivals in United States professional and amateur sports

League	Name of fan fest	Year	Event
Major League Baseball	All-Star Fan Fest	1991	All Star Game
National Football League	NFL Experience	1992	Super Bowl
National Basketball Association	NBA Jam Session	1993	All-Star Weekend
NASCAR	NASCAR World	1994	Brickyard 400
National Hockey League	NHL FANtasy	1996	All-Star Weekend
Major League Soccer	Soccer Celebration	1996	All-Star Game
National Association of Basketball Coaches	Fan Jam	1993	Men's Final Four
NCAA	Hoops City	1997	Men's and Women's Final Four

As we enter the twenty-first century, the advanced use of technology to market and enhance the sport event experience has arrived. Systems that integrate emerging Wi-Fi and on-demand technologies with the internet are becoming the norm. Fans attending a sport event can tap into a wireless network from anywhere in the stadium using a handheld device that, among other things, will allow them to view on-demand instant replays from various cameras; access real-time analytical and graphic player, team, and game statistics; order food and merchandise; learn from interactive rulebooks and playbooks; play interactive games with and against other users; send email and graphic e-postcards; bid on in-stadium auction items; check traffic for the drive home; and make reservations at nearby restaurants.

In a competitive industry where fans have a vast number of entertainment choices, sport properties are discovering the need to create special marketing programs that reach beyond the playing field. If special efforts are made to bring the sport and its stars directly to fans, sport properties have greater opportunities to develop the relationships and positive associations required for long-term growth. This growth shows the need for sport marketing professions to

341

move beyond sport consumer relationships (SCRMs) to capture the sport consumer. Consumers want more for their money, and are looking for multiple experiences. Embracing the concept of sport consumer experiences will allow the sport marketing professional the means to meet the needs and wants of the twenty-first-century sport consumer.

"Alternative" sports: lifestyle marketing and the resulting cultural impact

Alternative sports is more than just competitions, challenges, and races – it is a lifestyle that millions of participants have embraced. Alternative sport participants do more than just participate in the sport; they live it. These sports are an extension of their lives, rather than just a way to take part in physical activity.

Especially with the youth subcultures, there are signs and styles that are easily interpretable. Subcultural style indicates which group the individual belongs to, and distinguishes that group from the mainstream. This concept is the foundation for much of the work in sport consumer research and subcultures.

"Culture" and "lifestyle" are ways to describe the alternative sport scene. It is not only the activity or sport in which an individual participates; it is the entire culture. As an example, if you are a skateboarder, being a part of that culture means that you not only skate; it also means you look like a skater, dress like a skater, and participate in the culture of a skater. This concept has been documented in the movie *Dogtown and the Z-Boys*.

Previous consumer research about sport subcultures has focused on shared ethos, boundary maintenance, and hierarchical structure based on members' demonstrated commitment. Shared ethos or the shared cultural meanings of the group help to define the subculture. Shared ethos for participants of alternative sports would be individualism, rebellion, and anti-establishment. Boundary maintenance is the way members consume market goods to demonstrate acceptable behaviors to the group. Examples of market goods for alternative sports would include specific brands of skateboards, snowboards, clothing, and music.

The hierarchical structure refers to an order based on a set of criteria set by the subculture. The hierarchical structure for alternative sports would be driven by the top national stars in the various sports, the first and most notable being Tony Hawk in the 1990s and early 2000s. The next group in the hierarchical structure would be the local and regional stars from the sport. The final group in the structure would be the local "stars" from the skate park, snow park, or beach. These individuals are the ones who are reading the most current magazines, visiting the most "cool" websites, wearing the "in" clothing, and listening to the newest bands.

Boundary maintenance and the purchase of goods are what drive the commercial aspect of alternative sports. Youth, the target segment of these companies, are becoming more sophisticated in their purchase decisions. Kids seek inherent truth in products. If brand communications lie, and the product fails to do what is said it will do, the product will be rejected. The purchasing power of the youth market can be very powerful. Numerous studies show that 60 percent of parents state their children have some say in the purchase of food, clothes, leisure, and gifts. In addition, over 80 percent of teens control what they wear and what they do in their leisure time.

Understanding this unique sport market is critical to success. This has resulted in a direct relationship between culture and alternative sports. In the movie *Dogtown and the Z Boys*, a

342

documentary that took a hard look at how surfing values, style, and culture morphed into the alternative sport of skateboarding for an outlaw gang of Southern California beach kids in the 1970s, exemplifies just how important culture and lifestyle was to alternative sports, and continues to be today. The movie portrays that it was more than just the sport; it was the art, the music, and the culture of the scene in Dogtown, a shabby area of Santa Monica, California, that attracted people to participate in the sport and over the years create their own niche market.

Alternative sports, more importantly action sports such as skateboarding, snowboarding, and BMX, not only feed into the culture that performs these sports, but they are simultaneously fueled by this culture. It is a give-and-take relationship that is only a part of this side of the sports industry. Alternative sport is more than just the sport; it is about respecting the tradition upon which the sports were founded. The tradition, which is culture, style, and value based, is one that is not seen in the mainstream sports side of the industry. It is this type of lifestyle, within these types of sports, that makes alternative sports stand out from mainstream sports such as soccer and baseball.

Sport marketing companies across the country have gotten the message, and many companies are now specializing in marketing for alternative sports. One such company, Fuse Integrated Sports Marketing, of Burlington, Vermont, is a marketing/advertising agency that connects brands with the youth market through alternative sports. Agencies like this are succeeding because of the growing impact these types of sports are having on today's youth culture. No longer is it a myth that tattooed kids with long hair and baggy jeans are racing down a street on wooden planks attached to wheels.

Why do alternative sports fit in so perfectly with the youth culture and mainstream sports do not? The answer is simple: alternative sports are lifestyle driven. There is more to alternative sports than playing a game and going home after. It is more about hanging out with friends, listening to music, and wearing clothes than it is about listening to a coach and wearing a uniform. This is because the youth subculture – especially those who participate in alternative sports, prefer the individuality and freedom of the activities. In the past, kids played team sports in seasons. During the summer it was baseball season. In the fall it was soccer season. In the winter it was football season. This never gave kids a sense of individuality or identity. They were constantly switching sports according to the time of year. Alternative sports are not like this. Even if a kid cannot snowboard in the summer because of the lack of snow, he or she can still listen to music and wear clothes associated with the culture. Children can have their own identity year round.

RECOVERY SPORT MARKETING

Recovery sport marketing is the actual or potential regaining, restoration, or improvement of something lost or taken away as a result of a significantly negative situation or event. In sport marketing, this recovery is often accomplished through the transfer of goods and services from sport organizations to consumers. The history of recovery marketing is found mainly in the areas of hospitality, travel, and tourism, and the negative scenario most often focused on is natural disasters including hurricanes, cyclones, typhoons, tsunamis, and earthquakes. Much of the focus of the recovery marketing is on crisis management, then market recovery through destination communications. For example, if a hurricane were to hit a Caribbean island, the first focus would be on coordinating the problems created by the crisis. Then a plan would be implemented to repair major infrastructure and tourist attractions, followed immediately by communicating with the world that the island is open for business – since without tourism most of these economies would collapse.

For the sport industry, sport marketers must focus on preparing for these negative scenarios ahead of time in order to ensure recovery in a timely manner. This is very similar to what is done in risk management planning – that is, to identify and assess potential risks; define each in terms of severity and frequency; create a plan to deal with the situation should it occur; and determine the best way to communicate with the public through marketing communications and promotion both during and after the crisis to keep consumers informed. For sport marketers, this last step is crucial, because controlling the flow of information and through which communication channels information should be communicated can mean the difference between success and failure. Sport marketers have to determine the overall impact of the crisis on brand image and organizational reputation. More importantly, the sport marketer must determine what changes have to be made in marketing during recovery as compared to during normal operations. This includes the level of marketing and promotions that should be conducted during the crisis – ranging from no changes to the need to reduce (not eliminate) the demand for a product or service through de-marketing until the sport organization returns to an acceptable level of operations. This should be part of any strategic marketing plan, but unfortunately this is not done on a regular basis in sport marketing. Much like the concept of marketing myopia discussed earlier in the book, there is a lack of foresight in many sport marketing efforts, especially in contemplating the negative.

In an article published by Burton and Howard in 2000 titled "Recovery Strategies for Sports Marketers: The Marketing of Sports Involves Unscripted Moments Delivered by Unpredictable Individuals and Uncontrollable Events," they stated three major facts:

1   Those employed in sport marketing must be prepared for unexpected, often negative actions that jeopardize a sport organization's brand equity.
2   The negative actions tend to inflame public opinion or alter fan perceptions.
3   These events tend to create an immediate economic reaction that can distract senior management and impede organizational performance.

Logically, recovery marketing, in the form of crisis and marketing communications, may be utilized for numerous negative situations including scandals, illegal activities, and sanctions from governing bodies. However, over the past decade there have been numerous other negative scenarios where the application of recovery marketing has been implemented in the sport industry, including natural disasters, work stoppages, folding and re-establishment of teams and leagues, poor performance and relegations, and loss of hallmark event bids.

Natural disasters

In 2005, Hurricane Katrina hit the Gulf Coast region of Louisiana, Mississippi, Alabama, and Florida in the United States. Among the worst-hit areas was the city of New Orleans, home to numerous professional sport organizations, including the NFL's New Orleans Saints and the NBA's New Orleans Hornets. Each team has its unique challenges, especially since the city permanently lost nearly 50 percent of its residents, and the teams played games away from New Orleans for more than a year (Saints for one season; Hornets for two). The Saints had the biggest challenge to overcome – not only did they play games away from New Orleans for one year, there was a negative stigma related to their stadium, the Superdome, which was both damaged by the storm but also was a shelter used to house displaced residents, and the owner talked openly about possibly not returning to the city and moving the team to the San Antonio Alamodome. Fortunately, the city of New Orleans, the state of Louisiana, and the National Football League all engaged in a recovery marketing plan that included securing a $300 million bond to repair the facility; working with the ownership group to entice them to stay in the city and become a symbol of the rebuilding of the city; and creating a marketing campaign through the "Bringing Back New Orleans Commission" to get individuals and corporations to embrace the team. While in the short term there were successes in individual support for the team (they sold a record number of season tickets for the 2006 season), corporate support from sponsorships and specialty seating sales was at only 60 percent capacity. However, the ownership did not look at the short term; it focused strategically on the future with significant players' moves (especially signing quarterback Drew Brees), improving the product on the field, and continuing significant work in the community to be involved with the rebuilding of the city. Fast forward five years to the end of 2011 – the team are one of the best in the NFL, they were the 2009 Super Bowl Champions, and they now have a naming rights sponsor for their facility – the Mercedes-Benz Superdome.

With regard to the New Orleans Hornets, they had one significant challenge. Their arena was damaged to the point where they played 95 percent of their games out of New Orleans for two years – and in Oklahoma City, which was over 700 miles away. Their presence in the city of New Orleans was very limited, both because they moved temporarily to Oklahoma City, but also they were only starting to build brand awareness in the city after they had moved there three years earlier from Charlotte. When the team returned to New Orleans for the 2007 to 2008 season, the recovery marketing plan was a combined effort between the team and the NBA. The Hornets, recognizing the significant change in the city post-Katrina, sought to connect with returning business, fans, and newcomers to the fan base by instituting special discounting ticketing plans. The NBA chipped in with a marketing campaign focused on bringing basketball back to New Orleans. However, while the team had some success on the court and through marketing efforts centered on their superstar point guard Chris Paul, they continued to struggle in connecting with the city. Many believe this was because the owner at the time, George Shinn, was an outsider who really did not have a vested interest in the community of New Orleans (he was a North Carolina businessman who moved the Hornets from Charlotte to New Orleans because his image was tarnished in Charlotte due to sexual assault allegations). Eventually, the NBA bought the team from George Shinn in December 2010 for US$300 million, traded Chris Paul to the Los Angeles Clippers in October 2011, and then sold the team for $338 million in April 2012 to Tom Benson . . . the owner of the New Orleans Saints!

Work stoppages

A work stoppage is when an organization temporarily ceases to operate due to a strike or a lockout. A strike is when employees temporary stop working either to express a grievance or enforce a demand. For example, in 1994 to 1995, Major League Baseball players went on strike (refused to play games) because they believed the owners and the league were guilty of unfair labor practices, in addition to a new collective bargaining agreement not being in place. A lockout is when management denies employment to workers during a dispute related to terms of that employment. In 1998, the NBA owners and league locked out their players when the players' union would not agree to changes to the league's salary cap system and caps on individual player salaries. In 2004, the NHL owners and league wanted to institute a hard salary cap as part of the new collective bargaining agreement. The players declined, and the NHL became the first league to cancel an entire season. In 2010, the NBA owners and league once again locked out its players after the expiration of the collective bargaining agreement when the two sides could not agree on the division of revenue and new salary cap structure.

Any time a league has a work stoppage there will be negative effects in the eyes of the consumer. This is especially relevant considering many of the arguments for these stoppages are money related, and the owners and athletes are receiving exorbitant salaries as compared to the majority of the general public. As a result, when the league plans to return to operations, there is a need to implement a recovery marketing plan to get the fans back into the seats. Some leagues have done a poor job, while others have been prepared for recovery. MLB had no such plan in place after its strike, which resulted in significant fan backlash, reductions in revenue, and crippled numerous small market teams. The NBA has a fairly solid recovery marketing plan in place, and has used it after both of its lockouts (1999 and 2010). Their plan focuses on re-launching the league as a cooperative effort between ownership, players, coaches, sport marketing professionals, and public relations managers. In reaching a consensus between all parties, the entire organizational structure from league to individual teams focuses on a similar message that can address fan apathy, disappointment, and anger. For the NBA, these marketing efforts are sincere and direct, and are applied based on the type of scenario – in 1998 to 1999 it was a shortened 50-game season that also resulted in the cancellation of the All-Star Game; in 2010 to 2011 it was a shortened 66-game season that started with a quintuple-header (five games) on Christmas Day. For the NHL lockout, it was quite a challenge because they became the first team in United States sports history to cancel a season due to lockout; professional hockey was only the fifth most popular sport in the country (behind NFL, NASCAR, MLB, and NBA); and with the global influx of players many went back to their home countries in Europe and Russia to play. The NHL used many traditional marketing efforts to bring fans and players back, with limited success except in traditional hockey cities. They have struggled to get a significant national hockey contract on mainstream TV since losing the ESPN deal as a result of the lockout, but that has recently changed with the new contract with NBC and the launch of the NBC Sports Network. Many players decided to stay overseas to play in their own countries, or decided to join the newly created Kontinental Hockey League (KHL) in 2008. Four teams (Los Angeles, Pittsburgh, Ottawa, and Buffalo) have gone through bankruptcies since the lockout; and alone between 2011 and 2012, one team (Dallas) entered into bankruptcy at the start of the season, with another team (New Jersey) appearing to be headed towards bankruptcy at the end of the season. Finally, one team (Atlanta) relocated to Winnipeg in Canada.

Folding and re-establishment of teams and leagues

With the prospect of relocations of teams, such as in the NBA when the Charlotte Hornets moved to New Orleans in 2002 and the Seattle Supersonics moved to Oklahoma City in 2008, and in the NHL when the Atlanta Thrashers moved to Winnipeg, Manitoba, Canada in 2010, it is inevitable that a city may need to engage in a recovery marketing effort. As of the 2010 to 2011 season, the only city that had successfully implemented a recovery marketing plan was Charlotte. When the Hornets left for New Orleans at the end of the 2001 to 2002 season, there were numerous reasons for this, including the owner (George Shinn) being run out of town because of sexual assault allegations and continued disagreements with politicians, the city's unwillingness to build a new arena, and a resulting decrease in fan base. The city of Charlotte went to work immediately after learning of the possibility that the Hornets would relocate. They worked with the NBA to immediately be granted an expansion franchise, marketing the city as a viable proposition despite the problems related to the previous ownership and promising that a new arena would be built. The NBA agreed, awarding them the franchise that became the Charlotte Bobcats, and started to play in the Charlotte Coliseum in 2004. The new arena, currently called the Time Warner Cable Arena, opened in 2005.

According to Howard and Crompton (2003):

> When a city loses a sports franchise, it may create the impression that local businessmen and politicians are incompetent, that the community is declining or a "loser," and that its residents lack civic pride. Indeed, it may be worse for a city's image to lose a major event or major league team than never to have had one at all.

As a result, municipalities often engage in a recovery marketing plan to both improve that image and hopefully attract a "replacement" sport franchise. Over the past ten years, while there have been no professional sports relocations in baseball, football, or hockey from one United States city to another, the NBA has had two. The Charlotte Hornets moved to New Orleans, and the city actively engaged in a recovery marketing plan that resulted in getting the expansion franchise Charlotte Bobcats two years later. The Seattle SuperSonics moved to Oklahoma City in 2008, and the city is currently actively engaged in a recovery marketing plan that has the goal of securing an expansion team within five years.

As far as leagues are concerned, a good example is the Arena Football League (AFL). The AFL folded in 2008 due to the inability to agree on a feasible economic and business plan for future operations, and its subsequent filing of Chapter 7 bankruptcy. The following year, the developmental league (af2) ceased operations because none of the teams would commit to the following year while potential restructuring of the AFL was ongoing. This restructuring took place in 2010 with the return of the Arena Football League – starting its first year with a combination of former AFL and af2 franchises. The focus of the league's recovery marketing efforts is not fully known as of yet; however, judging by the initial results of its stronger business model, expanding into markets where there were successful AFL and af2 franchises in the past, and signing a contract with the NFL Network to broadcast games, it seems that the league is headed in the right direction for the 2012 season with 17 teams.

Poor performance and relegations

Teams that struggle on the field often have resulting reductions in revenue due to decreased gate receipts and concession sales. However, in some sport leagues around the world, poor performance on the field results in relegation to a lower division, and the need to recover to get back to the top level of play. For example, in the English Premier League (EPL) in soccer, the last three teams on the ladder/in the standings are relegated to the Football League Championship (or effectively one division lower), and three teams are elevated to the Premier League. When teams are relegated, it affects the entire organizational structure, and in many cases the supporters and community they reside in, as the teams in these communities bring significant economic impact to their regions. Enacting a proper recovery marketing plan can prevent long-term impacts of these relegations which may include decreases in attendance, memberships, community support, and sponsorships; reductions in revenues and assets; decreases in economic impact, community perception, brand equity, and image; and an increase in poor player attitudes and behaviors. One good example of successful recovery was Newcastle United, which was relegated in 2009 but then moved back up in 2010. The team had a strategic recovery plan in place to secure promotion on the first attempt because it recognized the considerable challenge it would face financially without the significant influx of money from the EPL's television contracts. The team reduced operating costs while maintaining a Premier League quality squad, and implemented a marketing plan that maintained memberships, attendance, and sponsorships.

Loss of hallmark event bids

Another interesting application of recovery marketing in sport could be for municipalities that spend up to ten years and millions of dollars on trying to secure a bid to host the Olympics, but come up short. In October 2009, Rio de Janeiro, Brazil was awarded the 2016 Summer Olympic Games, beating Chicago, Illinois; Tokyo, Japan; and Madrid, Spain. How does a city recover not only from being denied hosting the largest and most prolific sporting event in the world, but from the loss of money, sometimes up to US$100 million, that could have been spent elsewhere? In general, each municipality should implement recovery marketing by utilizing its bid documents to prove to its communities, external sporting organizations, and the world that its cities are top-notch destinations for major sporting, cultural, and social events in the future. For example, Madrid has failed in its bid for both the 2012 and 2016 Olympics, but used the documents for future Olympics and FIFA World Cup bids, as well as to secure the 2008 World Junior Table Tennis Championships and the 2008 World Synchronized Swimming Championships. At the very least, if recovery marketing efforts cannot be used to secure future events, the information embedded in the documents should be modified and used to enhance the community from whence the bid came. In the case of Munich, Germany, its failed bid document for the 2018 Winter Olympics is being used as a framework for the urban development and planning for the city of Munich and the administrative district of Garmisch-Partenkirchen.

SOCIAL SPORT MARKETING

Social marketing is a concept first articulated in 1971 by Philip Kotlar and Gerald Zaltman as a means to promote social objectives and causes more effectively. They believed that social marketing had the potential to be the catalyst for addressing the disparity between traditional marketing and concepts whose foundation are in the social sciences such as social change, social reform, and social policies. Social marketing is a significant means to address communication, conceptualization, and intellectual gaps between customers and organizations in terms of goals, values, and outcomes assessment.

Much of the framework of social marketing focuses on how marketing can be utilized as a catalyst and conduit for change in terms of emphasizing social goals as a part of normal business operations. As such, sport organizations need to recognize the value of social marketing as part of their normal marketing management operations. Reasons include:

- Social marketing recognizes the importance of the customer's role in meeting sport marketing social goals of the organization.
- Social marketing focuses on the exchange process of both products and services between companies and customers.
- Most market research strategies related to segmentation and consumer analysis have their foundations in social marketing.
- Most message designs for advertising and other promotional strategies are focused on social marketing.
- The partnerships and management of distribution channels need to take into account social marketing.
- The integration of marketing mix elements with each other (instead of looking at each individually) in terms of planning, implementation, and management of marketing plans is central to social marketing.
- The entire process of decision making, problem solving, outcomes assessment, and evaluation methodologies are all an implementation of social marketing strategies.

Does social marketing offer the conduit to affect fundamental rethinking and changes in behaviors for "the greater good?" The following benefits of social marketing are offered as points of support:

- Social "goodness" does not lend itself to keeping score – it can be of benefit to all, from the sport organization to the consumer, and beyond.
- Social marketing, if applied properly, can be profitable for a sport organization.
- Social marketing is "value added," which can provide a competitive advantage for sport organizations.
- Social marketing is active and inclusive, which expands the potential customer base for sport organizations.
- Social marketing provides the opportunity to stylize the traditional marketing mix from simple segmentation and targeting to a differentiated strategy that is unique as compared to other sport organizations competing for the same customers.
- Social marketing is theory based and informed, which may then be utilized by sport marketers to validate and enhance the practical application of sport marketing concepts.

Social marketing, as a result of the increased influence of social responsibility, has undergone significant growth over the past two decades in the sport industry. Yet, even with this reported growth, many efforts to operationalize social marketing and socially responsible sport-sponsored programs in particular, as well as sport philanthropy efforts in general, are still in their infancy of development, with great up-side potential for growth and enhancement. However, some significant advances have been made in recent years that have benefited the sport business industry. The evolution of social marketing concepts such as social responsibility, cause-related marketing, and sport philanthropy have been actively tied to sport sponsorships as components to add benefits for people and communities, increase brand awareness as a social contributor, and create new brand platforms with social benefits embedded in their implementation.

One of the most significant social marketing efforts actually started many years before Kotlar and Zaltman articulated the concept. Since 1938, the Professional Golfers Association (PGA) Tour has led the way with charitable and social contributions in coordination with its golf tournaments. In 2005, the Association reached the goal of the "Drive to a Billion" campaign, and now has its eyes set on contributing the next billion by 2015 through its numerous local, regional, and national charities in coordination with all of the tours (PGA TOUR, Champions Tour, Nationwide Tour). Probably the most significant part of this social marketing effort is that even in a significant time of economic downturn in the late 2000s and early 2010s, sponsors have been able to justify their spending on sport sponsorships with the PGA because of these social marketing efforts.

As a result, from a sport marketing perspective, social marketing can be profitable and revenue enhancing, provides unique opportunities to build a sport property's brand, and offers sponsors a more significant return on investment strategy to justify their sponsorship decisions. Examples of other cause-related charitable giving social marketing programs that are being utilized by sport organizations are listed in Table 15.2.

From a management perspective, creating partnerships between sport properties and charitable causes is an increasingly important management topic of discussion in sport executive front offices. With the majority of teams in the MLB, NBA, NFL, NHL, and NASCAR now supporting charitable foundations, and most major sport organizations overseeing their own programs, sport marketers are continually involved with planning, refining, and developing new social marketing programs to better connect their organizations with their targeted communities. In terms of sport sociology and sport psychology, social marketing impacts upon the broader community, its citizenry, and shapes perceptions of organizations that engage in and are committed to community-building activities. From a sport finance, law, and economics perspective, social marketing engages these subdisciplines as well, since many of the sport league and professional sport organizations have established non-profit foundations and charitable arms, with commensurate legal, tax, revenue, and expense reconciliation, and economic impact considerations. As a result, sport marketers must now take into account the wide-ranging, cross-disciplinary, community-centric influence that social marketing has on sport organizations going forward.

Table 15.2 Cause-related charitable giving social marketing programs by sport organizations

Sport property	Brand	Recipient cause(s)	Giving as of end of 2011 (US$)
National Football League	NFL Play 60 NFL Youth Football Fund NFL Charities	Youth United Way Breast Cancer	115 million annually
Major League Baseball	Reviving Baseball in Inner Cities Welcome Back Veterans	Boys' and Girls' Clubs of America ALS Association Habitat for Humanity	100 million annually
PGA Tour	Together, Anything's Possible	Determined by tournament	100 million annually
Lance Armstrong Foundation	Livestrong	Cancer	40 million annually
National Basketball Association	NBA Cares Basketball Without Borders Day of Service Read to Achieve Green Week	Youth Environmental issues Community service	25 million annually
Chick-Fil-A Bowl	Play It Smart	Team Scholarship funds	1.2 million annually
Major League Soccer	MLS WORKS	Nothing But Nets Active Bodies, Active Minds FIFA's Goal Program	1 million annually
National Hockey League	Hockey Fights Cancer	Cancer	600,000 annually
World Tennis Association	First Serve	UNESCO Habitat for Humanity	100,000 annually
National Association of Basketball Coaches	Coaches vs. Cancer	American Cancer Society	45 million since inception in 1993
American Football Coaches Association	Coach to Cure MD	Muscular Dystrophy	Over 1 million since inception in 2008
Women's Basketball Coaches Association	Kay Yow Cancer Fund Pink Zone/Play4Kay	Breast Cancer	3.3 million since inception in 2007
Andre Agassi Foundation for Education	Grand Slam for Children	Charter School in Nevada State and National Education Policy Advocacy	150 million since inception in 1994

Source: From Schwarz, E. C. and Branch, D. D. (2011). Social marketing as a catalyst for building new relationships between sport practitioners and academicians. *Journal of Applied Marketing Theory* 2(2): 56–67.

CONCLUSION

While there are probably numerous sociological concepts in sport marketing, three of the emerging topics are discussed in this chapter. Relationship sport marketing centers on extending the marketing communication process beyond basic advertising and sales promotional techniques by building long-term value with customers through continued interactions, and experience sport marketing seeks to employ marketing efforts that integrate the sport brand as being an integral part of the lifestyle and culture of the consumer. Recovery sport marketing is the regaining, restoration, or improvement of a market as a result of a significantly negative situation or event including natural disasters, work stoppages, folding and re-establishment of teams and leagues, poor performance and relegations, and loss of hallmark event bids. Social sport marketing seeks to promote social objectives and causes, and how marketing can be utilized as a catalyst and conduit for change in terms of emphasizing social goals as a part of normal business operations.

There are significant implications for sport marketers in each area. In relationship and experience marketing, there has been a dramatic shift in both areas over the past decade. With relationship marketing, there has been an evolution from creating quality customer service and building good face-to-face relationships with customers in a product-based society to becoming more collaborative through social networking, internet, and mobile communication channels through a service-based economy. Relationship marketing has further evolved from outbound efforts that focus on market research demographic and customer service data to include inbound data obtained through public relations, social media, and other internet and mobile communication platforms. This has resulted in the creation of new technologies to collect and measure this information – in the form of full-service customer relationship marketing management programs that help connect all parts of a sport organization and create more synergistic use of information for marketing efforts. As far as experience marketing is concerned, sport marketers must recognize the need to offer value beyond the core sport product and its extensions. In addition, sport marketers must understand that customers do not just want sport organizations to be simply a conduit to an event or activity; they want enhanced experiences that integrate the sport organization within the lifestyle and culture of consumers.

The need for addressing recovery marketing, especially during times of crisis, comes from the increased market-oriented strategies that are being implemented by sport businesses to maintain a competitive advantage. The role of the sport marketer in coordinating all internal and external constituencies of the sport organization in the decision-making and problem-solving processes for communicating and marketing during and after the crisis is crucial. By not having a comprehensive sport marketing recovery plan that includes (1) plans for rebuilding, redevelopment and renewal; (2) quality research that identifies and assesses the level of recovery needed, the risks, and the behaviors of stakeholders; (3) processes to control communication to the public about the crisis; (4) methods for implementing and managing a sport marketing recovery and restoration campaign; and (5) putting in place an outcomes assessment plan that enhances strengths, improves on weaknesses, identifies future opportunities, and recognizes threats to continued recovery, the road to recovery for a sport organization will be significantly hampered.

Sport marketers must also recognize that the social marketing effort of sport organizations is a vital catalyst to contributing to the greater good in their community, and there is really no other single marketing vehicle, platform, tool, or opportunity that provides the mutual benefits afforded by engaging in social marketing programs. At the heart of social marketing is relationship building with the community for the intended purpose of affecting some tangible social good, while enticing the population to engage with them – with the extra added benefit that they may also become future customers. In addition, sport organizations are always exploring new ways to provide value-added benefits to their corporate partners, as sponsors are looking for ways to not only substantiate their return on investment, but also finding new platforms to activate and leverage their sponsorship through more socially responsible outreach initiatives.

FROM THEORY TO PRACTICE

DANIEL E. BALLOU, DIRECTOR OF SPORTS SALES AND MARKETING
Albuquerque Convention and Visitors Bureau,
Albuquerque, New Mexico

After earning my Bachelor's degree, I went to work for a large trucking company for three years. My day-to-day schedule consisted of scheduling deliveries and freight pick-ups with five or six city drivers, getting the freight loaded on an over-the-road trailer, and off to a relay station where the freight would be unloaded and shipped to points far and wide. While sitting in my office in Topeka, Kansas, I had an epiphany one day and I asked myself, "Is this really what I want to do with my career?"

The one thing I had always enjoyed, from my days of early youth to today, was athletics. While sitting in that office, I decided I was going to pursue a career in sports. I did not know how, or in what area, but the important thing I did was to begin the process, and that process started with the cultivation of relationships.

In those days there were very few universities offering degrees related to sport, so getting to know someone who was already in the industry was paramount in trying to start a career in athletics. I would argue that your own network development is equally important today (but the modes of communication and the prerequisites available have changed drastically). I walked into the athletics department at Kansas State University, was able to get an appointment with the Sports Information Director (at that time), and told him I was willing to do anything from sweeping floors, to emptying trash cans in order to get a foot in the door. As you continue reading this article, ask yourself if you are willing to do the same and in what way you will start the process of building relationships.

I was fortunate enough to land a graduate assistantship in the K-State Sports Information Office, and six months into the position, one of the assistant directors left for another job and I was promoted to that position, my first full-time gig in athletics. During the time I was doing my assistantship, and during that first full-time job, I really started developing professional relationships with on-air talent and television production crews, administrators and coaches from competing schools, and a wide variety of people with whom I came into contact. This opened my eyes about relationship-building opportunities and I began using my own system of what later was coined "Relationship Marketing." In those days, it was as much about marketing me.

After spending several years in collegiate athletics, I used some of the relationships I had developed to land my current position of Sports Marketing Director for the Albuquerque Convention and Visitors Bureau. This position allows me to be involved in a wide variety of sports events, from a very high level like the NCAA Men's and Women's Basketball Championships, the USA Track and Field National Indoor Championships, a collegiate bowl game, and many others, all the way down to youth events at the youngest levels. My job in sports destination marketing helps employ people all over Albuquerque in the hospitality industry. If I am doing my job well, hotel and restaurant workers are being hired, our local attractions are being utilized, and direct spending dollars are being generated. Relationship marketing helps all this to occur.

Marketing can never be just about making the sale (although that is the ultimate goal). Relationship marketing, certainly in my work as a sports destination marketer, is about being in it for the long haul. Because the sports industry is intertwined, and because a lot of business is initiated by word-of-mouth campaigns, the ability to develop relationships with customers cannot be overstated. Our goal as marketers is to get buyers on to the consumption escalator in a consistent pattern of moving higher, which equates to buying more. The worst thing that can happen to a marketer is to get customers on to the consumption escalator, but not to take the time to cultivate relationships, and the customer steps off your escalator and on to your competitors' doorstep.

As someone who has been in the athletics marketing industry for a long time, I can attest that it is much easier to keep clients coming back, and perhaps increasing their purchasing decisions through the use of developed relationships. Marketers who do not have the wherewithal to develop relationships will find themselves continually in positions of having to uncover new business each and every renewal cycle. As a future marketing professional, that is a situation you do not want to be in. Get clients on board (or many of you will inherit existing clients), show them how important their business is, and get to know exactly what their objectives are in working with your organization. By establishing this type of relationship, show them you truly care about their initiatives and thank them for buying into what you are offering, and help them connect with an untapped market or improve existing market share.

Developing new business each year is extremely important, because new customers can eventually become long-term customers, but do not forget about the client who has been a consistent investor in you and your organization. If you start taking your existing customers for granted, you may find yourself in situations of crisis mode in looking for new business. Most successful sports organizations, be it at the professional, collegiate, youth, or amateur level, have relationships with long-standing clients who stay with an organization through the winning and losing and through the comings and goings of players and coaches, due to the relationships the two organizations have.

Finally, take advantage of the social networking tools available today, and stay on top of advances in technology. These are opportunities that can help maintain professional relationships and lead to long-term, consistent growth.

GLOSSARY

Accounting information system: *see* internal reports.

Adaptation: the ability to make change or modification.

Advanced ticket sales: tickets that are purchased by customers before the day of the event.

Advertisements: paid public announcements about a product or service through the print, broadcast, or electronic media that are designed to attract public attention and subsequent purchase.

Advertising: involves paid, non-personal communications about a sport product or service through the print, broadcast, or electronic media that are designed to attract public attention and subsequent purchase.

Advertising campaigns: a series of advertisement messages with a single mission and theme that are promoted through a variety of media options during a specified time frame.

Advertising strategy: the formulation of an advertising message that communicates the brand's value proposition, its primary benefit, or how it can solve the consumer's problem.

Affect referral decision rule: sport consumers make a sport product choice based on previously established overall ratings of the sport product. These ratings are directly affected by brand awareness, advertisement, salesperson influence, emotions, feelings, and moods.

Affective: the attitudes, feelings, and emotions directed toward a sport activity.

Aftermarketing: a visionary sales process that encourages salespersons to communicate and service the sport ticket holders after the purchase is completed.

Aggregate marketing factors: the indicators of the appeal of the sport product or service in the specific segment or category.

Alternative dispute resolution: the collection of methods (negotiation, mediation, arbitration) utilized to hear disagreements and determine an appropriate ruling about a situation.

Ambush marketing: the attempt by a third party to create a direct or indirect association with a sport event or its participants without their approval, hence denying official sponsors, suppliers, and partners parts of the commercial value derived from the "official" designation.

Amotivation: where there is no motivational influence intrinsically or extrinsically.

Analysis of variance: a difference analysis statistical method that assesses whether the means of more than two groups are statistically different than each other.

Analytical skills: proficiency in utilizing logical and critical thinking to understand the needs, wants and desires of the sport consumer.

Anonymity: assures the respondents that they will not be identified in conjunction with the data collected or the study.

ANOVA: abbreviation for analysis of variance.

Antiquity: the period of history from 3000 BC until the fall of the Roman Empire around 476 (this is the period prior to the Middle Ages).

Arbitration: the process of two parties agreeing to give an independent third party the power to make a decision based on the facts of the dispute.

Arbitrator: an independent third party who oversees a hearing to determine the facts of a dispute and who is authorized and given the power by all parties involved to make a decision that is final and binding.

Associative statistics: used to evaluate whether two specific variables within a study are related.

Athlete endorsement: a type of athlete sponsorship where the athlete is describing his or her personal association with the product or service.

Athlete sponsorship: where a corporation seeks to become affiliated with an athlete to secure the rights to market his or her association and reap the benefits of that association.

Atmospherics: the design of visual communications in an environment, such as lighting, colors, and music, to entice the sport consumer's perceptual and emotional responses to purchase the sport product or service.

Attitude: the state of mind or behavioral predisposition that is consistently favorable or unfavorable with respect to a product or situation.

Augmented reality: a virtual system that allows users to see a different reality through their viewport on their smartphone.

Awareness: the measurement of the percent of the target market that knows about the organization's products and/or services, including customer recall as related to brand recognition, brand features, or brand positioning.

B2B: business-to-business.

B2C: business-to-consumer.

Backorders: an unfilled customer order in demand, immediate or past due, against an item whose current stock level is insufficient to satisfy demand.

Balanced scorecards: where companies establish their most important financial goals as well as goals throughout the company and use supply chain metrics to identify achievements.

Balanced sourcing: a retailer which balances its purchases between two or more suppliers.

Bandwidth: the amount of information that can be passed through a communication channel at one time.

Behavioral: the actions or reactions directly related to the internal and external stimuli which sport provides.

Behavioral incentives: inducements that are made to consumers to entice them to purchase a product or service based on a perceptual relationship created between the consumer and the product or service.

Benefit selling: the creation of new opportunities, conditions, or perks that will counteract the objections a potential customer may have about a product or service, and offers additional value to the consumer.

Brand: a name, term, design, symbol, or feature that identifies one sport product or service as being different from another.

Brand loyalty: a consumer's preference to buy a particular brand in a product category.

Broadcast sponsorship: where a corporation purchases an association with specific sport programming via the radio or television.

Brokering sites: a website that acts as an intermediary between one sport business wanting a product or service, and another business seeking to provide such a product.

Business: individuals or organizations that seek to make a profit by providing products and services that satisfy the needs, wants, and desires of the consumer.

Business-to-business: refers to the transactions, collaborations, and business interactions that occur between two organizations.

Business-to-consumer: focuses on the transactions between businesses and consumers.

Buying process: the steps involved in making a decision to make a purchase – including identifying the need, searching for products or services that satisfied that need, evaluating options, making a decision, purchasing the product or service, and eventually re-evaluating the decision to determine whether to make the same purchase again or to change.

C2B: consumer-to-business.

C2C: consumer-to-consumer.

Case studies: published accounts of situations that have occurred to a business or industry, allowing the sport marketer to obtain a first-hand view of a similar situation and see how another organization dealt with the circumstances.

Category attractiveness analysis: developing a general understanding of the market segment category in which the sport organization chooses to operate, and whether the continued investment in that segment will yield an appropriate return.

Causal research: collection and analysis of information utilizing experimentation and simulations to determine the cause-and-effect relationship between the sport organization and the problem at hand; it is extremely complex because there is no certainty that the results are not being influenced by other variables.

Cause-related marketing: the process of creating a relationship between a sport organization and a specific social cause.

Center of gravity approach: the law of the country that has the most significant relationship to a given situation has jurisdiction.

Chi-square: an associative statistical method also known as a "goodness of fit" test; it seeks to take the obtained frequencies from the sample and compare them to the statistical hypothesis.

Classical antiquity: the period of history that started during the seventh century BC, during the time of growth in Europe, the Middle East, and North Africa, starting with the poetry of Homer, running through the rise of Christianity, and ending at the fall of the Roman Empire.

Classical conditioning: the process of using an existing relationship between a stimulus and response to bring about the learning of the same response to a different stimulus.

Click streams: the tracking of the sequence of pages visited by a customer after the initial interaction.

Climate: the attitudes, standards, or environmental conditions that affect sport marketing efforts.

Closed-ended questions: when the sport marketing researcher provides specific options of answers for the respondent.

Cluster sampling: a probability sampling method where the population is divided into groups, any of which could be considered as a representative sample.

Cognitive: the process of acquiring knowledge about an activity.

Cognitive abilities: the perceptual and intellectual capabilities of individuals including comprehension, judgment, learning, memory, and reasoning

Commerce: an organization's ability to sell products and services using its website, including the collecting of items in a "shopping cart," and payments through secure websites.

Communication management: the planning, implementing, supervising, evaluation, and modification of the various methods of communication internal and external to a sport organization.

Communication skills: the set of abilities that allows an individual to convey information that can be received and understood by another individual.

Commitment: the process by which an individual is emotionally or intellectually bound to a course of action.

Community: the ability to interact with other users including email, chat rooms, and discussion boards.

Community relations: the process of the sport organization interacting and connecting with the target population within a specific area.

Compensatory decision rule: how a consumer evaluates each sport product in terms of each important attribute, and then chooses the sport product or brand with the highest overall rating.

Competition sourcing: where suppliers study the nature of the activity, and then determine the best performance for the given activity without input from customers – including elimination of an activity, modification of a product or service for greater efficiency, or outsourcing to another department, division, or company.

Competitive set: the process of determining the direct competitors to a sport organization in the specific product or service area.

Competitor-orientated pricing: a result of researching what one's competitors are charging, and reacting accordingly. You may decide to charge the same, to undercut, or to present your service as better in some way, so that you can charge more.

Computer-assisted telephone interviews (CATI): where survey questions pop up on a computer screen, the interviewer reads the question to the respondent, the respondent gives the answer, and the interviewer enters the answer into the computer.

Computer networks: the system of data-processing points that is interconnected to communicate data between and through the network, most often with the end-point being a computer.

Concentrated sport marketing: focusing on one specific group of sport consumers; also known as niche marketing.

Concentrated strategy: a single-segment strategy where one market segment is served with one marketing mix; often the strategy of choice for smaller companies with limited resources.

Confidentiality: where the researcher knows the individual respondents, but the name of the respondent will not be divulged, or information related to the study not attached to the individual, without the expressed consent of the respondent.

Conjunctive decision rule: the sport consumer establishing a minimally acceptable grade for each attribute evaluated. For each sport product that falls below the established grade on any attribute, that sport product is eliminated from purchase consideration.

Connection: the ability for websites to link to other websites.

Consumer: an individual or organization that purchases or obtains goods and services for direct use or ownership.

Consumer-based integration: the involvement of the buyers and users of products and services as an integral part of the promotional process.

Consumerism: involves the systematic efforts of sport organizations, including individual sport marketers and sport marketing groups/departments, to protect the rights of consumers.

Consumer-to-business: where the consumer initiates the transaction process by soliciting organizations to compete for the individual's business.

Consumer-to-consumer: involves transactions between customers.

Content: the actual text, pictures, graphics, audio, and video found on a website that provides information to the user.

360

Context: the functionality and aesthetically pleasing look of a website, including the ease of navigation, and the use of appropriate graphics, colors, and design features.

Convenience sampling: a non-probability sampling method where the sport marketing researcher goes to a high-traffic area such as a mall or shopping center to survey potential respondents.

Conversion rates: the measurements utilized to calculate how many viewers of a web page actually do what the organization wants.

Coordinated integration: how all operational aspects of the organization work together to promote the products, services, and/or the organization itself.

Corporate social responsibility: focuses on the responsibility sport organizations have to society beyond that of investors and stakeholders to include philanthropy, volunteerism, and any other efforts that foster relationships that enhance society.

Correlation coefficient: *see* Pearson product moment correlation.

Cost management: the consideration of competitive manufacturing and logistics costs by optimizing the amount of stored materials, keeping capacities filled, achieving economical purchasing prices, and ensuring efficient transport and storage processes.

Cost-orientated pricing: a result of researching the costs, and then assessing prices, bearing in mind what percentage of profit the corporation desires.

Cost per engagement: the fee paid by a promoter to Twitter when someone retweets, replies to, clicks, or favorites a promoted tweet.

CPE: cost per engagement.

Creative brief: a document designed to inspire copy-writers by channeling their creative efforts toward a solution that will serve the interest of the client, and represents an informal pact between client and advertising agency that signifies agreement on what an advertising campaign is intended to accomplish.

Crisis communication: a contingency plan that is based on existing communication resources and operational capabilities, and which allows sport marketing professionals to respond effectively to a crisis related to the sport organization.

Cross-business integration: where the organization must coordinate with the information technologies of suppliers, sport consumers, and web-based marketplaces.

Cross-impact analysis: examining the relationships between outcomes.

Cross-sectional studies: studies that measure factors from a sample within a population at a specific point in time.

Cross-tabulations: an associative statistical method that involves basic tabular comparisons using raw data, frequencies, or percentages.

CSR: corporate social responsibility.

Culture: the principal attitudes, behaviors, values, beliefs, and customs that typify the functioning of a society.

Customary pricing: when the sport retailer sets prices for goods and services and seeks to maintain them for an extended period.

Customer service: the behaviors exhibited by salespersons during their interaction with customers, including the general assistance provided before and after the sale.

Customization: the ability of a website to adapt and modify itself based on the wants, needs, and desires of the user.

Database management: the process of developing an organized collection of demographic, geographic, and other personal data (usually through a computerized program), and using that information to maximize sales efforts.

Data mining: the process of collecting and analyzing data from non-traditional perspectives, categorizing the data, and summarizing relationships.

Decline stage: the final stage of the sport product and service life cycle; the point when a sport product or service becomes obsolete.

Delivery: the concept of producing or achieving what is desired or expected by the consumer.

Demand-orientated pricing: a result of researching what the market will bear. This means the corporation could charge more for a service which is seen as being value-added or elite.

Demographics: the categories of traits that characterize a group of people. The generic categories that most sport marketing professional look at are age, gender, household size, annual income, and geographic location. In sport marketing, especially with the expansion of global influences, these concepts are expanded beyond the traditional concepts to include culture, subculture, cross-culture, and social setting.

Descriptive research: collection and analysis of information that describes the "who, what, when, where, and how" of a potential problem; the information is very factual and accurate, but does not take into account the cause of the situation.

Descriptive statistics: uses basic data reduction and summarization (mean, median, mode, frequency distribution, range, standard deviation) to describe the respondents, the sample, and the population.

Dichotomous: a method used in closed-ended questions where the respondent is required to answer from a choice of two responses, such as yes or no, or (a) or (b).

Difference analysis: a method utilized when there are variations that exist between targeted groups – uses t-tests and ANOVAs for statistical measurement.

Differentiated sport marketing: focuses on two or more different sport consumer groups with divergent retailing approaches for each group.

Differentiated strategy: a selective specialization or multiple-segment strategy where different marketing mixes are offered to different segments.

Differentiation: the concept of creating and demonstrating distinct and specialized char-acteristics of sport products and services as compared to those of the competitors. The concept of being distinct and specialized.

362

Direct costs: those which can be associated directly with the product or service.

Direct promotional strategy: the actual process of identifying customers, connecting with them, increasing their awareness and interest in the product or service being offered, and persuading them to make a purchase.

Direct sport marketing: a variety of sport retailing in which the sport consumer is first exposed to a sport product through a non-personal medium such as a catalog, television commercial, or infomercial, then orders the sport product by mail, phone, fax, or internet.

Diversification: spreading out business activities and investments.

Domestic: sport marketing efforts focused internally (one country).

Downward integration: the movement of information throughout the entire organization using information technologies.

DSS: decision support system.

Eaves: a fictional currency that is invested in people who are influential in their industry.

E-business: an all-encompassing term that covers the internal information technology processes of an organization including human resources, finance, inventory management, product development, and risk management.

E-commerce: the external information technology processes of an organization including the marketing and sales functions.

Ego: the balancing part of the mind between primitiveness and morality, which includes internal and external consciousness, individual character differences, and the relationship between emotions and actions.

Ekecheiria: roughly translated means "Olympic Truce."

Elasticity of demand: the sensitivity sport consumers have to pricing changes and the relationship to the quantity of sport product they will buy.

Empire Avenue: a stock market for social people where you can invest a fictional currency called Eaves in people who are influential in their industry.

Endorsements: the use of high-profile individuals such as athletes, actors, and prominent businesspersons to use their notoriety or position to assist an organization in promoting or selling its products or services, with the result being an enhanced image because of the association.

Environmental marketing: marketing focused on the natural environment, the ecological environment, and the concept of greening in terms of developing products, pricing strategies, promotion activities, and delivery methods that do not damage the natural environment.

E-procurement: where the purchasing function is often outsourced to a third party.

Escalator concept: utilized to represent the movement of consumers to higher levels of involvement with a specified product.

Ethics: the philosophical study of moral values and rules.

Ethical behavior: attitudes focused on what is "good" or "right."

Ethical management: a comprehensive program that continuously improves thinking and behavior patterns and not just some high-visibility issues and ethics policies.

Event sponsorship: creating an association between a corporation and a sport event.

Evoked set: the sport product to which sport consumers give their greatest consideration.

Exclusivity: the guarantee that the products or services of the sponsoring organization will be the only type in that category to have an association with the sport organization.

Experience surveys: refers to collecting information from those who are considered to be experts in the field of interest as a result of being a part of a direct network, through recommendations of members of the direct network, or from research conducted about the area related to the research questions or objectives.

Experimentation: the process by which an independent variable is controlled and manipulated in order to determine the change effect on a dependent variable.

Exploratory research: collection and analysis of information when there is little or no information about an opportunity or threat; it is the most difficult method of research because it is impossible to create a plan of action in advance, instead working with impressions and assumptions based on personal experience or expertise.

External climate: the analysis of the climate of an organization in terms of the economy, social networking, legal and political forces, and social and ethical influences.

External organizational image: involves the perceptions of individuals from outside an organization regarding their view of that organization.

Extrinsic motivation: involves rewards or incentives used by an individual to bring about desired behavior in another person.

Facebook: a social networking service and network where users can create a personal profile, add other users as friends, exchange messages, and join common-interest user groups.

Facility sponsorship: naming rights agreements for stadiums, arenas, and other sport facilities.

Factual knowledge: information that can be easily researched through secondary resources.

Fixed costs: those costs which are the same whatever the usage.

Focus groups: an interview that involves eight to twelve people at the same time in the same group, and is used to evaluate products and services, or to test new concepts.

Formal scanning: a systematic search for information where there is a specific goal for the intelligence gathering; involves a narrow scope, but is less rigorous than a full marketing research effort.

Frequency distribution: the number of times a value occurs during the study.

Full market coverage: where an organization attempts to serve the entire market by means of either a mass market strategy or a differentiated strategy.

Functional integration: how the design or operations of the product, service, and/or organization can be utilized to effectively promote it.

Geolocation: a social media platform that uses the global position system (GPS) on a smartphone to check into a service; the service will then show the connection where the user is located.

Global: a comprehensive term that refers to worldwide involvement. For this text, it will specifically refer to sport marketing efforts that involve more than ten countries and usually a minimum of three continents.

Global sport marketing: sport organizations that take the international distribution of products and services to more of a worldwide level by grouping countries into marketing units based on similar economics, political environments, legal structures, or cultural compositions, and developing sport marketing strategies and plans for each unit.

Global sport marketing strategy: strategy that views the world as one big market and seeks to define and target similarities between various cultures around the world, with the eventual goal being to create a diversified marketing strategy that will allow the sport organization to compete in any market in the world.

Goodness of fit test: *see* chi-square.

Green marketing: *see* environmental marketing.

Grouping of contacts approach: the law of the country that is most concerned with the outcome of the case has jurisdiction.

Growth stage: the third stage of the sport product and service life cycle; the point in the cycle when the company with the best product, price, and/or service rises to the top, and maximizes sales and profit.

Guerrilla marketing: the use of promotional-based marketing techniques with a low budget.

High-analytical decision makers: individuals who break down problems into smaller parts, resulting in a set of causal relationships, and then the decision variables are manipulated to address those relationships with the goal of reaching decisions that will provide optimal success for the sport organization.

Hits: the number of times an individual goes to a web page.

Horizontal integration: the internal processes needed to bring sport products and services to market through an e-business structure.

Hyperlinks: text or graphics placed on a web page to provide cross-referenced materials for the user.

Hypothesis testing: the articulated expectation of the sport organization, the sport marketer, or the sport marketing researcher.

Id: the primary process of the unconscious mind that focuses on gratification (such as instant gratification and release) and primitive instinctual urges (such as sexuality and aggression).

Ideal self: who the consumer wants to be.

Image integration: the relationship between the opinion of consumers and the promotion of the sport product, service, and/or organization.

Impression: the receipt of third-party exposure through the media to create an association between the product or service being promoted and the reader (print or internet), listener (radio and TV), or viewer (TV or live).

Incentives: the benefits or reduced costs that are offered to motivate a sport consumer to purchase the specified sport product or service.

Indirect promotional strategy: all the methods whereby an individual or organization can create, convey, and place messages in the mind of the prospective customer.

Individualization: the customization of products and services as a function of personalized communications between the consumer and the company.

Inept set: the sport product that the sport consumer excludes from purchase consideration.

Inert set: the sport product that the sport consumer is indifferent toward because it is perceived to have no significant advantage.

Inferential statistics: used to generalize the results and draw conclusions simply based on the population characteristics and the data collected.

Infomediaries: a website that publishes trade and industry standards about an industry for those who operate in that industry.

Informal scanning: involves a limited, unstructured effort in collecting data for a specific goal; usually involves making inquiries to individuals on an impromptu basis.

Infrequent foreign sport marketing: sport organizations that dabble in foreign markets as a result of a surplus of products or a temporary increase in demand.

Integrated brand promotion: the use of multiple promotional tools in a coordinated manner to build and maintain overall awareness, identity, and preference for sport products, services, and the associated brands.

Interactivity: the ability of consumers to have additional two-way communication with companies and marketers.

Intermodal: the use of containers or sending freight via containers that are easily transferred from ship to railcar to truck as needed, without repacking.

Internal audit: the sport marketing professional must conduct an appraisal of the internal operations and systems of the sport organization to observe and evaluate its efficiency and effectiveness in quality delivery of products and services, appropriate risk management practices, and financial control.

Internal climate: the analysis of the climate of an organization in terms of organizational structure, culture, and change.

Internal development: the first stage of the sport product and service life cycle; involves an idea of a new product or service, or a new twist to an existing product or service.

Internal Marketing: involves the perceptions of individuals from inside an organization and how they view that organization.

Internal Reports: the accounting information system for a sport organization, including asset and liability management, revenue and expense operations, and administration of owner's equity.

Internal reports system: a component of the sport marketing information system that involves information that is generated by the internal operations of the sport organization.

International: refers to those efforts that extend beyond national boundaries and involve two or more nations. For this text, it will specifically refer to sport marketing efforts that involve at least two countries to a maximum of ten, with the countries being within one or two continents.

International sport marketing: sport organizations that actively engage in marketing in various markets by developing a multi-domestic sport market orientation and creating an individual sport marketing strategy and program for each country.

International sport marketing strategy: strategy that focuses on cross-cultural differences and that each individual culture requires a separate sport marketing strategy adapted to the individual cultures.

Internet: the worldwide system of publicly accessible computer networks that transmit data by a process called packet switching to standardized Internet Protocol (IP) addresses.

Internet Protocol addresses: the unique identifiers of a computer.

Interpretive knowledge: the meaning of facts within a society.

Interviews: person-administered surveys where the interviewer reads the questions to respondents either in person or on the telephone, and then records the answers.

Intrinsic motivation: the desire to satisfy natural needs and interests, knowledge, accomplishment, and experiences.

Introduction to market: the second stage of the sport product and service life cycle; the point at which a sport organization puts its product or service into action and starts to capture market share.

Inventory turns: the number of times a company's inventory cycles turn over per year.

Involvement: a close connection with something.

IP: abbreviation for internet protocol.

Judgment sampling: a non-probability sampling method used when sport marketing researchers use either their own opinion or that of someone considered to be an expert, to determine who will be a part of the sample.

Just-in-time manufacturing: the concept of receiving timely and accurate supply chain information which allows the company to make or ship only as much of a product as there is a market for.

Key performance indicators: those factors that influence the effectiveness of products and processes.

KISS approach: a method incorporating simple rules within the marketing strategy to allow for easy reactions to changes in the environment.

Knowledge management: the methods utilized to create, gather, classify, modify, and apply knowledge about consumer values and beliefs to achieve goals and objectives.

Knowledge skills: the ability to gather, organize, and share information.

KPI: key performance indicators.

KRA: key result areas.

KSF: key success factors.

Lateral integration: the movement of information between an organization and the consumer or business partners.

Law of the forum: *see* Lex Fori theory.

Lex Fori theory: the law of the country in which a court action is brought has jurisdiction.

Licensing: the creation of a strategic alliance in which the manufacturer of a sport product gives permission to a second party to manufacturer that product in return for specific royalties or payments.

Life cycle: the attitudes, values, and beliefs of individual sport consumers change as they transition through life.

Lifestyle inventory: a system of measurement used in sport marketing research that centers on the measurement of psychographic data by taking into account the values and personality traits of people as reflected in their unique activities, interests, and opinions toward their work, leisure time, and purchases.

LinkedIn: a business-related social networking site utilized for professional networking.

Local broadcasting contracts: agreements that cover events of and games played by the individual sport organization; are usually for multiple years, and may include such additional broadcasts as pre-game and post-game shows.

Logistics: the coordination of the receipt of orders from customers, developing a network of warehouses, picking carriers to get products to customers, and setting up an invoicing system to receive payments.

Longitudinal studies: studies that measure factors from a sample within a population repeatedly over a period of time.

Long-term value analysis: a method for evaluating what that sport consumer is worth to the sport organization in terms of sales and profit over a period of time; usually refers to a minimum of three years, but can be as long as a lifetime.

Low-analytical decision makers: individuals who look at a problem as an absolute, and seek feasible solutions to the entire problem based only on past experiences and previously solved problems.

Main conversion: enticing the consumer to take action such as making a purchase or contacting the organization for more information.

368

Marginal cost: the total cost that is incurred based on the quantity produced.

Marginal value: the worth to the sport organization of producing one more unit of the product in comparison to other products.

Marketing: the functions involved in the transfer of goods and services from the producer to the consumer. The focal point of these functions is in three specific areas known as the three Cs of marketing analysis: the consumer, the company itself, and the competition.

Marketing concept: a consumer-oriented philosophy which suggests that satisfaction of consumer needs provides the focus for product development and marketing strategy to enable the firm to meet its own organizational goals.

Marketing construct: the item which is to be examined or measured.

Marketing logistics: the management of the relationship between the marketing and logistical concepts, in order to unify their respective strategies within the context of the wider supply chain.

Marketing relativism: this principle focuses on the realization that the sport marketing efforts are usually based on strategies, values, and beliefs formulated from experience and knowledge.

Market potential: the process of estimating the maximum possible sales of a sport product or service so that a sport organization gains valuable knowledge about the amount of sport product or service to make available.

Market share: the proportion of a market that you supply.

Market specialization: where an organization specializes in serving a particular market segment, and offers that segment an array of different products.

Market tracking studies: studies that measure one or more variables over a period of time using data available from other research studies.

Mass market strategy: where a single undifferentiated marketing mix is offered to the entire market.

Mass sport marketing: where goods and services are available for sale to an extensive group of sport consumers.

Maturity: the fourth stage of the sport product and service life cycle; refers to the time at which the sport product or service has maximized profits and is seeking to maintain a stable place in the market.

Mean: the average value of a set of numbers (sum of all responses/number of respondents).

Median: the middle value of a distribution (50th percentile).

Media relations: the activities that involve working directly with individuals responsible for the production of mass media including news, features, public service announcements, and sponsored programming.

Mediation: the process of bringing an independent person into a negotiation to hear both sides and assist the two parties to reach a mutually agreeable solution.

Mediator: the independent neutral third party brought in to hear both sides of a dispute. Mediators have no legal standing to make a decision on behalf of the facts.

Merger: the union of two or more separately owned business entities.

Metrics: the indicators that marketing professionals utilize to evaluate an organization's impact on the environment, and its level of progress and success.

Microconversions: tracking the specific behavior a marketer would like to see the consumer do to become more involved with the product or service being offered.

MIS: marketing information system.

Mission: developing appropriate goals and objectives to operate under, based on an understanding of the philosophy of the sport organization (its values and beliefs).

Mode: the value occurring most frequently in the data.

Modified Likert scale: a system of measurement utilized in sport marketing research in which respondents are asked to indicate their degree of agreement or disagreement on a symmetric agree–disagree scale for each of a series of statements. The most common form is the 5-point scale.

Motivation: influence that initiates the drive to satisfy wants and needs.

Motive: an emotion or psychological need that acts to stimulate an action.

Multinational sport marketing strategy: *see* international sport marketing strategy.

Multiple-category: a method used in closed-ended questions where there are more than two response options.

Mystery shopping: *see* secret shopping.

National broadcasting contracts: agreements with a series of local radio or television networks to broadcast the games of leagues; usually multiple-year deals, and broadcasting dollars are split evenly across all teams within a league.

Negotiations: the process utilized by two parties to resolve disputes or to complete transactions.

New economy: the use of information, communication, and digital technologies for manufacturing, selling, and distributing products and services.

Niche: a special area of demand for a product or service.

No direct foreign sport marketing: sport organizations that are not involved in marketing efforts outside their own country.

Non-compensatory decision rule: the positive evaluation of an attribute of a sport product does not counteract a negative evaluation of another attribute belonging to the same product.

Non-probability sampling: a sampling category when there is no way to guarantee the representation in the sample.

Official sponsor: refers to the sport organization's public acknowledgment of the association between the sponsor and the organization.

Offshoring: the transference of manufacturing, customer service centers, and other labor-intensive work to other nations.

Online communication: the ongoing dialogue between users and the website including customer service requests, email notifications of specials and opportunities, and instant messaging.

Online offering: the products, services, or information to be placed on the internet and World Wide Web.

Open-ended questions: when the sport marketing researcher provides no answer options.

Operant conditioning: sometimes also called instrumental conditioning, this is where no automatic stimulus-response relationship is involved, so the sport consumer must first be induced to engage in the desired behavior and then this behavior must be reinforced.

Operational definition: how a construct will be measured; is usually presented in a question format that will be used in a specific measuring tool.

Opinion leadership: the process by which the sport marketer, or the opinion leader, informally influences the consumption actions or attitudes of sport consumers.

Order-to-payment cycle: the focal point of the internal records system; includes all the activities associated with the completion of a business transaction.

Organizational culture: the shared values and norms exhibited by a given group in response to adapting to the external environment and the internal integration of the organization.

Organizational image: the combination of how the internal organization believes others view the organization, and the beliefs and perceptions the external organization actually has of the organization.

Organizational skills: expertise in planning and managing the sport product and service information in an efficient and effective manner.

Overheads: costs a business incurs so that production is continued. Overheads can be cut if limits to production are made, or if production is halted completely, although some overheads are incurred whether or not there is production.

Packet switching: the method of moving data through computer networks in the most efficient and effective manner possible by splitting the data into smaller units, each labeled with the destination address, sent individually, and reassembled at the destination.

Panel: a group of individuals who have agreed to being involved with market research studies at periodic intervals to measure changes over time with a consistent sample.

Pareto Principle (80/20 Rule): a rule that assumes that 20 percent of customers generate 80 percent of sales or that 80 percent of merchandise comes from 20 percent of the vendors.

Participants: individuals who take part in an activity.

Participant consumer behavior: actions performed when searching for, participating in, or evaluating the sport activities consumers believe will satisfy their needs.

Partnership sourcing: the commitment between customers and suppliers to create a long-term relationship based on understood and agreeable objectives that work toward maximizing capability and competitiveness.

Pearson Product moment correlation: an associative statistical method also known as the correlation coefficient; creates a linear association between two variables.

Perceived self: how the sport consumer believes he or she is viewed by others.

Perceptions: involves gaining an understanding of the individual values, attitudes, needs, and expectations of the sport consumer by scanning, gathering, assessing, and interpreting those insights.

Personal contact: one-on-one communication between a representative of the sport organization and the sport consumer that should result in achieving promotional objectives ranging from providing information about products and services, to generating sales.

Personality: the unique and personal psychological characteristics of individuals which reflects how they respond to their social environment.

Place: the method of distributing the product to consumers.

Plan: the strategy for managing all the resources that go toward meeting customer demand for your product or service.

Pluralistic research: when both qualitative and quantitative data are used concurrently.

Point-of-purchase displays: special exhibits involving a product or service at the point of sale, such as cardboard cut-outs, end caps, kiosks, and signage.

Point-of-sale systems: a sales information computer system for internal reports that provides sport marketing professionals with more comprehensive information at their fingertips by offering instant access to information about their prospects and customers.

Population: refers to the entire group that is defined as being under study as per the research questions.

POP: point of purchase.

POS: point of sale.

Positioning: the process of influencing the perceptions of potential and current customers about the image of the company and its products and services. This is accomplished by applying the four Ps of marketing, with the goal of strategically placing the product or service firmly in the mind of the consumer.

Predictive statistics: used in prediction and forecasting of the future by evaluating previously collected data.

Price: the value a consumer equates to a good or service, or the amount of money or goods asked for in exchange for something else.

Price-based incentives: benefits derived from lowering the retail price of a product or service.

Price/quality matrix: the relationship between price and quality in positioning the sport product as compared to others.

Primary data: information collected by the sport marketer specifically for the research project; normally collected via personal contact, by mail, telephone, email, or face-to-face.

Primary intelligence: information collected by the sport organization through direct contact with customers, the distribution network, competitive analysis, and the internal sport organization itself.

Probability sampling: a sampling category utilizing random selection from the known population.

Processing power: the amount of information that can be handled by a website at any given time.

Product: tangible (goods) or intangible (services) merchandise.

Production: the schedule of activities necessary for making, testing, packaging, and preparation for delivery.

Product specialization: where an organization specializes in a particular product or service, and tailors the product or service to different market segments.

Projective techniques: used to allow respondents to verbalize their true opinions or beliefs about products and services.

Promotions: an element of the sport marketing mix that involves communicating information about the sport product or service to consumers.

Promotional integration: the actual creation and delivery of the promotional message that involves defining how the message is to reach the consumer, ensuring that the promotional message will be received and understood, and that the promotional message will lead to the purchase of a product or service.

Prospecting: the process of identifying potential customers to purchase products and services.

Publicity: the use of unpaid, non-personal promotion of a sport product or service through a third party that publishes print media or presents information through radio, television, or the internet.

Publicity campaign: the use of communications, activities, and media coverage to convey specific information to a targeted market over a specific period of time.

Public relations: the collection of activities, communications, and media coverage that convey what the sport organization is and what it has to offer, all in the effort to enhance its image and prestige.

Puffery: refers to exaggerated, subjective claims that cannot be proven true or false.

Purchasing: the process of acquiring products and services to help meet the goals and objectives of a sport organization.

Qualitative research: involves collecting, analyzing, and interpreting data by observing what people do, or how they answer open-ended questions utilizing a small number of respondents that represent a segment of the population, and focusing on the qualities of a sport product or service by articulating the values and beliefs they perceive the specific brand to have.

Quantitative research: involves collecting, analyzing, and interpreting data collected from a larger sample via a structured questionnaire or survey, with the data being analyzed in statistical terms, and the results produced in a numeric form.

Questionnaire: a form containing a set of questions used to gather information for a survey.

Quota: a number or percentage that constitutes an upper limit (such as maximum inventory available), or in most cases for sales, a targeted minimum.

Quota sampling: a non-probability sampling method that seeks to balance the proportion of selected respondent characteristics by setting quotas on how many individuals from a specific group can respond.

Radio frequency identification (RFID): a digital technology that can tell what the product is, where it has been, when it expires, whatever information someone wishes to program by global positioning satellites.

Range: the distance between the lowest value and the highest value in a distribution.

Recovery marketing: the actual or potential regaining, restoration, or improvement of something lost or taken away as a result of a significantly negative situation or event.

Reference group self: how the sport consumer interacts with his or her reference group.

Referrals: recommendations made by one individual to another about a specific product, service, or organization.

Referral sampling: a non-probability sampling method where the respondents to a survey are also asked to identify other individuals who would likely qualify to take part in the survey.

Regression: a predictive statistical method used to measure a dependent variable and its relationship to one (bivariate) or more (multiple) independent variables.

Regular foreign sport marketing: sport organizations that have a permanent presence outside national borders, but their primary market (50% or above) is domestic.

Relationship management integration: how all aspects work cooperatively with each other to effectively and efficiently promote the product, service, or organization.

Reliability: the ability to show that the results of the experiment are trustworthy, and, if the same experiment were run again, the results would be either similar or comparable.

Renvoi: where a court utilizes its own laws, and has the option of adopting the center-of-gravity laws from another country.

Research method: a plan for a study that steers the collection and analysis of information gathered.

Resource system: the process of selecting and utilizing resources to provide the benefits valued by the consumer.

Return on equity: the amount of profit earned on an organization's common stock over a given period, which tells investors how effectively their money is being utilized by the organization.

Return on investment: the amount of profit earned based on the quantity of resources used to produce the profit.

Returns: the network for receiving defective and excess products back from customers and supporting customers who have problems with delivered products.

Revenue models: the methods of securing earnings for the sport organization.

RFID: abbreviation for radio frequency identification.

RFM: recency, frequency, monetary.

RFM analysis: a method for evaluating the most profitable customers for the sport organization based on: (1) if the customer has purchased recently; (2) how often the customer has made a purchase; and (3) how much the customer spends with the sport organization.

ROE: *see* return on equity.

ROI: *see* return on investment.

Royalties: a share of income, in accordance with the terms of a license agreement, paid by a licensor for the right to make, use, or sell a product or service.

Sales force: the individuals responsible for selling sport products and services.

Sales incentives: the offering of a premium to attract first-time or bulk buyers of products and/or services, but more often are used to reward those repeat customers.

Sales management: the process of directing and controlling the sales force, and achieving the desired level of exchanges between the sport organization and sport consumers.

Sales pitch: a communication process where the salesperson outlines and explains the benefits of a product or service to potential customers in order to stimulate interest and motivate them to make a purchase.

Sales process: the steps that focus on taking the sport products and services available for sale, and developing the best methods for luring the sport consumer to make a purchase.

Sales promotion: a unique promotional method that is utilized to generate immediate interest in a product or service.

Sample: the most basic element of sport marketing research, as it is the factors taken from a small group that is representative of the characteristics of an entire population.

Sample frame: a master list of the entire population.

Sample frame error: the degree to which the sample frame does not encompass the entire population.

Saturation: the fifth stage of the sport product and service life cycle; the stage when gaining market share begins to slow.

Scale: a standard of measure developed by the sport marketing researcher.

Scaled-response questions: when the sport marketing researcher develops a scale and the answers from the respondents are based on both their perception and the scale defined.

Scanning: the collection of intelligence acquired through informal observations and conversations.

Scientific methodology: the process by which one gains information through a process of observation, developing a hypothesis, implementing some type of research to determine the appropriate course of action, and evaluating the results to draw conclusions, select courses of action or inaction, and modify the research and start again.

Screening: the process by which a researcher can conduct a preliminary appraisal of the potential respondent to determine his or her suitability for the study.

SCVNGR: a mobile gaming platform that allows brands and institutions to create treks that send their users on what is basically a scavenger hunt, and the challenges that players face while they are exploring the world around them can also lead to real-world rewards.

Season ticket equivalencies: the combination of season tickets sold and partial season ticket packages.

Secondary data: information that has been collected by another source or for another purpose prior to the current research project, and is being evaluated for use to solve the problem at hand.

Secondary data analysis: involves using existing data that have been collected by another source or for another purpose prior to the current research project.

Secondary intelligence: information collected by the sport organization from previous published sources such as books, trade journals, newspapers, and reliable sources on the internet.

Secret shopping: a tool utilized in market research to investigate products and services of competitors by sending individuals to act as buyers.

Segmentation: the concept of dividing a large, diverse group with multiple attributes into smaller groups with distinctive characteristics.

Segment factors: the underlying opportunities and threats that affect the segment or category.

Self-administered survey: a survey where an individual respondent completes the form on his or her own.

Self-concept: a concept that includes a consumer's ideal self, perceived self, and reference group self.

Semi-focused scanning: when there is no specific intelligence being sought or goal to attain, but a general inquiry is conducted to discover any piece of intelligence that may become evident.

Sense-and-respond approach: a method utilized to respond swiftly to changes in the market as a result of strategic thinking needing to be intuitive, reactionary, and simple.

Servicing: a process that involves a salesperson providing work or a duty to a customer in response to a need or demand, and then creating a relationship that helps a customer make an initial or repeat purchase.

Shopping intercept: a survey method utilized when a researcher stops shoppers at malls, supermarkets, outlets, and other retail establishments to get individual opinions.

Simple random sampling: a probability sampling method where a chance method is used to guarantee each member of the population an equal chance to be selected into the sample.

Single sourcing: the retailer who concentrates most of its stock purchases in one wholesale supplier.

Skip interval: a number representing how many names would be skipped when selecting the sample; it is calculated by taking the entire population list, and dividing it by the desired sample size.

Socialization: the process by which individuals acquire attitudes, values, and actions which are appropriate to members of a particular culture.

Social marketing: a concept first articulated in 1971 by Philip Kotlar and Gerald Zaltman as a means to promote social objectives and causes more effectively; they believed that social marketing had the potential to be the catalyst for addressing the disparity between traditional marketing and concepts whose foundations are in the social sciences such as social change, social reform, and social policies.

Social media: websites that allow the users to construct a public or semi-public profile within a bounded system, articulate a list of other users with whom they share a connection, and view and traverse their list of connections and those made by others within the system.

Social networking: *see* social media.

Social responsibility: *see* corporate social responsibility.

Sourcing: choosing suppliers that will deliver the goods and services you need to create your product.

Spam: unsolicited email.

Spectators: individuals who observe a performance, such as a sporting event.

Sponsee: the term that refers to the sport brand that desires to enter into an agreement with a corporate sponsor.

Sponsor: a term that refers to the corporation that desires to enter into an agreement with a sport organization.

Sponsorship: the relationship between a corporation and a sport organization as a tool to develop brand image and customer loyalty as a result of the association.

Sport: activities, experiences, or business enterprises that center on athletics, health and wellness, recreation, and leisure time opportunities. It is an all-inclusive term covering all aspects that go beyond the playing field, including all the various operations that make the games happen.

Sport advertising: one of the primary elements of the promotional mix that involves the process of attracting public attention to a sport product or sport business through paid announcements in the print, broadcast, or electronic media.

Sport business ethics: the values and principles within a commercial setting that apply to those individuals engaged in commerce.

Sport consumer relations: the use of various methodologies, information technologies, and internet capabilities that help entities organize and manage the interaction between the sport consumer and the sport organization.

Sport consumer relationship management (SCRM): the use of various methodologies, information technologies, and internet capabilities that help sport entities organize and manage sport consumer relationships. The goal of SCRM is to develop a system that all members of the sport marketing effort can utilize to access information about sport products and strive toward meeting the needs and wants of sport consumers.

Sport governing bodies: sport organizations that are responsible for developing the rule structure for the specific activity as well as organizing competitions at levels from local youth to international.

Sport journalism: encompasses all types of reportage and media coverage of current events in the world of sport.

Sport management: the collection of skills related to the planning, organizing, directing, controlling, budgeting, leading, and evaluation of an organization or department whose primary product or service is related to sport and its related functions.

Sport marketing decision support system: a component of the sport marketing information system that encompasses the primary and secondary data previously collected by the sport organization, the tools and techniques utilized to interpret those data, and the process by which that information is used in the decision-making process.

Sport marketing information system: a structure that consists of all aspects of the sport organization (people, equipment, goals and objectives, policies and procedures, etc.) being responsible for gathering, organizing, analyzing, evaluating, and distributing marketing information across the sport organization for the purpose of efficient and effective decision making.

Sport marketing intelligence system: a component of the sport marketing information system that involves the procedures and sources that the organization utilize to obtain everyday information about developments regarding external opportunities and threats.

Sport marketing planning process: involves the development of the sport organization's products and services marketing strategies, including the tactics and programs to be implemented during the lifespan of the plan.

Sport marketing research: the collection and analysis of information about sport consumers, market niches, and the effectiveness of sport marketing initiatives.

Sport market opportunity analysis framework: a methodology utilized by marketers to identify and evaluate the attractiveness of an opportunity in the marketplace.

Sport organization resource planning: assimilating all functions of an organization through information technology methods to become more efficient and effective in planning, manufacturing, marketing, and selling sport products and services.

Sport product: a bundle of attributes which are bought or sold.

Sport product and service life cycle: the defined stages that a sport product goes through during its lifespan. The six stages are initial development, introduction to the market, growth, maturity, saturation, and decline.

Sport product and service management: focuses on the approach taken by sport marketers and organizations to define and market their products and services.

Sport promotional mix: advertising, sponsorship, public relations, licensing, personal contact, incentives, and atmospherics.

Sport promotional strategy: the process of building brand loyalty and product credibility, developing image, and positioning the brand.

Sport retail management: the process of directing and controlling the business activities related to the sale of the sport product to consumers for their personal consumption.

Sports: refers to individual, dual, and team sports activities such as soccer, baseball, golf, and tennis.

Sports information: the gathering of results and other pertinent sporting information on individuals, teams, departments, and leagues.

Sport service: the process of providing quality, value, and satisfaction to the sport consumer.

Sport sponsorship: acquiring the rights to be affiliated with a sport product or event in order to obtain benefits from that association.

Standard deviation: measures the spread of values throughout the data – for a normal curve, which is used most often, the mid-point is the mean and the standard deviation is measured from that point.

Stakeholders: those with a vested interest in the outcomes of a sport marketing effort.

Stakeholder-based integration: how the ownership and employees of an organization have a vested interest in the efficient promotion of the product, service, and/or organization.

Standard error: an inferential statistical method used to measure the variability in the sample distribution: calculated by taking the standard deviation from the mean and dividing by the total number of respondents (SD/N).

STPD: abbreviation for segmentation, targeting, positioning, and delivery.

Strategic philanthropy: the social obligation an organization has to be a good corporate citizen by contributing to the improvement of the quality of life of people ranging from an individual or community to society as a whole.

Strategic plan: a comprehensive and integrated plan that is designed to look at the long-term projections of a business.

Stratified sampling: a probability sampling method where there is a large divergence in the population that would cause a skewed distribution.

Superego: the morality of an individual, which in turn formulates the ethical framework of individual values, beliefs, and codes of conduct.

Supply chain management: the process of coordinating the movement of sport products, sport services, and other pertinent information from raw materials to manufacturer to wholesaler to retailer, and eventually to the sport consumer.

Supply chain metrics: a set of measurements that helps the company to understand how well it is operating over a given period of time.

Support media: the use of non-traditional media efforts to connect with members of the target audience who have not been reached through traditional media (print, radio, television).

Survey: a form used to collect information from respondents about their attitudes, values, opinions, and beliefs via telephone, mail, face-to-face, and online.

SWOT: acronym for strengths, weaknesses, opportunities, and threats.

Systematic sampling: a probability sampling method that starts with a list of the entire population. Each is given a number, a skip interval is calculated, and names from the list are entered into the sample based on the skip interval.

Targeting: finding the best way to get a product's image into the minds of consumers, and hence entice the consumer to purchase the product.

Team sponsorship: agreement between a corporate partner and a team; usually more appropriate for local or regional companies that have smaller marketing budgets but have a desire to become the official sponsor of a team.

Technology integration: the modification of the traditional processes of order handling, purchasing, and customer services with the specific needs of the consumers and the unique abilities of the organization in mind.

Telemarketing: marketing goods and services by telephone.

Testimonials: the words and experiences of past users of the products or services being promoted.

Test marketing: the process of determining the sales potential of a new product or service, or the acceptance of a product previously entered into the marketplace.

Third-party logistics: services added on to regular transportation activities, including freight forwarding, which is the handling of freight from one form of transport to another.

Time management skills: the ability to control time.

Transactional data: information collected from the exchange process between a buyer and a seller.

Trend-impact analysis: a forecasting method that allows sport marketing researchers and the organization to track trends.

t test: a difference analysis statistical method that assesses whether the means of the two groups are statistically different than each other.

Tweets: the text-based posts viewed through Twitter.

Twitter: an online social networking and micro-blogging service where users can send and read text-based posts of up to 140 characters.

Unfocused scanning: exposure to information the sport marketing professionals deem to be useful based on what they have read, heard, or seen.

Uniform resource locators: more commonly known as main web addresses, they are the actual location of an internet item.

Upselling: the movement of customers from less profitable products or services in a specific category to either a more profitable one in the same category, or into another, more profitable category.

URL: abbreviation for uniform resource locators.

User interface: the ability to create a digital representation of the theme of the store, the ease with which the consumer can navigate around the website, and provide a pleasurable experience for the consumer.

Validity: the ability to show the accuracy of the methodology, and that the results are logical, reasonable, and sound.

Value: what the consumer is willing to pay for a product; or an amount of goods, services or money that is a fair price or return for something of an equivalent amount.

Value chain: the activities adding value directly to the consumer while adding indirect value through the support of other organizational operations.

Value propositions: how an organization will differentiate itself to consumers in terms of the value to be offered.

Variable costs: those which vary according to usage.

Variable pricing: when a sport retailer changes its prices as a result of changes in costs or demand.

Vertical integration: the speed with which information is delivered through internal and external information technology processes.

Virality: the probability that a social media or networking message is forwarded or sent along to other users.

Viral marketing: seeks to pass marketing messages about the sport marketer to as many people as possible, creating the potential for exponential growth in the influence the sport marketer has, as well as exposure of the sport product.

Word-of-mouth: spoken communication that does not come from the primary party.

World Wide Web: the collection of interconnected documents that are connected by uniform resource locators (URLs) and hyperlinks.

WWW: abbreviation for World Wide Web.

BIBLIOGRAPHY

CHAPTER ONE: INTRODUCTION TO SPORT MARKETING

Branch, D. (2002). *Sport Marketing Quarterly*: A journal designed for the business of marketing sport. *Sport Marketing Quarterly* 11(2): 80–83.

Cunningham, G. B. and Kwon, H. (2003). The theory of planned behaviour and intentions to attend a sport event. *Sport Management Review* 6(2): 127–145.

Desensi, J. T., Kelley, D. R., Blanton, M. D., and Beitel, P. A. (1990). Sport management curricular evaluation and needs assessment: A multifaceted approach. *Journal of Sport Management* 4(1): 31–58.

Ferrell, O. C., Hirt, G., and Ferrell, L. (2011). *Business: A Changing World*, 8th edn. New York: McGraw-Hill.

Horch, H. D. and Schutte, N. (2003). Competencies of sport managers in German sport clubs and sport federations. *Managing Leisure* 8(2): 70–84.

Kotlar, P. and Armstrong, G. (2010). *Principles of Marketing*, 13th edn. Upper Saddle River, NJ: Prentice Hall.

Larson, P., Tonge, R., and Lewis, A. (2007). Strategic planning and design in the service sector. *Management Decision* 45(2): 180–195.

Meenaghan, T. and O'Sullivan, P. (1999). Playpower: sports meets marketing. *European Journal of Marketing* 33(3–4): 241–249.

Pedersen, P. M., Parks, J. B., Quarterman, J., and Thibault, L. (2011). *Contemporary Sport Management*, 4th edn. Champaign, IL: Human Kinetics.

Pitts, B. G. (2002). Teaching sport marketing: Notes from the trenches. *Sport Marketing Quarterly* 11(4): 255–260.

Pitts, B. G., Fielding, L. W., and Miller, L. K. (1994). Industry segmentation theory and the sport industry: Developing a sport industry segment model. *Sport Marketing Quarterly* 3(1): 15–24.

Reh, J. F. (2005). Pareto's principle: the 80–20 rule. *Business Credit* 106(7): 76.

Sanders, R. (1987). The Pareto principle: Its use and abuse. *Journal of Consumer Marketing* 4(1): 47–50.

Shank, M. D. (2009). *Sports Marketing: A Strategic Perspective*, 4th edn. Upper Saddle River, NJ: Pearson Prentice Hall.

Slack, T. and Parent, M. M. (2005). *Understanding Sport Organizations: The Application of Organization Theory*, 2nd edn. Champaign, IL: Human Kinetics.

CHAPTER TWO: MANAGING THE SPORT MARKETING MIX

Apostolopoulou, A. and Biggers, M. (2010). Positioning the New Orleans Hornets in the "who dat" city. *Sport Marketing Quarterly* 19(4): 229–234.

Branch, D. (2008). The Charlotte Bobcats: (Re) launching of a new (old) NBA franchise. *Sport Marketing Quarterly* 17(1): 57–62.

Burton, R. and Howard, D. (1999). Professional sports leagues: Marketing mix mayhem. *Marketing Management* 8(1): 36–46.

Evans, J. (2011, October 15). Kasey Keller's retirement party draws crowd of 64,140. *The Seattle Times*. Available online: <http://seattletimes.nwsource.com/html/sounders/2016516460_keller16.html> (accessed 20 February 2012).

Fans choose Seattle Sounders FC as name for city's new MLS team. (2008, April 8). *Sports Business Journal*. Available online: <http://www.sportsbusinessdaily.com/Daily/Issues/2008/04/Issue-137/Franchises/Fans-Choose-Seattle-Sounders-FC-As-Name-For-Citys-New-MLSTeam.aspx?hl=Sports% 20Online%20Of%20The%20Year&sc>. (accessed 20 February 2012).

Farrey, T. (1994, June 15). Seattle misses first MLS cut: But bid isn't dead. *The Seattle Times*. Available online: <http://community.seattletimes.nwsource.com/archive/?date=19940615&slug=1915706> (accessed February 20, 2012).

Fullerton, S. and Merz, G. R. (2008). The four domains of sports marketing: A conceptual framework. *Sport Marketing Quarterly* 17(2): 90–108.

Helms, M. M. and Nixon, J. (2010). Exploring SWOT analysis: where are we now? A review of academic research from the last decade. *Journal of Strategy and Management* 3(3): 215–251.

Kotlar, P. and Armstrong, G. (2010). *Principles of Marketing*, 13th edn. Upper Saddle River, NJ: Prentice Hall.

Pedersen, P. M., Parks, J. B., Quarterman, J., and Thibault, L. (2011). *Contemporary Sport Management*, 4th edn. Champaign, IL: Human Kinetics.

Romero, J. M. (2008, May 17). Sounders FC announce fan association. *The Seattle Times*. Available online:<http://seattletimes.nwsource.com/html/sounders/2004420604_sounders17.html> (accessed February 21, 2012).

Ryan, T. J. (2005). Marketing mix. *Sporting Goods Business* 38(12): 22.

Seattle Sounders again lead MLS in attendance. (2011, October 15). *Sporting News*. Available online: <http://aol.sportingnews.com/soccer/story/2011-10-15/seattle-sounders-again-lead-mls-in-attendance> (accessed February 21, 2012).

Sharples, T. (2009, August 2). Soccer in Seattle: A new kind of football team woos fans. *Time*. Available online: <http://www.time.com/time/printout/0,8816,1912539,00.html#> (accessed February 20, 2012).

Stotlar, D. K. (2005a). Developing a marketing plan framework. In *Developing Successful Sport Marketing Plans*, edited by D. K. Stotlar. Morgantown, WV: Fitness Information Technology.

Stotlar, D. K. (2005b). Marketing mix. In *Developing Successful Sport Marketing Plans*, edited by D. K. Stotlar. Morgantown, WV: Fitness Information Technology.

Westerbeek, H. M. and Shilbury, D. (1999). Increasing the focus on "place" in the marketing mix for facility dependent sport services. *Sport Management Review* 2(1): 1–23.

CHAPTER THREE: SOCIAL RESPONSIBILITY AND ETHICS IN SPORT MARKETING

Babiak, K. (2010). The role and relevance of corporate social responsibility in sport: A view from the top. *Journal of Management & Organization* 16(4): 528–549.

Bhattacharya, C. B., Korschun, D., and Sen, S. (2008). Strengthening stakeholder–company relationships through mutually beneficial corporate social responsibility initiatives. *Journal of Business Ethics* 85(S2): 257–272.

Carroll, A. B. and Buchholtz, A. K. (2011). *Business and Society: Ethics and Stakeholder Management*, 8th edn. Mason, OH: South-Western Cenage Learning.

Dahlsrud, A. (2008). How corporate social responsibility is defined: An analysis of 37 definitions. *Corporate Social Responsibility and Environmental Management* 15(1): 1–13.

Ferrell, O. C., Gonzalez-Padron, T. L., Hult, G. T. M., and Maignan, I. (2010). From market orientation to stakeholder orientation. *Journal of Public Policy & Marketing* 29(1): 93–96.

Kerin, R. A., Berkowitz, E. N., Hartley, S. W., and Rudelius, W. (2006). *Marketing*, 8th edn. New York: McGraw-Hill.

Kim, K. T., Kwak, D. H., and Kim, Y. K. (2010). The impact of cause-related marketing (CRM) in spectator sport. *Journal of Management & Organization* 16(4): 515–527.

McAlister, D. T. and Ferrell, L. (2002). The role of strategic philanthropy in marketing strategy. *European Journal of Marketing* 36(5/6): 689–705.

Mowen, J. C. and Minor, M. (2001). *Consumer Behavior: A Framework*. Upper Saddle River, NJ: Prentice Hall.

Nalewaik, A. and Venters, V. (2009). Cost benefits of building green. *Cost Engineering* 51(2): 28–34.

O'Riordan, L. and Fairbrass, J. (2008). Corporate social responsibility (CSR): Models and theories in stakeholder dialogue. *Journal of Business Ethics* 83(4): 745–758.

Ottman, J. (2011). *The New Rules of Green Marketing: Strategies, Tools, and Inspiration for Sustainable Branding*. San Francisco, CA: Berrett-Koehler Publishers.

Pfahl, M. E. (2010). Strategic issues associated with the development of internal sustainability teams in sport and recreation organizations: A framework for action and sustainable environmental performance. *International Journal of Sport Management Recreation & Tourism* 6(1): 37–61.

Ratten, V. (2010). The future of sports management: A social responsibility, philanthropy and entrepreneurship perspective. *Journal of Management & Organization* 16(4): 488–494.

Rupp, D. E., Williams, C. A., and Aguilera, R. V. (2011). Increasing corporate social responsibility through stakeholder value internalization (and the catalyzing effect of new governance): An application of organizational justices, self-determination, and social influence theories. In *Managerial Ethics: The Psychology of Morality*, edited by M. Schminke. London: Routledge/Psychology Press.

San Francisco Giants. (2012). AT&T Park Information. Retrieved from http://sanfrancisco.giants.mlb.com.

Sweeney, L. and Coughlan, J. (2008). Do different industries report corporate social responsibility differently? An investigation through the lens of stakeholder theory. *Journal of Marketing Communications* 14(2): 113–124.

Walsh, B. (2011, June 30). Ranking North America's greenest cities. *TIME Magazine*. Retrieved from http://ecocentric.blogs.time.com.

Yani-de-Soriano, M. and Slater, S. (2009). Revisiting Drucker's theory: Has consumerism led to the overuse of marketing? *Journal of Management History* 15(4): 452–466.

CHAPTER FOUR: SPORT MARKETING RESEARCH AND INFORMATION SYSTEMS

Achenbaum, A. A. (2001). When good research goes bad. *Marketing Research* 13(4): 13–15.

Achenreiner, G. (2001). Marketing research in the "real" world: Are we teaching students what they need to know? *Marketing Education Review* 11(1): 15–25.

Ashill, N. J. and Jobber, D. (2001). Defining the needs of senior marketing executives: An exploratory study. *Qualitative Marketing Research: An International Journal* 4(1): 52–61.

Ashill, N. J. and Jobber, D. (1999). The impact of environmental uncertainty perceptions, decision-maker characteristics and work environment characteristics on the perceived usefulness of marketing information systems (MkIS): A conceptual framework. *Journal of Marketing Management* 15(6): 519–540.

Barnes Reports. (2012). *The 2012 Worldwide Spectator Sports Industry: Industry and Market Report*. Rockville, MD: C. Barnes and Company.

Coderre, F., St-Laurent, N., and Mathieu, A. (2004). Comparison of the quality of qualitative data obtained through telephone, postal and email surveys. *International Journal of Market Research* 46(3): 347–357.

Defining Business Objectives. (2003). *Journal of Government Financial Management* 52(4): 26.

Deveney, S. (2005). It's learning how to pan for gold in the data mine below the statistical surface. *Sporting News* 229(34): 28–29.

Evans, M. (2000). Marketing information and research. In *Oxford Textbook of Marketing*, edited by K. Blois. Oxford: Oxford University Press.

Filo, K. and Funk, D. C. (2005). Congruence between attractive product features and virtual content delivery for internet marketing communication. *Sport Marketing Quarterly* 14(2): 112–122.

Garver, M. S. (2002). Using data mining for customer satisfaction research. *Marketing Research* 14(1): 8–12.

Henderson, N. R. (2005). Twelve steps to better research. *Marketing Research* 17(2): 36–37.

Hess, R. L., Rubin, R. S., and West, L. A. Jr. (2004). Geographic information systems as a marketing information system technology. *Decision Support Systems* 38(2): 197–212.

Ilyashenko, S. M. (2004). The definition of necessary and sufficient information accumulation level to substantiate a choice of enterprise's market opportunities directions development. *Problems and Perspectives in Management* (1): 138–153.

Jackson, T. W. (2005). CRM: From "art to science". *Journal of Database Marketing and Customer Strategy* 13(1): 76–92.

Leonidou, L. C. and Theodosiou, M. (2004). The export marketing information system: An integration of the extent knowledge. *Journal of World Business* 39(1): 12–36.

Li, E. Y., McLeod, R. Jr., and Rogers, J. C. (2001). Marketing information systems in Fortune 500 companies: A longitudinal analysis of 1980, 1990, and 2000. *Information and Management* 38(5): 307–322.

Lilien, G. L., Rangaswamy, A., Van Bruggen, G. H., and Starke, K. (2004). DSS effectiveness in marketing resource allocation decisions: Reality vs. perception. *Information Systems Research* 15(3): 216–235.

McDaniel, C. D. and Gates, R. (2010). *Marketing Research Essentials*, 8th edn. Hoboken, NJ: John Wiley & Sons.

Morgan, M. J. and Summers, J. (2004). Sport consumption: Exploring the duality of constructs in experiential research. In *Sharing Best Practices in Sport Marketing: The Sport Marketing Association's Inaugural Book of Papers*, edited by B. G. Pitts. Morgantown, WV: Fitness Information Technology.

Moser, A. (2005). Take steps to avoid misused research pitfalls. *Marketing News* 39(15): 27.

Plunkett's Sports Industry Almanac. (2012 edn). Houston: Plunkett Research.

Raab, D. M. (2004). Business intelligence systems for marketers. *DM Review* 14(8): 68–69.

Ryals, L. (2003). Creating profitable customers through the magic of data mining. *Journal of Targeting, Measurement and Analysis for Marketing* 11(4): 343–349.

Shaw, R. (2001). Marketing decision support: a new discipline for dot.coms and dinosaurs. *Journal of Targeting, Measurement and Analysis for Marketing* 10(1): 5–8.

Sports Marketing and the Beverage Industry by the Beverage Marketing Corporation. (2005 edn). New York: Beverage Marketing Corporation.

Swaddling, D. C. and Miller, C. (2003). Understanding tomorrow's customers. *Marketing Management* 12(5): 31–35.

Taylor, T. (1999). Audience info the key to sports marketers. *Marketing News* 33(2): 10.

The 2006 Sports Business Market Research Handbook. Loganville, GA: Richard K. Miller and Associates.

Turauskas, L. and Vaitkuniene, Z. (2004). Planning and conducting focus group discussions in marketing research. *Problems and Perspectives in Management* (2): 304–308.

Vriens, M. (2003). Strategic research design. *Marketing Research* 15(4): 21–25.

Wyner, G. A. (2004a). Narrowing the gap. *Marketing Research* 16(1): 6–7.

Wyner, G. A. (2004b). The right metrics. *Marketing Research* 16(2): 6–7.

Wyner, G. A. (2005). Research road maps. *Marketing Research* 17(2): 6–7.

CHAPTER FIVE: SPORT CONSUMER BEHAVIOR

Armstrong, K. L. (2002). Race and consumption behavior: A preliminary investigation of a black consumers' sport motivation scale. *Journal of Sport Behavior* 25(4): 309–330.

Bennett, G., Sagas, M., and Dees, W. (2006). Media preferences of action sports consumers: Differences between Generation X and Y. *Sport Marketing Quarterly* 15(1): 40–49.

Brandish, C. and Lathrop, A. H. (2001). Girl power: Examining the female pre-teen and teen as a distinct segment of the sport marketplace. *Sport Marketing Quarterly* 10(1): 19–24.

Eastman, J. K., Eastman, A. D., and Eastman, K. L. (2002). Insurance sales agents and the internet: The relationship between opinion leadership, subjective knowledge, and internet attitudes. *Journal of Marketing Management* 18(3–4): 259–285.

EPM Entertainment Marketing Sourcebook. (2009–2010 edn). New York: EPM Communications, Inc.

Erikson, E. (1993). *Childhood and Society.* New York: W. W. Norton & Company.

Funk, D. C. and James, J. D. (2004a). Exploring origins of involvement: Understanding the relationship between consumer motives and involvement with professional sport teams. *Leisure Sciences* 26(1): 35–61.

Funk, D. C. and James, J. D. (2004b). The fan attitude network (FAN) model: Exploring attitude formation and change among sport consumers. *Sport Management Review* 7(1): 1–26.

Funk, D. C., Ridinger, L. L., and Moorman, A. M. (2002). Understanding consumer support: Extending the sport interest inventory (SII) to examine individual differences among women's professional sport consumers. *Sport Management Review* 6(1): 1–32.

Funk, D. C., Mahony, D. F., and Havitz, M. E. (2003). Sport consumer behavior: Assessment and direction. *Sport Marketing Quarterly* 12(4): 200–205.

Geng, L., Lockhart, B., Blackmore, C., and Andrus, R. (1996). Sport marketing strategy: A consumer behavior case analysis in China. *Multinational Business Review*. Available online: <http://www.findarticles.com/p/articles/mi_qa3674/ is_199604/ai_n8756626> (accessed March 17, 2006).

Goldsmith, R. E. and De Witt, T. S. (2003). The predictive validity of an opinion leadership scale. *Journal of Marketing Theory and Practice* 11(1): 28–35.

Green, B. C. (2001). Leveraging subculture and identity to promote sport events. *Sport Management Review* 4(1): 1–19.

Griffin, C. (2002). Identity check: Today's action sports consumer is the kid next door, and to understand him, just dial into youth culture. *Sporting Goods Business* 35(9): 18.

Hawkins, D. I., Best, R. J., and Mothersbaugh, D. L. (2006). *Consumer Behavior: Building Marketing Strategy*, 10th edn. Columbus, OH: McGraw-Hill/Irwin.

Henry, P. C. (2005). Social class, market situation and consumers' metaphors of (dis)empowerment. *Journal of Consumer Research* 31(4): 766–778.

Herek, M. (2002). Living the lifestyle. *Sporting Goods Business* 35(9): 32–33.

James, J. D. and Ross, S. D. (2004). Comparing sport consumer motivations across multiple sports. *Sport Marketing Quarterly* 13(1): 17–25.

James, J. D., Kolbe, R. H., and Trail, G. T. (2002). Psychological connection to a new sport team: Building or maintaining the consumer base? *Sport Marketing Quarterly* 11(4): 215–225.

Kahle, L. R., Aiken, D., Dalakas, V., and Duncan, M. (2003). Men's versus women's collegiate basketball customers: Attitudinal favorableness and the environment. *International Journal of Sports Marketing and Sponsorship* 5(2): 145–159.

Kwok, S. and Uncles, M. (2005). Sales promotion effectiveness: The impact of consumer differences at an ethnic-group level. *Journal of Product and Brand Management* 14(3): 170–186.

Kwon, H. H. and Trail, G. T. (2001). Sport fan motivation: A comparison of American students and international students. *Sport Marketing Quarterly* 10(3): 147–155.

Kwon, H. H. and Armstrong, K. L. (2002). Factors influencing impulse buying of sport team licensed merchandise. *Sport Marketing Quarterly* 11(3): 151–163.

Kwon, H. H. and Armstrong, K. L. (2004). An exploration of the construct of psychological attachment to a sport team among students: A multidimensional approach. *Sport Marketing Quarterly* 13(2): 94–103.

Lam, S. S. K. and Schaubroeck, J. (2000). A field experiment testing frontline opinion leaders as change agents. *Journal of Applied Psychology* 85(6): 987–995.

Lane, W. R., King, K., and Reichart, T. (2011). *Kleppner's Advertising Procedure*, 18th edn. Upper Saddle River, NJ: Pearson Education.

Lou, Y.-C. and Chen, S. F. S. (2002). Order effects on social attitude in an Eastern culture: Implications for cross-cultural consumer research. *Advances in Consumer Research* 29(1): 386.

Marsick, V. J. and Watkins, K. E. (2001). Informal and incidental learning. *New Directions for Adult and Continuing Education* 89: 25–34.

Miller, T. (1998). Global segments from "strivers" to "creatives". *Marketing News* 32(5): 11–12.

Painter, G., Deutsch, D., and Overholt, B. J. (1998). *Alfred Adler: As We Remember Him*, 2nd edn. Hershey, PA: North American Society of Adlerian Psychology.

Pelletier, L. G. (1995). Toward a new measure of intrinsic motivation, extrinsic motivation, and amotivation in sports: The sport motivation scale (SMS). *Journal of Sport and Exercise Psychology* 17: 35–53.

Quick, S. (2000). Contemporary sport consumers: Some implications of linking fan typology with key spectator variables. *Sport Marketing Quarterly* 9(3): 149–156.

Schiffman, L. and Kanuk, L. L. (2010). *Consumer Behavior*, 10th edn. Upper Saddle River, NJ: Prentice Hall.

Stewart, B., Smith, A. C. T., and Nicholson, M. (2003). Sport consumer typologies: A critical review. *Sport Marketing Quarterly* 12(4): 206–216.

Tokuyama, S. and Greenwell, T. C. (2011). Examining similarities and differences in consumer motivation for playing and watching soccer. *Sport Marketing Quarterly* 20(3): 148–156.

Trail, G. T. and James, J. D. (2001). The motivation scale for sport consumption: Assessment of the scale's psychometric properties. *Journal of Sport Behavior* 24(1): 108–127.

Trail, G. T., Fink, J. S., and Anderson, D. F. (2003a). Sport spectator consumption behavior. *Sport Marketing Quarterly* 12(1): 8–17.

Trail, G. T., Robinson, M. J., Dick, R. J., and Gillentine, A. J. (2003b). Motives and points of attachment: Fans versus spectators in intercollegiate athletics. *Sport Marketing Quarterly* 12(4): 217–227.

Trail, G. T., Anderson, D. F., and Fink, J. S. (2005). Consumer satisfaction and identity theory: A model of sport spectator conative loyalty. *Sport Marketing Quarterly* 14(2): 98–111.

Trail, G. T., Robinson, M. J., and Kim, Y. K. (2008). Sport consumer behavior: A test for group differences on structural constraints. *Sport Marketing Quarterly* 17(4): 190–200.

Van Ossalaer, S. M. J., Janiszewski, C., Mick, D. G., and Kardes, F. R. (2001). Two ways of learning brand association. *Journal of Consumer Research* 28(2): 202–223.

Verma, D. P. S. and Kapoor, S. (2003). Dimensions of buying roles in family decision making. *IIMB Management Review* 15(4): 7–14.

Volkov, M., Morgan, M. J., and Summers, J. (2005). Consumer complaint behaviour in sport consumption. In *Where Sport Marketing Theory Meets Practice: Selected Papers from the Second Annual Conference of the Sport Marketing Association*, edited by B. G. Pitts. Morgantown, WV: Fitness Information Technology.

Woodall, T. (2004). Why marketers don't market: Rethinking offensive and defensive archetypes. *Journal of Marketing Management* 20(5–6): 559–576.

Wooten, D. B. (1995). One-of-a-kind full house: Some consequences of ethnic and gender distinctiveness. *Journal of Consumer Psychology* 4(3): 205–224.

Zbar, J. D. (2002). Racing sponsors get room to stretch. *Advertising Age* 73(43): 8–9.

CHAPTER SIX: SPORT PRODUCT AND LOGISTICAL MANAGEMENT

Anderson, J. C. and Narus, J. A. (2003). Selectively pursuing more of your customer business. *MIT Sloan Management Review* 44(3): 42–49.

Archetti, E. P. (1998). El potrero y el pibe: territorio y pertenencia en el imaginario del fútbol argentino. *Nueva Sociadad* 154: 101–119.

Archetti, E. P. (1999). *Masculinities: Football, Polo, and the Tango in Argentina*. New York: Berg.

Barnes, R., ed. (2005). Looking down the line. *Do-It-Yourself Retailing* 189(2): 28.

Barrand, D. (2005). Sports marketing: When disaster strikes. *Marketing*: 35.

Bhonslay, M. (2004). Looming ahead: With the imminent demise of apparel import quotas, much of the industry is reorienting its sourcing towards China. *Sporting Goods Business* 37(12): 8–9.

Bhonslay, M. (2005). Lift lines: Alpine ski and snowboard gear for 2005/06 ascends the mountain with new technology. *Sporting Goods Business* 38(1): 28–32.

Brady, D. (2004). IMG: Show me the bottom line. *Business Week* 3891: 82.

Burke, M. (2004). X-treme economics. *Forbes* 172(15): 42.

Burton, R. (2005). Surf's up: Lessons from Down Under for sports leagues and media partners. *Mediaweek* 15(30): 17.

Carr, R. (2000). A plan to reduce supply chain time. *Sporting Goods Business* 33 (16): 7.

Cassidy, H. (2004). Tom Wilson/Craig Turnbull: Lunch pail set: Nothing but net. *Brandweek* 45(36): 42–45.

Chadwick, S., Semens, A., Schwarz, E. C., and Zhang, D. (2010). Economic Impact Report on Global Rugby, Part III: Strategic & Emerging Markets. Center for the International Business of Sport, Coventry University: Coventry, UK. Available online: <http://www.irb.com/mm/Document/NewsMedia/MediaZone/02/04/22/88/2042288_PDF.pdf> (accessed November 12, 2011).

Chandra, C. and Kumar, S. (2000). Supply chain management in theory and practice: A passing fad or a fundamental change? *Industrial Management and Data Systems* 100(3–4): 100–113.

Chatterjee, S. C., Hyvonen, S., and Anderson, E. (1995). Concentrated vs. balanced sourcing: An examination of retailer purchasing decisions in closed markets. *Journal of Retailing* 71(1): 23–46.

Clark, K. (2005). Multiple channels, one chain: Cabela's gets serious with supply chain management. *Chain Store Age* 81(5): 37A.

Desbordes, M. (2002). Empirical analysis of the innovation phenomena in the sports equipment industry. *Technology Analysis and Strategic Management* 14(4): 481–498.

Elliott, M. (2005). Bar codes are forever. *Industrial Engineer* 37(3): 28–29.

Facanha, C. and Horvath, A. (2005). Environmental assessment of logistics outsourcing. *Journal of Management in Engineering* 21(1): 27–37.

Flint, D. J., Woodruff, R. B., and Gardial, S. F. (2002). Exploring the phenomenon of customers' desired value change in a business-to-business context. *Journal of Marketing* 66(4): 102–117.

Forney, M. (2004). How Nike figured out China. *Time* 164(17): A8.

Gladden, J. M. and Funk, D. C. (2002). Developing an understanding of brand associations in team sport: Empirical evidence from consumers of professional sport. *Journal of Sport Management* 16(1): 54–81.

Gladden, J. M. and McDonald, M. (1999). Examining the importance of brand equity in professional sport. *Sport Marketing Quarterly* 8(1): 21–29.

Goldblatt, D. (2006). *The Ball is Round: A Global History of Soccer*. New York: Riverhead Books.

Green, B. C. and Muller, T. E. (2002). Positioning a youth sport camp: A brand mapping exercise. *Sport Management Review* 5(2): 179–200.

Greenfield, K. T. (2004). Bouncing back: A mogul hopes to revive the prospects for the megafirm of sports marketing. *Sports Illustrated* 101(14): 20.

Griffin, C. (2004). Keeping it real: Technology is bursting at the seams, but authenticity is gaining ground in marketing, as well. *Sporting Goods Business* 37(12): 30.

Harris, J. (2010). *Rugby Union and Globalization: An Odd-shaped World*. New York: Palgrave Macmillan.

Holmes, S. (2003). Nike. *Business Week* (3859): 98.

Holmes, S. and Bernstein, A. (2004). The new Nike. *Business Week* 3900: 78–86.

Janoff, B. (2004a). Dilemma of sports marketing; ATP swings deal for deuce. *Brandweek* 45(41): 12.

Janoff, B. (2004b). MLB safe at home with Ameriquest as new partner: Mortgage firm builds sports marketing with teams, All-Star Game. *Brandweek* 45(16): 8.

Janoff, B. (2004c). The world not according to Kobe. *Brandweek* 45(2): 20–23.

Kinsella, B. (2005). Delivering the goods. *Industrial Engineer* 37(3): 24–30.

Kulp, S. C., Lee, H. L., and Ofek, E. (2004). Manufacturer benefits from information integration with retail customers. *Management Science* 50(4): 431–444.

Lancioni, R. A., Smith, M. F., and Oliva, T. A. (2000). The role of the internet in supply chain management. *Industrial Marketing Management* 29(1): 45–56.

Leand, J. (2004). Dog fights: A pack of small vendors are shaking up the industry in a big way. *Sporting Goods Business* 37(9): 26–27.

Lehmann, D. R. and Winer, R. S. (2004). *Product Management*, 4th edn. New York: McGraw-Hill.

Linnett, R. (2003a). Fox sports specialty: Product 'immersion'; net inks tie-ins with Snapple. *Advertising Age* 74(3): 3.

Linnett, R. (2003b). Upfront: ESPN web property hawked in upfront. *Advertising Age* 74(23): 61.

Lowry, T. (2003). The NFL Machine: Behind a thrilling season is a hard-nosed business run with military precision. *Business Week* 3817: 86.

Mangan, J. A. (1998). *The Games Ethic and Imperialism: Aspects of the Diffusion of an Ideal*. London: Frank Cass.

Mangan, J. A. (2002). The early evolution of modern sport in Latin America: A mainly English middle-class inspiration? In *Sport in Latin American Society: Past and Present*, edited by J. A. Mangan and L. P. DaCosta. London: Frank Cass.

Mason, D. S. (1999). What is the sports product and who buys it? The marketing of professional sports leagues. *European Journal of Marketing* 33(3–4): 402–418.

McGivney, A. (2003). Our bodies, our gear. *Backpacker* 31(5): 92.

Meenaghan, T. and O'Sullivan, P. (1999). Playpower: sports meets marketing. *European Journal of Marketing* 33(3–4): 241–249.

Melville, G. (2005). Gym dandy. *Money* 34(2): 128–132.

Mollenkopf, D., Gibson, A., and Ozanne, L. (2000). The integration of marketing and logistics functions: An empirical examination of New Zealand firms. *Journal of Business Logistics* 21(2): 89–112.

389

bibliography

Moore, P. (1999). Help for special Olympics. *Tech Directions* 59(1): 13.

Morgan, P. (2003). Commonwealth Games public transport wins. *Logistics and Transport Focus* 5(3): 29–35.

Newell, K. (2003). A uniform(ed) decision: Making the right choices for team apparel. *Coach and Athletic Director* 73(3): 46–50.

Palmer, I. (2004). Adidas steps up to open platform in consolidation project. *Computing Canada* 30(17): 25.

Panayides, P. M. (2002). Economic organization of intermodal transport. *Transport Reviews* 22(4): 401–414.

Parrish, C. and Zorrilla, D. (2012). Rugby Union Football in Argentina. In *Sports Around the World: History, Culture, & Practice* (Vol. 3), edited by J. Nauright and C. Parrish. Santa Barbara, CA: ABC-Clio.

Persons, D. (2001). Local inventor's brainchild on a roll. *Community College Week* 13(14): 10.

Powell, M. (2001). Technology and sporting goods. *Sporting Goods Business* 34(6): 17.

Richelieu, A. (2004). A new brand world for sports teams. In *Sharing Best Practices in Sport Marketing: The Sport Marketing Association's Inaugural Book of Papers*, edited by B. G. Pitts. Morgantown, WV: Fitness Information Technology.

Rodríguez, M. G. (2005). The place of women in Argentinian football. *International Journal of the History of Sport* 22(2): 231–245.

Ryan, H. F. (2008). The development of rugby in the River Plate region: Irish influences. *Irish Migration Studies in Latin America* 6 (1): 29–38.

Schottmiler, P. (2000). Time to exchange: The new sporting goods supply chain. *Sporting Goods Business* 33(5): 14.

Siemieniuch, C. E., Waddell, F. N., and Sinclair, M. A. (1999). The role of "partnership" in supply chain management for fast-moving consumer goods: A case study. *International Journal of Logistics* 2(1): 87–101.

Smith, F. O. (2005). RFID, realistically speaking. *Manufacturing Business Technology* 23(10): 2–6.

Sowinski, L. L. (2003). Skating his way to China. *World Trade* 16(11): 44–45.

Speer, J. K. (2002). Reebok International Ltd. *Bobbin* 44(4): 30–31.

Tang, N. K. H., Benton, H., Love, D., Albores, Ball, P., MacBryde, J., Boughton, N., and Drake, P. (2004). Developing an enterprise simulator to support electronic supply chain management for B2B electronic business. *Production Planning and Control* 15(6): 572–583.

Tenser, J. (2004). Endorser qualities count more than ever: The lure is strong, but athletes face resistance. *Advertising Age* 75(45): S2.

Thim, J. (2005). Performing plastics. *Chemistry and Industry* 3: 20–21.

Thomaselli, R. (2004). Will MLB sell space on player uniforms? With $500M in wings league can "never say never". *Advertising Age* 75(14): 3.

Unión Argentina de Rugby. http://www.uar.com.ar/.

Vaidyanathan, G. (2005). A framework for evaluating third-party logistics. *Communications of the ACM* 48(1): 89–94.

van Phan, K.-Q. (2006). Strategic offshoring from a decomposed COO's perspective: A cross-regional study of four product categories. *Journal of American Academy of Business* 8(2): 59–66.

Walzer, E. (2004). Getting personal: Product customization lets customers reveal their inner designer while vendors and retailers strengthen their on-line businesses. *Sporting Goods Business* 37(12): 50.

Walzer, E. (2005). Active fusion: The blending of sport and street style leads to subtle, sophisticated designs. *Sporting Goods Business* 38(12): 32–33.

Wang, G., Huang, S. H., and Dismukes, J. P. (2005). Manufacturing supply chain design and evaluation. *International Journal of Advanced Manufacturing Technology* 25(1–2): 93–100.

Yang, B. and Burns, N. D. (2003). Implications of postponement for the supply chain. *International Journal of Production Research* 41(9): 2075–2090.

Yiannakis, A. (1991). Training the sport marketer: A social science perspective. *Journal of Sport Behavior* 14(1): 61–68.

CHAPTER SEVEN: SALES MANAGEMENT IN SPORT

Ashworth, A. (2005). Accelerating sales performance for Visa by closing the communications gaps. *Journal of Financial Services Marketing* 9(4): 318–328.

Baldauf, A., Cravens, D. W., and Puercy, N. F. (2001). Examining business strategy, sales management, and salesperson antecedents of sales organization effectiveness. *Journal of Personal Selling and Sales Management* 21(2): 109–122.

Bundschuh, R. G. and Dezvane, T. M. (2003). How to make after-sales services pay off. *McKinsey Quarterly* 4: 116–127.

Carillo, F. and Guliano, P. (2001). Writer's notebook. *Public Relations Quarterly* 46(3): 48.

Clopton, S. W., Stoddard, J. E., and Clay, J. W. (2001). Salesperson characteristics affecting consumer complaint responses. *Journal of Consumer Behaviour* 1: 129–139.

Dixon, A. L. and Schertzer, S. M. B. (2005). Bouncing back: How salesperson optimism and self-efficacy influence attributions and behaviors following failure. *Journal of Personal Selling and Sales Management* 25(4): 361–369.

Fader, P. S., Hardie, B. G. S., and Chun-Yao, H. (2004). A dynamic changepoint model for new product sales forecasting. *Marketing Science* 23(1): 50–65.

Grapentine, T. (2005). Segmenting the sales force. *Marketing Management* 14(1): 29–34.

Grewal, D., Levy, M., and Marshall, G. W. (2002). Personal selling in retail settings: How does the internet and related technologies enable and limit successful selling? *Journal of Marketing Management* 18(3–4): 301–316.

Howard, D. and Crompton, J. (2004). Tactics used by sports organizations in the United States to increase ticket sales. *Managing Leisure* 9(2): 87–95.

James, J. D. and Ross, S. D. (2004). Comparing sport consumer motivations across multiple sports. *Sport Marketing Quarterly* 13(1): 17–25.

Johansson, U. (2001). Retail buying: Process, information and IT use: A conceptual framework. *International Review of Retail, Distribution and Consumer Research* 11(4): 329–357.

Johlke, M. C. and Duhan, D. F. (2001). Testing competing models of sales force communication. *Journal of Personal Selling and Sales Management* 21(4): 265–277.

Knight, C. (2004). Maximize the buying potential of current customers. *Sell!ng*: 12.

Kwok, S. and Uncles, M. (2005). Sales promotion effectiveness: The impact of consumer differences at an ethnic-group level. *Journal of Product and Brand Management* 14(3): 170–186.

Lassk, F. G., Marshall, G. W., Cravens, D. W., and Moncrief, W. C. (2001). Salesperson job involvement: A modern perspective and a new scale. *Journal of Personal Selling and Sales Management* 21(4): 291–302.

Locander, W. B. and Luechauer, D. L. (2005). Are we there yet? *Marketing Management* 14(6): 50–52.

Luiras, T. E. and Stanley, J. E. (2004). Bringing science to sales. *McKinsey Quarterly* 3: 16.

Mangan, K. S. (2003). Perfecting the sales pitch. *Chronicle of Higher Education* 49(24): A30–A31.

Marber, A., Wellen, P., and Posluszny, S. (2005). The merging of marketing and sports: A case study. *Marketing Management Journal* 15(1): 162–171.

Randall, E. J. and Randall, C. H. (2001). A current review of hiring techniques for sales personnel: The first steps in the sales management process. *Journal of Marketing Theory and Practice* 9(2): 70–83.

Rigsbee, E. R. (2002). The relationship you build with your prospects and customers is more important than the close. *Cost Engineering* 44(2): 40–41.

Rouzies, D., Anderson, E., Kohli, A. K., Michaels, R. E., Weitz, B. A., and Zoltners, A. A. (2005). Sales and marketing integration: A proposed framework. *Journal of Personal Selling and Sales Management* 25(2): 113–122.

Schwepker, C. and Good, D. J. (2004a). Marketing control and sales force customer orientation. *Journal of Personal Selling and Sales Management* 24(3): 167–179.

Schwepker, C. and Good, D. J. (2004b). Sales management practices: The impact of ethics on customer orientation, employment and performance. *Marketing Management Journal* 14(2): 134–147.

Washo, M. (2004). *Break into Sports Through Ticket Sales*. Bedford Park, IL: MMW Marketing.

CHAPTER EIGHT: RETAIL MANAGEMENT IN SPORT

Berman, B. and Evans, J. R. (2010). *Retail Management: A Strategic Approach*, 11th edn. Upper Saddle River, NJ: Pearson-Prentice Hall.

Chiang, W. K., Chhajed, D., and Hess, J. D. (2003). Direct marketing, indirect profits: A strategic analysis of dual-channel supply-chain design. *Management Science* 49(1): 1–20.

Friend, L. and Thompson, S. (2003). Identity, ethnicity, and gender: Using narratives to understand their meaning in retail shopping encounters. *Consumption, Markets and Culture* 6(1): 23–41.

Grewal, D., Levy, M., Mehrotra, A., and Sharma, A. (1999). Planning merchandising decisions to account for regional and product assortment differences. *Journal of Retailing* 75(3): 405–424.

Hansotia, B. J. and Rukstales, B. (2002). Direct marketing for multichannel retailers: Issues, challenges and solutions. *Journal of Database Management* 9(3): 259–266.

Irwin, R. L., Zwick, D., and Sutton, W. A. (1999). Assessing organizational attributes contributing to marketing excellence in American professional sport franchises. *Journal of Consumer Marketing* 16(6): 603–615.

Lam, S. L., Vandenbosch, M., Hulland, J., and Pearce, M. (2001). Evaluating promotions in shopping environments: Decomposing sales response into attraction, conversion, and spending effects. *Marketing Science* 20(2): 194–215.

Merrilees, B. and Fry, M. L. (2002). Corporate branding: A framework for e-retailers. *Corporate Reputation Review* 5(2–3): 213–225.

Newholm, T., McGoldrick, P., Keeling, K., Macaulay, L., and Doherty, J. (2004). Multistory trust and online retailer strategies. *International Review of Retail* 14(4): 437–456.

Nielsen Business Media Retail top 100: The most successful companies continue to stress efficient operations, carefully planned store openings, and a clear point of differentiation. (2002). *Sporting Goods Business* 35(6): 23.

Reynolds, K. E. and Beatty, S. E. (1999). Customer benefits and company consequences of customer–salesperson relationships in retailing. *Journal of Retailing* 75(1): 1–2.

Smolianov, P. and Shilbury, D. (2005). Examining integrated advertising and sponsorship in corporate marketing through televised sport. *Sport Marketing Quarterly* 14(4): 239–250.

Sparks, M., Chadwick, S., Schafmeister, G., Woratschek, H., Hurley, T., and Junya, F. (2005). Sport marketing around the world. *Sport Marketing Quarterly* 14(3): 197–199.

Steenhaut, S. and Van Kenhove, P. (2005). Relationship commitment and ethical consumer behavior in a retail setting: The case of receiving too much change at the checkout. *Journal of Business Ethics* 56(4): 335–353.

Vinod, B. (2005). Retail revenue management and the new paradigm of merchandise optimisation. *Journal of Revenue and Pricing Management* 3(4): 358–368.

Young, S. (2000). Putting the pieces together at the point of sale. *Marketing Research* 12(3): 32–36.

CHAPTER NINE: E-MARKETING MANAGEMENT IN SPORT

Bart, Y., Shankar, V., Sultan, F., and Urban, G. L. (2005). Are the drivers and role of online trust the same for all websites and consumers? A large-scale exploratory empirical study. *Journal of Marketing* 69(4): 133–152.

Brandish, C. (2001). Electronic commerce. *Sport Marketing Quarterly* 10(2): 114.

Carlson, J. and O'Cass, A. (2010). Exploring the relationships between e-service quality, satisfaction, attitudes and behaviours in content-driven e-service websites. *The Journal of Services Marketing* 24(2): 112–127.

Cavusgil, S. T. (2002). Extending the reach of e-business. *Marketing Management* 11(2): 24–29.

Farrelly, F., Quester, P., and Greyser, S. A. (2005). Defending the co-branding benefits of sponsorship B2B partnerships: The case of ambush marketing. *Journal of Advertising Research* 45(3): 339–348.

Fay, S. (2004). Partial-repeat bidding in the name-your-own-price channel. *Marketing Science* 23(3): 407–418.

Filo, K. and Funk, D. C. (2005). Congruence between attractive product features and virtual content delivery for internet marketing communication. *Sport Marketing Quarterly* 14(2): 112–122.

Gerrard, B. (2000). Media ownership of pro sports teams: Who are the winners and losers? *International Journal of Sports Marketing and Sponsorship* 2(3): 199–218.

Hunt, E. C. and Sproat, S. B. (2003). Blasting off into e-business. *Nursing* 33(12): 74–76.

Kegeng, X., Wilkinson, T., and Brouthers, L. E. (2002). The dark side of international e-commerce: Logistics. *Marketing Management Journal* 12(2): 123–134.

Margolis, N. (2005). Why is B2B so far ahead of B2C in the digital marketing arena? *Precision Marketing* 17(29): 14–15.

Owens, J. D. (2006). Electronic business: A business model can make the difference. *Management Services* 50(1): 24–28.

Perrott, B. (2005). Towards a manager's model for e-business strategy decisions. *Journal of General Management* 30(4): 73–89.

Rayport, J. F. and Jaworski, B. J. (2003). *Introduction to E-Commerce*, 2nd edn. New York: McGraw-Hill.

Robbins, S. (2005). In e-business, the value of every transaction increases. *Information Systems Management* 22(3): 85–86.

Rohm, A. J. and Sultan, F. (2004). The evolution of e-business. *Marketing Management* 13(1): 32–37.

Sharma, A. and Sheth, J. N. (2004). Web-based marketing: The coming revolution in marketing thought and strategy. *Journal of Business Research* 57(7): 696–702.

Stork, K. (2000). It pays to be different. *Purchasing* 128(3): 38.

Stotlar, D. K. (2000). Vertical integration in sport. *Journal of Sport Management* 14(1): 1–7.

Strader, T. J. and Ramaswami, S. N. (2002). The value of seller trustworthiness in C2C online markets. *Communications of the ACM* 45(12): 45–49.

Tobias, H. (2002). Using e-business strategy to gain advantage. *Journal of Database Management* 9(2): 132–136.

CHAPTER TEN: COMMUNICATION MANAGEMENT AND PROMOTIONS IN SPORT

Alexandris, K. and Kouthouris, C. (2005). Personal incentives for participation in summer children's camps: Investigating their relationships with satisfaction and loyalty. *Managing Leisure* 10(1): 39–53.

Andersson, T., Rustad, A., and Solberg, H. A. (2004). Local residents' monetary evaluation of sports events. *Managing Leisure* 9(3): 145–158.

Bakamitsos, G. A. and Siomkos, G. J. (2004). Context effects in marketing practice: The case of mood. *Journal of Consumer Behaviour* 3(4): 304–314.

Beaupre, A. (2003). Getting your customers to help with public relations. *Public Relations Tactics* 10(10): 9.

Boivin, C. (2005). Profiting from licensing without royalties. *Marketing Bulletin* 16: 109.

Bristow, D. and Schneider, K. (2003). The sports fan motivation scale: Development and testing. *Marketing Management Journal* 13(2): 115–121.

Brown, M. T. and Kreutzer, A. (2002). Reducing risk in promotion: The incorporation of risk management principles by sport marketers. *Sport Marketing Quarterly* 11(4): 252–254.

Chelladurai, P. (2006). *Human Resource Management in Sport and Recreation*, 2nd edn. Champaign, IL: Human Kinetics.

End, C. M., Kretschmar, J. M., and Dietz-Uhler, B. (2004). College students' perceptions of sports fandom as a social status determinant. *International Sports Journal* 8(1): 114–123.

Eroglu, S. A., Machleit, K. A., and Davis, L. M. (2001). An empirical study of online atmospherics and shopper responses. *Advances in Consumer Research* 28(1): 40.

Fink, J. S., Trail, G. T., and Anderson, D. F. (2002). Environmental factors associated with spectator attendance and sport consumption behavior: Gender and team differences. *Sport Marketing Quarterly* 11(1): 8–19.

Geary, D. L. (2005). The decline of media credibility and its impact on public relations. *Public Relations Quarterly* 50(3): 8–12.

Geiger, S. and Turley, D. (2005). Personal selling as a knowledge-based activity: Communities of practice in the sales force. *Irish Journal of Management* 26(1): 61–70.

Grady, J. (2005). University of Alabama case to test limits of trademark licensing in sport art cases. *Sport Marketing Quarterly* 14(4): 251–252.

Guiniven, J. (2005). Community relations: more than money. *Public Relations Tactics* 12(11): 6.

Hal Dean, D. (2002). Associating the corporation with a charitable event through sponsorship: Measuring the effects on corporate community relations. *Journal of Advertising* 31(4): 77–87.

Hardin, R. and Mcclung, S. (2002). Collegiate sports information: A profile of the profession. *Public Relations Quarterly* 47(2): 35–39.

Hoffman, K. D. and Turley, L. W. (2002). Atmospherics, service encounters, and consumer decision making: An integrative perspective. *Journal of Marketing Theory and Practice* 10(3): 33–47.

Hogue, J. (2000). How I spent my summer vacation: An intern's foray into sports marketing. *Public Relations Tactics* 7(9): 20.

Holt, R. (2000). The discourse ethics in sports print journalism. *Culture, Sport, Society* 3(3): 88–103.

Hopwood, M. (2005). Sports public relations: The strategic application of public relations to the business of sport. In *Where Sport Marketing Theory Meets Practice: Selected Papers from the Second Annual Conference of the Sport Marketing Association*, edited by B. G. Pitts. Morgantown, WV: Fitness Information Technology.

Hopwood, M. K. (2005). Applying the public relations function to the business of sport. *International Journal of Sports Marketing and Sponsorship* 6(3): 174–188.

Keller, K. L. (2001). Mastering the marketing communications mix: Micro and macro perspectives on integrated marketing communications. *Journal of Marketing Management* 17(7–8): 819–848.

Kurtzman, J. and Zauhar, J. (2005). Sports tourism consumer motivation. *Journal of Sports Tourism* 10(1): 21–31.

Kwok, S. and Uncles, M. (2005). Sales promotion effectiveness: The impact of consumer differences at an ethnic-group level. *Journal of Product and Brand Management* 14(3): 170–186.

Kwon, H. H. and Armstrong, K. L. (2002). Factors influencing impulse buying of sport team licensed merchandise. *Sport Marketing Quarterly* 11(3): 151–163.

Lam, S. Y., Vandenbosch, M., Hulland, J., and Pearce, M. (2001). Evaluating promotions in shopping environments: Decomposing sales response into attraction, conversion, and spending effects. *Marketing Science* 20(2): 194–215.

MacDonald, M. A., Milne, G. R., and Hong, J. (2002). Motivational factors for evaluating sport spectator and participant markets. *Sport Marketing Quarterly* 11(2): 100–113.

Milotic, D. (2003). The impact of fragrance on consumer choice. *Journal of Consumer Behaviour* 3(2): 179–191.

Neeley, S. (2005). Influences on consumer socialisation. *Young Consumers* 6(2): 63–69.

Samsup Jo, B. (2003). The portrayal of public relations in the news media. *Mass Communication and Society* 6(4): 397–411.

Schuler, M. (2004). Management of the organizational image: A method for organizational image configuration. *Corporate Reputation Review* 7(1): 37–53.

Schwarz, E. C. and Blais, D. (2005). How to get a minor league promotion major league publicity. In *Where Sport Marketing Theory Meets Practice: Selected Papers from the Second Annual Conference of the Sport Marketing Association*, edited by B. G. Pitts. Morgantown, WV: Fitness Information Technology.

Smith, J. M. and Ingham, A. G. (2003). On the waterfront: Retrospectives on the relationship between sport and communities. *Sociology of Sport Journal* 20(3): 252–274.

Stoldt, G. C., Dittmore, S. W., and Branvold, S. E. (2012). *Sport Public Relations: Managing Stakeholder Communication,* 2nd edn. Champaign, IL: Human Kinetics.

Stoldt, G. C., Miller, L. K., and Comfort, P. G. (2001). Through the eyes of athletics directors: Perceptions of sports information directors, and other public relations issues. *Sport Marketing Quarterly* 10(3): 164–172.

Ward, S., Bridges, K., and Chitty, B. (2005). Do incentives matter? An examination of on-line privacy concerns and willingness to provide personal and financial information. *Journal of Marketing Communications* 11(1): 21–40.

CHAPTER ELEVEN: SPORT ADVERTISING

Amato-McCoy, D. M. (2002). Pigskin passion! *Beverage Aisle* 11(9): 60–63.

Arens, W. F. (2005). *Contemporary Advertising*, 10th edn. New York: McGraw-Hill.

Bauer, H., Sauer, N. E., and Exler, S. (2005). The loyalty of German soccer fans: Does a team's brand image matter? *International Journal of Sports Marketing and Sponsorship* 7(1): 14–22.

Bhattacharjee, S. and Rao, G. (2006). Tackling ambush marketing: The need for regulation and analysing the present legislative and contractual efforts. *Sport in Society* 9(1): 128–149.

Chadwick, S. (2005). Sport marketing: A discipline for the mainstream. *International Journal of Sports Marketing and Sponsorship* 7(1): 7.

Charbonneau, J. and Garland, R. (2005). Talent, looks or brains? New Zealand advertising practitioners' views on celebrity and athlete endorsers. *Marketing Bulletin* 16: 1–10.

Clancy, K. J. and Kelly, L. (2001). Stemming the slide: A lesson from the Red Sox. *Brandweek* 42(14): 17.

Cousens, L., Babiak, K., and Slack, T. (2000). Adopting a relationship marketing paradigm: The case of the National Basketball Association. *International Journal of Sports Marketing and Sponsorship* 2(4): 331–355.

Coyle, P. (1999). NFL team scores big with DM game plan. *Direct Marketing* 62(3): 20–27.

Cuneen, J., Spencer, N. E., Ross, S. R., and Apostolopoulou, A. (2007). Advertising portrayals of Indy's female drivers: A perspective on the succession from Guthrie to Patrick. *Sport Marketing Quarterly* 16(4): 209–213, 215–217.

d'Astous, A. and Chnaoui, K. (2002). Consumer perception of sports apparel: The role of brand name, store name, price, and intended usage situation. *International Journal of Sports Marketing and Sponsorship* 4(2): 109–126.

Evans, D. M. and Smith, A. C. T. (2004). Internet sports marketing and competitive advantage for professional sports clubs: Bridging the gap between theory and practice. *International Journal of Sports Marketing and Sponsorship* 6(2): 86–98.

Gladden, J. M. and Funk, D. C. (2001). Understanding brand loyalty in professional sport: Examining the link between brand associations and brand loyalty. *International Journal of Sports Marketing and Sponsorship* 3(1): 67–94.

Grebert, C. and Farrelly, F. (2005). Interview with Carl Grebert, Brand Director Nike Asia Pacific. *International Journal of Sports Marketing and Sponsorship* 7(1): 10–13.

Green, B. C. (2002). Marketing the host city: Analyzing exposure generated by a sport event. *International Journal of Sports Marketing and Sponsorship* 4(4): 335–353.

Howard, D. and Burton, R. (2002). Sports marketing in a recession: It's a brand new game. *International Journal of Sports Marketing and Sponsorship* 4(1): 23–40.

Hyman, M. (2005). Branding the course: It doesn't come cheap, but golf tournament sponsorship earns valuable exposure. *Business Week* 3935: 96.

James, J. D. and Ridinger, L. L. (2002). Female and male sport fans: A comparison of sport consumption motives. *Journal of Sport Behavior* 25(3): 260–279.

Janoff, B. (2005). ESPN brands X games goods: ING NYC Marathon sets pace. *Brandweek* 46(25): 12.

Jowdy, E. and McDonald, M. (2002). Relationship marketing and interactive fan festivals: The Women's United Soccer Association's "Soccer Sensation". *International Journal of Sports Marketing and Sponsorship* 4(4): 295–311.

Lachowetz, T. and Gladden, J. (2002). A framework for understanding cause-related sport marketing programs. *International Journal of Sports Marketing and Sponsorship* 4(4): 313–333.

Lorenz, T. and Campbell, D. (2003). Brands treading over new ground: The demand for "sports lifestyle" products is booming. *Design Week* 18(24): 9.

Meikle, E. (2002). *Lawless Branding: Recent Developments in Trademark Law . . . FIFA Defends World Cup Against Pepsi Ambush Marketing*. Retrieved March 3, 2006 from http://www.brandchannel.com/features_effect.asp?pf_id=103.

Papadimitriou, D., Apostolopoulou, A., and Loukas, I. (2004). The role of perceived fit in fans' evaluation of sports brand extensions. *International Journal of Sports Marketing and Sponsorship* 6(1): 31–48.

Pritchard, M. P. and Negro, C. M. (2001). Sport loyalty programs and their impact on fan relationships. *International Journal of Sports Marketing and Sponsorship* 3(3): 317–338.

Richelieu, A. (2004). A new brand world for sports teams. In *Sharing Best Practices in Sport Marketing: The Sport Marketing Association's Inaugural Book of Papers*, edited by B. G. Pitts. Morgantown, WV: Fitness Information Technology.

Ruihley, B. J., Runyan, R. C., and Lear, K. E. (2010). The use of sport celebrities in advertising: A replication and extension. *Sport Marketing Quarterly* 19(3): 132–142.

Smolianov, P. and Shilbury, D. (2005). Examining integrated advertising and sponsorship in corporate marketing through televised sport. *Sport Marketing Quarterly* 14(4): 239–250.

Soderman, S. and Dolles, H. (2010). Sponsoring the Beijing Olympics: Patterns of sponsor advertising. *Asia Pacific Journal of Marketing and Logistics* 22(1): 8–24.

Stevens, J. A., Lathrop, A. H., and Brandish, C. L. (2003). "Who is your hero?" Implications for athlete endorsement strategies. *Sport Marketing Quarterly* 12(2): 103–110.

Stone, G., Joseph, M., and Jones, M. (2003). An exploratory study on the use of sports celebrities in advertising: A content analysis. *Sport Marketing Quarterly* 12(2): 94–102.

Thomaselli, R. (2004). Guarascio mixes up the NFL plays; Marketing QB's mandate: "Deliver value to business partners" of football league. *Advertising Age* 75(45): S2.

Thomaselli, R. (2005). Ambushing the Super Bowl. *Advertising Age* 76(26): 3, 57.

Vakratsas, D., Feinberg, F. M., Bass, F. M., and Kalyanaram, G. (2004). The shape of advertising response functions revisited: A model of dynamic probabilistic thresholds. *Marketing Science* 23(1): 109–119.

Yoon, S.-J. and Choi, Y. G. (2005). Determinant of successful sports advertisements: The effects of advertisement type, product type and sports model. *Journal of Brand Management* 12(3): 191–205.

CHAPTER TWELVE: SPORT SPONSORSHIP

Alexandris, K., Tsaousi, E., and James, J. (2007). Predicting sponsorship outcomes from attitudinal constructs: The case of a professional basketball event. *Sport Marketing Quarterly* 16(3): 130–139.

Amis, J. and Cornwell, T. B. (2005). *Global Sport Sponsorship*. Oxford: Berg Publishers.

Becker, O. K. (2003). Questioning the name games: An event study analysis of stadium naming rights sponsorship announcements. *International Journal of Sports Marketing and Sponsorship* 5(3): 181–192.

Bradish, C. L., Stephens, J. A., and Lathrop, A. H. (2003). National versus regional sports marketing: An interpretation of "think globally, act locally". *International Journal of Sports Marketing and Sponsorship* 5(3): 209–225.

Burton, R., Quester, P. G., and Farrelly, F. J. (1998). Organizational power games. *Marketing Management* 7(1): 26–36.

Cassidy, H. (2005). So you want to be an Olympic sponsor? *Brandweek* 46(40): 24–28.

Chadwick, S. (2002). The nature of commitment in sport sponsorship relations. *International Journal of Sports Marketing and Sponsorship* 4(3): 257–274.

Chadwick, S. and Thwaites, D. (2004). Advances in the management of sports sponsorship: Fact or fiction? Evidence from English professional soccer. *Journal of General Management* 30(1): 39–59.

Clark, J., Lachowetz, T., Irwin, R. L., and Schimmel, K. (2003). Business-to-business relationships and sport: Using sponsorship as a critical sales event. *International Journal of Sports Marketing and Sponsorship* 5(2): 129–144.

Cornwell, T. B., Relyea, G. E., Irwin, R. L., and Maignan, I. (2000). Understanding long-term effects of sports sponsorship: Role of experience, involvement, enthusiasm and clutter. *International Journal of Sports Marketing and Sponsorship* 2(2): 127–143.

Crompton, J. L. (2004). Conceptualization and alternate operationalizations of the measurement of sponsorship effectiveness in sport. *Leisure Studies* 23(3): 267–281.

Dalakas, V. and Rose, G. M. (2004). The impact of fan identification on consumer response to sponsorships. In *Sharing Best Practices in Sport Marketing: The Sport Marketing Association's Inaugural Book of Papers*, edited by B. G. Pitts. Morgantown, WV: Fitness Information Technology.

Doherty, A. and Murray, M. (2007). The strategic sponsorship process in a non-profit sport organization. *Sport Marketing Quarterly* 16(1): 49–59.

Doonar, J. (2004). Sponsorship is more than just a logo. *Brand Strategy* 185: 46–49.

Fahy, J., Farrelly, F., and Quester, P. (2004). Competitive advantage through sponsorship: A conceptual model and research propositions. *European Journal of Marketing* 38(8): 1013–1030.

Gladden, J. M. and Wolfe, R. (2001). Sponsorship of intercollegiate athletics: The importance of image matching. *International Journal of Sports Marketing and Sponsorship* 3(1): 41–65.

Goodman, C. (2006). Brands must make most of sponsorship chances. *New Media Age* 111(7): 7.

Gosnell, G. (1994). Banner policies at government-owned athletic stadiums: The First Amendment pitfalls. *Ohio State Law Journal* 55: 1143.

Grohs, R., Wagner, U., and Wsetecka, S. (2004). Assessing the effectiveness of sport sponsorships: an empirical examination. *Schmanlenbach Business Review* 56(2): 119–138.

Henseler, J., Wilson, B., and Westberg, K. (2011). Managers' perceptions of the impact of sport sponsorship on brand equity: Which aspects of the sponsorship matter most? *Sport Marketing Quarterly* 20(1): 7–21.

Hughes, S. and Shank, M. (2005). Defining scandal in sports: Media and corporate sponsor perspectives. *Sport Marketing Quarterly* 14(4): 207–216.

Irwin, R. L. and Asimakopoulos, M. K. (1992). An approach to the evaluation and selection of sport sponsorship proposals. *Sport Marketing Quarterly* 1(2): 43–51.

Irwin, R. L., Lachowetz, T., Cornwell, T. B., and Clark, J. S. (2003). Cause-related sport sponsorship: An assessment of spectator beliefs, attitudes, and behavioral intentions. *Sport Marketing Quarterly* 12(3): 131–139.

Lough, N. L. and Irwin, R. L. (2001). A comparative analysis of sponsorship objectives for US women's sport and traditional sport sponsorship. *Sport Marketing Quarterly* 10(4): 202–211.

McCawley, I. (2006). FIFA vows to stop unofficial World Cup sponsorship. *Marketing Week* 29(5): 15.

Mcgeer, B. (2003). Deciding when sponsorship can benefit a brand. *American Banker* 168(81): 8–9.

McKelvey, S. M. (2004). The growth in marketing alliances between US professional sport and legalised gambling entities: Are we putting sport consumers at risk? *Sport Management Review* 7(2): 193–210.

McKelvey, S. M. (2005). "Vice" sponsorships raise brand issues. *Brandweek* 46(7): 18.

Moler, C. (2000). Wanted: Not-for profit to take money . . . marketing through sponsorship. *Parks and Recreation* 35(9): 164–166, 169–172.

Olsen, E. (2010). Does sponsorship work in the same way in different sponsorship contexts? *European Journal of Marketing* 44(1/2): 180–199.

Papadimitriou, D., Apostolopoulou, A., and Dounis, T. (2008). Event sponsorship as a value creating strategy from brands. *The Journal of Product and Brand Management* 17(4): 212–222.

Pruitt, S. W., Cornwell, T. B., and Clark, J. M. (2004). The NASCAR phenomenon: Auto racing sponsorships and shareholder wealth. *Journal of Advertising Research* 44(3): 281–296.

Renard, N. and Sitz, L. (2011). Maximising sponsorship opportunities: A brand model approach. *The Journal of Product and Brand Management* 20(2): 121–129.

Scassa, T. (2011). Ambush marketing and the right of association: Clamping down on references to that big event with all the athletes in a couple of years. *Journal of Sport Management* 25(4): 354–370.

Slattery, J. and Pitts, B. G. (2002). Corporate sponsorship and season ticket holder attendees: An evaluation of changes in recall over the course of one American collegiate football season. *International Journal of Sports Marketing and Sponsorship* 4(2): 151–174.

Stotlar, D. K. (2005). *Developing Successful Sport Sponsorship Plans*, 2nd edn. Morgantown, WV: Fitness information Technology.

Verity, J. (2002). Maximising the marketing potential of sponsorship for global brands. *European Business Journal* 14(4): 161–173.

Willins, M. (2002). Maximize your exposure. *Aftermarket Business* 112(3): 41–43.

CHAPTER THIRTEEN: SOCIAL MEDIA AND NETWORKING IN THE SPORT INDUSTRY

Arena Football League. (2012). Arena Football League Facebook Page. Available online: <http://www.facebook.com/pages/Arena-Football-League/8649266837> (accessed February 16, 2012).

Boyd, D. M. and Ellison, N. B. (2007), Social network sites: Definition, history, and scholarship. *Journal of Computer-Mediated Communication* 13: 210–230.

Facebook. (2012a). Check-in deals. Available online: <http://www.facebook.com/help/?page=18685 1114696034> (accessed February 13, 2012).

Facebook. (2012b). Facebook ads for pages and events. Available online: <http://www.facebook.com/help/?page=202790293089857> (accessed February 16, 2012).

Facebook. (2012c). Page insights. Available online: <http://www.facebook.com/help?page=308377712530003> (accessed February 18, 2012).

Foursquare. (2012). What are Foursquare specials? Available online: <http://support.foursquare.com/entries/481480-what-are-foursquare-specials> (accessed February 17, 2012).

LinkedIn. (2012). About us. Available online: <http://press.linkedin.com/about> (accessed February 16, 2012).

Peck, J. (2007). 50 sports social networking websites. Available online: <http://www.jasonfpeck.com/2007/12/10/50-sports-social-networking-websites/> (accessed February 9, 2012).

Roettgers, J. (2011). Video gamers: TwitchTV wants you to quit your day job. Available online: <http://gigaom.com/video/twitchtv-partner-program/> (accessed February 16, 2012).

Saint, N. (2010). Foursquare competitor SCVNGR partners with Boston Celtics to give away season tickets. Available online: <http://www.businessinsider.com/scvngr-celtics-2010-10#> (accessed February 8, 2012).

SCVNGR. (2012). About us. Available online: <http://scvngr.com/about> (accessed February 21, 2012).

Sutton W. (2011). Looking forward: A vision for sport marketing inquiry and scholarship. *Sport Marketing Quarterly* 20(4): 242–248.

Taggert, S. and Vaynerchuk, A. J. (2010). Early proof that geolocation marketing will succeed [Web log message]. Retrieved from http://vaynermedia.com/2010/04/early-proof-that-geolocation-marketing-will-succeed/.

Twitter. (2012). Promoted tweets. Available online: <https://business.twitter.com/en/advertise/promoted-tweets/> (accessed February 16, 2012).

Williams, J. and Chinn, S. J. (2009). Using Web 2.0 to support the active learning experience. *Journal of Information Systems Education* 20(2): 165–174.

WNBA. (2012). WNBA Facebook page. Available online: <http://www.facebook.com/wnba> (accessed February 21, 2012).

CHAPTER FOURTEEN: INTERNATIONAL AND GLOBAL MARKETING IN SPORT

Bafour, F. (2003). It's time for a new playbook. *Business Week* (3849): 56.

Bairner, A. (2003). Globalization and sport: The nation strikes back. *Phi Kappa Phi Forum* 83(4): 34–37.

Bodet, G. and Chanavat, N. (2010). Building global football brand equity: Lessons from the Chinese market. *Asia Pacific Journal of Marketing and Logistics* 22(1): 55–66.

Boyd, T. C. and Shank, M. D. (2004). Athletes as product endorsers: The effect of gender and product relatedness. *Sport Marketing Quarterly* 13(2): 82–93.

Bradish, C. L., Stevens, J. A., and Lathrop, A. H. (2003). National versus regional sports marketing: An interpretation of "think globally, act locally". *International Journal of Sports Marketing and Sponsorship* 5(3): 209–225.

Brake, M. (1985). *Comparative Youth Subcultures: The Sociology of Youth Culture and Youth Subcultures in America*. London: Routledge.

Burton, R. (2000). SMQ profile/interview. *Sport Marketing Quarterly* 9(1): 5.

Cateora, P. R. and Graham, J. L. (2008). *International Marketing*, 14th edn. New York: McGraw-Hill.

Curran-Kelly, C. (2005). Stranger in a strange land: Using international student experiences to teach adaptation in global marketing. *Marketing Education Review* 15(2): 55–58.

Dayal-Gulati, A. and Lee, A. Y. (2004). *Kellogg on China: Strategies for Success*. Evanston, IL: Northwestern University Press.

Desens, C. and O'Reilly, D. (1994, December 5). The NBA's Fast Break overseas. *Business Week* 3402: 94.

Dickson, G., Phelps, S., and Waugh, D. (2010). Multi-level governance in an international strategic alliance: The plight of the Phoenix and the Asian football market. *Asia Pacific Journal of Marketing and Logistics* 22(1): 111–124.

Euchner, C. (2008, January/February). Hoop dreams. *The American*: 27–34.

Graves, B. (2003). In extreme sports, hardware and apparel are two sides of the same coin. *San Diego Business Journal* 36(3): 24–28.

Hewett, K. and Bearden, W. O. (2001). Dependence, trust, and relational behavior on the part of foreign subsidiary marketing operations: Implications for managing global marketing operations. *Journal of Marketing* 65(4): 51–66.

Huang, X. and Van de Vliert, E. (2004). A multilevel approach to investigating crossnational differences in negotiation processes. *International Negotiation* 9(3): 471–484.

International Program. (2005). National Basketball Association. Available online: <http://www.nba.com/jrnba/intl_programs.html> (accessed January 5, 2009).

Janoff, B. (2005, December 12). NBA marketing mantra: Think global, act local. *Brandweek* 45 (1): 11.

Kates, S. M. (2002). The protean quality of subcultural consumption: An ethnographic account of gay consumers. *Journal of Consumer Research* 29: 383–399.

Larmer, B. (2005, September 15). The center of the world. *Foreign Policy* 66–73.

Lombardo, J. (2008, May 12). AEG & NBA focus on China [Electronic version]. *Sports Business Journal* 1.

Marber, A., Wellen, P., and Posluszny, S. (2005). The merging of marketing and sports: A case study. *Marketing Management Journal* 15(1): 162–171.

Mayrhofer, U. (2004). International market entry: Does the home country affect entry mode decisions? *Journal of International Marketing* 12(4): 71–96.

McAuley, A. (2004). Seeking (marketing) virtue in globalisation. *Marketing Review* 4(3): 253–266.

McDonald, H., Karg, A. J., and Lock, D. (2010). Leveraging fans' global football allegiances to build domestic league support. *Asia Pacific Journal of Marketing and Logistics* 22(1): 67–89.

McGraw, D. (2000, May 1). NBA finals are no slam-dunk for TV. *U.S. News & World Report* 128(17).

NBA hopes to capitalize on basketball's popularity in China. (2008). *ESPN News*. Available online: <http://sports.espn.go.com/oly/summer08/basketball/news/story?id=3542013> (accessed January 5, 2009).

NBA Madness. (2008). National Basketball Association. Available online: <http://www.nba.com/madness2008> (accessed January 4, 2009).

Orejan, J. (2005). Understanding and adapting to cultural diversity in international sport marketing. In *Where Sport Marketing Theory Meets Practice: Selected Papers from the Second Annual Conference of the Sport Marketing Association*, edited by B. G. Pitts. Morgantown, WV: Fitness Information Technology.

Quelch, J. A. (2002). Does globalization have staying power? *Marketing Management* 11(2): 18–23.

Singh, S. (2005). Sports has world of opportunity to help others, help itself. *Sport Business Journal* 8(24): 25.

Styles, C. and Hersch, L. (2005). Executive insights: Relationship formation in international joint ventures. *Journal of International Marketing* 13(3): 105–134.

Till, B. D. and Shimp, T. A. (1998). Endorsers in advertising: The case of negative celebrity information. *Journal of Advertising* 27(1): 67–82.

Trachtenberg, J. A. (1989, January 23). Playing the global game. *Forbes* 23: 90.

Trompenaars, F. and Woolliams, P. (2004). *Marketing Across Cultures*. Hoboken, NJ: John Wiley and Sons.

Van Riper, T. (2008, August 15). America's most lucrative sports arenas. *Forbes*. Available online: <http://sports.yahoo.com/top/news?slug=ys-forbesarenas081508&prov=yhoo&type=lgns> (accessed June 20, 2009).

Wallace, T. (2002). Reaching global extremes? Are broadcasters' claims for X games' worldwide appeal justified? *SportBusiness International* (72): 9.

Westerbeek, H. (2010). *The Global Sport Business*. New York: Palgrave Macmillan.

Westerbeek, H. and Smith, A. (2003). *Sport Business in the Global Marketplace*. New York: Palgrave Macmillan.

Yu, L. (2003). The global-brand advantage. *MIT Sloan Management Review* 44(3): 13.

CHAPTER FIFTEEN: EMERGING SOCIOLOGICAL SPORT MARKETING CONCEPTS

Brake, M. (1985). *Comparative Youth Cultures: The Sociology of Youth Culture and Youth Subcultures in America*. London: Routledge.

Graves, B. (2003). In extreme sports, hardware and apparel are two sides of the same coin. *San Diego Business Journal* 36(3): 24–28.

International Olympic Committee. (2006). *IOC Guide on Sport, Environment and Sustainable Development*. Lausanne, Switzerland: International Olympic Committee.

Irwin, R., Lachowetz, T., and Clark, J. (2010). Cause-related sport marketing: Can this marketing strategy affect company decision-makers? *Journal of Management and Organization* 16(4): 550–556.

Jones, N. (2005). Rankings demonstrate the power of event marketing. *Event*: 8–10.

Jowdy, E. and McDonald, M. (2002). Relationship marketing and interactive fan festivals: The Women's United Soccer Association's "Soccer Sensation". *International Journal of Sports Marketing and Sponsorship* 4(4): 295–311.

Kincaid, J. (2002). *Customer Relationship Management: Getting It Right!* Upper Saddle River, NJ: Pearson Education.

Kiska, J. (2002). Customer experience management. *CMA Management* 76(7): 28–30.

Parr, R. (2002). The changing face of sports marketing. *Sport Marketing* (78): 16.

Peralta, S. (2001). *Dogtown and Z-Boys*. USA: Sony Picture Classics.

Ratten, V. (2010). The future of sports management: A social responsibility, philanthropy and entrepreneurship perspective. *Journal of Management and Organization* 16(4): 488–494.

Rovner, M. (2000). Brands need to keep their promises if they're to win the loyalty of US kids. *Kids Marketing Report* 1(25): 18.

Schmitt, B. H. (2003). *Customer Experience Management: A Revolutionary Approach to Connecting with your Customers*. Hoboken, NJ: John Wiley and Sons.

Schouten, J. W. and McAlexander, J. H. (1995). Subcultures of consumption: An ethnography of the new bikers. *Journal of Consumer Research* 22(1): 43–61.

Schwarz, E. C. (2009). Building a sense of community through sport programming and special events: The role of sport marketing in contributing to social capital. *International Journal of Entrepreneurship and Small Business* 7(4): 478–487.

Schwarz, E. C. (2010). The role of recovery marketing to recapture a sport market over the past decade: From travel and tourism to professional and amateur sport business. *Journal of Applied Marketing Theory* 1(2): 24–35.

Schwarz, E. C. and Branch, D. D. (2011). Social marketing as a catalyst for building new relationships between sport practitioners and academicians. *Journal of Applied Marketing Theory* 2(2): 56–67.

Smith, A, and Westerbeek, H. (2004). *The Sport Business Future*. New York: Palgrave Macmillan.

Stavros, C. and Westberg, K. (2009). Using triangulation and multiple case studies to advance relationship marketing. *Qualitative Market Research* 12(3): 3307–3320.

Stavros, C., Pope, N. K. L., and Winzar, H. (2008). Relationship marketing in Australian professional sport: An extension of the Shani framework. *Sport Marketing Quarterly* 17(3): 133–145.

Stevens, A. (2008). *Sustainable Sport*. London: SportBusiness Group.

Stewart-Allen, A. L. (2000). Building a successful brand experience: Lessons of the dome. *Marketing News* 34(16): 7.

Vancouver 2010/AISTS. (2009). *Sustainable Sport and Event Toolkit (SSET) v1.3b*. Lausanne, Switzerland: AISTS.

Waddell, R. (1994). Interactive sports fan festivals growing in size, popularity. *Amusement Business* 106(51): 59–60.

Waltner, C. (2000). CRM: The new game in town for professional sports. *InformationWeek* (801): 112–114.

Weinberger, J. (2004). Customers for life. *CRM Magazine* 8(7): 32–38.

INDEX

Numbers in **bold** refer to figures and tables

402

404

408